Augustine Wirth

Lenten Sermons

Augustine Wirth

Lenten Sermons

ISBN/EAN: 9783744742122

Printed in Europe, USA, Canada, Australia, Japan

Cover: Foto ©Lupo / pixelio.de

More available books at **www.hansebooks.com**

LENTEN SERMONS.

EDITED BY

REV. AUGUSTINE WIRTH, O. S. B.

FIRST EDITION.

ELIZABETH, N. J.
1891.

INDEX.

The Way of the Cross.

FIRST COURSE.

		PAGE
1.	Jesus is condemned to death	3
2.	Jesus takes the cross on his shoulders	9
3.	Jesus falls under the cross the first time	15
4.	Jesus meets his most afflicted Mother	21
5.	Simon of Cyrene assists Jesus in carrying the cross	26
6.	Veronica wipes the face of Jesus	32
7.	Jesus falls under the cross the second time	38

SECOND COURSE.

1.	Jesus consoles the women of Jerusalem who wept over him	44
2.	Jesus falls under the cross the third time	50
3.	Jesus is stript of his garments	57
4.	Jesus is nailed to the cross	63
5.	Jesus dies on the cross	67
6.	Jesus is taken down from the cross and laid in the lap of Mary	74
7.	Jesus is laid in the tomb	79

THIRD COURSE.

1.	Christ's sufferings for the salvation of mankind	89
2.	The mental sufferings of Christ	96
3.	The trial	104
4.	The denial of Peter	111
5.	The repentance of Peter	117
6.	The scourging at the pillar, the crowning with thorns, and the crucifixion of Christ.	123
7.	The Seven Last Words of Christ on the Cross	130

FOURTH COURSE.

1.	The washing of the Apostles' feet, Peter, Judas, and the questions of disciples	143
2.	The Garden of Gethsemane, the prayer, agony and bloody sweat of Christ, and the coming of the Angel	151
3.	Judas in the garden, the apprehension of Jesus Annas, the blow, Caiphas	158
4.	The interior sufferings of Christ, Peter's denial, Pilate, the despair of Judas, Herod, Barabbas	166
5.	The scourging, the crowning of Christ with thorns, and the derision	172
6.	*Ecce homo*, the sentence of death, the way of the cross from Jerusalem to Calvary.	179
7.	The crucifixion, the Seven Last Words, the death of Christ	187

Skeleton Sermons on the Seven Last Words.

FIFTH COURSE.

1.	Father, forgive them, for they know not what they do	199
2.	This day thou shalt be with me in paradise	202
3.	Woman, behold thy son. Son, behold thy mother	205
4.	My God, my God, why hast thou forsaken me?	208
5.	I thirst	210
6.	It is consummated	214
7.	Father, into thy hands I commend my spirit	218

From Mount Olivet to Mount Calvary.
Sixth Course.
1. Jesus on Mount Olivet... 223
2. Jesus betrayed by Judas, apprehended, and abandoned by his disciples.......... 230
3. Jesus before the high council of the Jews........ 236
4. Jesus before Pilate and Herod.... 243
5. Jesus sentenced to be crucified.. 249
6. Jesus carries the cross and is crucified thereon............................ 255
7. Good Friday... 260

Man's Relation to God.
Seventh Course.
1. Venial sin.. 267
2. Mortal sin... 273
3. The habit of sin... 278
4. Final Impenitence.... 284
5. Repentance... 290
6. God's mercy to the sinner.. 296
7. The threefold sacrifice of Christ...................................... 301

The Seven Last Words of Christ on the Cross.
Eighth Course.
1. The first word... 311
2. The second word 317
3. The third word 324
4. The fourth word... 331
5. The fifth word.. 337
6. The sixth word.. 343
7. The seventh word........ 349

Questions of the Soul.
Ninth Course.
1. What have you done? 357
2. What awaits you?.. 362
3. Is there no relief?... 367
4. How to begin ?.. 372
5. Will you delay?... 377
6. How glad you will be? 383
7. The dereliction of Jesus upon the cross............................... 387

ERRATA.

Page 260, fourteenth line from top: consummate should be consummated.
" 267, second line from top: thoughts should be thought.
" 275, seventeenth line from top: patieat should be patient.
" 277, eleventh line from bottom: Belchazzar should be Baltassar.
" 288, eighteenth line from bottom, read: harder than rock.
" 293, sixteenth line from bottom: is should be it.
" 300, ninth line from bottom: after good should be after a good.
" 304, tenth line from bottom: fever should be fervor.
" 307, third line from top, read: you number those gaping wounds.

THE FOURTEEN STATIONS
—OF—
THE WAY OF THE CROSS.

FIRST AND SECOND COURSE.

SEVEN SERMONS FOR EACH COURSE.

FIRST STATION.

JESUS IS CONDEMNED TO DEATH.

"Then Pilate delivered him to them to be crucified."—John 19 : 16.

Amongst the many lovely devotions which, like fair flowers, have sprung up in our holy Church, and constantly diffuse their fragrance throughout the vast garden of that tender mother, is one which most earnestly commends itself to the consideration of all who would fain linger by the side of the suffering Saviour, as he painfully wends his way up Calvary's steep ascent. This is the devotion of the "Way of the Cross" which originated in the following manner:

When but a few centuries had elapsed since the precious blood of our Redeemer was shed for us—his beloved children—pious Christians from all parts of the known world made pilgrimages to Jerusalem there to visit the holy places, and to retrace the path rendered sacred to us by the footprints of our divine Saviour, as he bent beneath the weight of his heavy cross.

After some time pictures representing the different scenes in the Passion were erected at certain distances from each other along this "Way of the Cross," and, before each, the faithful would pause for awhile in wrapt meditation upon the dolorous mystery which the picture so vividly brought to their minds. When, at a later period, the Saracens seized upon the Holy Land, and it was no longer possible to visit the places, so hallowed by the sufferings of a loving Saviour, the Christians, with the approbation of the Popes, erected station pictures at other places also, to afford the faithful a means of meditating on the Passion of Christ, and the first who did this were the Franciscans.

The deep hold which the devotion had taken upon the hearts of all fervent Catholics was soon manifested in the rapid and general diffusion, and there are very few churches to-day, upon the walls of which are not found pictures, commemorative of the sorrowful "Way of the Cross." Those who devoutly visited the stations of the Way of the Cross, gained many indulgences. The Popes Innocent XI. and XII., and Benedict XIII., granted these indulgences also to all those who visit the Stations erected by the Franciscans, and there devoutly venerate the bitter Passion and death of Christ. That you may perform the devotion of the Way of the Cross in a profitable manner, I shall give you a brief explanation on each of the fourteen stations. To-day we will represent to ourselves in the spirit of the First Station, which bears the inscription: *"Jesus is condemned to death,"* and consider two reasons why he was condemned to death, namely:

I. The human fear of Pontius Pilate, and
II. The inconstancy of the Jewish people.

"We adore thee, O Christ, and we bless thee. Because by the holy cross thou hast redeemed the world."

Part I.

Accompanied by his disciples our Blessed Lord repaired to Mount Olivet in the evening of Holy Thursday to begin his Passion, and there, in an agony, the bitterness of which it were indeed a vain attempt to depict, he was bathed in a bloody sweat and apprehended by his relentless foes. Like a criminal, deserving of death, he was led first to Annas where a rude servant dared to strike his divine and holy face, then to Caiphas where he was declared guilty of death. Then during the whole night he was so shockingly insulted and maltreated, that St. Jerome says: "The mockery and insult which were inflicted on Jesus during that night were so great that their enormity shall only be known on the day of judgment." When after a night of such humiliation and suffering, day dawned, our Good Friday, the Jews brought Jesus before Pilate, that he might condemn him to death: Let us now consider :

1. *The human fear of Pilate which caused him to condemn Christ to death.* Pilate before very long was firmly convinced that in the suffering Jesus he beheld an innocent victim, and, having still a due regard for what was right and just, he was willing to set him free. Having examined our Lord, he appeared before the Jews, and said to them : "I find no cause in this man."—Luke 23 : 14, but the Jews, so far from being satisfied with this assurance, insisted with unrelenting fury upon his death. Then Pilate had recourse to a most cruel means to save Jesus. "I will chastise him therefore and release him."—Luke 23 : 16. He thought that by applying the stinging lash to the tender flesh of our Saviour, the rage of the Jews would be appeased. Jesus therefore was scourged. This punishment, which was meted out by the Romans only upon slaves, and the vilest of malefactors was horrible, and many died while the torturers pursued their task. Picture to yourselves, O Christians! from six to eight men, human beings indeed, but with hearts destitute of one trace of humanity, who were permitted to exercise their cruel will against the Saviour of the world! They rudely tore off his clothing, bound him with ropes to a column, and two by two, relieved each other in the fiendish work. By this terrible

flagellation at which rods, whips and straps were mercilessly used, the body of Jesus was so lacerated that it appeared like one quivering wound. The prophet who in spirit saw Jesus thus mangled says of him : "From the sole of the foot unto the top of the head there is no soundness therein, wounds and bruises and swelling sores, they are not bound up, nor dressed, nor fomented with oil."—Is. 1 : 6.

After this painful scourging, the soldiers brought thorns and wove them into a crown, which they placed on the head of Christ, and O! what intolerable anguish thrilled through every nerve of our dear Saviour as they pressed those sharp points deep into that sacred head. And—O! refinement of malice !—they decked him out in a purple mantle, placed a reed in his hand and most shamefully mocked at our Lord. Thus bruised, reviled and maltreated, they again led him before Pilate who felt even *his* pagan heart thrill with pity to its very depths. O ! pitiful sight ! Pilate exclaimed "*Ecce Homo*!" Behold the man !—John 19 : 5. He imagined that the Jews would abandon their design, and no longer seek his death, but alas, he was deceived—he had not measured their hatred of Christ. "Crucify him ! Crucify him !" was the cry sent up from their dark, blood-thirsty hearts. Crucify him ! Crucify him ! they cried out—John 19 : 5; but Pilate made yet another attempt. A custom prevailed amongst the Jews which permitted them to liberate a malefactor, after he had been seized by the law, and they had the privilege of releasing whom they chose at Easter. Availing himself of this opportunity he led before them *Barabbas*, a criminal whose soul was stained with the guilt of robbery and murder. He could not think otherwise than that, when he asked them which of the two should be set free, their choice would be the innocent Jesus. "Whom will you that I release to you, Barabbas, or Jesus, who is called Christ?" (Matt. 27 : 17.) Ah ! Pilate had not fathomed the depth of their hatred for Christ. The Jews clamored loudly that Barabbas should be saved. *Barabbas*, whose hand was red with the blood of his fellow-man, preferred before Jesus! Behold the depths to which human fear caused the wretched Pilate to fall ! His craven spirit led him to fear that the Jews would denounce him to the Roman emperor, and that he would lose his office, his dignity, and it might be, his life. To avert such a danger he condemned innocence to death ! Of what atrocious injustice was he guilty, and all through human fear—Fear of man !

2. *The human fear of Christians which is the cause of the commission of so many sins in our days.* For the same reason one hesitates to call the attention of a friend or an acquaintance to his faults or admonish him to the pursuit of a better life. For this reason some even dare not go frequently to confession or receive often the precious body and blood of our Lord ; they shrink from visiting Jesus present in the Blessed Sacrament of the Altar, and are afraid to lead a retired—a holy life. They fear the

mocking smile and covert sneers of some friends who are wholly engrossed with the world, and human respect conquers again. For this reason instead of condemning discourses which violate religion, wound fraternal charity and put chastity itself to the blush, many dare not speak the word which might lead the conversation into another strain, and perhaps save a soul from perdition. It is human fear and human respect that frustrate unnumbered conversions. How many sinners are held captive in the bonds of sin through human fear; how many infidels and heretics are deterred from embracing the true faith. Should they renounce their errors and be converted, they would have to make it evident to the world by a change of life, and they recoil from encountering its sneers. They must give up some sinful companionship, or perhaps sever the ties of kindred and friendship, and the sacrifice seems too great in their eyes. O! how much good does human fear prevent,—how much evil does it cause!

Guard against nothing so much as against human fear. "Be not afraid of them that kill the body, and after that have no power that they can do * * * fear ye him who after he hath killed hath power to cast into hell."—Luke 12, 4, 5. Make a firm resolution never through human fear to do or to omit what would burden your conscience and violate the commandments of God. When it tempts you to sin think of Pilate who was led to condemn the Son of God to death, and thus won eternal damnation for his soul. Take courage, and let your hearts echo the words of the wise man: "He that feareth man shall quickly fall; he that trusted in the Lord shall be set on high."—Prov. 29 : 25.

Part II.

Another reason why Christ was condemned to death was the *inconstancy and fickleness of the Jewish people.*

1. *How incredible is the inconstancy of this people!* Jesus was always a favorite of the people; wherever he went great multitudes accompanied him; they listened with pleasure to his words and went so far in their enthusiasm as to proclaim him king on several occasions. The ambitious Scribes and Pharisees were right when, fired with indignation they exclaimed: "Do you see that we prevail nothing? Behold, the whole world is gone after him." — John 12: 19. And with what love, what veneration, what devotion, did they not regard him but a few short days before his death. The eager throng hastened forth to meet him, spread their garments in his path, and with palm branches waving aloft, were overjoyed to form the "Guard of Honor" of our Lord. Each tried to surpass the other in their marks of love and attention, and as they beheld the beautiful countenance of the Saviour, they cried out in their enthu-

siasm: "Hosanna to the Son of David! Blessed is he that cometh in the name of the Lord!" (Matt. 21 : 9.) A few days have passed, and what an incomprehensible change has that little time wrought in the hearts of these perverse children of men! They are entirely blinded, they know their Redeemer no longer, and deadly hate reigns in place of their devotion and love. Jesus stands before Pilate; the high-priests, Scribes and Pharisees demand his death and allege a multitude of false accusations and calumnies against him; they say that he is a false teacher, a demagogue, a rebel, who refuses obedience to Cæsar, a malefactor guilty of death. Pilate washes his hands with the solemn declaration: "I am innocent of the blood of this just man, look you to it," and the people answering cry: "His blood be upon us, and upon our children!"—Matt. 27 : 24, 29. Can anything more detestable, more abhorrent, more damnable than this inconstancy of the Jews be conceived! Have they not a thousand times deserved the punishments which God has visited upon them?

2. *But how great is also the inconstancy of many Christians!* Let us call to mind some particular season of grace, *e. g.*, a mission, a Jubilee. How many showed themselves the most fervent penitents. They avoided evil occasions, gave up their sinful familiarities with persons of the opposite sex, no longer visited the houses and societies in which they had so grievously offended God, they renounced impurity, gave up midnight revels, and firmly turned from the demon of drink. They no longer spent time and money at the gameing table, curses and blasphemies were no more heard from their lips. Obscene words were abandoned, they became reconciled with their enemies, avoided all kinds of injustice, and carefully guarded their hearts against sin. At the same time they were scrupulously observing their religious duties, they prayed, listened to the word of God and frequently received the Sacraments. Thus piously and penitently many Christians lived a longer or shorter time ago. How do they live now? Ah, they have returned to their old ways. The good resolutions which they made are forgotten, the zeal for penance has disappeared, frivolity and forgetfulness of God have again taken possession of their hearts. They again entertain sinful familiarities, frequent wicked houses and societies, drink, gamble, curse, swear, blaspheme, commit impurity, cheat, steal, in short, again commit the old sins and walk in the ways of vice. I need hardly say that they have lost all love for exercises of devotion and especially that they will not hear of the reception of the Sacraments. In what great danger is the salvation of such inconstant, wavering Christians! There is alas! every reason to fear that they will share the doom of the fickle-minded Jews who were rejected, and forsaken by the Lord. An inconstant Christian is in far greater danger of eternal fire than the sinner whose whole life has cried out to the Lord, "I will

not serve." An unchaste man may be moved, like David, who did penance for his adultery. A publican may renounce his injustices, like Zachæus, who restored fourfold the goods he had unjustly acquired and gave the half of all that he possessed to the poor. People who are sunk in the mire of iniquity can be converted like Mary Magdalene who bewailed her sins at the feet of Jesus. But of an Achab, who having been warned by Elias, did penance in sackcloth and ashes, and afterwards went to Bethel and sacrificed to Baal—of a Zedekias, who asked to know the will of the Lord of the Prophet Jeremiah, and shortly afterwards relapsed into his former blindness—of a Saul who, but a little while after he had known and repented of his injustice to David, persecuted him again and sought his life—of these we do not read that they were ever finally and truly converted, and their souls saved from the fires of hell. The words of St. Peter apply to such inconstant Christians: "If having fled from the pollution of the world through the knowledge of our Lord and Saviour Jesus Christ, being again entangled in them, they are overcome; their latter state is become unto them worse than the former. For it had been better for them not to have known the way of justice, than, after they have known it, to turn back from thy holy commandment, which was delivered to them."—2 Pet. 2: 20, 21. And Christ himself says: "No man putting his hand to the plough, and looking back, is fit for the kingdom of God."—Luke 9: 62. Supported by these divine words, St. Bernard also says: "Of those who after their conversion relapse into the old sins, become ungrateful for the divine grace received, and after laying hands to the plow, being of a lukewarm and carnal disposition, relapse, or after having known the truth, publicly apostatize and enter again upon the way of sin—of these you will find but few who after such a relapse return to the right path.

PERORATION.

What resolution should we make to-day at the first Station? Certainly this: Never to allow *human fear and inconstancy* to be our guides. Pilate acted contrary to his better knowledge and conscience in condemning Jesus to death. He did it from human fear. Let not the fear of man overcome us. Let us not permit human respect to gain the ascendency in our hearts. Let us crush it, trample upon it, and resolve to die rather than yield to its power; to incur the hatred of the world, and shed our blood rather than offend our loving Saviour. Let us detest the inconstancy of the Jews. Let us not be reeds, driven about by every wind, but guard against every relapse into sin. He only will receive the crown who perseveres unto the end. Let us resolve to be constant in the service of God, and let us bewail our weakness and unfaithfulness with penitential tears, crying out: "Jesus Christ crucified, have mercy on us." Amen.

SECOND STATION.

JESUS TAKES THE CROSS UPON HIS SHOULDERS.

"*And they took Jesus, and led him forth, and bearing his own cross, he went forth to that place which is called Calvary.*—*John 19: 16, 17.*

The feeling of pity which, for a time, touched the heart of the Roman Governor at the sight of the suffering Saviour was as transitory as it was futile,—and Pontius Pilate, yielding, through human fear, to the demands of the Jews, has condemned Jesus to the death of the cross. The preparations for the Crucifixion are all made; carpenters hew a long and heavy cross and carry it before the Governor's palace, others bring nails, ropes, hammers, ladders and various things requisite for its completion. Rushing towards our Saviour in mad haste the servants and soldiers tear off the purple mantle, with which in bitter mockery, they had decked him, and rudely clothe him in his own garments again. That they might the better drag him to death they put a rope about his loins, and commanded him to take the cross upon his shoulders.

Second Station. *Jesus takes the cross upon his shoulders.* To this mystery of the Passion we shall to-day direct our attention and consider that Jesus took the cross upon his shoulders and carried it,

  I. *With patience; and*
  II. *With joy.*

PART I.

1. *Jesus Christ takes the cross upon his shoulders and carries it with patience, although it is in itself very heavy, as well as because of the sins of the world.*

(a) *The cross was very heavy in itself.* It had been put together in haste of rude, hewed wood; its perpendicular beam measured, as St. Bonaventure and others report, fifteen feet, and the cross beam, eight feet; it was a load burdensome enough for any strong, robust man. How heavy, then, must it have been for the Redeemer, already weakened by the loss of so much blood! Under the most cruel and inhuman treatment he had been dragged from one place to another, and not a minute's rest had been allowed him during the preceding night; the loss of blood and the pains of his cruel flagellation had completely exhausted him; moreover, the terrible strokes of the scourging had so bruised and lacerated his back and shoulders, that the least pressure caused him the most intense pains. From this it is evident, what a heavy load the cross must have been for our divine Saviour, and what violent pain he must have experienced when it was laid thereupon.

(*b*) *But the sins of the world rendered the cross still heavier.* There are living upon the earth over a hundred millions of men, who on an average die within the space of thirty years, thereby making room for as many and even more descendants. Though the earth was not as much populated before the coming of Christ, as it is at the present day, still we may safely say that the number of men who have lived from the beginning of the world until now surpasses hundreds of millions, and that, until "time shall be no more," an equally great throng shall live and die. Let us assume something entirely different from the actual state of affairs— that every man, during every day, offends his Creator by only one sin, and in about thirty years, he will have been guilty of ten thousand sins! These sins may be venial—they may be mortal—but *ten thousand* will be the number they will reach! Now if we compute this number of sins for all men that have ever lived from the beginning of the world, and shall live to the end of time, we obtain a number of sins, which no longer amounts to millions and billions, and of which we can no longer form an idea, because of the immense multitude. Behold all these sins together with the cross were laid upon his shoulders, and Jesus, the Lamb of God, was compelled to take them and carry them with the cross. Therefore St. Peter writes: "Who his own self bore our sins in his body upon the tree, that we being dead to sin should live to justice."—1. Pet. 2 : 24. Now, if so many of the Saints were so deeply grieved at the sins which are committed in the world, who can comprehend the sorrow which Jesus experienced, when he saw the cross, laden with so many sins, lying before him? And who will be able to describe his consternation and terror, when he took this terrible load upon his shoulders!

(*c*) *Nevertheless he takes the cross upon his shoulders with patience.* He offers himself as a sacrifice to his heavenly Father with the greatest willingness, and heeding not the pain and smarting of his lacerated shoulders, he patiently takes up the cross. He does it with joy, he is eager to carry it to Calvary that he might point out to *us* the dolorous "Way of the Cross." The prophet Isaiah (53 : 7) had said of him: "He was offered because it was his own will, and he opened not his mouth: he shall be led as a sheep to the slaughter, and shall be dumb as a lamb before his shearer, and he shall not open his mouth." His body writhes under the terrible load, and all his members tremble, but he complains not, he laments not, but prays even now as on Mount Olivet: "Father, not my will, but thine be done."—Luke 22 : 42.

2. *We too, must carry our cross with patience. And why?* Since the trail of the serpent penetrated the fair garden of Eden, and sin cast its shadow o'er its beautiful groves, the earth has resembled one vast cemetery where tombstones meet our eye wheresoever we turn, and crosses perpetually arise. Poverty and destitution, sickness and pain, oppression, persecution, and a thousand other spiritual and corporal calamities afflict men, force from them heavy sighs, and cause tears unceasingly to flow from their eyes. Job was right in saying: "Man born of a woman, living for a short time, is filled with many miseries."—Job 14 : 1.

(*a*) *Because it is only when the cross is borne in patience that it is meritorious.* Simply to carry the cross of itself does not lead to heaven, its value depends upon the patience with which it is borne. There is no doubt but that many who had heavy crosses on earth are now in hell, their cross afforded them no blessing because they did not carry it with patience and resignation to the will of God. St. Gregory says, that as patience in suffering is a sign of election, impatience is a mark of condemnation. And Christ himself says: "In your patience you shall possess your souls."—Luke 21 : 19. Recognizing, as we do, this truth, O Christians, is it not utterly opposed to every dictate of reason for us to rebel against carrying the cross? Not only does it avail nothing in removing its weight from our shoulders but we lose all the merit that a sweet and gentle patience would have gained for us, for heaven. Let us never forget that the patience with which we carry the cross upon earth turns to bright gems for our heavenly crown, and the greater the patience, the more brightly those gems will glitter therein.

(*b*) *Because Christ has carried his most heavy cross with the most perfect patience.* Some ancient chronicle has handed down the story of a noble maiden, over whose head but a few sunny years had passed, when she felt her heart drawn to a more intimate union with God, and resolved to serve him in one of the most austere Orders of the Church. To try her vocation the Superioress gave her a graphic description of all she would have to undergo, conducted her in spirit to all the apartments of the community, and showed her only such things as were calculated to terrify human sensuality. The maiden, who seemed deeply impressed, and visibly agitated at the communication of the holy Religious, remained silent. "My daughter," said the sister, "you do not answer." "I have but one question to ask," replied the undaunted postulant. "Are there crucifixes in the convent?" "O! surely, my child; turn your eyes whithersoever you will, they cannot fail to rest upon that reminder of our Saviour's immeasurable love." O! then," replied the fervent girl, "what more could I ask? Should my courage seem to falter, let me but glance at the image of my crucified Saviour, and that look will increase it a thousand fold." My brethren, crucifixes are not wanting to us, faith and devotion have placed them everywhere for our veneration. When a heavy cross presses upon you, follow the example of this ardent soul, cast a look upon your crucified Redeemer, and contemplate the unconquerable patience with which Jesus carried his cross; and you will most certainly be encouraged to carry yours with patience, since for love of you Christ bore a far heavier one. Should we be called upon to endure opprobrium or insult, let us think of the scorn, the ignominy, the outrages which Jesus suffered for love of us, and we will accept it not only patiently, but with joy. That which at first wounded our hearts like sharp thorns will diffuse the fragrance of roses for us, so powerful is one thought of the cross.

Part II.

When Jesus saw the cross he stretched out his hands streaming with blood, he embraced it affectionately, kissed it, and with joy took it upon his shoulders.

1. *When our dear Saviour took the cross upon himself, why did he accept the heavy burden not only with patience, but with a holy joy, animating his divine and adorable heart?* He was animated solely by the love which burned in that heart for the human race, and by the mercy which he longed to exercise upon man. The sole heritage of our first parents was *sin.* Through that sin with which we entered the world, and with the actual sins which, when we attained the use of reason, we committed ourselves; we were plunged into an abyss of misery from which it seemed impossible to emerge. Deprived of sanctifying grace, we languished in the servitude of the devil, heaven was closed against us, and endless misery seemed our portion forever. What rendered our lot still more deplorable was the impossibility of raising ourselves from our fall by our own exertions and of again obtaining God's love, grace and friendship. Left to ourselves, nothing remained for us but to live and die in the state of disgrace and sin and to be cast away forever. Jesus knew our misery and our inability to help ourselves, and having compassion on us, he resolved to redeem us. Since according to the divine decree the work of redemption could not be accomplished except by his death on the cross, his heart rejoiced when he saw before him the instrument of our redemption. He did not think of the weight of the cross, nor of the inexpressible pains in which he would die; his merciful love had before his eyes only the precious fruits, which would ripen for us upon it, therefore, with the greatest desire

he stretched out his hands streaming with blood, embraced it, kissed it and with joy took it upon his mangled and bleeding shoulders.

2. *O that we also, imitating Jesus, would take up our cross and carry it not only with patience but also with joy!* Why?

(*a*) *Because the cross disengages and detaches our hearts from the world, and directs our thoughts to eternal goods.* Take for example, a sick person, lying wearily upon his bed of pain, scarcely able to move his aching limbs, or, when fever seizes him, tossing restlessly from side to side, unable to find any ease. What a change takes place in him! The glow that once illumined life's pathway has faded,—riches and earthly goods avail him not, for he has no power to enjoy. He recalls the sea of pleasure into which he once plunged, and disgust takes possession of his soul—he now believes that Solomon rightly termed terrestrial things "vanity and affliction of spirit." He is utterly indifferent and sad. Even the passions, under whose fierce sway he lived, lose their power and die under the pressure of the cross. What a change takes place in him! That fire of revenge which flamed in the breast of that angry man when he walked forth in the full vigor of health and strength dies away, and his trembling hand readily clasps the hand of one whom he once hated for some real or fancied wrong, but whom he now welcomes as a friend. The proud man, who, before the withering blight of a sudden illness laid him low, held himself, in arrogance, far above other men, now feels the power of one who holds him in "the hollow of his hand," and humbles himself before the Lord. The unchaste man who has dared to ignore that his soul has been made in the image and likeness of God, who was steeped in the mire of unholy pleasures, now humbles himself under the heavy weight of the cross, and even the unbeliever, beneath its shadow, turns to God, crying out, "I believe, Lord! O! help thou my unbelief!" Thus the cross is to innumerable sinners and worldly people the means of the salvation of their souls.

(*b*) *Because the cross confirms us in virtue.* The more strokes of the hammer you give to the nail, the more deeply it sinks into the wood, and the more firmly it is imbedded therein, the more enduring will be its hold, so too, the more keenly a pious Christian has, with Jesus, to bear and suffer, the more thoroughly will his virtue be confirmed. Let us only think of ourselves. How soon does the fervor of our piety diminish, how speedily our zeal for virtue disappear, how lukewarm and tepid we become when prosperity attends on all we undertake, and life seems one long summer day undimmed by sorrow, grief, disease or care! It is, therefore, very salutary, nay, often necessary, that tribulations come upon us from time to time. Thereby we are moved, the soul which has grown languid is animated anew, and fidelity to God takes a deeper root in our heart. Moreover the cross is especially calculated to detach us from creatures which could weaken our constancy, it awakens and preserves within us a salutary diffidence in ourselves, compels us to watch and pray, and to employ other necessary and useful means for preserving God's grace in our heart. In general the cross affords an opportunity for the practice and increase of many Christian virtues. In sufferings and afflictions faith becomes more living, more steadfast, love more ardent, devotion more fervent, humility and resignation cast their roots deep, deep into the inmost recesses of our souls, and produce fruits far more precious and rare.

(c) *Because the cross increases our glory in heaven.* Since, like fire, it purifies us from the dross of sin and revives our fervor in virtue, and since it extirpates self-love and inflames within us the love of God, it enables us to enrich ourselves with merits in this life, and to gain hereafter a great reward. Hence, St. Gregory the Great says: "If an innocent man is punished with scourges, the treasure of his merits is increased by his patience. The soul of the elect, indeed, withers now, but it becomes green hereafter in the exultation of beatitude."

(d) *Finally, because the Saints have given us the most beautiful example in carrying their cross.* Far from rejecting the cross, they accepted it with the greatest willingness from the hand of God, and carried it with a joyful heart. Thus, "the Apostles went from the presence of the council rejoicing, that they were accounted worthy to suffer reproach for the name of Jesus."—Acts 5 : 41. St. Teresa used to say : "Lord, let me suffer or die ;" and St. Mary Magdalene of Pazzi's prayer was "Let me suffer and not die." St. Francis of Assisium called pains and sickness his brothers and sisters, poverty and contempt, his dearest daughters. When St. Francis Xavier was in Lisbon, he was grieved because everything went according to his desires and wishes, and he was anxious lest he might fall from the state of grace, if freed from every cross. Whenever a calamity befel him, he used to exclaim : "Yet more O! Lord, yet more!" Often in tribulations he prayed : "Lord, take not this cross from me, unless you send one far more bitter to take its place." Whenever in their sufferings and tribulations the Saints were tempted by a want of faith, they at once consoled themselves with the words of the Apostle: "The present tribulation, which is momentary and light, worketh for us above measure exceedingly an eternal weight of glory."—2. Cor. 4 : 17.

PERORATION.

This should be for us also an inexhaustible source of comfort and consolation in every tribulation and difficulty. Our cross weighs upon us only for a time, but the reward which follows will be eternal. Let us look upon Jesus; heavy was the cross which he carried; he carries it no longer, it glitters in his hand as an emblem of victory over death and hell, and has acquired for his humanity the glory of heaven. What a happiness for us, if, like Jesus, we carry our cross during the short time of our earthly pilgrimage, like him we shall also be so glorified in heaven. Let us, then, to-day, prostrate ourselves again before Jesus in the Second Station of the Way of the Cross, and pray with heart and lips: How could I be a friend of Christ if I am an enemy of the cross? O dear, O precious cross! I embrace thee, I kiss thee, I joyfully accept thee from the hand of God. Far be it from me to glory in anything but the cross. By it the world shall be crucified to me, and I to the world, that I may belong to thee, O Jesus, to thee alone, to thee entirely—to thee completely, to thee with my whole heart and soul! Amen.

THIRD STATION.

JESUS FALLS BENEATH THE CROSS THE FIRST TIME.

"Have mercy on me, O God, for man has trodden me under foot."
—*Ps. 55 : 1.*

The fiat of death has gone forth, and Jesus, taking the heavy burden of the cross upon those mangled shoulders, still suffering from the cruel scourging they had undergone, goes forth to the place of execution prepared to shed his precious blood for us in such anguish as had never before been known in the world. On his way to death a rude throng of soldiers close around him, they torment him with their sharp swords and huge clubs, and a vast crowd of turbulent human beings precede and follow him to Mount Calvary. Many of the most prominent among the Jews,—many priests, scribes, and pharisees formed part of the multitude which pressed around the Saviour, as he painfully struggled on to the mount. They followed Jesus as he walked wearily on, but not to aid or comfort him in his sorrow. No! they strove rather to mock him—to insult—to revile. Their faces indicate the venom which embitters their hearts, as they cry out in tones of exultant joy: "At last he is in our power, never more to escape, for before long we shall see him die on the cross." Let us also accompany this mournful train, and stopping at the Third Station consider *how Jesus falls beneath the cross the first time.* Why did Jesus fall so painfully? For two reasons.

I. *Because of the superabundance of his suffering, which we have inflicted upon him by our sins;*

II. *Because of the unfruitfulness of his Passion, in regard to those sinners who will not desist from their sins.*

PART I.

As the first reason, why Christ on his way to death had so painful a fall, we may assume *the superabundance of suffering which we have inflicted upon him.* The suffering of Jesus was twofold.

1. *Interior.*

(*a*) The martyrs in the midst of all their torture enjoyed divine consolation; God sustained them in their sufferings, consoled and strengthened them. It was this divine assistance which gave unto them a courage which no human aid could give, upheld them as the horrid instruments of torture were displayed before them, and enabled them even to regard with holy joy. It was this which sent them exultantly forth to death, as if they were going to a nuptial banquet, and caused them to bear the most cruel tortures in a manner that astonished even their executioners. It was this aid which bade them look calmly upon the sword, the rack, the cruel wheel, and smile at the savage beasts thirsting for blood, let loose by savage men. It was this divine consolation which enabled the holy deacon Lawrence, when the red hot bars of the gridiron caused him the most intense pain, to jest and say with a smile, as he lay helplessly there: "I am roasted sufficiently, take O! tyrant and eat." But it was not thus with Christ, when loaded with the cross he went to Calvary to die for us. The heavenly Father looked upon him as a victim who, because he had taken upon himself the guilt of sin, deserved punishment; he therefore withdrew all consolation from his humanity, so that he could even now exclaim, as afterwards on the cross: "My God, my God, why hast thou forsaken me."—Matt. 27: 46. Neither did he receive any consolation from man on his difficult way of the cross. The disciples whom he loved had abandoned him, the people, to whom he had done untold good, had forgotten his many benefits, and even wished for his death, and the proud leaders among the Jews, had sworn inveterate and perpetual enmity to him. Therefore Christ could truly say with David: "I looked for one that would grieve together with me, but there was none: and for one that would comfort me, and I found none."—Ps. 68: 21. Now, who can comprehend what the most Sacred Heart of Jesus suffered in being thus deprived of all consolation, and forsaken by God and man on his way to death, amid such inexpressible bodily pains! yes, when he was mocked, blasphemed, insulted, and abused by his enemies! Can a greater affliction be imagined? Can we wonder that, exhausted and powerless, he fell to the ground beneath the load of the cross?

(b) This interior suffering, this utter abandonment and dereliction, our dear Lord wished to take upon himself for the atonement of our sins, whereby God is offended in so many ways. But if, in their reckless folly, men neglect to avail themselves of the merits of Christ, so superabundantly presented to them—if they persistently refuse to give up their evil ways, and year after year go on in this impenitent way—to them shall be meted out some portion of that anguish of soul and utter abandonment which crushed Jesus to the earth on his way to the cross. When they come to die, they will call for their former friends and companions of sin, and implore their help, but these will turn away with indifference, or it may be with a shudder at the near presence of death, and abandon them to their desolation of soul. They will seek consolation of the world, but the world will refuse them its caresses, and will do nothing for their relief. They will, perhaps, turn to God, but alas! may we not fear with too much reason, that those menacing words of the Holy Ghost will find a verification equally terrible and just;—that to them will be said: "Because I called, and you refused: I stretched out my hand; and there was none that regarded. You have despised all my counsel, and have neglected my reprehensions. I also will laugh in your destruction; and I will mock when that shall come to you which you feared."—Prov. 1: 24, 25. Consider this unhappy end of the impenitent sinner. O! try to escape the fearful fate by a thorough and immediate amendment of life.

2. *Exterior.*

(a) When criminals are in prison; or already condemned to death, they are generally treated with mildness and consideration. Just the reverse was the case with Christ. Scarce had the basest treachery betrayed him into the hands of his enemies than he is forced to submit to one kind of ill-treatment after another, he is dragged before Annas, Caiphas, Pilate, and Herod, buffetted, scourged most inhumanly, a crown of thorns is put on his head, and during the whole night from Holy Thursday to Good Friday they allow him not a moment's repose. They never grow tired of mocking, blaspheming and tormenting him. And yet in the face of such multiplied, such agonizing sufferings, after an exhaustion so entire, that life seemed indeed passing away, Jesus takes the cross upon his shoulders in order to carry it to Calvary's Mount. Is it, therefore, astonishing, that after a short space he wavers, and falls prostrate to the ground?

(b) Recognize herein the enormity of sin, for after all it is sin only that is the cause of the sufferings of Jesus in general as also of this painful fall in particular: "He was wounded for our iniquities, he was bruised for our sins."—Is. 53 : 5. Now if God does not spare even his only beloved Son, having taken the sins of the world upon himself, but subjects him to the full severity of his justice, can it be something insignificant, can it be only a matter of little moment to commit mortal sins and to relapse into them again and again? Basilius, a notorious emperor of the Orient, while out one day, enjoying the pleasures of the chase, meeting an elk of extraordinary size, rushed upon him and endeavored to slay him with a lance. The elk, however, by means of his antler caught the emperor at his cincture, lifted him on high, and was about to dash him to the ground, when a nobleman in the vicinity noticing the peril of his sovereign, hastened to his rescue and saved his life. Every one praised the heroic act of the nobleman and believed that the emperor would richly reward him. But what did he do? The infamous wretch, whose pride could not endure to be under obligations to any one for a benefit, ordered his devoted subject, under the pretext of having sought his life, to be beheaded. Do not people who commit mortal sins act more wickedly and ungratefully towards Jesus than did this emperor towards the nobleman who saved his life? Is it not a most grievous offence against our divine Saviour, if, instead of being thankful to him for the grace of Redemption, we crucify him anew? Behold our suffering Saviour thus wearied unto death, and lying prostrate beneath the weight of the cross, let us reflect what a terrible thing sin is, and let us make the resolution henceforth to lead a penitential life, and to die rather than offend him again by mortal sin.

PART II.

Another reason why Christ on his way to Calvary's Mount fell in so painful a manner was, without doubt, the unfruitfulness of his Passion in so many impenitent sinners. To convince ourselves of this, let us consider,

1. *The love of Jesus for men.* No mother loves her only child as Jesus loved us, for as the prophet Jeremiah assures us, he loved us with an eternal love. Is not his incarnation even a proof of his infinite love! Or is it not an evidence of his infinite love for us, when for our redemption he exchanged heaven for earth, walked among us in the form of a servant, and for thirty years led a life of poverty, contempt and humiliations? Was it not loving us with an infinite love, when, finally, he suffered the most bitter death of the cross, in order to reconcile us with God, and rescue us from eternal damnation? And what love shone forth in his demeanor towards sinners, with what affection he sought them out all through his earthly career! How condescending was he not towards the Samaritan woman, how mercifully did he not treat the adulteress, whom the Jews wished to stone to death, how affectionately he received Magdalene, that

notorious public sinner, how compassionately and forgivingly he looked at Peter, who had denied him three times! He rejected not even the murderer on the cross, but in the last hour of his life gave him the consoling assurance: "This day thou shalt be with me in paradise."—Luke 23: 43. Evidence of the love of Jesus for us sinful men, and of his desire to save us, are also the parables of the good shepherd, who leaves the ninety-nine sheep in the desert and goes after the lost one, till he finds it, and having found it, rejoices over it; of the woman who seeks the lost groat with the greatest anxiety, and when she has found it, shows it to her friends and neighbors, saying: "Rejoice with me, because I found the groat which I had lost."—Luke 15: 9. Because Christ loved men with an ineffable love, he longed, during his whole life upon earth, for the day on which he could accomplish the work of redemption; for this reason he said to his disciples at the last supper: "With desire I have desired to eat this pasch with you before I suffer."—Luke 23: 15.

2. *His foreknowledge that his bitter Passion and death would be fruitless for the greater part of mankind.* By virtue of his omniscience he foresaw, that the majority of Jews and pagans would persevere in voluntary blindness and, therefore, remain for ever excluded from the kingdom of God; he foresaw that many Catholics would apostatize from the true faith, and thereby be eternally lost; he foresaw that the majority of Catholics would fail to become partakers of the merits of his Passion, and in consequence be eternally lost. While Christ, on the way of the cross, by reason of his omniscience represented to himself the people of all times, he was forced to say to himself: "I love men with such a devoted love, and I have done and suffered so much for them, I am even now on my way to die for them,, and what will be the result of all my sacrifices? Fruitless with so many are my instructions, my benefits, my miracles, and all the suffering of my earthly life; fruitless is my agony and my bloody sweat on Mount Olivet; fruitless the numberless insults, ignominies, and pains which I endured at my scourging and crowning with thorns; fruitless my going unto death, and the blood which I am about to shed on the cross. And before my eyes rise up the vast number of the unchaste who will not abandon the base pleasures which have cost me such bitter pain, I behold even the many avaricious men who will continue to hold their hoarded wealth as *God*. I weep for the unjust who deem it a trifle to defraud their fellow men, and sigh over the unforgiving who still cherish the enmities that eat into their very hearts. I see numbers who will permit sloth to take entire possession of their whole being, who will not exert themselves to repay *my* labors, but let my precious blood be shed in vain. All—all—place earthly cares and joys above their eternal salvation—they will not do penance—they will live in sin—And as they live, so shall they die." Now when Christ, on the one hand, loved

men so much, and therefore wished to save them in every possible way, and on the other hand saw, that nevertheless by far the greatest number would be delivered to eternal perdition, an inexpressible sadness and sorrow, more oppressive than the cross which he carried, weighed upon his most sacred heart, with every step his strength decreased, and at length, completely exhausted, he fell fainting to the ground.

3. *Ah, how many there may be amongst us, who were the cause of Christ's sorrowful fall on the way to Calvary!* How many there are who thoughtlessly violate the commandments of God and the precepts of the Church, and thereby offend him more and more with each succeeding day. They have so many means at their disposal, but they either do not avail themselves of them or abuse them, thus rendering themselves far more guilty in the sight of God. Many sermons are preached during the year; if by each sermon only one soul would be converted, in a short time there would be no more sinners, they are remembered at every Sacrifice of the Mass, many Christian pray for them, and often receive the bread of life in their behalf. They always have an opportunity, especially on Sundays and holydays, of reconciling themselves to God by a worthy reception of the Sacraments, yet they do not amend their life, but persevere in sin, and no grace is powerful enough to recall them from their evil ways. How was it possible for Christ, laden with the cross, not to have fallen to the ground on account of these sinners? If you live among Christians, with whom the merits of the Passion and death of Christ seem lost, on account of their continued impenitence, tell them to place themselves near the Third Station and there to reflect that Jesus on account of that impenitence, fell beneath the cross. Parents, say to your dissipated son, your wayward daughter: For your sake Christ fell beneath the cross. O! Christians, say to all impenitent sinners: It was *you* who hastened the fall of our dear Lord,— Through *you* he bent and fell beneath the weight of the cross,—Yet it was not that weight but your sins which cast his sacred form to the ground,— *you* have caused this first painful fall.

PERORATION.

Look at the picture of this Third Station where the loving Saviour lies prostrate beneath his cross. A livid paleness overspreads his holy face and the blood, forced out by the sharp points of the thorns, which form his crown runs in a red stream to the ground. One emaciated hand rests on the ground, the other clings to the cross to show that he loves its weight. Note how the cruel Jews urge him to rise, and then seriously ask yourselves this question, "Can it be that I too am the cause of Christ's sorrowful fall? We all, perhaps, have reason to answer in the affirmative, and confess: Yes, I am the cause, and on my account Christ fell thus painfully to the ground. Though at present we live in the state of grace, yet in years past we have often contaminated our conscience and offended God by thought, word, deed and omission. Whether we are sinners or penitents, let us prostrate ourselves at the Third Station, strike our breast and sigh contritely : " Jesus Christ crucified, have mercy on us ! " Amen.

FOURTH STATION.

JESUS MEETS HIS MOST AFFLICTED MOTHER.

" O all ye that pass by the way, attend, and see if there be any sorrow like to my sorrow."—Lam. I : 12.

Christ having somewhat recovered from his painful fall, with one mighty effort of love, summons his remaining strength, takes the heavy cross upon his shoulders and amid the rude jeers of the multitude, resumes, with faltering steps, his sorrowful way to Mount Calvary. But how hard did this journey become for him before he arrived at its end! Mary, knowing her dearest Son to be in the hands of his enemies, has no longer any rest or peace, she must see him and accompany him on his way to death; in order to afford him all possible relief in his dire need and abandonment. That she may not be prevented in her mission of love, she hastens with her faithful companions along a route which leads more quickly to the mount of sorrows, and waits at a spot by which the mournful procession must pass. She has not long to wait, savage cries fill the air, Christ, bent beneath the burden of the cross, surrounded by soldiers and accompanied by a great multitude of people, approaches and meets his mother. Let us consider with heartfelt sympathy in this meeting of Mother and Son under the most afflicting circumstances,

    I. The sorrow of the Son, and
    II. The sorrow of the Mother.

PART I.

That we may, at least to some extent, realize the greatness of the anguish which overwhelmed our divine Saviour when, on his way to Calvary, he met his most afflicted mother, let us consider,

    1. *That he loved her most tenderly* Now to measure the depth of love, mercy, and compassion of his adorable heart would be a deed scarce within

the compass of man. No heart ever beat in any human breast, save that of his beloved mother, which so throbbed with pity at the sorrows of us children of men, and he was ever ready to comfort those who wept. Thus in the city of Naim, a youth was carried out, the only son of a widow. Jesus seeing the mother of the dead youth in the deepest grief is at once moved with compassion; drawing near to her, exclaims: "Weep not." Then he bade the dead youth arise, renewed the light in his darkened eyes, replaced the livid hues of death with the warm color of life, and restored him living, to the mother, who could scarce contain herself for joy. Shortly before his own death, he stands at the grave of Lazarus in Bethany; the death of this man and the affliction of those present, grieve him so much that he himself sighs, and is moved to tears.—John 11 : 33-35. Such a sympathizing, feeling heart had our divine Lord for the sufferings of others. Yes, so sympathizing, compassionate and tender a heart had our Lord, that even for the misfortunes of his enemies he was moved, and the destruction of Jerusalem brought tears to his eyes. At the sight of this city, whose end is to be so deplorable, he cannot restrain his tears : "Seeing the city he wept over it."—Luke 19 : 41. Still more; even with his murderers he had mercy, and from the cross spoke those words of love and forgiveness : "Father, forgive them, for they know not what they do."—Luke 33 : 34. Now when Jesus was so affectionate towards all men, even towards his enemies, Oh, what anguish must have pierced his heart when he met under such afflicting circumstances his mother, whom he so tenderly loved. His sorrow was great when the terrible scourges lacerated his body, when the sharp, pointed thorns penetrated deeply into his head, and when weighed down by the cross he fell prostrate to the ground, but the agony which the sight of his afflicted mother caused him was incomparably greater, and we may well believe what St. Bridget says : "When Jesus saw his mother in such affliction, the sorrow he experienced on her account was so great that, from this exceeding grief for her, he ceased to feel the intolerable pain of his wounds."

2. *That he was unable, in her deep affliction, to offer her any comfort or consolation.* It is true, this was not impossible to him, for even in his deepest humiliation, he, being the Son of God, was almighty, he had only to will, and Mary's intense sorrow would have been changed into the greatest joy. Nevertheless, as in accordance with the decree of his divine Wisdom, he had ordained that his most holy mother should take an active part in this Passion and death ; in this sense he was not able to raise her up in her sorrow and console her. Though, according to his human will, he desired to comfort his afflicted mother, his divine will prevented it, and it demanded of him to accomplish the work of Redemption under all its painful, aggravating circumstances and to drink the chalice of bitterness to

the very dregs. Although he loved his dearest mother—this best of sons—with a love that surpassed all the combined affection of all earth's devoted children, he could not help her. Truly, meeting his most beloved mother under such circumstances, he could exclaim with the prophet: "O all ye that pass by the way, attend, and see if there be any sorrow like to my sorrow!"

3. *Application.* Christian sons and daughters, look upon the Fourth Station and learn from your Saviour, how you too should tenderly love your parents, and share with them both joy and sorrow, prosperity and adversity. Although they are not as good and perfect as Mary, the best of all mothers, yet they deserve all your love and gratitude, for after God they are your greatest benefactors. Reflect upon all the good they have done you in body and soul, think of all the trouble and solicitude you have caused them, the labor and pain they have endured for your sake. It would be ingratitude beyond description, should you forget the benefits they have heaped upon you from earliest infancy, or repay them with rudeness and ill-treatment! O! hard indeed would be the hearts of those children who, forgetful of the constant care given them by tender parents in their helpless childhood would neglect those dear ones when sickness, sorrow, or old age calls for their most devoted filial care. And yet there are such children. A good tree nourishes many fruits and causes them to grow and ripen. But as soon as they are mature they burden the tree, bend it to the ground and break off many branches, yea, would even destroy it altogether, were it not supported by props. Do many children act otherwise? Having been reared by their parents not without care of which one can scarcely form any idea, and trouble of which it were vain to attempt a description, they cause them nothing but sorrow and grief. They have no patience with their frailties, treat them harshly and rudely, and too often neglect them, and permit want and misery to enter their doors. How fittingly does the old adage in such cases come in to play: "Parents can support five, six and more children, but five, six, and even more children often are not sufficient to support an aged father and mother." They willingly see their parents depart this life, in order to have no longer any care and expense with them. Such God-forsaken, ungrateful children certainly incur a great responsibility before God and have reason to fear, that in them will be fulfilled the words of the Holy Ghost: "Of what an evil-fame is he that forsaketh his father? And he is cursed of God that angereth his mother."—Eccles. 3: 18. Beware then, Christian children, of such conduct toward your parents, treat them with reverence, mildness, and forbearance, though they should not be without fault, love them most tenderly and let them want for nothing in their sickness or old age. —Consider the words of the Lord: "Son, support the old age of thy father; and grieve him not in his life: and if his understanding fail, have

patience with him, and despise him not when thou art in thy strength : for the relieving of the father shall not be forgotten."—Eccles. 3 : 14, 15.

Part II.

Great, ineffably great, was the sorrow of the Blessed Virgin, Mother of God, when she met Jesus almost sinking beneath the burden of the cross. The magnitude of this sorrow will become manifest to us when we consider,

1. *The person who carries the cross.* Compassionate hearts sympathize with the misery of others and on beholding it can scarcely refrain from tears. Thus the women of Jerusalsm wept when they saw Jesus laden with the cross, and accompanied him to the place of execution. wherefore he said to them : "Daughters of Jerusalem, weep not over me ; but weep for yourselves and for your children."—Luke 23 : 28. How much more intense is the grief if the suffering person is no stranger, but a relative, or a child ! How much did not Jacob lament, when the bloody coat of Joseph was exhibited to him and he was told that a wild beast had devoured him ! Inconsolable in his grief, he exclaimed : "I will go down to my son into hell (limbo) mourning."—Gen. 37 : 35. What must have been Mary's anguish when she saw her son in the hands of his murderers led to crucifixion ! When her grief was so profound during the three days of her beloved child's loss at Jerusalem, that in her sorrow she thus pathetically said to Jesus : "Son, why hast thou done so to us ? Behold thy father and I have sought thee sorrowing ; "—Luke 2 : 48 ; what must have been her sufferings at the Fourth Station when she saw him so terribly maltreated, and knew that he was to die on the cross? How truly St. Bernardine says : "At the sight of her Son Mary experienced a sorrow so great that if it had been equally divided among all men they would have died."

2. *His suffering form.* Ah, the most beautiful amongst the sons of men has no longer any form or beauty, he is the most despised and abject of men, a man of sorrows, like to a leper, whom the Lord has bruised for our sins.—Is. 53 : 2–5. His head is crowned with thorns, his eyes are swollen and full of dust, tears and blood, his countenance is disfigured with spittle, perspiration, wounds and blood, his garment is soiled and reddened with blood, upon his mangled shoulders lies the heavy cross, the terrible instrument of his Passion, the weight of which presses him to the ground, in short he is a most pitiable object to behold. Add to this the horrible curses and imprecations of the soldiers, the mockery of the Scribes and Pharisees, the clamor and noise of the rabble, and you have but a faint idea of how Mary beholds her Son ! Pilate, a pagan, seeing him, has compassion on him, and exclaims : "*Ecce Homo!*" Behold the man ! If the cold heart of a pagan is touched, how must the most tender,

loving mother's heart feel! O, at the Fourth Station of the Way of the Cross the prophetic words of St. Simeon were fulfilled in Mary to the very letter: "Thy own soul a sword shall pierce."—Luke 2: 35. On account of this sorrow Mary is justly called "The Queen of Martyrs."

3. *Application.* In our Blessed Mother parents have a most admirable example of the living interest they should take in the necessities of their children, and the relief they should afford them as far as they are able, Christian charity and the obligations inseparable from their state in life alike impose this duty upon them, and to neglect it renders them guilty before God of sins against justice and charity.

(*a*) *For the temporal welfare of their children.* Many parents have a number of children, and to provide for the many needs of those little ones, requires diligent and constant labor, wearisome toil from early morn until late at night. But how do many act? Yielding to the demon of sloth, and reckless of the fatal consequences, they ruthlessly squander the precious time which should be devoted to work. Or the father will, perhaps, throw away his last penny for drink—or gamble with the money which should clothe and feed his wife and little ones. Though the wife and children suffer the utmost need, though they have no clothes to cover themselves fittingly, no bread to stay their hunger, the dissipated father cares not, provided his wants are gratified. To such fathers the words of the Apostle apply: "If any man have not care of his own, and especially of those of his house, he hath denied the faith, and is worse than an infidel."—I. Tim. 5: 8.

(*b*) *For their spiritual welfare.* Many parents act contrary to their duty in this regard. Their children frequently, even in early life manifest great levity and conduct which foreshadows the worst results. The years bring no reform, alas, they become more degenerate as they grow older. Prayer, going to church, receiving the Sacraments and all religious exercises are distasteful to them; they plunge themselves into a life of worldliness and dissipation, and give free scope to all their sinful lusts and desires. With such children parents should have no compassion, they should act toward them with severity; for they are in a fair way of becoming miserable for time and eternity. But no; they allow their son, their daughter to go the way that leads to perdition, and are even indignant with those who condemn their wicked conduct, and who endeavor to win them from their evil ways. Are there not parents who find constant fault with teachers, who punish their mischievous little ones at school? Are there not parents who resist the rules and regulations which are made for the good of children? Are there not parents who reprehend priests for forbidding unseasonable hours, drinking, gambling and dancing? O the blindness of fathers, the folly of some mothers, who would scorn the imputation of not loving their children, and yet they have not a spark of true love for them in their hearts. Ah no! they are the enemies of those immortal beings, they have no compassion, they would destroy whom a just judge will require at their hands. What a responsibility is theirs, because their children on account of neglected discipline offend God in many ways, and perhaps are eternally lost.

PERORATION.

Parents and children, assemble to-day before the Fourth Station of the Way of the Cross, consider the sorrow of Jesus and Mary in their meeting and make firm resolutions to fulfill conscientiously the duties which belong to your respective states of life. Children, love your parents, honor them, obey them; if they are bent under the sorows of years, have patience with them and assist them according to your ability, and rejoice if God still leaves them—a precious legacy!—with you a little longer that you may repay, at least, a part of your debt to them while they are still with you on earth. Parents, have a true, Christian love for your children, be solicitous for their spiritual and temporal welfare and put forth all your energy in order to bring them up in the love and fear of God, and faithful members of his holy Church. Such a love as exists between parent and child should reign amongst you all. Let us, according to the admonition of the Apostle, put on the bowels of mercy, assist one another in our necessities according to our ability and promote our temporal and eternal welfare. But because with the best will we cannot help ourselves or others without the assistance of God's grace, let us have recourse to Jesus the fountain of all consolation and help, and pray with humility and confidence: "Jesus Christ crucified, have mercy on us." Amen.

FIFTH STATION.

SIMON OF CYRENE ASSISTS JESUS IN CARRYING THE CROSS.

"*And they forced one Simon of Cyrene to take up his cross.*"—*Mark 15 : 21.*

Thanks be to God. The fury with which the divine Saviour has been persecuted ceases by degrees, and human feelings seem at last to have entered the hearts of his relentless foes. Even the rude soldiers manifest some mercy and compassion, for they take the heavy load of the cross from his shoulders and place it upon a certain Simon of Cyrene. "And they forced one Simon of Cyrene to take up *His* cross." Now that the intolerable load has been removed, and the lacerated shoulders released from its pressure he can perhaps regain some small part of his fast vanishing strength, and the more easily reach the spot where the last drop of his blood will be shed for us, *sinners*, whom he so tenderly loves. Human hearts have procured him this mitigation. But think you that the cross was removed from the shoulders of the exhausted Saviour from a motive of mercy and compassion? Alas! no! his enemies had no mercy—no pity in their hearts—It was done lest their hate should be deprived of its victim—lest Christ, unable to bear the load, should falter and fall, and die before he reached the scene of his crucifixion. Hate alone inspired those cruel men to take the cross from Jesus and give it to the Cyrenian.—Let us to-day place ourselves at the Fifth Station of the Way of the Cross, over which are written the words: "Simon of Cyrene assists Jesus in carrying the cross," and consider,

I. The reasons which Simon had for not carrying the cross, and
II. The reasons which nevertheless induced him to carry it.

Part I.

1. Suppose that even Simon carried the cross for Jesus more from compulsion than voluntarily, he nevertheless merits some consideration, on account of the reasons which he had for not carrying it, and of which I shall mention only these three :

(*a*) *His business.* He was a farmer, and had to earn his bread in the sweat of his brow. Consequently when he drew near the mournful procession, he had no idea of joining the crowd, but, as the Gospel especially makes mention, he only wished to pass by so as to lose no time from his work. Therefore, when he was hastening home, and was confronted by the noisy crowd with the word that he was to take the cross and to carry it for Jesus, he could readily have made an excuse: "I have no time, you see yourselves, I have just come from work and cannot be detained. There are many idlers here who will lose nothing by carrying the cross, put it upon one of them." Thus, or in similar words, Simon could have escaped the unwelcome task they would impose upon him, and gone away whithersoever he desired.

(*b*) *The disgrace of carrying the cross.* The cross was an instrument of death for malefactors of the lowest class, and he who had to die upon it was considered as cursed by God and man. "Cursed is every one that hangeth on a tree."—Gal. 3 : 13. How mortifying then for Simon to be thus forced to carry the cross for our Saviour, who was considered a criminal; yes, it was a *disgrace*, even, for Christ was regarded amongst all malefactors, the chief.

(c) *The fatigue of carrying the cross.* The weight of the cross was enormous, Jesus had already fallen beneath the load, and could carry it no farther ; the way to Calvary was steep, and Simon, without doubt, was already wearied by hard work. He was anxious to reach his home for a much-needed repast, he wished to refresh himself before returning to his laborious task, and lo ! a task far more arduous and repugnant was offered him, and, eventually almost forced, upon his unwilling hands.

2. We are called upon and invited, not by the soldiers, but by Jesus Christ himself, to carry the cross. "If any man will come after me, let him deny himself and take up his cross, and follow me."—Matt. 16 : 24. Being Christians, we are obliged to carry the cross, that is, to undergo mortifications and labors, without which it is impossible to lead a pious life. But many Christians will not consent to this,

(a) *On account of their temporal affairs.* Entirely carried away by the pressure of temporal affairs, and utterly engrossed by their business, or pleasures, as the case may be, they do not take time to think of the salvation of their soul, and to comply with those religious duties which, as Catholics, it is incumbent upon them to fulfill. But so far from complying with those obligations, each succeding year finds them given up to distractions, and alas! oblivious of "those things which are above," they toil and plan, and scheme, and ever it is from day to day, *the world*. They resemble busy Martha, who was careful about many things, whilst she neglected the one thing necessary. They never think of saying their daily prayers. If on Sunday they do not entirely neglect the precept of hearing Mass, a low Mass suffices for their devotion, and thus, perhaps, a year elapses without their having even once been present to receive instruction through the word of God. They do not think of confession until the paschal precept reminds them that now indeed *they must*, and then they delay receiving the Sacraments until the Easter time is almost over. And why? Because as they allege, they have no time. O rather let them acknowledge their want of zeal in doing good, and confess that the will to perform their duties is lacking. If other Christians, who might well nigh sink beneath the pressure of all that duty compels them to do at home, find time for all and *more* than their absolute obligations of religion, why cannot they? Look at the noble example of Louis IX of France who, with the affairs of a kingdom to control yet found time for every duty he owed to God.

(*b*) *On account of the contumely of which they are afraid, if they zealously follow Jesus and endeavor to lead a holy life.* Too often alas! in our day there is a certain obloquy attached to the rigid observance of God's commandments, and the precepts of the Church, while to show one's self a fervent zealous Catholic is to become a subject for remark and reproach. What contempt follows those who wish to lead a more than ordinarily pious life! Their virtue is suspected, they themselves are insulted, they are slandered—derided and mocked at by the votaries of the world. This fatal fear of being made the subject of remark, the apprehension of being ridiculed, deters many from the rigid observance of their religious exercises. It makes them model their lives according to the manner of their worldly minded associates. They are influenced by that bane of so many Christians: " " *What will they say of me ?* " Human respect! What will they think if I act so differently from their mode of life? It is the fashion of the world, I must act this way, otherwise I should be overwhelmed with mortification. When I hear irreligious, unchaste discourses, I am really displeased, but have to listen to them for fear of mockery and contempt. I would like to go frequently to confession and Communion, and to hear Mass regularly, but if I did I should be exposed to unkind remarks and all kinds of abuse. Thus people think and speak, and it is but too true that many Christians, from a false shame and for fear of the judgment of the world, act in direct opposition to the voice of conscience, and despise the Cross on which their loving Saviour died. O, that such Christians would consider the words of Christ: "Whosoever shall deny me before men, I will also deny him before my Father who is in heaven."—Matt. 10: 33. "Whosoever shall be ashamed of me, and of my words, in this adulterous and sinful generation, the Son of Man also shall be ashamed of him, when he shall come in the glory of his Father, with the holy angels." —Mark 8 : 38.

(*c*) *On account of the hardships and difficulties attendant upon the following of Christ.* It cannot be denied that to walk with Jesus along the dolorous way of the cross, in other words to follow him and lead a mortified pious life most assuredly is hard and demands many a painful sacrifice, which poor, weak human nature often shrinks from undertaking. Christ himself says : " The kingdom of heaven suffereth violence, and the violent bear it away." —Matt. 11 : 12. And again : "How narrow is the gate, and strait is the way, which leadeth to life ; and few there are who find it."—Matt. 7 : 14. A pious Christian must continually carry his cross, mortify the flesh with its concupiscences, renounce the sinful pleasures of the world, take upon himself the difficulties of the service of God, atone by penitential works for the insults he has offered to him, and carefully guard against a relapse. At the sight of so many hardships, difficulties and sacrifices, many Christians are discouraged and cannot resolve upon earnestly beginning to carry the cross after Christ. O, the blindness and infatuation of such people; they do not consider that God commands nothing impossible, that his grace supports our weakness and effectually sustains us in all that is necessary for salvation, that there is difficulty only when one is entering upon a life of piety and that the consolation and peace enjoyed by the faithful servants of God sweeten all bitterness and render what would be otherwise heavy and hard, so light and easy that it becomes their chief joy to walk in the footsteps of their suffering Lord.

Part II.

1. Three reasons in particular, may have induced Simon of Cyrene to carry the cross for Christ:

(*a*) *Compulsion.* He refused at first to carry the cross for Christ, but his resistance was vain; for he was compelled by the soldiers to do as they wished. "They forced one Simon of Cyrene to take up the cross for Jesus," says the Gospel. When he found them so determined, and saw that his objections were all unheeded, he yielded to necessity and carried the cross.

(*b*) *Compassion.* Simon beheld the most piteous and pathetic sight, ever witnessed in the world, before his very eyes, that of the tortured Redeemer weakened, bruised, wounded, and covered with dust and blood. He felt that if he refused aid in this extremity, the Saviour would soon give up and die beneath the heavy weight of the cross, and kinder sentiments were awakened in his heart. Although he was not perfectly convinced of his innocence, yet a feeling of sympathy was awakened in him; he, therefore, resisted the soldiers no longer, but took up the cross and put it upon his own shoulders. He did this the more readily as the patience with which Jesus Christ bore every hardship, his eyes raised to heaven, his silence, and his whole conduct convinced him more and more of the innocence of the Saviour.

(*c*) *The shortness of the way.* Turning his glance in the direction of Calvary, Simon saw that the journey was almost completed, and that he would soon reach the summit of the mount. He said to himself: I will no longer resist, in a few minutes it will be over, and I shall lay down the cross, and with the consciousness of having performed a work of mercy, can return to my work.

2. *Application.*

(*a*) "God will have all men to be saved," (1.Tim. 2 : 4), but because many are not willing to do what is required for salvation, he does what the soldiers did who forced Simon to take up the cross, he forces them by tribulations and sufferings to serve him. There are alas! but too many who resemble a clock which works only when it is loaded with a weight, or water which can be preserved from corruption only by the strength and virtue of salt. How many sinners do we not find who owe their conversion to crosses and afflictions! Adam and Eve, the brothers of Joseph, Manasses, and the man who was afflicted with an infirmity for thirty-eight years, and thousands of others would probably have continued in sin, if God had not recalled them from their evil ways by strewing with thorns the pathway which formerly had been bordered with roses. Such is also the case to-day. Man, who, when the sunshine of prosperity illumines his life, easily forgets God and deviates from the right path, is called back upon it, when its brightness is overshadowed by the clouds of affliction. He detaches his heart from the deceitful world, repents of his errors and reforms his life, and is ever after a true lover of the cross. The tribulations with which God visits us are, therefore, especial proofs of his love and are frequently the only means of salvation for the sinner. Let us not, then, complain of sufferings and afflictions, but receive them patiently and bear them as long as it pleases God to afflict us, mindful of the words of the Apostle: "Whom the Lord loveth he chastiseth, and he scourgeth every son whom he receiveth."—Heb. 12 : 6.

(*b*) One glance upon our suffering Saviour should stimulate us to patience. "My God," says St. Alphonsus, "how is it possible that he who looks at his Saviour, who beholds his God die in a sea of sufferings, can become impatient in his sufferings, nay, how is it possible for him not to wish, for the love for his Lord, to endure all possible pains!" St. Magdalene of Pazzi says: "The greatest pain is agreeable when one looks upon Jesus on the cross." And St. Bernard says: "He who loves his crucified Saviour never murmurs or complains in sufferings and tribulations." In all your trials, sufferings and afflictions look up to Jesus on the cross and consider what he has suffered, and with what heavenly patience he has endured everything, and it will certainly not be hard for you to follow him on the Way of the Cross.

(*c*) When Simon of Cyrene took up the cross, he consoled himself with the thought: The end is very near at hand, the way to Calvary is not long, I shall soon be there. Can we not also console ourselves with this thought when we are visited with sufferings and afflictions, or when to follow Christ on the way of mortification and self-denial appears hard to us? O yes, for what is our life upon earth but a shadow which quickly passes, a flower that blossoms to-day and withers to-morrow. Some of us may yet live thirty years, others twenty, others ten, others five, some perhaps only one year, one month, one day. How quickly will this time pass! Even supposing that for some the years will extend to a period of fifty or sixty? It is a long time to look forward to, but what are those years compared to eternity? Not one moment! "for a thousand years in thy sight (O eternal God) are as yesterday which is past."—Ps. 89 : 4. And, behold, if in this short space of time you carry the cross after your Saviour, you will enter with him into glory, for if we suffer with him we shall be glorified with him.—Rom. 8 : 17. O where is the Christian who, considering this consoling truth, will refuse to follow Jesus Christ on the way of the cross, with patience and constancy.

PERORATION.

O Jesus, our crucified Lord and Saviour, we know and take to heart what thou hast said : "He that taketh not this cross and followeth me, is not worthy of me."—Matt. 10: 38. Meditating then upon the Fifth Station let us make the firm resolution to carry the cross after Jesus, to walk in his footsteps and to follow him that we may one day participate in his glory in heaven. Amen.

SIXTH STATION.

VERONICA WIPES THE FACE OF JESUS.

"*Do good to the just; and thou shalt find great recompense.*"—*Ecclus 12: 2.*

In the Sixth Station of the cross we behold Jesus still painfully pursuing his steps along the dolorous way, whilst his tormentors urge him to greater speed in their eagerness to put him to death. His sacred countenance is so disfigured by dust and blood, that it can scarcely be recognized, and his whole appearance so indicative of the deepest dejection that it touched the heart of a pious matron, who, burning with the desire to help the divine sufferer, offers him her veil that he might wipe his sacred face! It is not known who this good woman was, we cannot even give her name with certainty. Some call her *Berenice*, others say that her name was *Seraphia*, and that she was the wife of a certain councilman, named Sirach. We know her best by the name "Veronica," however, and love to contemplate the kind act which even on earth, met with so magnanimous a reward. *Veronica* signifies "the true picture." The name was given her because Christ when he wiped his face imprinted on the veil the picture of his most holy

SIXTH STATION.

countenance. Let us meditate to-day on this event. Placing ourselves beneath the Sixth Station, which bears the inscription: "*Veronica wipes the face of Jesus,*" let us consider for our edification,

I. *What act of charity Veronica did to Christ, and*
II. *What recompense she received from him for it.*

PART I.

1. At first sight the act of charity which Veronica did to Christ in presenting him her veil to wipe his face, does not appear as something great, but we shall judge otherwise when we consider,

(a) *The great love with which she came to the relief of Christ in his abandonment.* There is no doubt that Veronica was of the number of those who acknowledged Christ as the Redeemer, promised and sent by God, and that she adhered to him with a believing, faithful heart. How she trembled when she heard that he was condemned to death and would be led to Calvary to be crucified! She started at once on her way, hastened to Mount Calvary and took a position at a place from which she could see the mournful train as it passed. O! what anguish stirred her heart to its deepest depths when the rabble drew nigh, and in the midst of a rude, jeering mob, she saw Christ almost fainting under the heavy load of the cross. Tears dimmed her eyes as she beheld the cold clammy drops of perspiration, mingled with blood and dust, which covered the holy face of our Lord—of him, the king of heaven and earth! Her compassionate heart would have rejoiced could she have rescued the innocent sufferer from his merciless foes, but as this would be an impossibility, she did at least what she could. She approached Jesus and with the greatest reverence wiped his face with her veil in order thereby to mitigate his sufferings. This certainly was an act of charity which, because of the loving wish which prompted it is entitled to our earnest commendation.

(b) *The obstacles which she had to overcome in the performance of this act of charity.* The divine Saviour was surrounded only by men who hated him with a most intense hatred, and who took the greatest pleasure in aggravating his way to death as much as possible. With what contempt must this good woman have been treated when she pressed forward to wipe the face of Jesus! Some said that she had lost her senses, because she wiped the face of a malefactor with her costly veil, others rudely pushed her back, with loud curses and threats. And what did the priests, the Scribes, the Pharisees do? Their dark and angry glances betrayed their indignation and wrath, and they bitterly denounced her as deserving of the expulsion from the synagogue which would probably follow her "mad act." Thus we see how Veronica's kind deed gained for her derision, persecution and insult, but regardless of all else save her mission of love, she hesitated not until it was accomplished. There were difficulties in her path—there were obstacles in the way—but in the face of all she performed this deed of charity inspired by love.

2. *Application.*

(*a*) What a beautiful example does not Veronica give us for our consideration! The service of God is attended with difficulties. Christ himself says: "If any man will come after me, let him deny himself, and take up his cross, and follow me."—Matt. 16 : 24. He who wishes to live as a good, pious, practical Christian, must be prepared to suffer contempt, insult, derision and persecution, and to endure much that is not only not pleasant, but decidedly the reverse, and often very difficult to bear.

(*b*) In these obstacles we find the reason why so many Christians, forgetful of all that Jesus endured for them, become faithless to Christ, and enter the enemy's camp. Alas, how many poor weak souls does human respect lure from their allegiance to Christ! Like the Apostles, who could not be too devoted in their adherence to their divine Master when sunshine seemed to gild his way, but who, when the dark clouds of adversity appeared, left him and fled, they too fail in the hour of trial. They lack good will; they find pleasure in good and detest and hate that which is evil, they serve God in time of prosperity and joyfully walk in the path of virtue; but in time of adversity, when a sacrifice is required of them for Christ's sake, they become discouraged, cowardly surrender and make a dishonorable peace with the enemies of the cross. Whence this weakness? Ah! their love for God is still weak and imperfect. If their love for Christ were as ardent as was Veronica's, let the difficulties in the way of their salvation seem ever so insurmountable, they would persevere until they were all set aside. "Love is as strong as death, many waters cannot quench charity," (Cant. 8 : 17), for charity beareth all things, endureth all things.—1. Cor. 13 : 7. He who loves God above all things can exclaim with St. Paul: "Who shall separate us from the love of Christ? Shall tribulation? or distress? or famine? or nakedness? or danger? or persecution? or the sword?"—Rom. 8 : 35. Let us daily ask Jesus for this strong, conquering love, that we may adhere to him with equal fidelity in the days of adversity as well as in those of prosperity.

PART II.

Veronica through devotion and compassion for Jesus offered the veil from her head, that he might wipe the sweat from off his brow, and he deigned to imprint his sacred countenance upon the cloth. In truth, a great recompense for the act of charity which Veronica performed; for he thereby gave her,

1. *The most touching evidence of his love.* The more precious in our estimation is the gift we bestow upon another, the greater is the degree of affection we manifest towards the favored one. Thus Jonathan divested himself of his own garments and gave them, together with his arrow, sword and cincture, to his friend David as a sign of his affection and love for him. The dearer to us is the gift which we give to another, the more we express our love for him, and demonstrate the high place he holds in our esteem. Now there is nothing in closer relation to us, and of greater value in our own eyes, than our own portrait. By giving it to one we give him, as it were, ourselves. When, therefore, our divine Lord permitted Veronica to possess the impression of his holy face, it was a certain mark that he found her worthy of his approval and love. Thereby he distinguished and preferred her to the weeping women of Jerusalem, to whom he gave no other sign of his love than to say to them, that they should not weep over him, but for themselves and for their children.—Luke 23 : 28.

(*a*) What a grace for Veronica that Jesus gave her the impression of his sacred countenance, thereby assuring her of his love! What treasure is more valuable and more desirable than the love of Jesus! He who possesses this inestimable treasure enjoys even here below the greatest happiness, for he enjoys a peace which surpasses all conception and which the world with its ephemeral joys and fleeting treasures, may try, but try all vainly to give. Even in sufferings and tribulations he can say with the Apostle : "I am filled with comfort, I exceedingly abound with joy in all our tribulation."—2. Cor. 7 : 4. And what an unspeakable felicity is reserved for him in the next life? There he will enjoy a beatitude incomprehensible in its greatness and eternal in its duration : "The eye hath not seen, nor ear heard, neither hath it entered into the heart of man, what things God hath prepared for them that love him."—1. Cor. 2 : 9.

(*b*) *An excellent means for a return of love.* So exceedingly precious in the eyes of devoted and loving children are the portraits of their dead parents that they value them as their dearest earthly possessions. Looking at them vividly recalls the tender solicitude with which that dear father—that cherished mother watched over them during life, and they weep tears of gratitude—of sorrow—of love. At the same time they vividly remember the salutary lessons and admonitions given them by their father and mother and they renew their resolutions to live according to them as long as life lasts. Good children do this, the picture of their parents is to them not only a dear keepsake, but also a powerful incentive to a virtuous life.

We cannot doubt that Veronica thought and felt thus before the image of Jesus. O, I think I see her look at this wonderful picture and contemplate it for hours at a time. When she represented to herself the bitter Passion and death of Christ, the fire of love would ardently inflame her heart, and full of emotion she would exclaim : "O Jesus, how much thou hast done and suffered in order to redeem us miserable sinners ! In gratitude to thee for this infinite love I devote my whole love to thee!" And this she did; she offered herself as a sacrifice to Jesus, and for the remainder of her life, the greatest trials and hardships were joyfully endured for his sake. All the days of her life she served him with a fidelity that knew no wavering, and now it is her happy lot to see her Saviour face to face. In wrapt adoration she can gaze constantly on the reality of what she so cherished upon earth.

2. *Application.*

(*a*) We possess the same means which incited Veronica to the love of Jesus Christ. The "Ecce Homo," that touching picture of the crucified, the MAN OF SORROWS is within the reach of all, and he that can resist the pleading look in its sad eyes must be obdurate and hard-hearted in the extreme. He that contemplates this picture with attention and in the light of faith, would prove himself, indeed, destitute of every human feeling, if he would remain cold and insensible to all emotion. History proves that even the most careless people and the greatest sinners become contrite, totally changed and inflamed with the love of God. Hippolitus, a pious priest of Florence, had a painting of the "Ecce Homo." It was his constant practice to devote several hours daily to the contemplation of this picture, and to meditation upon the love and suffering which it recalled. His heart would overflow with gratitude, as he dwelt upon every detail of that infinite love which caused a God to shed his precious blood for sinful man. Whilst thus engaged he attracted the gaze of a proud vain woman who lived opposite, and who was scandalized thinking that he was regarding his own features in a mirror, Unable to resist her curiosity she asked him to show her the remarkable mirror which so frequently engrossed his attention. The priest willingly complied with the request. He took the picture and brought it to the house of this vain daughter of the world. Seeing the image of our Redeemer, with a crown of thorns on his head, tears in his eyes, his lips purple, his face covered with spittle, perspiration and dust, and in such a pitiable state that he scarcely resembled a man, she was struck with terror and deeply moved. The priest said: "Behold the mirror which you desired to see; in it all should daily contemplate themselves. If this mirror makes no impression upon you and does not move your heart to conversion, you are lost. Contemplate in this sacred countenance how much your Redeemer suffered on account of your pride and vanity. Behold with your own eyes him, before whom on the day of judgment you must give a rigorous account of all whom you have scandalized and seduced." These words made so powerful an impression upon her that she began to weep bitterly for her sins and contritely prostrating herself before the priest, she implored pardon for them, resolved to lead a Christian life, renounced the world, and, in a convent, became a model for all.

(*b*) Follow the example of this penitent. Look often at the picture of the crucifixion, but let not your eyes turn away from it unmoved. It will be a meditation most profitable to the soul. You will understand the great evil of sin and will resolve to love and serve Jesus who has done and suffered so much for your sake. Look upon the picture of your crucified Saviour, particularly in time of temptation and when in danger of committing sin. If you have to suffer injustice and persecution, if anger and hatred arise in your heart, look upon the crucifix and consider, what ignominy and abuse Jesus suffered for love of you, and you will overcome all desire of revenge and remain meek. If great tribulations afflict you, look at the crucifix and contemplate the inexhaustible patience with which Christ suffered and you will regain courage and resign yourself to the will of God. If you are tempted to pride, to impurity or to any other sin, look at the crucifix, and consider what Jesus had to suffer on account of our sins, and take to heart the words: "If in the green wood they do these things, what shall be done in the dry;" (Luke 23 : 31); thus with the help of God's grace you will overcome every temptation and with constancy walk in the path of virtue.

PERORATION.

Yes, according to the example of Veronica and other pious Christians, often look at the image of the suffering and dying Redeemer; contemplate yourselves in this mirror of all virtue and perfection, and you will be greatly stimulated to avoid every sin and to serve God with renewed fervor. Thus the pictures of the Passion will be to you as to Veronica a great gift of grace, and you may hope that you will one day behold in heaven him, upon whose picture you so often looked with loving sorrow here below. Amen.

SEVENTH STATION.

JESUS FALLS BENEATH THE CROSS THE SECOND TIME.

"Being pushed, I was overturned that I might fall."—Ps. 117 : 13.

We are again assembled to-day to direct our attention to the divine Saviour who for love us died the most painful death, for the narrative of the Passion and death of Christ must be to us a story "ever ancient, yet always new," and we cannot weary of hearing how our dear Redeemer purchased for us heaven and its joys by the cross. And of the many subjects of meditation presented by our watchful mother the Church, there is none more salutary than the devout contemplation of all that Jesus has done and suffered for our sake. Herein we learn not only God's severe justice which spared not his only begotten Son; but having pledged him for sinners, delivered him up to the most painful death, but we also behold with a clearer conviction that infinite love and mercy which moved God to sacrifice the dearest object of his love, that the sinful human race might be redeemed. We are stimulated to renounce sin, to serve God and to enter upon a holy life and to secure the salvation of our immortal souls. For this reason the holy Fathers and spiritual writers urgently recommend the meditation on the Passion and death of Christ, and St. Albert the Great says that to meditate daily on the Passion of Christ is more profitable than to fast on bread and water every Friday throughout the year, to discipline oneself severely and to recite all the psalms from beginning to end. Let us place ourselves at the Seventh Station, over which is written: "*Jesus falls beneath the cross the second time,*" and let us consider what was the cause of this fall, I find two reasons, in particular:

I. *The cruelty of his enemies, and*
II. *The faithlessness of his friends.*

PART I.

Once again we behold the wearied and well-nigh expiring Saviour waver beneath a burden far too heavy, a load which has already caused him one painful fall. He vainly seeks to recover himself, the weight overpowers him, he falls with his holy face to the earth. Why does he fall again to the ground, from which he had but a few moments ago risen from his first fall? You need not question long; the first cause was the *cruelty of his enemies.*

SEVENTH STATION.

1. *They had not the least compassion on him.* The very criminal on his way to the death penalty is treated with consideration and his pathway smoothed by a certain degree of kindness, so that his last hour of life may not be bitter and hard. He is placed in a wagon or carriage, by his side is a priest who whispers words of solace, bids him take courage, prays *with* him, and *for* him, that he may be preserved from despair. A breathless silence seems to pervade the very air, so profoundly quiet are the spectators, and they evince the greatest sympathy, especially if he die a penitent death. But how is Jesus treated with the cross on his shoulders? Is his dolorous way to Calvary's Mount alleviated, is the adorable Son of God treated better than a malefactor? We must answer these questions absolutely in the negative. They have compassion on Barabbas, the robber and murderer, compassion on the two thieves, but they have no compassion on Jesus; all who conduct and accompany him to death are his sworn enemies, who vie with one another in making his way to death as painful as possible. The leaders of the Jewish people, the Scribes and Pharisees, blaspheme and calumniate him and every moment seems an hour until they see their divine victim expire on the cross. The degenerate people, too, who in great multitudes accompany him, desire his death, and anxiously look forward to the moment when he is to be crucified. On his way to Calvary, with the exception of Mary, his ever loving mother, and a few pious women who, although their hearts longed to comfort him, could accomplish nothing to give him relief, no one had any compassion, no one would in any way alleviate his sorrowful journey to death. His sacred brow was throbbing beneath the thorns, and his tender feet were bleeding, bruised, and torn. His tottering form was bending with the weight of the cross, which seemed to grow heavier with every step he took. O! truly could he say with the Psalmist: "I looked for one that would grieve together with me, but there was none: and for one that would comfort me, and I found none."—Ps. 68 : 21.

Application. Had you been present at the time when Jesus laden with the cross went to Calvary, would you, too, have had no mercy, no compassion on him? Certainly you would have had. With Veronica you would have offered him fine linen to wipe his holy face; with Simon of Cyrene, assisted him in carrying his cross and with the women of Jerusalem who wept over him, you at least would have mingled your tears. What you would have done then, you can do even to-day, you can prove in deed that you have compassion on Jesus, your suffering and dying Redeemer. One day, when the pitiless storms of a hard winter swept over the earth, and many perished from cold, the following incident is related of St. Martin, afterwards bishop of Tours. He was marching through the country with other officers and soldiers, when he met at the gate of the city of Amiens a poor man, almost naked, trembling and shivering with cold, begging an alms of those who passed by. Martin, seeing that those who went before him took no notice of the poor mendicant, thought he was reserved for himself. On account of his charities to others he had nothing left but his arms and the clothes he wore; Yet drawing his sword, he cut his cloak in two pieces, gave one to the beggar and wrapped himself up in the other half. But what happened? A divine vision appeared to him during the night, and he recognized Jesus Christ in the poor mendicant he had befriended. Our Lord was wrapped in the half of the mantle which the saint had given away, telling him to look well at it and say whether he knew it, our Lord said to him: "Martin, yet a catechumen, has clothed me with his garment." Do you know now how you should have compassion? Be charitable to the needy and afflicted. Christ receives what you do to others, as done to himself, for he says: "Amen, I say to you, as long as you did it to one of these my least brethren you did it to me."—Matt. 25: 40.

2. *He is treated most unmercifully.* Did you ever see a man whipping his horses unmercifully, when they could not draw the load he had in his cruelty imposed upon them? Such is the treatment that Jesus received. He cannot, how much soever he may try, carry the load any farther, his knees tremble, his form sways hither and thither, a few moments and he will fall. This arouses the fury of his enemies anew. The cruel torturers when they observe his weakness behave like madmen, they strike and drag him forward with ropes which they had fastened round his loins, and, in their rage, presume so far as to kick the Son of God. Under such cruel tortures he loses the remnant of his strength, and falls as one dead to the ground with the heavy weight of the cross upon his bruised and bleeding body. "He falls the second time beneath the heavy load of the cross."

Application. Guard against nothing so much as against being unmerciful towards your fellow-men, especially towards the poor, the needy and the afflicted. Be assured that great as is the delight which God takes in Christians who practice works of mercy towards their fellow-men, so equally great is the displeasure with which he regards those who have no heart and feeling for the needs of their neighbor and uncharitably thrust him from their doors when he asks their assistance. The inhabitants of a certain city in Posen were condemned by the enemy to pay so enormous a sum as an indemnification, that it seemed impossible to raise the amount. There lived in the city a woman, the widow of a prince, who possessed a fabulous amount of wealth; at the cost of some deprivation to herself she could have defrayed the whole amount, which the poor citizens altogether were not able to pay. They humbly asked her for help but were repulsed. So urgent was the necessity, so deplorable was their condition that they begged again and yet again, but with no effect; the unmerciful woman locked herself in the house and refused to see any one. Some time elapsed and, the house still remaining unopened, they began to wonder what had become of her. It was decided to force open the doors, and O! what a terrible spectacle met their gaze! The wretched creature was crouching near a box of gold, *dead,* but staring at it, apparently, as if fascinated by its glitter. One rigid hand clutched the box in an icy clasp, the other held the key,—Yes, she had gone before her judge. Her countenance wore a repulsive look in death, her eyes had in them the stony glare of one whose last moments were filled with despair. O! who can depict her horror! What must have been her final doom? For all reply look to the parable of Dives and Lazarus (Luke 16: 20) as well as to the sentence pronounced by Christ upon the unmerciful.—Matt. 25: 21. Far from showing yourself destitute of mercy and compassion towards the poor and needy, be rather charitable towards them and assist them in word and deed, considering the words of Christ: "Blessed are the merciful, for they shall obtain mercy."—Matt. 5: 7.

PART II.

Jesus Christ fell the second time on account of the *unfaithfulness of his friends.* Our oft-repeated sins are the cause of his fall.

1. When our divine Saviour with the heavy load of the cross upon his shoulders was on the way to Calvary's Mount, his thoughts rested upon the friends whom he loved so tenderly, and who had received such numerous benefits at his hands. He recalled the touching evidence of the love and loyalty which had never been wanting from them and his heart was sorrowful, almost "unto death," for now all were disloyal to him. We can well imagine then, how this thought became for him a source of the bitterest grief, and how it immeasurably increased his dejection as he sadly pursued his way to the mount. Peter had reiterated his denial with an oath. Poor weak apostle! He was the most emphatic of all in his assurances of fidelity to his master, he declared that though all should forsake Jesus he would never desert him, and yet at the first moment of temptation he fell! The other disciples too, who, at the Last Supper, had assured him that they would live and die with him, took to flight when they saw his enemies surround him, and in their terror fled, daring not to show themselves before men. And the inhabitants of Jerusalem! What of them? But a few short days before they had welcomed him with enthusiasm, spread their rich robes as a carpet in his path, and waved the graceful palm branch aloft. Ah! now thoroughly blinded they forget how they cried, Hosanna to the Son of David! Blessed is he that cometh in the name of the Lord! Hosanna in the highest.—Matt. 21: 17. Instead, from lip to lip pass the cruel words: "Away with him! away with him!

Crucify him! crucify him!—John 19 : 15. During his public life Christ had rendered assistance to numberless unfortunate persons and conferred on them all manner of benefits, now there is not one among them who would dare to take his part, all remained away from him and were silent, some even joined in the cry of murder which resounds through the air. Should not such base treachery deeply afflict and wound the heart of Christ! Nay must not this treachery of his friends have been more painful to him than even the cruelty of his enemies? Who could doubt it? Nothing inflicts a deeper wound upon the human heart than the treachery of friends. When Cæsar recognized his friend Brutus, upon whom he had lavished so much kindness, among the conspirators who fell upon him with sharp daggers, his strength left him and mournfully exclaiming: "And thou, too, Brutus!" he covered his face with the toga, and without any further resistance suffered himself to be wounded unto death. Thus it was with our divine Saviour; when he remembered the treachery of his friends to whom he had done so much good, an anguish so intense seized his soul that his strength failed him and he fell a second time beneath the weight of the cross.

2. How is it with us? Does not the accusing voice of conscience tell us that we, too, have been accessory to this second painful fall of our dear Lord? Yes, many of us, forgetful of his great love have left,

(*a*) *The ways of innocence and have sinned.* Perhaps a short time ago they walked in holiness and purity of morals, and were happy in the knowledge of never having lost their baptismal innocence. But how do matters stand with them now? Ah, their love for God has grown cold, the Holy Ghost no longer reigns in their hearts. Instead of fair gardens, lovely with the flowers of virtue, behold! they have become desolate plains—they have committed mortal sin, and the evil spirit rules with full sway. Should the angel of death summon them to depart in this unhappy state, they would most surely be cast into the fiery abyss of the damned. O, how deplorable is the lot of such Christians! Is it any wonder that Jesus faltered with pain and grief of mind, and fell to the ground on his way to Calvary, when he thought of their sad fall from the state of grace? O unfortunate souls, can nothing touch you, can you not be moved to consider the pain you have caused your suffering Saviour by the loss of baptismal grace? Will you not rise from your fall by a true repentance, and thus rescue your soul from eternal perdition. But you who are so happy as to possess baptismal innocence, preserve it as your most precious treasure. and "watch and pray, that you enter not into temptation."—Matt. 26 : 41.

(*b*) *The way of penance and have sinned again.* Absalom, David's degenerate son, had killed his brother Ammon. This was a great affliction for his aged father, who loved all his children most tenderly. Absalom fled that he might escape the punishment of which he was most deserving ; but, repenting of his crime, he presumed on the affection so lavishly poured out upon by his father, and implored his pardon, whereupon, not only was his wickedness freely forgiven, but David fully reinstated him in his favor, (2. Kings 14,) but what did the ungrateful child do shortly afterwards? He forgot all the love of his father and rebelled against him, being desirous of usurping his sceptre and crown. Now judge for yourselves: was not Absalom a man who merits our entire detestation? Did he not deserve the death he met with at the hand of Joab, who thrust three lances into his black treacherous heart ? But however grievously Absalom erred by his repeated crime towards his father, the relapsing sinner commits a greater crime. Why? Evidently because he renders himself guilty of the greatest ingratitude towards God whom he offends anew after having been pardoned by him. Tertullian says : "A sinner, who, having received from God the remission of his crimes, again relapses into them, prefers the devil himself to God ; for since God by means of sanctifying grace has entered into the heart of the penitent sinner according to the words of the Evangelist : 'We know that we have passed from death to life,'—1. John 3 : 15; such a sinner, who dares to offend God anew, makes, as it were, a comparison between God and the devil, and, finally, by his resolutions to sin actually passes the sentence : that the one of the two for whom he declares himself must be the better." What an infatuation, to prefer the devil to God ! Relapse into sin, above all when it becomes of frequent occurence places our salvation in most imminent peril, and why? Because by yielding to sin we grow weaker while our passions wax stronger, the devil acquires a certain dominion over us, and the grace of God recedes farther and farther from our souls. Hence, St. Bernard says : "As the relapse into a bodily sickness is worse than the first attack, so it is with the relapse into sin. "And St. Augustine says : " Did Christ give sight twice to a blind man? Did he twice heal the man sick of the palsy? Did he twice raise the same dead man to life ? The Sacred Scripture speaks of only one healing, that we should fear to relapse into sin." It was this ingratitude and this danger of our soul's salvation, which so deeply oppressed the heart of our Lord on his way of the cross that he fell the second time to the ground. Consider this, you relapsing sinners, humbly ask pardon of Jesus for the pain which you have caused him by your infidelity and resolve to amend your life and henceforth to walk with constancy on the way of penance.

PERORATION.

Let us all, sinners and just, devoutly meditate on this second fall of Christ so exceedingly painful, which was caused by the cruelty of his enemies and the treachery and unfaithfulness of his friends. Let us detest from the inmost recesses of our heart, the inhuman cruelty with which the Jews maltreated our divine Saviour, but let us also detest our own infidelity of which we have been guilty, let us vow to him a thorough amendment and cry out in the words of the Way of the Cross: "Jesus! have mercy on us. Stretch out thy hand, that its strengthening grasp may support us in our weakness and so aid us that we may never again relapse into our former sins. We have said it, and this very moment we shall begin the work of our conversion in all earnestness. Do thou O Jesus, assist us with thy grace without which we can do nothing, that we may faithfully keep our resolution." Amen.

EIGHTH STATION.

JESUS CONSOLES THE WOMEN OF JERUSALEM WHO WEPT OVER HIM.

"Daughters of Jerusalem, weep not over me: but weep for yourselves and for your children.—Luke 23 : 28.

Jesus having fallen the second time under the weight of the cross lies prostrate on the ground. This pitiful sight, so far from moving the soldiers to pity, increases their rage to the point of madness, while they curse and blaspheme in so loud a manner that the Mount resounds with the imprecations which pour in torrents from their lips; with their unholy hands they dare to strike Jesus, and savagely pull him with the ropes fastened around his loins until they succeed in raising him once more upon his feet. The women of Jerusalem who follow the mournful train are profoundly touched on account of his painful fall, and observing the cruelty with which his cruel enemies treat him, they can no longer repress their sorrow, but burst forth into violent sobbing, while their tears seemed as if they would never cease to flow. Jesus hearing their cries and lamentations turns and addresses them in these earnest words: "Daughters of Jerusalem, weep not over me; but weep for yourselves and for your children." We will make a short meditation on this circumstance in the Passion of Christ. Turn your eyes upon the Eighth Station, which bears the inscription : *"Jesus consoles the women of Jerusalem who wept over him,"* and consider :

    I. The tears which the women wept over Jesus, and
    II. The words which Jesus spoke to the women.

Eighth Station.

Part 1.

The Eighth Station also affords us some degree of consolation. We see there the women of Jerusalem, who had compassion for Jesus and wept sorrowful tears for his woes. The tears of those women however do not merit our undivided approval, for

1. *They flowed from a natural cause.*

(*a*) There was indeed nothing to elicit surprise or remark in these women weeping over our Saviour; the sight of him was enough to excite sympathy in the heart of every one who had not lost all feeling for the woes of others. If even the pagan Pilate, when he saw before him the Saviour, scourged, crowned with thorns and most inhumanly abused, exclaimed in sadness and sympathy: "*Ecce Homo!* Behold the man!" how could women, who are by nature much more tenderhearted and sympathetic than men, have refrained from weeping at the sight of his pitiable condition? It was but fitting that the women of Jerusalem should shed those tears of compassion, but they should also have investigated the cause of the deplorable misery into which he was plunged. And what was this cause? Alas! no other than their sins, the sins of the world. "He was wounded for our iniquities, he was bruised for our sins."—Is. 53 : 5. Sin lifted the heavy cross and placed it on the lacerated shoulders of our Lord. Sin ultimately is the sole cause that he had to carry it to the sorrowful mount. Sin, accursed sin, drove the nails to fasten him thereupon, and left him to suffer and die. The women of Jerusalem did not consider this; they wept only from natural tenderness of heart, nothing was farther from their thoughts than to repent and bewail their sins as the cause of Christ's painful journey to Calvary. Hence their tears were profitless and would not avert the judgments of God, which were to come upon Jerusalem.

Application. Do not many Christians resemble these women? They sigh, moan, lament and weep, but not for or on account of their sins, but on account of the temporal evils which they have brought upon themselves by their sinful life. A daughter is deeply dejected. Why? Because, through her scandalous conduct, she has lost her honor and good name and must henceforth dwell, poor and forsaken, beneath the shadow of a blighting shame and disgrace. A wayward son who, in some midnight brawl, has wounded or even taken the life of his adversary, grieves and his despair even forces the tears from his eyes. Why? Because a lawsuit, with its attendant expenses is inevitable, while a prison or, perhaps, even the gallows looms up before his eyes. The inebriate whose passion for drink has brought upon him an incurable malady—laments in his trouble and weeps. Why: Because he can no longer hope to recover his health, and because he dreads approaching death. Thus there are many Christians who sigh, moan and weep, but without benefit to themselves, without fruit before God, because their sighs and tears have no reference to sin as an offence against God, but only to the evil consequences of sin. The repentance that proceeds from a hatred of sin and love of God is a true repentance. "but the sorrow of the world worketh death."—2. Cor. 7 : 10.

2. *They were not efficacious.*

(*a*) The women of Jerusalem wept over Jesns, but we do not read that they made any exertions towards alleviating his misery or procuring him any comfort. The wife of Pilate, who urged her husband to liberate Jesus, Simon of Cyrene, who notwithstanding he carried the cross more from compulsion, than free will, Veronica who, offered him her veil, that he might wipe his face, which was covered with spittle, dust, perspiration and blood, all merit more praise than the women of Jerusalem.

Application. The world affords many instances of such conduct as that of the women of Jerusalem. Occasionally men are aroused to a lively sense of the wrong they have done, and feel keenly the misery they have brought upon themselves by sin. A fleeting wish for something better and nobler animates them, they occasionally long to do right and resolve to amend their life. They weep and sorrowfully sigh over their transgressions. This indeed is good and proves that the seeds of repentance have been planted in the heart, but if they do nothing further, if they continue still to wallow in the mire of their gross and flagrant excesses, O! believe me, the seed, far from fruitifying, will wither and die; they do not renounce sin and enter upon the way of penance, if they continue in the same indifference and tepidity in the service of God, and if the same abuse of divine grace and the same love of the world find place in their soul, all their tears and sighs are of no profit; their tears resemble blossoms which fall off before they develop the fruit, The tears must be followed by deeds, we must avoid what we bewail. See for example, all true penitents: Mary Magdalene, Peter, St. Margaret of Cortona. Weep, then, for your sins, you have reason to tremble at the recollection of them; but do not stop there, be not content with useless tears, bid farewell to sin, control your passions, root out your pernicious habits and do all that is necessary in order to amend your life. Only in such a way will your penance be pleasing to God.

3. *They were of short duration.*

(*a*) The tears of these women soon ceased to flow, they wept only while the sufferings of Jesus were vividly before them. The adage " out of sight, out of mind," was only too soon verified in their regard. They left Mount Calvary, the scene of such sorrow and anguish, and no sooner had they turned away than their grief was a thing of the past. They laughed, jested, and resumed the ordinary routine of life, utterly forgetful of what they had seen. This, indeed, was most reprehensible. Tears and sorrow of such brief duration could not be pleasing to our Lord. More acceptable to him were the tears of St. Peter and St. Mary Magdalene, who never ceased to weep for their sins.

Application. Therefore your sorrow for having offended God must endure while life remains, if not exteriorly, at least, interiorly, and each succeeding day must be marked by some penitential act. Christ demands this, saying : "Sin no more, lest some worse thing happen to thee." He who repeats the sins of which he has repented, is no penitent, but a scoffer; he who commits again the sins which he bewailed, runs the risk of being eternally rejected as a relapsing sinner; for "no man putting his hand to the plough, and looking back, is fit for the kingdom of God."— Luke 9; 62. Only he whose feet never wander from the straight and narrow path, shall enter into the glory of heaven. Witnesses: All holy penitents.

Part II.

The Gospel says of Jesus on his way of the cross : "There followed him a great multitude of people and of women; who bewailed and lamented him. But Jesus, turning to them, said : Daughters of Jerusalem, weep not over me; but weep for yourselves and for your children. For, behold, the days shall come, wherein they will say: Blessed are the barren, and the wombs that have not borne, and the paps that have not given suck. Then shall they begin to say to the mountains : Fall upon us: and to the hills : Cover us. For if in the green wood they do these things, what shall be done in the dry ?"—Luke 23 : 27–32. In these words the divine Saviour foretells an event, which would be so terrible that the lot of those barren women who were considered so unhappy would be preferable to that of the fruitful mothers whose homes were made glad by the voices of many children; he prophesies an event of a nature so appalling that people would look upon even a sudden death as a blessed means by which to evade its horrors. Let us now consider how this prophecy of the Lord,

1. *Was fulfilled in Jerusalem.* Thirty-eight years after the death of Christ the clamor of war is heard and the Roman General, Titus, with a great army appeared before the gates of Jerusalem, firmly determined to chastise the Jews for their continual sedition. The first thing he did was to cast a trench about the city, thus preventing those unhappy creatures

within its walls either from leaving, or receiving aid from without. In a few weeks the provisions in Jerusalem were consumed, and famine began to exercise its ravages so severely, that the inhabitants were reduced to the necessity of eating the most disgusting things. The gardens hitherto so fragrant with the perfume of the rarest flowers, so lovely in their arrangement, and so spacious in their dimensions, became in a short time like arid wastes without a blade of grass to greet the eye, Not the tiniest plant or shrub was left, everything was devoured by a people driven frantic by hunger. Mothers even ate their own offspring. The number of those that died of hunger and disease is estimated to be 600,000. Daily might be witnessed the terrible sight of dead bodies being hurled over the walls, for it became impossible to give them sepulture, and they were left to moulder and decay in the trenches. Five hundred prisoners were crucified every day in order to intimidate the inhabitants of Jerusalem to surrender. The wretched inhabitants resisted for five months, but their efforts to withstand their powerful assailants were vain, and in despair they hopelessly desisted. Thousands of the Jews fell by the swords of the furious Roman soldiers, blood flowed in torrents through the streets of the city; the city itself was pilaged and the temple set on fire. The massacre of the inhabitants appears to us to be exaggerated when we read the numbers, although the truth is verified by the concurrent testimonies of the Jewish and heathen historians who calculate the number of deaths from hunger, disease and the sword to be over a million. The entire city was reduced to ashes, and not a stone was left upon a stone. When Titus, after taking the city, rode among the ruins and saw the great number of dead he sighed and raised his hands toward heaven, saying: "I am innocent of this misery. It is the Lord who has done this, not I." Here we see fulfilled Christ's prophecy to the women of Jerusalem: "Daughters of Jerusalem, weep not over me; but weep for yourselves and your children."

2. *Let us consider how this prophecy is fulfilled in impenitent sinners.*

(a) *The impenitent sinner on his deathbed.* Let us call up before us the terrible picture it presents. He has heaped sin upon sin during his past life, and the worm which never dies is gnawing at his heart, but alas! it is remorse, not contrition. His dim eyes over which the film of death is already gathering behold the most frightful spectres turn whithersoever they will. Now it is the inspirations he has neglected, then the promises he has broken, and finally the many years now lost and gone forever, rush before his mind. He who shrank from reflection in the flush of health and strength, *now* can meditate on the past and the present. Where are the companions of his pleasures, the friends who flattered and encouraged him in his evil ways? They have abandoned him! He cries and moans, a cold sweat is stealing over him, his breath is failing, he frequently faints away. He lies there forsaken by the world, whose delights he can no longer promote, in pains too great for his undisciplined heart to endure he tosses from side to side. It is the agony of death! His eyes, at last, open to the truth of eternity, of which, during his life, he made but little account, and he sighs with Antiochus: "Into how much tribulation am I come, and into what floods of sorrow, wherein now I am : I that was pleasant and beloved in my power."—1. Mach. 6 : 11. Glancing into the future, terror seizes his unhappy soul, for dawning faith tells him : "The death of the wicked is very evil."—Ps. 33 : 22. He exclaims : "How I have misspent my life! What will become of me in a few moments! And disturbed by confusion, fear and despair his soul departs from the body to appear with empty hands before his Judge. St. Gregory the Great relates the following of a certain Chrysontius, who was a man of great wealth but of very bad morals, and who had spent his life in entire forgetfulness of God and eternity. Sickness came upon him at last, and when he lay terrified at the near approach of his last hour, he cried to the evil spirits who visibly appeared to him in order to snatch him away : "Give me time, give me time till to-morrow!" But they said : "You fool, you beg for time now, you had plenty of time but you misused it to your own destruction, time is no longer yours. The wretch ceased not to cry and begged for help. One of his sons, named Maximus, being with him at the time, Chrysontius cried out to him : "My son, help me, Maximus, help me!" Whilst writhing in contortions and wailing like a despairing man, he breathed his last. Such is the unhappy death of the impenitent sinner.

(*b*) *And what awaits him after death ?* How will that unfortunate soul tremble, what inexpressible anguish, when separating from the body, it beholds legions of horrible demons waiting with horrid eagerness to drag it with them to hell, with its tortures and flames. It will strive to re-enter the body, but in vain, an invisible power urges it forward and places it before the judgment-seat of God. O who can describe the anguish of the soul at that terrible moment! When our first parents heard the voice of God speaking to them in paradise after they had sinned, they did not tremble as much as the sinner now trembles before the eternal Judge. He must now give an account of the sins he has committed during the whole course of his life, those sins equal in number to the grains of sand which lie scattered along the shores of the sea, of the good he has neglected to do, the graces he has abused, the scandals he has given, the souls he has ruined, in short, of everything whereby he has offended God. What will he do? Will he defend himself? Alas! no, he is silent. Now the Judge pronounces sentence upon him : Depart from me, you cursed, into everlasting fire, which is prepared for the devil and his associates! What a thunderbolt for the sinner! He is to depart forever from God, to be for ever excluded from heaven; he is to depart into everlasting fire, where in company of the evil spirits and of the damned, he will be tormented for all eternity. The sentence is passed, the instant that reveals it sees its fulfillment; the demons rush with a mad fury, like tigers fiercely wrangling for their prey, and fall upon the lost spirit to hurl it into the terrible abyss of the damned where it will suffer nameless torments, as long as God shall be God, for an eternity which will never end. Such is the end of the impenitent sinner, more terrible than that of the Jews at the destruction of Jerusalem.

PERORATION.

We may also apply to ourselves the words of Christ: "Daughters of Jerusalem, weep not over me: but weep for yourselves and your children." They were spoken for all men of all times, that by a speedy and thorough repentance they may avail themselves of the proffered graces and escape eternal perdition. Let us prostrate ourselves before Jesus at the Eighth Station, bewail our sins and pray with a contrite and humble heart: O Jesus, who shall give water to our head, and a torrent of tears to our eyes that day and night we may bewail our sins! We beg thee through thy bitter and bloody tears to give us the grace of tears and to soften our hearts in such a manner, that in bitter sorrow we may bewail thy sufferings and our sins all the days of our life. Amen.

NINTH STATION.

JESUS FALLS BENEATH THE CROSS THE THIRD TIME.

"He fell flat on the ground.—Mark 14 : 35.

The words which Jesus spoke to the weeping women of Jerusalem on his painful journey to Calvary's Mount, were the last warning he gave the Jews for their conversion. Once more he placed before their eyes the terrible judgments of God, which would be visited upon them, if they did not bring forth fruits worthy of penance. Had they been mindful of this final warning, had they believed in the Saviour, they would have found mercy, and Jerusalem would not have been destroyed. "The Lord beareth patiently for your sake, not willing that any should perish, but that all should return to penance;" (2. Pet. 3 : 9,) but the Jews remained obdurate. So far from responding to the loving words of Christ, a torrent of blasphemy poured forth from their lips as they hurried him on to Mount Calvary. He

Ninth Station.

had, with painful efforts, almost gained the summit, when, as the spot chosen for his crucifixion, rose to view, he faltered and fell a third time to the earth. This enraged the brutal soldiers, and excited them to the verge of madness. They dragged the Son of God from the ground, and with fresh insults, goaded him and bade him go on with his heavy and wearisome load. Let us look at the Ninth Station, which bears the inscription : *Jesus falls beneath the cross the third time*, and consider, that this fall was occasioned,

    I. By the ill-treatment of his enemies, and
    II. By the fear of approaching death.

Part I.

Our divine Saviour fell beneath the cross the third time *on account of the ill-treatment which he received at the hands of his enemies on his way to Calvary*. Who can adequately describe this ill-treatment and abuse ? The cruel scourging had accomplished its end only too well, and the crown of thorns fulfilled its mission of torture as fully as malice could have hoped, yet those wretches will allow their divine victim no rest. He is compelled to walk under the weight of a cross so heavy that a man in the full flush of health might well have hesitated to carry it, even a few steps. Nay, with help even none would have borne it up Calvary's steep and rugged ascent, for the path to that sacred spot is hard, and in every sense a dolorous way. It would have been arduous enough for Christ to have ascended without any load, and behold, he has to carry the heavy load of the cross. One would naturally think that the Jews and the soldiers would have treated him humanely and rendered the carriage of the cross as easy as possible for him. But no, their hearts seem to have lost the last spark of human feeling, they scoff at the thought of affording him the slightest alleviation, so far from even giving him sympathy, they strive to strew more thorns in his path to the Mount. When worn out with fatigue he would fain seek but a few moments rest, their curses and blasphemies are terrible to hear, and like a beast of burden they drive him onward with kicks and blows. When, overcome by weakness, he falls to the ground he dare not remain, they drag him up and goad him onward, and he has scarcely risen from his fall when he must again take the cross upon his mangled shoulders. Not contented with this, in their malice they add many other injuries. With the rope fastened about his loins they pull him hither and thither, strike his cheeks with their fists, and jostle the crown so that the long, sharp thorns pierce more deeply into his sacred head ; some shake the cross, others stand on the end that touches the ground, that the load may become heavier and the pressure greater. What he endured on his way to Calvary surpasses our comprehension, but we shall be amazed, when it will be made manifest to us on the day of judgment. We need not, therefore, wonder that Jesus fell the third time beneath the weight of the cross.

2. *Application.* Our life here below is also a way of the cross, we have many enemies who frequently cause our fall.

(*a*) *Who are these enemies? The world, the flesh, and the devil* is a dangerous enemy, for it hates God and abhors all that is good, casts many snares for us by its representations, bad examples and scandals and is ever on the alert in various ways to entice us from the service of God. And when it adds to the number of its votaries it loves to clothe each new captive in the livery of its slaves. St. John warns us against it when he writes: "Love not the world nor those things which are in the world. If any man love the world the charity of the Father is not in him. For all that is in the world, is the concupiscence of the flesh, the concupiscence of the eyes, and the pride of life."—1. John 2 : 15, 16. *The flesh* or concupiscence, a result of original sin, has for its object to lure man from "the things which are above" to gross and sensual delights, so that the way of virtue seems rude and hard, and that of sin so pleasant that he lingers therein. It is, alas the heritage of which Holy Writ thus discourses, "the imagination and thought of man's heart are prone to evil from his youth."—Gen. 8 : 21. And : "Every man is tempted, drawn away by his own concupiscence."—James 1 : 14. The foe who, however, works most ruin to mankind is *the devil*, his most dangerous enemy is *Satan*. He would rejoice to draw the whole world from the service of God. So envious is the fiend that we can gain the heaven that he has lost. He constantly seeks to ruin our souls. He it was who in the guise of a serpent tempted our first parents to sin, and has ever since been the sworn enemy of man. He seduced men to the most abominable idolatry and the most shameless vices, yea, even presumed to approach Christ himself and thrice dared to tempt the Son of God. St. Peter calls him a roaring lion who goes about seeking whom he may devour.—1. Pet. 5 : 8. And St. Paul writes: "Put you on the armor of God, that you may be able to stand against the snares of the devil. For our wrestling is not against flesh and blood; but against principalities and powers; against the rulers of the world of this darkness; against the spirits of wickedness in the high places."—Ephes. 6 : 11, 12.

(*b*) *What means must we employ that these enemies may not cause our fall?* Particularly these two: *Watchfulness and prayer,* according to the admonition of Christ: "Watch ye, and pray, that you may not enter into temptation. The spirit, indeed, is willing, but the flesh weak."—Matt.

26 : 41. We must *watch*, that is, exercise constant vigilance as to all that passes within and without us that we may perceive the first shadow of peril, and guard against the dark waves of danger that encompass and threaten to overwhelm our soul. By neglecting this vigilance, and failing to co-operate with the inspirations of God, a soul which has been the object of his favors, may nevertheless be lost. He who relying on his former dispositions does not carefully watch over himself will soon fall into sin. David, because he failed to guard his eyes, committed the heinous sins of murder and adultery. Dina imprudently entered the city of Sichem, and lost her innocence; Peter, yielding to a fatal curiosity, gains entrance to a place where he encounted a wicked crowd, and what followed? He cruelly denied Christ. How many there may be among us, who for the want of vigilance have grievously sinned? Instead of banishing the very shadow of that sinful thought, you were careless and what followed? Complacency, and complacency gave way to delectation, delectation to consent, consent to gratification. Remember that the kingdom of heaven suffereth violence, and that the saints never reached the glory of canonization without one long effort which never ceased on earth. The salvation of man depends upon vigilance and co-operation with grace. In the practice of virtue you can never say with certainty that you will be faithful to-morrow because you have been faithful to-day. One unfortunate occasion is sufficient to cause your eternal ruin. Therefore watch, that you enter not into temptation. Life is a warfare—Ah! justly may it be looked upon as one constant temptation—a perpetual battle wherein there is no truce. Remember, then, that watchful prudence, circumspection and prayer are necessary if we wish not to be led into temptation.

(*c*) We must *pray*. When through prayer we fervently implore God's grace, our divine Lord, imparts to us those interior lights which so illumine the inmost recesses of the soul that we at once recognize the cunning assaults of our spiritual enemies and obtain strength to resist them with determination. St. Augustine says: "As long as you pray you may be assured that the divine mercy will not fail to come to your succor. And St. Chrysostom says: "The roar of the lion does not drive away the wild beast, as does the prayer of the just man all enemies." We read that the solitaries of the olden time were one day called upon to assemble from their cells in the desert of Egypt that each might give his opinion as to the exercise most essential for every Christian in order to obtain eternal salvation. They unanimously agreed that it was none other than fervent, persevering prayer. Hence they resolved, that each of them should often say with David: "O God, come to my assistance; O Lord, make haste to help me."—Ps. 69: 2. Be fervent, then, in prayer, and do not omit to cry to God for help in every temptation, that you may not fall.

Part II.

Another reason why Jesus fell the third time beneath the cross was without doubt the agony he suffered at the thought of *the approach of death.*

1. There is deeply implanted in man an inherent terror of death, because the separation caused by death between the soul and the body is so unnatural. When God created man he munificently intended to endow him with immortality both of body and soul. He placed him in the garden of paradise where he might have lived in perfect happiness, and when his time had come he would have been translated body and soul into heaven without tasting the bitterness of death. Death is a consequence of and a punishment for, an act of disobedience against the law of God. It is not a blessing but an evil, and even those who have led holy lives tremble at the thought of crossing the dark river which leads to the eternal shore. St. Arsenius on his death-bed was seized with a fear so great that his disciples who knew well how faithfully he had labored in the service of his Master, said to him: "And you, too, O! father?" they exclaimed; "do you shudder at the near approach of death?" But he said to them: "Yes, children, this is no new fear, I have feared this hour all the days of my life." Since Jesus Christ was not only God, but also man, and as man wished to suffer and die, is it natural that he, too, experienced the terrors of death, and so much the more as by his omniscience he foresaw what a painful death was awaiting him. Let us consider this a little more minutely in the Ninth Station. Under abuses the most horrible and sufferings the most intense he had arrived almost at the summit of Calvary and reached the spot where he was to be crucified. At a few paces from him he sees workmen drill a hole into the rock for his cross. Each harrowing detail of the preparations for the last terrible scene are present to his view,, he beholds the vast throng impatiently waiting for his approach. And as he draws near, crowned with thorns, and blood trickling fast to the ground, they cry: "He is coming—we shall not have long to wait—we can witness his death!" In this moment all the tortures and sufferings that accompany that death are vividly presented to his mind. He beholds the rude mob looking on while his tormentors tear off his clothing and present him almost naked to the jeers of the crowd He sees how they stretch him on the hard bed of the cross, how his hands and feet are extended and cruelly pierced through with nails, he sees how the cross is erected and fastened in the opening, how he hangs upon it for three hours in the utmost abandonment and a sea of suffering, how he, finally bows his head and dies. Who can picture even faintly the anguish of the meek Saviour at the representation of all these circumstances of his Passion and death. If, when death's dark shadow rose but dimly before him in the garden of Olives, the thought could force drops of blood from every pore of his sacred

body, and cause him to cry out in his anguish: "My soul is sorrowful even unto death," how much more agonizing must have been his terror at its near approach! Can we wonder that no strength is left him and that he falls to the ground beneath the weight of the cross?

2. *Application.* Let us sympathize with our Redeemer, sorrowful unto death, and lying prostrate on the ground; but let us also reflect upon our own condition, and try to present vividly to our minds the truth that our last hour is fast approaching, and that sooner or later it will come. O! supreme moment of death which decides our eternal fate!

(*a*) *For time.* As long as we live the salvation of our soul is in our own hands, we can lay up a treasure of merits for heaven and prepare ourselves for eternity. Even if we have the misfortune to forfeit the grace of God by mortal sin, there is rescue in store for us, we need only seek pardon at the tribunal of mercy to find grace and forgiveness with a merciful God. But when the last breath has left our pale lips, and we lie cold and still in death, alas! closed for us are the portals of grace, forever closed, 'tis too late, we cannot enter in! The moment we are no more the words of St. John in the Apocalyse apply to us: "The angel lifted up his hands to heaven and he swore by him that liveth for ever and ever: That time shall be no more."—Apoc. 10: 5, 6. O what an important thing it is to die! And yet there are Christians whose lives are one constant whirl of dissipation, and who acting as if they were to live on earth forever, give no thought to their eternal salvation, and who never trouble themselves about dying. How negligent they are in doing good! They squander away the "acceptable season," they turn with indifference from the devotions held during the ecclesiastical year, they care not for prayer either public or private, and when they do pray, it is with the utmost indifference and a want of fervor that renders their prayers rather an insult than an act of homage to God. The reading of a spiritual book is to them an intolerable task, and they avoid, when, they can do so, listening to the word of God in church. They allow months, nay, even years to pass without confession and Communion. They have so many opportunities to put their conscience in order and to reconcile themselves to God by a good confession, but they suffer these opportunities to pass until finally "the night cometh in which no man can work" and they realize what a bitter thing it to lose the Lord, their God. How can I anticipate, how can I describe their feelings in the other world! What untold misery lies hidden in those mournful words. Alas! of what folly have I been guilty! In my life I had long series of years, in which I might have become a saint, but I would not. Preparation for a good death was the last thought which ever presented itself to my mind, and now I have no time to atone for any neglect and to save my soul.

(*b*) *For eternity.* "If the tree fall to the south, or to the north, in what place soever it shall fall there shall it be."—Eccles. 11 : 3. In eternity there is no change, in what state soever man dies, in that will he remain forever. It is now more than five thousand years since the death of the fratricide Cain. Because he persevered in his impenitence to the last, he was damned and has been burning in hell for over five thousand years. During all this long time there has been no day, no hour, no moment in which his situation has been changed, or his sufferings been, in the least, interrupted or mitigated. How excruciating must have been the torture he has endured during all these long series of years, but after five thousand years more have elapsed, nay, after millions and millions of years have passed, his lot and the lot of all the damned will still be the same, ever the same torments, the same hopelessness, the same despair. What a terrible state! But the destiny of the blessed is, also, unalterable. Over eighteen hundred years have passed away since when St. Peter and St. Paul gave up their lives for Christ, the portals of heaven opened wide to receive them. Who can describe the joy, the happiness which these Apostles have enjoyed without any interruption as century after century rolled by! And who can form an adequate idea of the joy and happiness which they with all the elect shall continue to enjoy throughout the ages to come—for all eternity, without any interruption. O how much depends on death, on that last moment of our life, which holds within its depths our fate for all eternity! On it depends our happiness or misery for an endless eternity. Do you believe in your impending fate? Why then do you live as if you were never to die? What folly it is for the sake of a wretched momentary pleasure in this life to run the risk of dying a miserable death and commencing a life of misery that will never terminate. Remember Lot's wife. Remember death; it is certain; prepare for it that you may escape a miserable eternity.

PERORATION.

O! then ponder often upon death, and forget not to go down in thought to the narrow home, the last resting place of the dead. Behold the havoc wrought by the crawling worms of corruption! O! it will then be an easy task to give up the world, and its allurements and to ward off the shadow of sin ere it fall upon your soul. The frequent and oft-renewed remembrance of death will be to you a shield, from which all the arrows of your spiritual enemies will rebound, especially if you are watchful and invoke God's help in very temptation. But because you have hitherto failed to do this on many occasions, and have, therefore, sinned grievously, prostrate yourself before Jesus in the Ninth Station and full of sorrow and compunction of heart, pray: O most merciful Jesus, we thank thee, that thou didst not permit us to die in our sins, nor bury us as we have deserved, in the abyss of hell. We beseech thee by the merits of this thy third most painful fall, to pardon our frequent relapses and our long continuance in sin; and may the thought of these thy sufferings make us detest our sins more and more thoroughly, and persevere in good to the end. Amen.

TENTH STATION.

JESUS IS STRIPT OF HIS GARMENTS.

"They have parted my garments among them; and upon my vesture they have cast lots."—John 19 : 24.

When Jesus Christ had fallen beneath the cross the third time, when he lay there, faint and exhausted, an object of derision and reproach, it seemed as though he would lie prostrate till death despoiled his captors of their prey. But he did not die, the immeasurable depth of his love for us made him desire to suffer still more, he wished to die the most ignominious death of the cross, therefore, with one mighty effort he arose from his painful position, and took the cross upon his shoulders; his love gave him strength to carry it till he reached the place where he was to be nailed to it. He stands upon Calvary, on that mountain which is connected with Mount Moria, on which Isaac, his prototype, was to be slaughtered; on that mountain where our first parent Adam, as Origen and St. Athanasius relate, is buried; on that mountain where the head of the infernal serpent is to be crushed, sin blotted out, and divine justice satisfied by a superabundant satisfaction. "And they came to a place that is called Golgotha, which is the place of Calvary."—Matt. 27 : 33. Let us consider at this Station:

I. The corporal denudation of Jesus Christ, and
II. The spiritual denudation of the Christian.

PART I.

When our divine Saviour had reached the spot where he was to be crucified, he was stript of his garments, and oh!

1. *With what great pain!*

(*a*) According to the Roman law, the malefactors who were condemned to the death of crucifixion were to be deprived of their garments, and the soldiers who executed the sentence received them as their portion. Christ too, who, in every respect, was treated as the greatest malefactor, had to submit to this law. The soldiers then began to strip him of his garments. With rude haste they first tore off the cloak under which our divine Saviour wore a seamless garment, tightly fitting his body. This had been the work of his dear mother, a labor of love for her beloved Son. This garment was only open at the throat and had to be drawn over the head. But now however this could never be accomplished on account of the great crown whose thorns still pressed deep into his head. The crown of thorns, therefore, had to be first removed. How painful this must have been to Jesus! If we draw out a splinter which has penetrated somewhat deeply into the flesh how hard to bear the suffering that ensues! How intense then must have been the torture of our divine Saviour, when the long, sharp thorns which had penetrated deeply into his head, and had remained there, were drawn out. Meditate on the indescribable agonies which our Lord thus endured, and at the same time think of the unchaste thoughts and desires with which you have so often wounded his sorrowful heart. Ah! on account of these shameless thoughts and desires the most holy head of our Lord has been so painfully tortured by the crown of thorns and its removal. From the very depths of your heart deplore these sins; and resolve henceforth to fight against and banish all impure thoughts and desires, that you may not contaminate your conscience with sin.

(*b*) Having removed the crown of thorns, the soldiers began to strip him of his clothes. His whole body was mangled and full of wounds and blood, his garment adhered to it, especially to his lacerated shoulders and back, for it was *there* that the rough wood of the cross had pressed most heavily. How unprecedented must have been the pain caused when they tore away this garment from our Lord. The lightest touch would have caused a smart, picture if you can the agony consequent on its being cruelly pulled over his head. The narrative of the martyrdom of St. Bartholomew, and of other martyrs, who were flayed alive, is so thrilling that the very thought of such torture causes a shudder. But no less painful was the torture which Christ endured when he was stript of his clothes, which adhered to every part of his body, and by which operation pieces of skin and flesh were torn off, and his wounds renewed, and made to bleed afresh.

O! then take deeply to heart the sufferings of your Redeemer, and shun all effeminacy of the flesh and sins of lust, for it was on account of these sins of effeminancy that Christ had to endure what was so abhorrent to his feelings, to be stript naked before the gazes of an immense multitude of people. Whenever you are tempted to impurity, the sight of that divine

Victim whose raiment was so cruelly taken away, and who stands, a pleading, wounded dove, should banish the vile thought from your heart.

2. *With what great ignominy!*

(*a*) Innate and deeply implanted in the human heart is the feeling which ranks modesty and decorum amongst the highest obligations. It impels every one with proper self-respect to endure any thing rather than permit any improper uncovering of his person. Even the Gentiles had this feeling of modesty, for Plutarch relates that in a certain city of Greece suicide had, at one time, become so prevalent among the female sex that the authorities no longer knew how to put a stop to it. They finally passed an ordinance that the bodies of the suicides should be stript naked, exposed to the pnblic gaze and burnt. This ordinance was successful, for no sooner was it publicly proclaimed, than the terrible mania for suicide died away. All shuddered at the punishment of being exposed naked to public view. The pagans even, who were given to the most abominable debaucheries, awarded the most exalted place to the virtue of modesty. And how dear, how precious was it not esteemed by the early Christians. They would rather endure the greatest tortures and the most cruel death, than the ignominy of being stript naked. No matter how fiercely the executioners might torture them, their first care was to avoid the least indecorum in this regard. St. Perpetua, a noble Roman lady, over whose head but twenty brief years had passed, was hurled to the ground by a wild cow, which rushed at her in a terrible rage. Almost dead she perceived that the angry beast had torn the covering from her side with its horns. But even in her extremity she quickly drew her robe together, thus carefully guarding her modesty in death. Now you can form some faint idea of the pain which the Sacred Heart of Jesus felt when the rude soldiers tore off his clothing, and in a state of nakedness exposed him to the curious gaze of an immense multitude. Sorrowfully he looked to the ground and sighed : "Thou, (O Lord), knowest my reproach, and my confusion, and my shame."—Ps. 68 : 20.

(*b*) It is the opinion of spiritual writers that our Lord took upon himself this ignominy of nakedness especially on account of the abominable vice of impurity. "When a man," says a Father of the Church, "yields to pride, it is a man indeed that sins, but he sins like an angel ; when he succumbs to avarice, it is a man indeed that sins, but he sins like a man ; but if he gives himself up to impurity, he does not sin as an angel or a man, but as a beast." O what a detestable vice is impurity, since it so deeply degrades man, who is created to the likeness of God, placing him upon a level with the brute creatures.

Part II.

The corporal denudation of Jesus Christ serves as a lesson to us, that we must spiritually denude ourselves if we wish to be his true followers, and with him to possess the eternal joys of heaven. Wherein does this spiritual denudation consist? In this, that we divest ourselves—

1. *Of all love of sin.* It suffices not to refrain from the actual commission of sin; we must have no voluntary inclination to it; we must hate and destest all evil from our heart. God regards the heart, the seat of love or hatred. As long as the love of evil holds sway within our heart we displease him, although externally we may do nothing wrong. Everything depends upon the internal justice, without it, all exercises of virtue and good works are as a shell without a kernel, tinsel without value. He who, for instance, does not commit the vice of impurity in deed, but loves it and would commit it if he had an opportunity, or entertains with pleasure unchaste representations and desires, is anything but chaste before God; on the contrary, he is to be numbered among the unchaste, and, unless his sinful mind and disposition become thoroughly changed, he can hope for nothing after death, but to be cast into the fire of hell.

Reflect how matters stand with you. Have you put off the old man, all perverse will, all love for sin, as you put off a garment? Can you say in truth, evil is abhorrent to my soul, and my only joy is in that which is good; my heart, my whole undivided heart belongs to God. If you can in all sincerity make this assertion, O! happy beyond measure are you! You are on the path which will inevitably lead to heaven! and its portals will be open to receive you when you die. But sad indeed and deplorable would it be for you, if you still cherished your evil desires, and still turned your will away from God; for should you persevere in your perverse inclinations, you could not be saved.

2. *All inordinate love of the world.* A soldier who in the faithful service which, for many years, he had rendered his prince left no time for the one thing necessary, when, one day, sickness stood at his door, leading Death. The prince, who was very much attached to him, visited him on his death-bed and bade him ask any favor of him he desired. The sick man replied that the prince, in recompense for the many years during which his chief thought had been to promote the royal interests, should obtain for him the grace either to escape death, or to be relieved of his terrible pains for at least an hour, and, finally, after leaving this world, to be admitted into heaven. The prince, with tears in his eyes, said: "My dear friend, to grant you this favor is not in my power." The soldier sorrowfully sighed; "In vain have I labored, in vain have I served you so long. Had I served my God as long and faithfully as I have served my prince, he would give me heaven

as a recompense. Alas! of what great folly have I been guilty, that I have spent my years and have made no provision for my soul, for a happy eternity." Alas! how many Christians who have lived many years in the world, and have not spent them for God, will, like this soldier, bitterly regret the time they have squandered without any regard for their souls. All the time that has not been spent for God is lost time. They are now attached to the world and to worldly things, they are enamored with them, they hardly ever think of the affair of their salvation. From time to time they have a few transitory desires of conversion, but delay their repentance until their death-bed, and only resolve to abandon sin when sin has abandoned them, when they are no longer able to commit it, and thus their case is as hopeless as that of the soldier. If, however, a worldly advantage is to be gained, they are all life and activity, they spare no labor, no pains, whereas in the service of God the least sacrifice seems so enormous that they make *none*. They omit their morning and evening prayers, neglect to hear the word of God on Sundays and holydays, and to receive the Sacraments, they never enter into themselves and never ask themselves whether the way they go leads to heaven or to hell. There can be only one result from all this. Their hearts become so infatuated with the world that they utterly cast aside all care for their souls. With the most heinous sins they walk serenely through life until death brings them torments of endless duration in the fiery prison of hell—

Beware, then, of being ruled by the love of the world. Consider the words of Christ : "What doth it profit a man, if he gain the whole world, and lose his own soul."—Matt. 16: 26. What folly would it be, if, for the sake of such fleeting, vain, worldly goods, you would plunge yourselves into eternal perdition! Walk in the path trodden by the many who now shine forth, glorious Saints in the realms of the blessed. God's holy service, and their eternal salvation were their most important affairs whilst on earth. "Vanity of vanities, and all is vanity, besides loving God and serving him alone. It is the highest wisdom to despise the world and to tend to heavenly kingdoms. It is vanity to seek after riches which must perish, it is vanity to be ambitious of honors, it is vanity to follow the lusts of the flesh, it is vanity to mind only this present life, and not to look forward unto those things which are to come. It is vanity to love that which passes with all speed, and not to hasten thither where everlasting joy remains."—Imit. Christ, book 1, ch. 1. Think not however that it is forbidden to exercise a due amount of care in acquiring the goods of this world. No! but all else must be subservient to the salvation of your soul. You must render everything else subordinate to this. As the sunflower never swerves from the direction where it can bask in the vivifying rays of the sun, so let the Christian constantly turn his gaze to that bright home above, the abode of the blessed and always be guided by the thought of what is eternal. Shun, therefore, everything injurious to the salvation of your soul, and avail yourselves of temporal goods in such a way that you may still gain everlasting bliss.

3. *All inordinate self-love,* which consists in seeking agreeable and sensual things, in gratifying the passions and leading an easy life. Christ demands self-denial and mortification of his followers: "If any man will come after me, let him deny himself, and take up his cross, and follow me."—Matt. 16: 24. The Apostle also writes: "They who are Christ's, have crucified their flesh with the vices and concupiscences."—Gal. 5: 24. He, therefore, who has put off inordinate self-love, subjects his body to mortifications and denies it everything that could entice it to lust and unfit him for the service of God. Thus St. Paul chastised his body, and brought it into the subjection of the spirit, that after having preached to others, he, himself, might not become a cast away.—1. Cor. 9: 27. St. Francis of Assisium led a very mortified life. The earth was generally his bed, he slept in a sitting posture, the head resting upon a piece of wood or stone. What he ate was seldom cooked, he never drank anything else than water, and even that in the smallest quantity, let the heat be ever so oppressive. Our Lord does not ask such austerity from *us*, but nothing can release us from the duty of avoiding whatever is sinful and prohibited, and turning from whatever might entice us to sin. To crush down this most inveterate enemy, inordinate self-love, it is also necessary to deny our own will, and cheerfully to comply with all that God requires of us and to which obedience obliges us. If we have freed ourselves of all inordinate self-love, we will be truly humble, will not seek the praise of men, prefer to be rather last than first, yield to the will of others, and when obedience demands of us a sacrifice, let not one murmur escape our lips.

PERORATION.

Herein consists the spiritual denudation of the Christian. We must put off all love of sin by the renovation of our mind and the amendment of our heart, put off all inordinate love of the world by the contempt of all earthly things and an earnest solicitude for what is eternal, divest ourselves of all inordinate self-love by the mortification of all sensuality and self-will. True, this spiritual divesting is something more than the idle play of children with their gilded toys. The path to it is weary, and often hard, but we can arrive thereat, for with God's grace we can do all things. Consider the Saints who have accomplished this spiritual denudation, and let their example stimulate us to imitation. Let us look at Jesus in the Tenth Station, and consider the pains and ignominy which he suffered when his clothes were torn from his body, that we may not despise the difficulties connected with our spiritual denudation. "Yes, O Jesus, may we put off the old man and put on the new, who is according to thy pleasure, wish and will. Though it should be hard for us, we will not spare our flesh; divested of all earthly things, and attached to thee alone, we desire to die, that we may live eternally with thee." Amen.

ELEVENTH STATION.

JESUS IS NAILED TO THE CROSS.

"They crucified him."—Luke 23: 33.

Amid a scene of confusion, and almost fainting, behold! Jesus has gained the summit of the mount. His executioners are preparing for the last dread sacrifice, the time for the crucifixion has come. Having dug a hole on the top of Mount Calvary, they carried the cross to the spot where they intended to crucify Jesus and placed it in such position that the cavity they had prepared for it would only too readily receive the heavy load which he had borne through the hot streets und up the weary hill. Ah! there it lay, the hard rough bed of the cross, whilst scattered around were the various instruments selected for the torture of our Lord. The hammers, the ropes, the nails, carefully guarded by those brutal murderers, who were less like rational beings than fiends. The very air was polluted with their blasphemies. Rendered still more ferocious by drink and scarcely half clothed, they gloated over their terrible task. They had brought a vase containing vinegar and gall, a mixture which looked like wine, and which was given to malefactors before executing the sentence of death that they might not feel the approaching tortures, and to smooth the painful pathway to death. They offered it to our Lord, he tasted it, but would not drink; (Matt. 27, 34) for he wished to die without the least mitigation of the pains of death. Now begins the most horrid tragedy which the world has ever witnessed, the Crucifixion of Christ. The Eleventh Station, *Jesus is nailed to the cross.* Let us consider

I. The nailing of his hands, and
II. The nailing of his feet, to the cross.

PART I.

Jesus had suffered much on his journey to Mount Calvary, but indescribably greater are the sufferings that still await him. Let us consider,

1. *The nailing of his hands.*

(a) His murderers then imperiously commanded Jesus to place his wounded form upon the cross. They had rudely pulled it from his shoulders and placed it in such position that they might easily nail him thereupon. Jesus, patient as a lamb, which is dumb before its shearer, (*Is.* 53: 7) extends his sacred body on the cross. Hard was his bed when as a child of poverty he came into the world; for a crib was his cradle, and hay and straw his bed; hard was his bed in the days of his earthly life, for he had not, as he himself assures us, where to lay his head, but infinitely harder is his bed now, when he lies down to die. Jesus is placed on the cross; and *why?* O! for a few brief moments will he not repose his weary limbs? The poorest vagrant, weary and footsore, casts down his bundle, in the sultry summer noon, and rests for awhile upon the soft cool grass. Ah! no! our divine Lord seeks no rest, he is placed upon the cross that the cruel nails may do their work. "Stretch forth your hands that we may thrust deep therein these sharp and pointed nails." And the meek lamb of God, the powerful Lord of heaven and earth complied with the cruel request. Seizing his right arm they dragged it to the hole prepared for the nail, and having tied it tightly down with a cord, one of them dared to kneel upon his sacred chest, a second held his hand flat, and a third eagerly sought for a nail longer and sharper than the rest, pressed it on the open palm of that adorable hand, which had ever been ready to bestow blessings and favors upon the ungrateful Jews, and with a great iron hammer drove the point with such force into the flesh, that it went far into the wood of the cross. One agonizing moan half escaped those quivering lips, whilst his precious blood streamed, unheeded upon the arms of the executioners. The size of the nails employed in fastening our Lord to the cross was unusually large, the heads about the size of a silver dollar, and the thickness, that of a man's thumb, while the points came through at the back of the cross. When the executioners had nailed the right hand of our Lord, seeing that his left did not reach the hole they had bored to receive the nail, they violently seized his left arm and steadied their feet against the cross, whilst they pulled the left hand violently until it reached the place prepared for it. It would seem that the agony experienced by our Lord at this dreadful—nay fiendish—process could scarcely be surpassed at any stage of the sufferings he had endured. His breast heaved, and his legs were violently contracted. They again knelt upon him, tied down his arms, and drove the second nail into his left hand. His sacred blood streamed forth anew, and pitiful moans attested his pain. Each blow of the hammer forced them from his lips, but nothing could move the hardhearted executioners to the slightest commiseration.

2. *The cause of this painful nailing.*

Our Lord suffers this indescribable agony of the nailing of his hands to the cross on account of the sins with which the souls of men are disfigured in various ways *by the abuse of their hands.* We have received them from a beneficent God as another means of serving him and performing acts of kindness to our neighbor, whilst they are of incalculable benefit to ourselves. But too often they are perverted from the use for which they were given us. Even Christians dare to use their hands in a manner most displeasing to their Creator by committing many sins and vices. For is it not a most flagrant misuse when they make unjust attacks upon the property of others, rob and steal; when they are so quick with the cruel blow, and even wound and murder their fellow men? Is it not a violation of their use to do servile work on Sundays and holydays instead of going to church and praying; to be guilty of unchaste touches on their own persons, touches which are abominable in the sight of God and in the eyes of every honorable person, or to collect and disseminate the miasma contained in those books so destructive to innocence and purity of heart, to religion and morality which abound at the present time?

Have you, perhaps, been amongst those who heaped blows upon our Saviour by the various sins committed with your hands? O, reflect, and if it be so, make an act of contrition, humbly ask pardon of him and promise to amend your life. Henceforth, employ your hands according to the will of God in labor, prayer, the practice of good works, and especially, works of mercy and charity. Should the tempter come with his evil suggestions to use your hands so that they would reopen the wounds in those of Jesus, remember the pains which your Lord suffered when those sharp nails were driven deep in his flesh, and beseech him to give you grace to overcome the temptation and not to offend him by any sin.

Part II.

The nailing of the hands to the cross was followed by the nailing of the feet. Let us now consider,

1. *The nailing of the feet to the cross.* The executioners had fastened a piece of wood to the lower portion of the cross beneath where the feet of Jesus would be nailed, that thus the weight of his body might not rest upon the wounds of his hands, as also to prevent the bones of his feet from being broken when nailed to the cross. A hole had been pierced in

this piece of wood to receive the nail when driven through his feet, and there was likewise a little hollow place for his heels. These precautions were only another proof that his torturers were the personification of malice, for they feared that his wounds might be torn open by the weight of his body, and that he would, by dying before he had borne all the agony they wished to inflict upon him, deprive them of the cruel sight of each new pain. The whole body of our Lord had been dragged upward, and contracted by the violent manner in which the executioners had stretched out his arms, and his knees were bent up; they, therefore, flattened and tied them down tightly with cords; but soon perceiving that his feet did not reach the piece of wood which was placed for them to rest upon, their fury raged with terrible force. Some proposed making fresh holes for the nails which pierced his hands, as it would be very difficult to remove the piece of wood, but the others violently opposed this and continued to vociferate: He will not stretch himself out, but we will make him. These words were accompanied with the most fearful oaths and imprecations, and, having fastened a rope to his right leg, they pulled it violently until it reached the wood and then tied it down as tightly as possible. The agony which Jesus suffered from this violent tension was indescribable; so intense that the words, "My God, my God!" escaped his lips, but the monsters increased his pain by tying his chest and arms to the cross, lest the hands should be torn from the nails. They then fastened his left foot over his right foot, having first bored a hole through them with a pointed instrumet, because they could not be placed in such a position as to be nailed together at once. They, next, took a very long nail and drove it completely through both feet into the wood of the cross, which operation was more than usually painful, on account of his body being stretched so unnaturally. How terrible is it not! O, Christians, to think that before the nail was driven through the bruised feet and the hard wood, *thirty-six* blows of the hammer were required. Who can even faintly depict the anguish which racked that sacred body as each blow inflicted a new pain? Every blow penetrated marrow and bone, his heart heaved and trembled, his breathing became slower, paleness covered his face, and there was not a nerve or artery in his body that was not torn with the most violent pain.

2. *The cause of the painful nailing of his feet.* No questions are needed here, for it is but too evident why the feet of Jesus were fastened in so painful a manner to the cross. It was the *sins* which *men commit with their feet.* God has given us feet that, in the observance of his holy commands, we should not deviate from the narrow path which leads to heavenly bliss. And yet, alas! the great majority prefer the broad and pleasant road whose end is death. Ask yourselves whether your feet have not often wandered through places where no thought of God's interests or your duty ever entered your mind, but where you could gratify some vile passion,

and wound anew the bruised feet of your suffering Lord. It was Sunday morning, and conscience urged you to go to Mass, whither you knew well that it was your duty to go. Alas! how many of you went to some den of iniquity to spend the time during the holy sacrifice in drinking or in idle conversation, while Christians who realized the value of their souls knelt before God's altar in prayer and listened to his divine voice in church. It was night, and after the turmoil of the day you should have sought repose, but many of you walked forbidden ways and offended God with the most grievous sins. Alas! many of you have taken steps for purposes which will press heavily on your hearts when called upon to take your last step— the step into eternity. Deplorable, indeed, is the condition of those unfortunate ones who misuse their feet to offend God and always walk in evil paths, for alas! where else can their wanderings terminate but in that abyss where darkness and everlasting horror prevail?

PERORATION.

Reflect well on this, and if your conscience reproaches you that your feet have led you into various sins, with hearts full of sorrow, look upon this Eleventh Station and with the deepest humility implore God's pardon for your sins. With Mary Magdalen prostrate yourselves at the feet of your Lord, and, with her, bathe them with penitent tears, while you promise that henceforth you will walk in the path of virtue. Yes, O Jesus, this shall be the fruit of our meditation to-day: We will never again employ our hands or feet in evil ways; on the contrary, we are resolved to follow thee on the rough road of mortification and penance that we may be permitted to follow thee into the eternal glory of heaven. Amen.

TWELFTH STATION.

JESUS DIES ON THE CROSS.

"*And bowing his head he gave up the ghost*"—*John 19 : 30.*

Let us place ourselves again in spirit on Mount Calvary and contemplate Jesus on his bed of pain. His hands and feet are nailed to the cross. No words can even faintly give an idea of that pain, but the ingenuity of malice has devised still greater sufferings, and a new torture is prepared for our Lord. When those wretched creatures had completed his crucifixion, they tied ropes to the trunk of the cross, and fastening their ends to a long beam which was fixed firmly in the ground at a little distance, they raised up the cross. Some of their number supported it, while others pushed its foot towards the hole prepared for it—the heavy cross fell into this opening with a frightful shock—Jesus uttered a faint cry—his wounds were torn open in the most fearful manner, and the precious blood gushed forth, then, *as now*, trampled upon by the unthinking crowd. They pushed the cross to get it thoroughly into the hole, and caused it to vibrate still more by planting five stakes around it to support it. Christ is thus exalted, and, as a malefactor, hangs on a gibbet between heaven and earth. Let us place ourselves at the Twelfth Station, which bears the inscription : *Jesus dies on the cross*, and consider,

 I. The victory which Jesus won on the cross.
 II. The victory which we, too, must win.

Part I.

From the severe struggle which Christ had to endure on the cross he came forth as conqueror,

 1. In the struggle against his unutterable bodily pains.

(*a*) How intense are the pains which Jesus suffers on the cross! There is not a spot of his sacred head that is free from pain. Alas! the thorns have made it one quivering wound, his face is swollen and disfigured by blows, his chest is distended and raised in such a manner that it were easy to number his bones, his back is lacerated, his hands and his feet pierced through with nails and fastened to the cross—in a word, his whole aspect is such as makes him appear to us as a man of sorrows. And in these nameless sufferings he cannot procure for himself the least mitigation. His head pains him, but if he wished to remove the thorns, the nails hold his hands fast to the cross; his hands and feet ache and smart, but if he should try to find relief, alas! he is bound fast by the nails; his back and chest cause him absolute torture, but he cannot move—*our sins* keep him nailed to the cross. Imagine how our Lord must have suffered, to remain so long unable to lie or sit, to walk or stand, and with the whole weight of his body perforce suspended by these three nails. His members are growing weaker by the long hanging, and, the wounds made by the nails having become larger, with every moment the pain grows more excessive, but, alas! he must drain the bitter cup to the dregs. As St. Alphonsus remarks, Jesus endures the pangs of death every moment, and we may say that he suffers death as often as there are moments in the three hours during which he hung upon the cross. The terrible thorns in his diadem of pain pressed into his head and prevented his raising it even for a moment without the most intense suffering; his mouth was parched and half open from exhaustion, and his waving locks and beard clotted with blood. His chest was torn with stripes and wounds, and his elbows, wrists and shoulders so violently distended as to be almost dislocated. The precious blood never ceased flowing from the gaping wounds in his hands, and his flesh was so torn from his ribs that you might almost number them. His legs, thighs, and arms were stretched almost to dislocation, while the flesh and muscles were completely laid bare that every bone was visible, and his whole body covered with black, livid and gaping wounds. The blood which issued from his wounds was at first red, but by degrees it became rather like water, and the whole appearance of the body was that of a corpse ready to be placed in the grave. Thus Jesus on the cross could truly exclaim in the words of the prophet: "O all ye that pass by the way, attend, and see if there be any sorrow like to my sorrow."—Lament. 1 : 12.

(*b*) Yet, notwithstanding the horrible wounds, the like of which no man ever endured, notwithstanding the ignominy to which he was reduced, there still remained that inexpressible look of dignity and goodness which had ever filled all beholders with awe. Indescribable as are his pains—no complaint, no murmur, no despondent word comes from his lips; he does not make the least exertion to be freed from his torture; he remains on the cross, and with constancy perseveres to the last moment. Though his hands and feet and every member of his body suffer unspeakable pains, he does not complain; as in the Garden of Olives, so now on the cross, he suffers with resignation and bows to the will of his heavenly Father.

2. *In the struggle against the wickedness of his enemies.*

(*a*) You who have walked step by step with our beloved Saviour along the dolorous way of the cross, whose hearts have gone forth in sympathy with his bitter sorrows, may think that at the sight of his countless pains the fury of his enemies would have subsided and given place to feelings of compassion and mercy; for it is peculiar to the human heart to be satisfied when it sees the object of its hatred destroyed. But no, the leaders of the Jews far from feeling the least commiseration for the crucified Saviour, on the contrary emulate one another in blaspheming and mocking him in his misery and abandonment. "Vah," some of them said, "thou who destroyest the temple of God, and in three days buildest it up again, save thy own self; if thou be the Son of God, come down from the cross." Others sneeringly exclaimed: " He saved others; himself he cannot save. If he be the king of Israel, let him now come down from the cross, and we will believe him. He trusted in God; let him deliver him now, if he will have him; for he said, "I am the Son of God."—Matt. 27; 40-43. How painful such blasphemies must have been to our crucified Saviour! What pain his Sacred Heart must have suffered when in this last supreme hour he was mocked by his own creatures and not even granted the privilege of dying in peace!

(*b*) What is Christ's conduct towards his enemies? Does he burn with holy indignation at their wicked behavior? Does he from the cross hurl curses upon his heartless scoffers or destroy them with the breath of his mouth? Ah! no; Jesus, the Eternal Love, does not do this. He does not regard the injury inflicted upon him, but their immortal souls and the judgment awaiting them, and, full of compassion and commiseration, he lovingly pleads for his murderers, saying: "*Father, forgive them, for they know not what they do.*"—Luke 23 : 34. O love of my Jesus, what a good fight thou hast fought, what a glorious victory thou hast won! O, millions of thy servants, who are despised and persecuted in the world, look upon thy struggle, and, in thy victory, conquer.

3. In the struggle against the dejection of his heart.

(*a*) The Apostles and martyrs, it is true, had to endure a hard struggle in the hour of their death, for they were most cruelly tortured. When we read of the sufferings which many of them had to undergo for the sake of their faith, we shudder and can scarcely believe it possible that they could suffer such torments. But then, in all their struggles and sufferings these Saints enjoyed divine consolation, and it was this that raised their drooping spirits, strengthened them and sweetened the most bitter pains. But how different is the manner in which our crucified Saviour suffers! He is destitute of all heavenly consolation, for he voluntarily parted with it that he might, to its fullest extent, suffer the bitterness of death. His heavenly Father withdraws himself from him, as it were, and no longer allows him to enjoy the sweetness of his presence. His soul, like his body, is overshadowed by the densest darkness, and not a ray of heavenly light penetrates into his agonizing heart. His humanity shudders at this and breaks forth into the plaintiff cry: "*My God! my God! why hast thou forsaken me.*"—Matt. 27 : 46.

(*b*) Let us not believe, however, that this plaintive cry showed that the deep interior anguish of our Redeemer had conquered. Let us not think that he had at last faltered, and would, with despondent heart, meet his death. No, he only complains, and that in a loud voice, that we may fully understand what an inexpressible pain for him is this deprivation of all divine consolation, and realize the depth of a love, which impelled him voluntarily to undergo this pain in order to render our death less painful. He does not waver a moment in his confidence in God, even in the hour of his greatest abandonment he is perfectly resigned to the will of his heavenly Father, therefore, after a short pause he exclaims: "*Father, into thy hands I commend my spirit.*"—Luke 25: 45.

Part II.

Being disciples of Christ crucified, with him we must fight and conquer,

1. *In the tribulations of this life.*

(*a*) Sufferings are our portion in this life; for since sin has found entrance into the world, it brought them sad heritage in its train. That this earth is no longer the fair garden into which our first parents entered, the paradise full of bright and beautiful sights which God permitted them to enjoy is well known to us all. That it is a vale of tears where pleasure is always attended by pain, is too evident to us children of men. The first act of the babe that leaves its mother's womb, is to utter a feeble wail, as if already conscious that it must shed many tears on its journey through life. And when man lies on his death-bed, ah! when do his lips part in laughter? he sighs, moans and groans, while bitter tears flow from his breaking eyes. Ah! how many sufferings and tribulations there are in the world! How many suffer the greatest poverty all their life! Great is the number of diseases, and scarcely a day passes on which we are not overtaken by a greater or less indisposition. How many cares and difficulties are connected with the duties of our state of life! Heat and cold, hunger and thirst, fatigue and night-watches, and accompanying all these are many disquietudes and vexations. Job indeed spoke truly when he said: "Man born of a woman, living for a short time, is filled with many miseries."—Job 14: 1.

(*b*) How should we act in the midst of these sufferings and tribulations? Should we lose patience and courage, and despondently murmur against God? Ah! no, that would be wrong and sinful. Though the cross laid upon us may seem almost too heavy, we must bear it with resignation; "for patience is necessary for us; that, doing the will of God, we may receive the promise."—Heb. 10: 36. In the days of tribulation let us arm ourselves with the weapon of patience, and beg our divine Saviour through the pains he endured for love of us on the cross, to grant us resignation to his holy will; and let us carry the cross with constancy as long as it pleases him, remembering the words of St. James: "Blessed is the man that endureth temptation: for when he hath been proved, he shall receive the crown of life, which God hath promised to them that love him."—1: 12.

2. *In the injuries and offences which are offered to us by our fellow-men.*

(*a*) It costs a struggle to suffer patiently and to grant an *entire* pardon to those who offend us, for it is repugnant to our self-love which abhors the thought of yielding and forgiving. But as Christians it is our strict duty to love all men, even our enemies and those who offend us, and to return them good for evil. Our divine Lord emphatically says: "But I say to you: Love your enemies: do good to them that hate you: and pray for them that persecute and calumniate you."—Matt. 5: 44. We also know well that it is vain for us to expect forgiveness of God, unless we forgive from our heart: "If you will not forgive men, neither will your Father forgive you your sins." And we daily pray: "Forgive us our trespasses as we forgive them that trespass against us." We would be guilty of falsehood before God, if we refused to forgive those who offend us, and would, as it were, demand of him to refuse his forgiveness to us.

(b) To forgive our enemies and those who offend us entails frequently a hard struggle; nature revolts against it, but if we have a good will, with the grace of God, which he is always most willing to give, we shall overcome nature and conquer. Consider the many Christians who have won this victory. St. Stephen, that holy youth, first flower of martyrdom in the garden of the Church, prayed for his murderers in the moment of death: "Lord, lay not this sin to their charge."—Acts 7: 59. St. Francis of Sales was grossly insulted by two men, but so far from being angry he cast himself on his knees and humbly asked their pardon, though he had in no way injured or offended them. With such admirable examples before you, you should say with St. Augustine: "If these could do it, why not I?" Courage then. Wage a ceaseless war against all temptations of hatred and ill-will, and consider what a glorious recompense is awaiting you, if you check every desire of revenge and cultivate kindness towards those who offend you, for Christ assures us: "Blessed are you when men shall revile you, and persecute you, and shall say all manner of evil against you falsely, for my sake; rejoice and be exceedingly glad, because your reward is very great in heaven."—Matt. 5: 12.

3. *In the disconsolate state of mind.*

(a) "This state," says St. Alphonsus, "is the most sensitive and is the severest pain which a pious Christian can suffer in this world." As long as he is favored with divine consolation, no affliction grieves him; derision, contempt, pains, privations and persecutions are rather welcomed by him because they afford him an opportunity of making a sacrifice to his Redeemer and of becoming conformable to him. But to feel that his heart is an arid waste, where he can discover no flower of fervor, to know that the bright sunshine of holy desires no longer illumines it, and to realize that there is no consolation for him in any religious exercise, not even in Holy Communion, is a trial very difficult to bear. Still more wretched is he when he thinks that God has abandoned him and will no longer acknowledge him as his child.

Thus St. Francis of Sales when seventeen years old was tempted by the terrible thought that God, from all eternity, had decreed to condemn him to hell, and that, do what he might, he could not escape this terrible fate. This temptation lasted all through one weary month, till it pleased God to lift the cloud from his soul through the intercession of Mary. We read similar incidents in the life of St. Theresa, St. Rose of Lima, St. Margaret of Cortona and of many other Saints. As a rule, God generally visits with interior sufferings those who aspire to higher perfection and often withdraws his consolation from them for a time.

(*b*) Now, if God should find it expedient to let you taste a few drops of the bitter chalice, which Jesus and many Saints had to drink, do not lose courage, arm yourself and fight manfully, and you will come forth victorious from the contest. Arm yourself with humility, acknowledge and confess that the chastisement is on account of your sins, but too well merited; arm yourself with courage and confidence in the conviction that God will not abandon you; arm yourself with prayer by continuing your exercises of devotion, though you should feel no devotion; and, finally, arm yourself with sincerity by candidly disclosing the state of your soul to your confessor and doing what he prescribes for you.

PERORATION.

Therefore, go forth to battle with courage and prove yourselves worthy soldiers of Christ, who on the cross won so glorious a victory over his pains, over his enemies, and over his abandonment. Should sufferings and tribulations overwhelm you, do not despond, put your confidence in God and full of resignation pray: "Thy will be done on earth as it is in heaven." If you are offended, let no thought of hatred and revenge arise in you, but forgive, as God, also, has forgiven you. Should you be deprived of sensible devotion and become disconsolate in the exercise of your religious duties, resign yourself to the will of God and serve him with equal fidelity in good as well as in evil days. Blessed are you, if you thus fight and conquer, you shall triumph with your crucified Redeemer for ever in heaven. Amen.

THIRTEENTH STATION.

JESUS IS TAKEN DOWN FROM THE CROSS AND LAID IN THE LAP OF MARY.

"*They took the body of Jesus, and bound it in linen clothes with the spices.*"
—*John 19: 40.*

Jesus has expired on the cross. It is three o'clock in the afternoon; according to the law of Moses (Deut. 21: 23) which commanded that the burial of those crucified should take place on the same day, haste was necessary in order to take the body of Christ down from the cross. As those who were crucified frequently did not die for some time the executioners broke their legs and chest in order to hasten death. This was to be done, too, in the case of Jesus. When, however, they saw that he was already dead they did not break his legs, but one of the soldiers opened his side with a spear and immediately there came out blood and water. These things were done, that the Scripture might be fulfilled: "You shall not break a bone of him," (Ex. 12: 46), and again: "They shall look upon him whom they have pierced."—Zach. 12: 10. Preparations were now being made for taking the lifeless body of Christ down from the cross. The Thirteenth Station represents this mystery to us: *Jesus is taken down from the cross and laid in the lap of Mary.* At this Station we will consider two points:

I. *Jesus is taken down from the cross.*
II. *He is laid in the lap of Mary.*

PART I.

Jesus Christ being dead on the cross, Joseph of Arimathea, a member of the Sanhedrim, went to Pilate with the request that his body might be given into his charge. Had he not taken this precaution Christ would have been interred on Calvary as were the two criminals executed at the same time. No fitting interment would have been given to those precious remains. Pilate, having convinced himself of the death of Christ, did not hesitate to give the body to Joseph, who, with his friend Nicodemus, likewise a member of the great council, went to Mount Calvary. There, in the presence of the Mother of Jesus and some pious women and disciples, they took down the body of Christ. Then, according to a revelation of St. Bridget, they tenderly bore the mangled form to a rock, on which they spread out linen of the most exquisite fineness, cleansed our divine Saviour from all dust and blood, anointed him with precious spices and prepared him for his burial. Herein Joseph and Nicodemus give us a beautiful example of a *strong and generous love for Jesus.*

1. Of a strong love.

(*a*) "Love is strong as death," (Cant. 8 : 6) for, like death, it can be deterred by no obstacle; "it hopeth all, endureth all."—I. Cor. 13 : 7. Such was the love of Joseph and Nicodemus for Jesus. The great council long before had issued its imperious decree which threatened our Saviour's adherents with expulsion from the Jewish church, and some who, notwithstanding this, still favored his cause had been ignominiously expelled. These two devoted friends had to expect the same, and, it might be, a punishment still more severe. They knew well that by interesting themselves in surrounding the burial of our Saviour's body with whatever tokens of respect they could command they would incur the hatred of the Scribes and Pharisees and expose themselves to hard, life-long persecutions. But these considerations did not deter them from the good work. Their ardent love of Christ made them willing to sacrifice all they possessed, honor, dignity, property, and even life.

(*b*) O, should not the noble example of these two faithful friends of Christ bring the blush of shame to the cheek of the majority of Christians? They are never wanting in words : "Jesus, for thee I live; Jesus, for thee I die," is often heard from their lips, but they shrink from even the smallest sacrifice for the love of Christ. They are tempted to anger, impurity, hatred, aversion toward their neighbor. For love of Christ they should struggle against, and overcome, these temptations, but they yield and thereby sin. Is this a strong love? They are in a society where irreligious discourses take place. It is their duty to manifest their displeasure at such discourses and to show themselves practical Catholics, but through fear of giving offence they do not utter a word, and thereby exteriorly consent to what they interiorly disapprove of. They let their fear of ridicule and raillery conquer their dread of offending God. Is this a strong love? They have made their confession and promised God and their confessor never again to commit this or that sin, but a few days have scarcely passed by when they relapse into their former sinful life, and their resolutions of amendment are cast to the winds. Is this a strong love? How deplorable the condition of such cowardly, wavering Christians. To them are applicable the words of Christ : "He that loveth father or mother more than me, is not worthy of me; and he that loveth son or daughter more than me is not worthy of me.—Matt. 10 : 37. Consider this and endeavor so to love Christ that you can say in truth : "Who shall separate us from the love of Christ? shall tribulation? or distress? or famine? or nakedness? or danger? or persecution? or the sword?"

2. *Of a generous love.*

(*a*) Joseph and Nicodemus had to draw largely from the golden store of their riches in order to have Christ's body taken from the cross and buried. They deemed themselves happy, however, to be permitted so great a privilege, and with the greatest joy procured what was necessary for the embalming and interment of the sacred body. "Joseph taking the body, wrapped it up in a clean linen cloth and laid it in his own new monument, which he had hewed out in a rock."—Matt. 27: 59, 60. Truly, a love, which we must not only admire but also imitate.

(*b*) How can we imitate the love of these two pious men? Opportunities are never wanting. There are churches, school-houses and orphanages to be built and maintained. Now, if you conscientiously guage your liberality by the extent of your means, and give, as freely as they will permit towards the support of your Catholic school and your church, you certainly perform an act of charity most pleasing to your Saviour. If you feed the hungry, clothe the naked, visit the sick, in general, if you relieve the needy and the afflicted Christ accepts these works of mercy as if done to himself. "Amen, I say to you, as long as you did it to one of these my least brethren, you did it to me."—Matt. 25: 40.

Part II.

Jesus is laid in the lap of Mary. It is an ancient tradition that the body of Jesus after the descent from the cross was laid in the lap Mary. St. Bridget testifies that Mary revealed this to her in these words: "When my Son had been taken down from the cross I took him like a leper into my bosom. His eyes were red and full of blood, his mouth was as cold as ice, his hands so stiff that they could not be bent. As he had hung on the cross, so they laid him in my bosom."

Let us consider,

1. *The grief of the divine Mother.* O! sad beyond the power of expresssion was the heart of this disconsolate mother when she contemplated the body of her Son! If it is true what St. Augustine says that the measure of the pains is the measure of love, and if it is certain that Mary loved her Son far more intimately and affectionately than any mother ever loved her only child,

you may imagine, how intense, how unspeakably cruel must have been the grief which pierced her soul when she gazed at those mangled remains. We can without hesitation assent to what a spiritual writer has said: "If we consider all the torments which the holy martyrs endured together, they were not as bitter as the sorrow which Mary experienced at the death of her most beloved Son. Mary, herself revealed her sorrow to St. Bridget in these words: "No man is able to express the grief I suffered when I had my Son in my bosom, I was like a mother in travail, whose members tremble, who is unable to breathe for very pain."

2. *Why she underwent this great grief.* For no other reason than her devoted love for us sinners. She was well aware that according to the decree of God our only hope of redemption was in Christ's death on the cross; therefore loving us most tenderly and wishing nothing more ardently than to behold reopened our pathway to heaven, she made a sacrifice of herself to God and even at the Incarnation of Jesus Christ gave her consent to his painful death. She does the same now that she has the body of her crucified Son in her lap. Suppressing her natural maternal feeling she again makes a sacrifice of Christ, and says: "My heart is ready to break with sorrow, but now I see those whom I so tenderly love, rescued from perdition, I see them reconciled with God and fit to enter into heaven, therefore, I love and praise thee, O God for having inflicted upon me this very great grief, for I esteem the salvation of men above all things.

Application. What a glorious example Mary gives us *that we, too, should sincerely love our fellow-men and be solicitous for their salvation.*

1. *Motives.* This love is our sacred duty. "He gave to every one commandment concerning his neighbor."—Ecclus. 17: 12. If it be incumbent upon us to promote even the temporal welfare of our neighbor, how much more must we be solicitous for the salvation of his soul, since the soul is inestimably more precious than the body and eternity more important than time. Consider the mighty efforts, the unceasing exertions of the Saints, all made that they might win wandering souls to Christ. St. Francis Xavier went to India and Japan, bearing innumerable hardships and dangers in order to bring the blind pagans to the knowledge of God. St. Paulinus sold himself into slavery in order to ransom the son of a widow and to preach the Gospel to infidels. St. Fidelis oftentimes incurred imminent danger by his sermons to heretics, and esteemed it the greatest privilege to die a martyr. The sacrifices made by these and thousands of other Saints are still made by the missionaries who go into distant parts of the world and disregarding labors and dangers preach the holy faith.

2. *Means.*

(*a*) *Words.* A word of instruction, of correction or of warning when spoken at an appropriate and well chosen time and with charity, excercises a great influence upon the human heart; the careless man abandons his negligent habits, the lukewarm become zealous, the sinner enters upon the way of penance. Examples: King Saul persecuted the innocent David unto death; but at the persuasion of his son Jonathan he desisted from his persecution and swore not to injure David.—1. Kings 19: 4, 5. David had grievously sinned, and, for a time, persevered in impenitence. Nathan came to him and showed him the greatness of his crimes, David at once opens his eyes to the true condition of his soul and repents of his sins.—2. Kings 12: 1, *et seq.* Never hesitate to speak such words when you have the least hope that they will be of any avail, and be assured that God will recompense you for this act of charity; for "they that instruct many to justice, shall shine as stars for all eternity."—Dan. 12: 3.

(*b*) *Good example.* A good example like a lovely song charms and enraptures every, even the most savage heart. The pious Christian feels himself sustained and strengthened by the good example of others to walk in the path of virtue; the lukewarm Christian looking at the bright example of some holy souls within his circle, gains inspiration to enter upon a new life and grows more fervent. The sinner who for years had turned every page in the dark record of vice turns from his evil ways and enters upon the way of penance. History also teaches us the effect of good example. The Centurion Cornelius asked and received baptism, and stimulated by his example his whole house embraced the Christian faith.—Acts 10: 48. The hermit Abraham spent years in trying to open the eyes of the infidels to the light of faith, but with no success. When, however, he received with patience the blows and ignominies which they inflicted upon him, they felt themselves drawn towards him by an irresistible power. "Behold," they said, "the patience of this man, behold his love for us, notwithstanding all the injuries and sufferings which we cause him he remains among us and continues to announce the Gospel. If his words were not from God, he certainly would not suffer so much for us. Come, then, and let us believe in the God whom he preaches." According to the admonition of Christ, therefore, "let your light so shine before men, that they may see your good works, and glorify your Father who is in heaven."—Matt. 5: 16.

(*c*) *Prayer,* than which as experience proves there is no more efficacious means for the salvation of souls. The prayer of Moses availed much. God had often decreed to punish the Israelites on account of their sins, but through the intercession of Moses he was again pacified and spared the people. Through the intercession of Abraham God would have spared the cities of Sodom and Gomorrah, if ten just men had been found therein. St. Augustine observes that St. Paul owed the grace of his conversion to St.

Stephen, who prayed for him whilst being stoned. St. Paul, himself, was convinced of the power of intercessory prayer, for he exhorts us, "that supplications, prayers, intercessions and thanksgiving be made for all who are in high stations that we may lead a quiet and a peaceful life, in all piety and chastity."—1. Tim. 2: 1, 2.

PERORATION.

Here is a wide field in which you can contribute your share towards the salvation of your fellow-men. Instruct them, correct them with all patience and doctrine, now with friendly, now with severe words, as in your prudence you deem it expedient and necessary; in everything shine before them with a good example and frequently commend them in your pious prayers to the love and mercy of God. If in such a manner you manifest your love for your neighbor you will do more good than you will ever know during life. You will strengthen the weak, excite Christian fervor in the hearts of the lukewarm, lead the sinners back to the way of penance and rescue many souls from perdition. You may be assured that God, who desires nothing more ardently than that all men be saved, will be pleased with your works of charity and will reward you for them with many graces in this life and with eternal beatitude in the next. Amen.

FOURTEENTH STATION.

JESUS IS LAID IN THE TOMB.

"Joseph taking his body, wrapped it up in a clean linen cloth; and laid it in his own new monument which he had hewed out in a rock.
—*Matt. 27: 59, 60.*

Mary the Mother of God had taken her Son after his descent from the cross into her bosom and once more contemplated all his wounds, although the effort produced an anguish far keener than any mother, before or since, has ever felt. But a new and greater grief was to follow. The sun is fast receding from view, the shadows of evening are beginning to fall, and the burial of Jesus must be hastened, because after the setting of the sun begins the Easter-feast on which no interment is permitted to take place. The two friends of our Saviour, Joseph and Nicodemus, make all the necessary arrangements for the burial. They wash the sacred body, anoint it with the precious ointments they had brought, wrap it up in fine linen and bury it in the new monument of Joseph of Arimathea. This is represented to us in the last Station of the Holy Way of the Cross, whereon we read: *Jesus is laid in the tomb. Let us consider,*

I. *The burial of Jesus in the new monument, and*
II. *His burial in our heart.*

PART I.

1. *The persons who follow the corpse to the grave.* Persons who have been prominent during life either by their goodness which has won for them admiration, or their wealth which has given them a high position, or their rank which entitles them to consideration are generally followed to the tomb by a long and imposing funeral train. An elegant casket contains the mortal remains, the bells are tolled, a long line of carriages, filled with people, accompany it to the grave. And if the deceased was some great, or mighty potentate, whole regiments attend in order to add to the solemnity of the funeral. Now if miserable men are buried with such great pomp, how magnificent should be the funeral of the Son of God! He is rich, immensely rich; for all the treasures of the immense universe are his; he is the ruler whose dominion extends over the whole visible creation and whom heaven and earth obey; he is a saint, before whose splendor the sanctity of Angels and Saints disappear as the light of the moon and the stars before the rays of the sun. Moreover, never before or since he dwelt upon earth had man so loving, so helpful a friend, for his whole life was one constant series of benefits to all; the poor loved him, for it was his delight to "load them with good things," the sick revered even the hem of his garment, for they knew he could restore them to health. The ignorant hailed the words of instruction from him as the parched earth drinks in the soft spring rain, and sinners, weary of tasting husks, could not withstand his pleading voice, as he bade them repent, and "sin no more." The funeral of so great, so noble, so generous, so perfect a being will doubtless surpass all similar demonstrations of respect ever known. All Judea and Samaria will be present and tears without number will be shed at his grave. Millions will weep for him, his heroic and magnanimous deeds will be told, and his praise will be on every one's lips. But what do I say? It will be even now as when, during life, he walked on earth. Few and humble were those who loved him dearly and truly, and when his eyes closed in death there were equally few whom he could claim as his true friends. He was the King of the Jews, but no Herod is there to pay him the last tribute of respect, no Pilate with reverend mien joins the throng; he was High-priest, but I see no priest, no Levite among the mourners; he was a Prophet, but I see no Scribe, no Pharisee hasten to pay this last act of regard towards one whom they had loved and esteemed. Who then form the vast crowd of mourners at the funeral of

Christ? Alas! His few but faithful friends alone attend. Mary, his most afflicted mother, Joseph of Arimathea, Nicodemus, St. John, one or two of the disciples, Mary Magdalene and a few pious women of Jerusalem. What a small unpretending funeral for so great a person!

Lesson. Such is the world. If Christ had pandered to the passions of the Jews and sanctioned their vices, or, at least, silently overlooked them, he would without doubt have had a most magnificent funeral and the marvels he wrought would have been reiterated all over the world. But because he was fearless in his condemnation of vice, and preached penance and self-denial as necessary virtues he incurred a hatred which pursued him unto death. He was condemned to the death awarded to malefactors, and could his enemies have gained their wish, they would have destroyed even his memory from the face of the earth. Do not value the praise and applause of the world, but be firm in your allegiance to Christ; the friendship of one pious soul is infinitely more precious, than the friendship of the world. When your lifeless form has been placed in the casket and is about to be borne to the silent city of the dead, if you have the fervent prayers of ten pious Christians, it will be of far greater benefit to you than would be the presence of a thousand worldly people at your grave, whose only motive in going is self interest, or who are prompted by a regard for propriety, and they will never think of saying an Our Father that, the time of probation being shortened, you may soon enter the realms of perpetual light, the mansions of heavenly bliss.

2. *The place of burial.* Christ was laid in a new sepulchre. The more prominent of the Jews had their own monuments, which often were very spacious and magnificent, and looked more like a dwelling than a grave. Joseph of Arimathea, too, had such a monument, for he was wealthy and a member of the great council. Christ having died on the cross, was to be buried like all other criminals, on Golgotha, that is, *the place of skulls,* in the valley Enon, a horrible place, where all the refuse of the city was thrown. But happily through the generosity of Joseph this great indignity did not take place. He conveyed the body of Christ to his own monument and deemed himself happy to be able to bury him there. Thus in a stranger's grave was the only refuge offered to Jesus; he who on the cross had not where to lay his holy head, had not even his own grave in the world, because he was not of the world.

Lesson. Do not set your heart and affections on the goods of this world, much less let them cause you to offend God. All earthly goods are vain, fleeting, perishable, and resemble a vapor which is seen a little while and then disappears.—James 4: 15. What else is our life here below but a drama, which will soon end; for "the figure of the world passeth away."

—1. Cor, 7: 31. He that plays the king, leaves behind the purple trailing robes. When the drama is at an end he that acted the king is king no more, and the master is no longer master. The sad hour of death puts an end to all glory, all nobility, all greatness and all possessions. Casimir, king of Poland died while at a banquet with the great ones of his kingdom. He was lifting a glass to his lips when death snatched it away; thus the drama ended for him. Celsus was killed after having been commander-in-chief only seven days, and the drama was at an end for him. Ladislas, king of Bohemia, a youth of eighteen years, was expecting his bride, a daughter of the king of France, and great preparations had been made for her reception, when behold! one morning a deadly faintness and intense pains attacked him, and caused his death. Messengers were despatched to convey the sad tidings to his bride that the end of the drama had come for him. You are only actors in the drama of life, in your own estimation you are of importance, but you are nothing, you are only acting your part. . You may imagine that you are rich, but the world deceives you, you are poor, you have nothing, because you brought nothing into this world, and as you came so shall you leave, the world claims all your possessions. Beware, therefore, on account of these vain, fleeting, perishable worldly goods, of burdening your conscience and of preparing for yourself a miserable eternity.

We Catholics enjoy a still greater privilege than did Joseph of Arimathea and Nicodemus, for we can bury Jesus, not only once, but as often as we please, and not in the earth, but in our heart. As often as we communicate, Jesus comes to us, our heart becomes his resting place. But that our heart may become a fitting dwelling place for our divine Saviour, it must resemble the monument in the garden of Joseph of Arimathea. This monument was, as we read in the Gospel (Matt. 27: 60),

1. *New.* It had been but lately hewed out, and no man had as yet been interred therein. Our heart must also be *new*, that Jesus may find there a worthy sepulchre. O! could you but see the repulsive appearance of a heart where sin has taken up its abode. The throne which God has erected is overthrown and demolished, the light of grace and with it the splendor of Christian virtues, is extinguished, and instead of Christ entering permanently in, he turns from it in horror. Satan has come, bringing with him sin and vice, and now it resembles a gloomy, dismal prison where crawling creeping things feed on the damp foul air. What an insult, therefore, do those Christians inflict upon their Saviour, who offer him an impure, sinful heart for his abode! They compel the God of all holiness to enter where sin and the devil dwell. Is not this insulting him in the grossest manner? Let us not wonder when the Apostle says: "He that eateth and drinketh unworthily, eateth and drinketh judgment to himself." —1. Cor. 11: 29. The very instant that man communicates unworthily, he renders himself guilty of eternal damnation.

Reflect well on this, and be careful that, at all times, but especially this year again at Easter, you make a worthy Communion. Renew your spirit, create for yourselves a new heart, cleanse it by a good confession from all sin, transform it into a fair garden all filled with the fragrant flowers of virtue, especially the blossoms of faith, love, humility and a holy desire of being united with Jesus. After such a preparation you may with confidence receive the Holy of holies into your heart, for he will find there an agreeable resting place.

2. *Hewed out in a rock.* The monument of Joseph of Arimathea which was hewed out in a rock, was, therefore, protected against all storms and afforded to the sacred body of Christ a secure habitation. *Firm as a rock* must also be your heart, no power of hell, no allurement of the flesh, no enticement of the world should have power to cause your disloyalty to the divine Saviour, who has entered into your heart and to whom you have given yourself whole and entire. At your Easter Communion think of the sepulchre of Christ hewed out in a rock, and whilst you live remain faithful to the resolution you have made. Walk with constancy in the way of God's commandments, in the way of virtue, and confiding in the assistance of divine grace, often say with the Apostle: "I am sure that neither death, nor life, nor Angels, nor principalities, nor powers, nor things present, nor things to come, nor might, nor height, nor depth, nor any other creature shall be able to separate me from the love of God which is in Christ Jesus our Lord.—Rom. 8: 38, 39.

3. *Closed with a heavy stone.* As we read in the Gospel, Joseph of Arimathea rolled a massive stone before the entrance of the monument. With such a stone you, too, must secure the entrance of your heart, that no enemy may enter and banish your Saviour. By this stone I understand,

(a) *The careful avoiding of whatever might cause a relapse into sin*, *i. e.*, the proximate occasion of sin. With those who do not shun the proximate occasion of sin, there is no true conversion, they will and must ere long relapse. It is difficult to be in the midst of fire and not burn, to have the opportunity to sin and not sin. St. Augustine says: "To love the proximate occasion, and to fall into sin are one and the same thing." "He that loveth danger, shall perish in it."—Ecclus. 3: 27. "He that toucheth pitch, shall be defiled with it."—13: 1, Example: Alipius, a friend of St. Augustine, had been a passionate lover of theatricals, which are so pernicious in their effects, but when faith began to penetrate his soul he generously resolved to abandon them. One day he met several friends who invited him to go with them, and who drew him after them as he resisted. He said: "You may drag my body into the theatre, but you cannot direct my mind and eyes to the play. I will, therefore, be present and absent at the same time." And he did, indeed, sit before the stage with his eyes closed, but suddenly, as an immense shout of applause burst upon his ears, in the same instant his old passion returned and he opened his eyes. He relapsed into his former sins and continued in this deplorable condition, till the hand of God totally changed him. Here you have unequivocal proof that he who does not shun the occasion of sin, does not avoid the actual sin. Experience: Whence does it come that drunkards, gamblers and the unchaste relapse into the mire of their iniquity? Because they do not avoid saloons, gambling houses and familiarity with persons of the opposite sex. Shun, therefore, the evil occasions, especially those which you know have heretofore been fatal to your perseverance. Though this should be difficult for you to accomplish, it must be done even though it should entail the sacrifice of your dearest treasures. The kingdom of heaven suffers violence, it is not for cowards, but for those valiant warrriors who know how to fight and gloriously conquer. "If they right eye cause thee to offend, pluck it out, and cast it from thee; for it is better for thee that one of thy members should perish, than that thy whole body should be cast into hell."—Matt. 5: 30.

(*b*) *A diligent use of the means of amendment.* Though a patient be convalescent, he must continue to take medicine, in order to build up his system. Thus it is with penitents, who, by nature, are weak and inclined to evil, and whose innate weakness has been much increased by their sinful life. They will find it impossible to avoid relapsing into their former evil ways, unless they have recourse to the following means. First, *prayer*, for this fortifies us with heavenly strength, that we may overcome all the enemies of our salvation. "Prayer," says St. Chrysostom, "is a saving anchor for him who is in danger of suffering shipwreck, an inexhaustible treasure for the poor, and an effectual medicine for him who desires to retain his health." Pray, therefore, without ceasing, but above all when the tempter tries to storm the citadel of your heart, for prayer is most necessary that we may drive him victoriously away. Another means for the preservation of grace is the frequent *reception of the Sacraments of Penance and the Blessed Euchrist.* The more frequently you, by a good confession, prepare to welcome the divine Savior in your heart, the weaker your evil inclinations become, the greater power the spirit obtains over the flesh, and the more graces you receive to overcome temptation and to remain steadfast in good. Another means is the *frequent renewal of our good resolutions.* If you wish to preserve fire in a stove, you must put fuel in from time to time. In like manner you must renew the good resolutions you have made at your confessions, that your zeal in virtue may not grow cold and give place to tepidity, the forerunner of a relapse. Finally, another means is the serious and frequent *consideration of the four last things*, according to the words: "In all thy works remember thy last end, and thou shalt never sin."—Ecclus. 7: 40.

PERORATION.

You know, now, how you are to bury your divine Savior in your heart. Cleanse it from every mortal sin, for he who is all purity can dwell only in a pure heart. If Christ has taken up his abode with you, promise him eternal love and fidelity, carefully shun the occasions of sin, and avail yourselves of the means of amendment. If you do this you may hope one day to reign with Jesus Christ, your Saviour and Redeemer, in heaven for all eternity. Amen.

LENTEN SERMONS.

THIRD COURSE.

SEVEN SERMONS.

SERMON I.

CHRIST'S SUFFERINGS FOR THE SALVATION OF MANKIND.

"He suffered under Pontius Pilate."—Apostle's Creed.

The bitter and rude contumelies of an ungrateful world, the sorrowful Passion and ignominious death which Jesus Christ suffered under Pontius Pilate for the salvation of mankind, form the great mystery which the Apostles make the subject matter of our meditation in the fourth article of the Creed; a mystery which includes not only the superabundance of the great love of the Father, who sacrificed the precious life of his only-begotten Son for us sinful men (John, ch. 3), but also the love of this divine Son, who laid down his life on the altar of the cross for mankind, urged, as it were, by his ineffable love for his ungrateful children. I have selected this mystery, namely those bitter outrages which so deeply wounded our divine Lord during his ignominious passion and death as the subject of our meditations during these penitential days. Before, however, entering upon the special circumstances of the dolorous Passion of our Blessed Redeemer, I shall speak of it in general, explaining to you—

    I. Who it was that suffered,
   II. For whom he suffered, and
  III. Why he suffered.

These three considerations are most necessary, and are of the greatest importance for those who would meditate with fruit on the Passion of Christ; for without meditating first on these three points, the history of the Passion of our Savior would be of little or no advantage to them.

    1. *Who is it that endured* such great sufferings, such bitter sorrows, such protracted agonies? Who is he? Is he a saint? No, he is more than a saint. Is he an angel? No; the highest angel in heaven bends low before his heavenly throne. He is no created spirit. Who is he? Listen. He that is suffering is God himself, God suffering. It is Jesus Christ, true God and true man. As man he was externally, so charming and amiable, that David says of him, (Ps. 44), "He was *beautiful above the sons of men.*" The author of the Canticles compares his head to the finest gold, his locks to branches of palm-trees, his eyes to the eyes of doves upon brooks of

waters, which are washed with milk, and sit beside the plentiful streams, his lips to lilies dropping with choice myrrh.—5: 11–13. He was adorned with such indescribable beauty and loveliness that at the very moment he appeared all shadows were lifted from the heart, while perfect peace and solace took their place. Humility sat upon him like a garment, and meekness had full possession of his heart, for he never opened his mouth to complain of the insults which were offered to him. He was most innocent; he never committed a sin, and in him neither malice nor delusion was found, whence he needed not to offer sacrifice for his own sins.—Heb. 7: 27. He was merciful above all the sons of men, for his whole course of life was one long exercise of kindly deeds and good offices to man. We may also add that his physical organization was so perfect, formed, as he was from the pure blood of the Immaculate Virgin through the agency of the Holy Spirit that he was most sensitive to every pain, and felt suffering to an extraordinary degree. Who can be so hard-hearted as to refuse the tenderest pity at the sight of so perfect a being mocked and insulted, whilst the precious blood which streaming from his sacred body so changes the beauty of his divine countenance that he was not like another man, as the Sacred Scripture says?

But this man who was treated so cruelly, and martyred without mercy, was also God. God begotten by God, the divine Light, which proceeds from the Father, true God and true man. The Apostle says: "He is the same, whom God hath appointed heir of all things, by whom he also made the world, who being the brightness of his glory, and the figure of his substance, and upholding all things, by the word of his power, sitteth at the right hand of his Majesty on high: being made so much better than the angels, who being perfectly happy in himself, begins and completes the happiness of the Saints.

It is the *Son of God*, who assumed human flesh, became man, endured agony untold and died for our sins. Yes, it is *the God of heaven and earth*, who is tormented until his blood bursts forth from every pore, and basely betrayed by one whom he considered his friend, dragged before wicked judges, derided and mocked, insulted, abused, scourged at the pillar, crowned with thorns and crucified. It is the *King of Glory*, who submits his divine form to the lash of his meanest slaves. It is the *Judge of the living and the dead*, who, condemned to death by an unjust sentence, is led forth with a heavy cross on his mangled shoulders to Mount Calvary; who, fastened to the cross between two highway robbers, suffers death on that infamous gibbet. Isaias (66: 8), exclaims: "Who hath ever heard such a thing; and who hath seen the like to this?" Had one of those bright spirits who stand before his throne undergone such excessive suffering, he would deserve the highest praise. Shall we not be lost in admiration at the thought? He that suffered is God, in comparison to whom man is nothing, and the whole universe like a dew-drop that glitters in the morning sun and disappears with its ardent ray. But the august Sufferer is far more than the highest angel in heaven. Jesus, that only-begotten Son of the heavenly Father, the Creator and sovereign Lord of heaven and earth, suffers and dies for our sins.

It is an article of our holy faith that the divine nature of the God-man has not suffered, because it being essentially unchangeable, cannot suffer. It was the humanity of Christ that suffered and died; but because the humanity is most intimately united to the divinity, and because there is but one person in Christ, namely, the divine, we are right in saying that he, the only-begotten Son of God, consubstantial with him, and equal to him in power, wisdom, majesty, and all other perfections, from eternity, has suffered, in time, persecution, contumely, torture, crucifixion and death. And as—making use of an example of St. Augustine's—a man is a philosopher only according to his soul—we say, without hesitation, the philosopher has become blind, has died, has been buried—things which concern only the body—so Jesus Christ is the Son of God and King of Glory only according to his divine nature; and yet, we are right in saying, God suffered, God was crucified, God died and was buried, though these things regard only the human nature of Christ; for although there are two natures in Christ, that is, the divine and the human, there are not two Christs, but one only, as in the philosopher, there are not two men, but one only, notwithstanding the two substances in him, soul and body. Whence it follows, that the same Jesus Christ, who is true God and true man, could be, and was, crowned with thorns and crucified. This was the admirable invention of God, the great miracle of his love, which caused Jesus, though incapable of suffering according to his divine nature, to suffer, uniting in the one person of the Word two natures, the human and the divine.

2. *For whom has the Son of God suffered?*

Was there perhaps some crime resting upon him of which he was conscious, and for which he alone could make amends? Or did the faint shadow of some imperfection dim his pure spirit, and require the cleansing which his precious blood alone could give! No; for who does not know, as the Apostle says, that he is sanctity itself, the stainless one, the most pure between whom and sinners, there is a vast, an impassable gulf? Who does not know that he was filled with so many and such great graces, as to render him incapable of sinning; that in him the fulness of the Deity dwelt corporally, and that God acknowledged him at his baptism as his well beloved Son? For whom, then, did he suffer, if he had no need to suffer for himself? He left the grandeur and splendor of his heavenly throne, assumed flesh in the womb of a Virgin, and, as a tiny babe, endured all the sufferings of his helpless condition. He accepted the bitter outrages heaped upon him by an ungrateful world. He offered himself a bleeding victim on the Cross of Calvary for us miserable sinners. Yes, Christ bore all this for our sake, for *us*, who, beside his infinite Majesty, are nothing but dust and ashes who, like the frail leaves of the forest trees, are whirled aloft, the sport of every wind. He suffered for us wicked, sinful creatures, who not only have no power to move and to prolong our lives, but are even incapable of conceiving a thought of ourselves. The Creator has suffered for his creatures, the Lord and Master, for his servants; the fullness of riches and power and majesty has suffered for us poor, weak, impotent men. But how is it possible to believe so stupendous a tale? The Creator willing to suffer for his creatures! We must believe it, because faith so teaches us. The Council of Nice commands us to confess: "I believe in one Lord, Jesus Christ, the Son of God, who for us men, and for our salvation was crucified, suffered, died, and was buried."

Let us imagine that a prince, burning with zeal to improve the condition of his subjects, and to relieve them from the sharp sting of poverty, should relinquish his purple, his crown and sceptre, and regarding neither pain, nor expense to accomplish his design, should brave the dangers of long, wearisome journeys, risk his life, nay, cheerfully die for the welfare of his people, would it not be a singular case? And yet Jesus has done what no prince or king ever did for his people. His goodness and mercy arrived at that superabundance of love to which the love of a prince for his people never aspired, nor ever will; and this great love for us appears the more admirable the greater the distance is between God and man, and the more it excels the relations of a prince to his subjects. He that was mighty conceals his immensity and all for love of us. He whose kingdom is the kingdom of all centuries, and whose dominion is over all generations, became the reproach of men and the outcast of the people.—Ps. 21. The prophet Isaiah calls him "a man of sorrows," and such he was; for his whole life was a life of sorrow. He took on his shoulders all our debts. It is true, he was not only man, but also God. One single sigh, one little prayer, one tiny drop of his most precious blood would more than have sufficed for the sins of a thousand worlds. But this dear Saviour chose rigorously to satisfy the justice of God, to be despised and to endure the most bitter pain, *all for us!* It was through this same love that he preferred to be considered the most abject of men, to be looked upon as wicked and vile. *This* was the prophet Isaiah's meaning in his prediction: "We have seen him despised and the most abject of men."

Was there naught in our poor weak nature to win for us so priceless a gift as God's love? Ah, no! but there was everything that aroused his anger against us. Besides our innate insignificance and littleness there was in us sin, which for a being of infinite purity should naturally suffice to arouse his hatred and anger against us. We are all conceived in sin and born children of wrath, and God beheld in us rebels whom his justice had to condemn. But notwithstanding our insignificance and unworthiness, our divine Saviour, out of mere goodness and mercy, became our mediator, took upon himself all our debts, and was ready to atone for them. Where is the man that would give his life for a criminal, when, as the Apostle says: there is not to be found one who would be willing to lay down his life for an innocent man! Christ did this. He died for criminals. He gave every drop of his precious blood that our salvation might be secured. He laid down his life not only for those who would repay him with devotion and gratitude, but for those also who would trample on the precious boon thus conferred. He was aware of this cruel return on the part of mankind; the very blackness of the ingratitude might have concealed it from man, but alas! it was only too clear to our Lord. He knew that the greater number, the vast majority, would reap no benefit from his sufferings, but he would also suffer for these ungrateful people. Had he suffered only for those who, after having obtained the garment of innocence by Baptism, would preserve it with jealousy; for those only who, after having recovered the friendship of God in the Sacrament of Penance, would guard it as their most precious treasure, for those only who going to distant lands would tell the heathens of the Creator who so loved them and increase his glory by winning those savage tribes to believe in him, amazing and incomprehensible would be his love. But how great must be our admiration when we consider that he suffered for those who live for months and years without devoting even a moment to the meditation of his Passion; who, instead of gaining souls for God, are the very means of perverting and destroying them by the scandal they give! And if it be the summit of heroic love to which man can aspire, to give his life for his friend, language fails to express the love of Christ, who gave his life for us who were not his friends, but his enemies. We were born slaves of sin, children of the devil, enemies of God, and yet Christ, becoming obedient unto death, atoned for our disobedience, died for our salvation, and by his death, recovered for us that bright inheritance which we had lost by sin, namely, *liberty, grace* and, the *right to heaven.*

Ere yet Christ had come into the world it was overshadowed by the deep night of spiritual darkness, and Satan held mankind under his sway. He ruled over the intellect or understanding, which was darkened by ignorance and error, holding it fast by chains which were forged in the fire of hell. He tyranized over the heart and will, enslaving them through pride, concupiscence and greed of gold. He had arrogated to himself the adoration which is due to God alone, and introduced idolatry into the world; magnificent fanes arose for the worship of false deities, incense was burnt before the idols of Satan, and parents immolated even their children to make him propitious to them. Jesus Christ, by his last words on the cross, "It is consummated," uttered his death-warrant and when he bowed his head and died, he gave the death stroke to the monarch of hell. The temples were shaken to their center, and the idols hurled mercilessly from their shrines, which henceforth would be devoted to the worship of God. Christ himself foretold that the prince of this world would be cast out. It was then that St. John saw the angel coming down from heaven, having the key of the bottomless pit, and a great chain in his hand who laid hold of the dragon, the old serpent, which is the devil and bound him, and cast him into the bottomless pit, and shut him up, and set a seal upon him, that he should no more seduce the nations.—Apoc. 20: 1–3. It was then that man was delivered from the power of darkness, and translated into the kingdom of God. That infernal spirit still rages against us, it is true, and seeks revenge because we have escaped from his power. He is likened to a dog that is tied by a short chain; he may bark at us, and terrify us with his sharp glistening teeth, but he cannot injure us unless we go within his reach, and should we, through our own negligence, receive a wound, an earnest reflection upon the Passion of Jesus Christ will be a powerful remedy against the poisonous bite of this furious Cerberus of hell.

Besides liberty, Christ has merited grace for us. All men were conceived in sin and born guilty of high treason against the divine majesty, objects of God's anger, and sentenced to be punished for an endless eternity. That God might reinstate man in his favor, and elevate him again to the state of grace, it was necessary to appease the divine wrath and to make full reparation and satisfaction for the offense committed against him; a sacrifice was required sufficient to free man from all that made him abominable in the sight of God, but who was able to make a sacrifice of such virtue and efficacy? It would not suffice to offer irrational animals for rational beings, for though the blood of goats and oxen cleansed the flesh according to the law of Moses, it was never able to cleanse the conscience, and to take away the sins of the world. There was nothing appropriate in offering irrational animals for the guilt of man: a man was required, who would offer himself for the rest of mankind as an expiation. A rational being must be immolated for rational beings. Over the broad earth there was not one human being whose soul had not been stained by sin, and could one equally guilty with the rest efface the transgressions of others? That the sacrifice might be a rational one a man was to be sacrificed; and that as a result of this sacrifice men might be cleansed from their sins, a man without sin must be offered. This man without sin was Jesus Christ, who, in a mysterious manner, was born of the Blessed Virgin Mary, by the agency of the Holy Ghost, and who was of the same nature as the rest of men, but free from the slightest shadow of sin. This God-man Christ, offered himself a bleeding expiation to his Father, saying to him at his entrance into the world: "Sacrifices and oblations, and holocausts for sin, thou hast not desired, neither are they pleasing to thee, which are offered to thee according to the law. Then said I: 'Behold, I come to do thy will, O God.'" —Heb. 10: 8, 9. In this *will* we are sanctified by means of the offering of the body of Jesus Christ. What was indeed impossible for any other sacrifice to accomplish, Christ accomplished by his Passion and death on the cross. He washed our souls in his blood, appeased God's wrath, and made peace between heaven and earth.

All men having contracted a heavy debt, divine justice required that the honor of which God had been deprived by sin, should be restored to him and this satisfaction no other save the God-man could bestow. The offence being offered to the infinite majesty of God, the atonement must be made by a person of infinite majesty, and this person could be no other than Jesus Christ, who, in the quality of true God and true man, taking on himself our guilt and the punishment due to it as man, was able to give it an infinite value as God. Offering himself, therefore, to his Father, he offered him a ransom which not only equalled our guilt, but outweighed it; wherefore, St. Paul says: that if the guilt was great, the grace was abundant. All the spiritual treasures, which in such superabundance are offered to us, the Sacraments which he instituted for our sake, the graces which we have received and still receive, are the fruits of that price which Jesus paid for us by his Passion and death; a price by which he recovered for us besides liberty and grace, the right to a home beyond the skies.

Jesus Christ endured these sufferings and a cruel death, not only to deliver us from the power of the devil, who unhappily had made us his slaves, not only to reconcile us to God, whose anger was aroused against us, but also to open a pathway for us into heaven. The Old Testament furnishes us with a beautiful figure of this particular favor. In the book of Numbers we read that God said to Moses: When you shall have passed over the Jordan, into the land of Canaan, determine what cities shall be for the refuge of fugitives who shed blood against their will. And when the fugitive shall be in them, the kinsman of him that is slain, may not have power to kill him, until he stand before the multitude and his cause be judged, and if he be found innocent, he shall be delivered from the hand of the avenger, and shall be brought back by sentence into the city whence he had fled, and he shall abide there until the death of the high-priest that is anointed with oil. God wished to say by this command that no one, though no stain had marred the pure whiteness of his soul, could be permitted to enter into heaven before the death of the eternal High-priest, who is Christ Jesus. Adam waited through the weary course of centuries, with his descendants, exiled from their heavenly home; even the Patriarchs and Prophets remained also excluded until the High-priest completed his sacrifice on the cross. It was then that the gates of heaven, which for four thousand years had been barred against mankind, were opened and remained open, and still remain open for all the souls that make themselves partakers of the merits of the Passion and death of Jesus Christ.

When the loving Saviour, the Holy One, the pure and spotless Redeemer chose to suffer persecutions, contumelies, tortures and death, is it not just that we, who are defiled by many sins and iniquities, should bear the sufferings of this life with patience and resignation to the will of God? When God suffered so much for us sinful men, is it right that we suffer nothing for our sins? Is it right that we renounce no pleasure for his sake, that we do not restrain our sinful inclinations? When Christ endured such anguish that we might be freed from the power of the devil, reinstated in the favor of his Father, and enabled to enter heaven by the pathway which he opened for us, is it right and prudent for us to re-enter the ranks of his enemy, to assume the livery of the devil and to close the heavenly portals against us? When God retired into the desert and fasted forty days and forty nights for our sakes, is it right that you should live in gluttony during this holy season? Will you do no penance for your sins? Some of you are, perhaps, dispensed from the rigorous observance of Lent, but you are not, and cannot be dispensed from the obligation of doing penance. One fast is incumbent upon you all. There is no dispensation from the fast of sin, it binds you all alike, young and old, sick and healthy, rich and poor, it binds all—in all places, at all times, during the whole course of their life. Now is the acceptable time, this is the day of salvation, the present is yours; by employing it well, you may escape a miserable eternity. Let us not suffer these days of grace to glide away unacceptable to God and unprofitable to ourselves, lest we die in our sins, a misfortune which God, in his infinite mercy, may avert from us all. Amen.

SERMON II.

THE MENTAL SUFFERINGS OF CHRIST.

"My soul is sorrowful even unto death."—Matt. 26 : 38.

The evil which the unhappy fall of our first parents brought on all mankind and with which all are infected, is threefold, as St. John says: All that is in the world is the concupiscence of the flesh, the concupiscence of the eyes, and the pride of life. Scarce had the forbidden fruit passed the lips of Adam than he recognized the transformation which had taken place over his affections and inclinations, there had passed an utter change, and this change affected all men. Inasmuch as he himself after the first sin, was drawn to sinful objects, for which, in the state of grace, he had no inordinate desire, so all his descendants are born with an inclination that draws them from spiritual and divine things to objects which are "of the earth earthly" and urges them to seek for terrestrial joys. Whence it comes that man sets his *consolation in the perishable goods* of this life, *his greatness in the attainment of honors and dignities,* and *his pleasure in the enjoyment of lust.* Alas! he plunges recklessly and most deplorably forward, becoming immersed in an ocean of happiness which he finds as empty as dead sea fruit. Jesus Christ, the second Adam, left the magnificence of heaven to free a world, which repaid his benefits with ingratitude, from all imperfection, places his tribulation against the vanity of human consolation, his love of contempt against the vanity of human greatness, his tortures and pains against the vanity of human pleasures. Abandoning himself to an interior anguish, suffering disgrace in his honor, and excruciating corporal pains, he made use of the right means to heal those three deadly wounds of which mankind was lying sick. *I shall speak to you to-day only of the interior sufferings which Jesus endured during the whole course of his life and, particularly, in the Garden of Olives.*

Having taken the last supper with his disciples, after which he instituted the Sacrament of the Blessed Eucharist, having given the commandment to love one another, and recommended to his heavenly Father in fervent prayer all who would believe in him, Jesus passed over the brook Cedron, which divides Jerusalem from Mount Olivet, where there was a garden, called the garden of Olives. Into the garden he went accompanied by his disciples. How different was this garden from the one in which God had placed the first man. In the garden of Paradise was the tree of life; in this Christ could pluck only the fruits of death. Through the former flowed the limpid waters of four lovely streams, which moistened the verdant grass, and rendered the place as fertile as it was charming to behold. Their musical murmur was but one of the many joys connected with Paradise. The garden of Olives, half hidden in the most desolate spot of the bleak, lonely mountain, was moistened by the tears and the blood of a God-man. The first presented a living picture of the happy state of the blessed, the second was a vivid type of the tortures which were the heritage that Adam's sin won for man. The first man was placed in Paradise to enjoy all possible pleasures, but the second went into this to endure the most intense agony and pain. Scarce had his sacred foot pressed the ground than, as the Scripture phrase expresses it, he was plunged into a sea of suffering, and so great an anguish arose in his soul that it would have killed him had not his omnipotence preserved him from death. A sadness so deep that not one ray of light could pierce its gloom, an exceeding great terror overwhelmed his beautiful soul. The waves of desolation swept over him and made him feel the pains that were to come, the more violently, the more he buried them *deep, deep,* in his sorrowful heart. At last that over-charged heart pathetically revealed its grief to his disciples when he said: "*My soul is sorrowful even unto death.*" But you will say: what? anguish, fear, and sorrow with the Lord, who is the comforter of the afflicted here, the joy and happiness of the Angels and Saints in heaven! Yes, and it was for our sakes that he became sorrowful unto death. He knew all the agony that was to come upon him; he had the shadow of the cross always before him, and had his sufferings foretold to his disciples in these words: "Behold, we go up to Jerusalem, where the Son of man shall be betrayed to the chief priests; and they shall condemn him to death, and they shall deliver him to the Gentiles, and they shall mock him, spit upon him, scourge and crucify him." He had told them that he would drink the bitter chalice, and be baptized by a hard baptism. He voluntarily offered himself as an expiation for the sins of mankind, and at his entrance into the world, he promised his Father this great and magnanimous sacrifice. Now the hour had come to taste of the bitter chalice, to receive the baptism of tribulation, to take the first step in the stupenduous sacrifice, and Jesus permitted himself to be seized with anguish, fear and sorrow, prostrate with his face on the earth. Think not that the courage of the divine Victim faltered, or that weakness caused this terrible conflict in his soul. This was an effect of his infinite love, which, in a miraculous manner, made these various affections enter therein. He was not confused and grieved by the weakness of his soul, but by the power of his love.

The greatest bodily suffering, and the bitterest desolation of spirit were alike welcome, the rage of the Jews and the cruelty of the executioners were able to torture his body only, his soul was beyond their reach. The scourging, the thorns, the nails, and all the instruments used by malice, wounded and lacerated his flesh, but could not destroy the peace of his soul. The excess of his love for mankind became the inventive executioner which devised a method whereby his mind also shared the torture of his bodily pains. It was that mighty love that deprived his soul of that sweetness into which, as in an ocean of bliss, it was plunged by the ecstatic enjoyment of God. It was his love for us which, after having taken the last vestige of solace from his soul, left it a prey to excruciating pains, and portrayed in vivid colors the sorrows that were to come. *The presentiment of an impending calamity is able to strike terror even into the most courageous heart.* The Sacred Scripture relates that the two servants of Pharao who were in prison with Joseph were thrown into a pitiable state of terror by a dream which they feared portended some evil. When the mere *apprehension* of such a thing could thus affect them we may imagine the inward anguish which the *certainty* of impending trouble and the clear knowledge of its circumstances would cause in man. And no man could fully know these like Jesus. Man, how much soever he may be afflicted in this world, is never wholly destitute of solace, nor always deprived of relief. Thus our merciful God treats us, his ungrateful and rebellious children. But has he not seemed less kind to his beloved Son, whose life in this world was an uninterrupted succession of afflictions from the crib to the cross? *Again, men suffer afflictions, but it is only during the time that they suffer them*, because they cannot tell what the future will bring. But Jesus having, as God, a knowledge of all that it held in its depths, had not one moment's ease while he lived. Besides the actual pains of the moment he felt the pangs of all those which were held in reserve, especially the outrages of his most sorrowful Passion; having always before his eyes his scourging at the pillar, his crowning with thorns, his crucifixion and death, with all the horrors of desolation that accompanied it.

The anguish and interior dereliction which the soul of Jesus endured in the garden of Olives, not only equalled the sufferings of the body, but were incomparably greater. It is true, the tortures which he endured in the members of his body during the time of his Passion, were manifold and cruel, but it was only during the time that he suffered them. First, he was scourged, then he was crowned with thorns; the executioners ceased from one kind of cruelty before they began another. How different soever the instruments of his executioners were, each one was calculated only to torture a certain part of his body. If an executioner were cruel and inventive enough to make a man feel various tortures at one and the same time, how much greater would be the pains. In such a manner the damned are punished. There is not one species of torture which the fire of hell does not inflict at one and the same time on those wretched lost souls, and, similarly, did the ardent fire of that love which Jesus had for man torture his soul in the garden of Olives. This inexpressible love made him feel, at one and the same time, the thorns and the nails with which he was fastened to the cross, so that he could say of himself what is written in the Psalms: "The tortures of hell have surrounded me." I know no figure, which will more vividly present to your minds the appalling situation in which our Saviour was placed in consequence of his foreknowledge of his future sufferings, than that of unhappy Job. Overwhelmed with sorrow, the afflicted man sat in the midst of those who had hastened, one after another to bring him tidings of great misfortunes and terrible catastrophies. One messenger said: "The oxen were ploughing, and the asses feeding beside them, and the Sabines rushed in and took all away and slew all thy servants with the sword, and I alone have escaped to tell thee." And while he was yet speaking, another came, saying: "The Chaldeans made three troops, and have fallen upon the camels and taken them; moreover, they have slain thy servants with the sword, and I alone have escaped to tell thee." He was yet speaking, when, behold, another came in and said: "Thy sons and daughters were eating and drinkiug wine in the house of their elder brother. A violent wind came on a sudden from the side of the desert, and shook the four corners of the house, and it fell upon thy children, and *they are all dead*, and I alone have escaped to tell thee." One alone of these calamities would have been sufflcient to depress his spirits, and you may easily imagine the impression which such an unprecedented array, at one and the same time smiting his ear and heart, would make on the unhappy man. He rent his garments, and overwhelmed by the thought of his misfortunes, fell down upon the ground. But multiplied as were his trials they were but a faint shadow of what Jesus endured. All the tortures and pains which the hatred and malice of the Jews could invent were mercilessly poured out upon him at once, and at the mere thought, he grew pale, trembled, and was filled with desolation and sadness. The terrible agony, the dread herald of death, was upon him, and was the greater because the sufferings still to come were so excessively cruel. And as to aggravate the misery of the afflicted Job, he was struck with a grievous ulcer, from the top of his head to the sole of his foot, so the horrid wounds of mankind were joined to the impending sufferings of the Redeemer, in order to increase his interior tortures. These wounds are the sins of men, so incalculable in number, and so awful in malice, that, with justice, they are called in the Sacred Scripture *streams of iniquity*. He bore all our iniquity, because God put on him all our guilt. He saw himself marked with the sign of sinners. The holy, the sinless-one might well be stricken with horror at the sight of so many and such grievous transgressions, and sink beneath a burden made up of the millions upon millions of sins of which mankind throughout all time had been, and would, until the end of the world, still be guilty, and of all those that will be committed to the end of time. He felt the disobedience of Adam, the fratricide of Cain, the adultery of David, the idolatry of Solomon, all the sins of impurity of Sodom aud Gomorrah, all the abominations of the Gentiles, all the ingratitude of the people of Israel, all the blasphemies that were ever uttered, all the horrible perjuries, sacrileges, debaucheries, homicides, and in fact, every kind of the basest crimes and iniquities were laid on his shoulders. What horror must have seized him, beholding so many and such great sins, and what torture to see himself laden with them! To understand the greatness of the desolation which the aspect of the sins of mankind produced in his soul we should be able to comprehend the greatness of sin. Ah, if it were given to us to know the greatness, the enormity and malice of mortal sin, we ourselves would be seized with horror, and wonder no more at what is related of some penitents, who, being enlightened by God, and comprehending the greatness and malice of mortal sin, became a prey to death. Now Christ had a perfect knowledge of the turpitude of sin, such as no other man can have, and knowing also the greatness and majesty of God, he clearly saw the malice and baseness of sin, by which God is most cruelly outraged and offended. What then must have been the torture of his oppressed heart, when the millions upon millions of sins, by which his Father was offended, were present before his eyes! He was grieved as much as all men together should have been grieved, because the sins of all men were resting on his shoulders.

We might, however, suppose that, when he was animated by the desire to redeem mankind by his Passion and death on the cross, this desire sweetened the bitterness which the knowledge of the future tortures and the sight of sin caused him. He knew that by his death on the cross he would destroy the kingdom of the devil, reconcile man with God, merit for him liberty and the right to heaven. Desiring the salvation of man so ardently, we might suppose, I say, that this consideration gave him great comfort in his sufferings. The thought of the combat making him sad, the certainty of the victory must have strengthened him, the foretaste of the tortures to which he was to submit, discouraging him, the superabundance of the fruits which he was to reap must have inspired him with courage, and trembling at the array of the many sins, by which God was offended, the thought, that, by his Passion and death, the glory of his Father would be re-established must have filled him with joy. But, this *very desire to glorify his Father and to save man, became to him a fountain of sorrows.* He longed, O! how unutterably, to destroy sin, and in the interests of this cherished aim he was willing to lay down his life, and to shed the last drop of his precious blood. Loving mankind with an eternal love, he longed that they all might know God and love him, and that through this knowledge and love, they might be saved. Alas! it was all the while but too apparent that his exertions would be useless for the greater part of mankind. He realized that his great sufferings would be, by the majority, unheeded, and that man would go on piling sin upon sin. He foresaw that, though many, that is, all are called, but few would be chosen. The vast multitude of heathens rose up before his eyes, and looking into the very depths of their stubborn hearts, he knew that they would close their eyes against the light of faith, and would refuse to give to God the adoration which was his due. Then too arose with clearest vision before his mind the many heretics, who, instead of seriously seeking the one true Church established by him, would follow their own systems, according as interest and prejudice would lead them, whose quest for *self* would be far more eager than their search after truth. Moreover, he saw many, even of the believers, for whom his holy doctrine would, alas! be a wasted boon; that they would derive no profit from it, but, leading a life, according to their inclinations, would prefer rather to offend God than break with the world. What anguish must this conviction have produced in his mind!

When a woman, after suffering great pains, brings forth a living child, such is her joy that she scarcely remembers the pains she endured. But if, after great labor, she brings forth a dead child, she is grieved and almost inconsolable. Jesus Christ was going to bring forth children of God in the garden of Olives, and foreseeing that so many would be lost he was sorely grieved. O! how bitterly sorrowful he was when he thought that his sufferings for man's eternal welfare, reaching even unto the ignominious death on the cross would, with the vast majority, be of no avail. Had he not realized that his precious blood would be shed in vain for so many who would not partcipate in the merits of his Passion, the pains would not have been so keenly felt. But a numberless multitude of people of every state, sex, and age, presented themselves before his mind, who notwithstanding the magnitude of his sufferings, would for ever remain excluded from the kingdom of heaven, and it was this that increased his sorrow, making it almost too great to be borne. He was, as it were, over and over telling himself the cruel truth: "I am shedding my blood for the salvation of all, yet only a few shall be saved. I am laying down my life to prepare an acceptable people for God, who would honor him by doing his holy will, but they will continue to live in sin, and never cease to dishonor and offend him. In vain do I labor, in vain do I exhaust my strength." In this state of depression he sought comfort and help from his heavenly Father; prostrate on the ground he prayed: "O my Father! if it is possible, let this chalice pass from me: nevertheless, not as I will, but as thou wilt." These words make known to us the interior contradiction that existed between the higher nature, which was ready to die, and the inferior, which feared, and longed to escape, the death which awaited him. Having finished his prayer, he said to his disciples: "Rise, let us go, behold, the hour is at hand: and the Son of man shall be betrayed into the hands of sinners. And as yet he spoke, behold Judas, one of the twelve, came, and with him a great multitude, with swords and clubs, sent from the chief priests and ancients of the people. And he that betrayed him gave them a sign saying: "Whomsoever I shall kiss, that is he." Ah! who can measure the extent to which this base treason increased the sorrow, the anguish of Jesus? What torture of mind was it for him to see himself betrayed by one of his disciples, to see himself betrayed with a kiss, the token of friendship, love and peace—betrayed for thirty pieces of silver, the ordinary price then paid for a common slave! O! the indscribable sweetness with which the Saviour addressed him: "Does my love for thee meet with the return of an ingratitude, the like of which was never known before, of a treachery and perfidiousness the basest of the base. Friend, whereto art thou come, Judas, dost thou betray the Son of man with a kiss? If an enemy had done this it would cause me no pain, but thou betrayest me, thou Judas, my beloved child, my apostle, thou who wert sitting with me at the same table. Ah, the prophecy is verified: 'He that eats bread with me raises his heel against me.'" Yes, of all the bitter phases of Christ's most bitter Passion, this treason on the part of his faithless apostle caused him the keenest pang, and nothing inflicted a greater blow than the thought: Judas prepares for himself eternal damnation, while I am enduring all for his salvation.

And now, my brethren, you have a faint picture of the interior anguish which Jesus endured in the garden of Olives. There are three reasons for this mental suffering, as already stated: the *impending painful death*, the *sins of the world*, and the *loss of so many souls*. He was willing, nay, *glad* to suffer the tortures of the body, even though his inferior nature beheld them with shuddering dread. The sins of mankind caused him an inexpressible anguish, he felt an overpowering sadness at the loss of so many souls, for who so well knew the value of an immortal soul? Should not this teach us to regard every trial which may arise in our path, and all the crosses which we meet during life as a means of liquidating the debt we have contracted with God? But, O my God, how different are our affections and feelings from those of thy divine Son! We know that we have sinned exceedingly, that we have sinned against heaven and earth, but the thought of atoning for our constant transgressions by walking in the way of the cross never seems to occur to our minds. Instead of accepting sickness, afflictions and the tribulations of this life with patience and resignation to the will of God, we complain and murmur against God, and thus impatience adds new sins to our list. O! what difference there is between the manner in which *we* look upon sin, and the form in which it appeared to our suffering Lord. We are wholly absorbed by the goods and pleasures of this world, think constantly on what is of "the earth earthly," and seldom raise our hearts to "the things which are above where Christ is." We scarcely ever consider what a terrible thing it is to offend the majesty of God, and hence, sin appears to us but a trifle. No marvel then, my brethren, that we are calm and unconcerned at the thought of our guilt, when Christ was troubled and confused, that we enjoy pleasures, when he was grieved, that we shed not a single tear when he shed blood. O! surely we cannot realize even faintly what sin is! If we did our whole life would become thoroughly changed.

Let us henceforth live in piety, in the fear and love of God; let us lovingly remember the grief and sorrow of Jesus, and let our great dread, our chief fear be to offend God. O! let me exhort you to sleep no longer in the arms of perdition, to remain no longer in the deplorable state of mortal sin, but to renounce sin, without any further delay? O! give up the criminal habits of cursing, swearing, blaspheming and all detestable vices which now enslave so many unhappy sinners, make them enemies of God, objects of his hatred, slaves of the devil, a scandal to religion, and a disgrace to the Church, amongst whose children they profess to be. O come, come all, Christ is waiting for you, his arms are outstretched to receive you, he calls you, he invites you, oh! come to the sure refuge of his precious wounds. If to-day, then, his voice sounds sweetly in your hearts, O! my brethren, respond to his call.

SERMON III.

THE TRIAL.

"I am a worm, and no man, the reproach of men, and the outcast of the people."—Ps. 21: 7.

As Christ placed his interior anguish as an unfailing cure for those vain and fleeting joys which captivate and engross man, so, too, he chose to endure outrage and disgrace to crush down human pride, which leads us to constantly seek distinction and honor. To try and realize the extent of these interior pains would be for us a vain attempt, because they were inward. *Here I am to do nothing else than to place before your eyes what the Evangelists relate.* You will see your Redeemer so dishonored, so humbled, and so debased that he could truly say by the mouth of the prophet: "I am a worm, and no man, the reproach of men, and the outcast of the people."—Ps. 21: 7.

The traitor Judas gave the sign, and the soldiers surrounded Jesus. They cruelly bound him as if he were a robber or a murderer; they bound him, I say, lest he should escape their hands, and conducted him into the city as conquerors rejoice after taking a prey, when they divide the spoils. —Is. 9: 3. O! pause one brief moment and consider the confusion, the deep shame of the God-man. He, who according to his human nature, in whose veins flowed the royal blood of David's honored house, and who, according to his divine nature, looked down from infinite heights upon all men and Angels, was taken by a set of the basest and lowest ruffians, and exposed to the scoffs and mockery of a most wicked and dissolute soldiery. The same hands that created heaven and earth, that gave motion to the planets and poised the universe, that performed so many miracles, were tied with ropes and, like a prisoner, all fettered with chains. The more exalted the rank and dignity of a man, the more heinous the affront that is offered him. Now can aught more outrageous be imagined than the insult which the God-man then received? Those wicked men laid their sacrilegious hands upon him, took him prisoner and treated him as the worst malefactor? The Creator chained by his creatures! Was there ever so wicked, so *atrocious* an act? But even this outrageous treatment he bore with meekness, although, had he asked aid, the Eternal Father would have sent more than twelve legions of Angels from their heavenly home. He had power to make his enemies recoil backward to the ground and to destroy them, but he would not—out of love for us sinful men. He allowed himself to be dishonored by the arrogance of these furious and bloodthirsty monsters. The measure was not yet full. And O! how his ignominy was intensified when the time approached for him to appear before Jerusalem in chains, and attended by the vilest rabble! But a few brief fleeting days had passed since he had entered Jerusalem in triumph. The loud hosannas and acclamations of the people, who believed in him and acknowledged him as the promised Messiah and Redeemer of the world rent the air, and their rich robes were spread in his path. Behold him now about to meet those people in chains, guarded by soldiers, and reviled as a man guilty of most heinous crimes. When the king of the Ammonites shaved off one-half of the beard and cut off one-half of the garments of the ambassadors of David and sent them away, their shame and confusion to appear before their king were so great that they stayed at Jericho till their beards were grown, then they returned to Jerusalem. And yet, they could expect kindness and sympathy both from monarch and subjects, and felt sure every one would scorn the wicked insult which Hannon, by violating the law of nations so shamefully, had offered to ambassadors. Far otherwise was it with our Saviour. When he was led into Jerusalem, weary, mournful, and guarded as a criminal, there was none who had compassion on him, and he received from the fickle people nothing but contempt. And those even who had listened to his heavenly doctrine, and beheld the many wonders he performed, regarded him as a crafty impostor, when, at the command of the high-priest, they beheld them bind the Redeemer, the friend of mankind. This was their mode of reasoning: the high-priest would not have acted in this manner if his impositions had not been discovered. They, therefore took it for granted that he was an impostor, and as such deserved the greatest punishment. The people cried out: "Behold, see there! Jesus of Nazareth, who preached a new doctrine and announced himself to be the promised Messiah; O! look they are dragging him to prison." O! Christians, let your own hearts tell the depths of ignominy and shame into which Christ sank as he listened to their words. After entering Jerusalem in so humiliating a manner, he was led to Annas, and from him to Caiphas, who was high-priest for that year. There the Pharisees, the Scribes, and the ancients of the people were assembled. The high-priest questioned him regarding his disciples and his doctrine. He thus made answer: "I have spoken openly to the world, I have always taught in the synagogue, and in the temple, whither all the Jews resort, and in secret I have spoken nothing. Why askest thou me? Ask them who have heard what I have spoken unto them; behold, they know what things I have said." And when he had thus spoken one of the hirelings standing near dared to strike Jesus, saying, "Answerest thou the high-priest so?" A wicked soldier gave Jesus a blow in his sacred face and reprimanded him for having answered the high-priest irreverently. Was Jesus not right in telling the high-priest to ask those who had heard him? Is not the evidence of others, rather than that of the criminal who is arraigned at the bar, to be weighed in a court of justice? Would they have believed him? That face which was transfigured on Mount Thabor and appeared as brilliant as the sun, the same face that ravishes the Saints, and before the splendor of which the Angels veil their faces with their wings, became the object of the insolence of a servant, a common soldier. This wicked servant had sufficient assurance before the eyes of the judge, of the court, and against every law, to abuse that innocent man, for even his bitterest foes dared not say that he had been found guilty. And not one of the whole assembly opened his lips at this act of disrespect to the Son of God. No one spoke, not even the judge, whose duty it certainly was to punish that servant for assuming to himself an authority which belonged not unto *him*, but to the judge. Christ, who came into this world not to make an ostentatious display of his omnipotence, was, indeed, grievously offended by such an indignity from so base and abject a source. But as his mission upon earth was to inculcate humility and patience he gave no evidence of anger, and would most probably have kept silence had not that servant accused him of violating the reverence due the high-priest. In order to leave no room for suspicion, and show that he had proper respect for the high-priest, he said: "If I have spoken ill, give testimony of the evil, but if well, why strikest thou me?" This answer should have sufficed to enlighten them and to soften their hearts.

Of all that assembly there was not one who thought of punishing that base hireling, who, full of insolence, had assumed to himself judicial authority before their eyes, by outrageously insulting Christ. Even the high-priest had not a word of reproach! Consumed with hatred towards Jesus, and eager to see him dead, and to have his memory obliterated from the earth, they deliberated how they might accomplish their wicked design under the pretence and appearance of justice. Hence, they sought false witnesses, who should accuse him of the crimes they alleged against him, that they might put him to death. Although many came with their tales of his guilt, their testimonies were so conflicting that they could not be considered sufficient to put him to death, thus verifying what the royal prophet says: "Many false witnesses have risen against me, and injustice hath betrayed itself." Last of all two witnesses came in and said: "We have heard this man say, I am able to destroy the temple of God, and in three days to rebuild it." The high-priest rising, and turning to Jesus, said: "Answerest thou nothing to the things which they witness against thee?" But Jesus held his peace. And the high-priest said to him: "I adjure thee by the living God, that thou tell us if thou be Christ the Son of God?" Jesus said: "Thou hast said *it*: Nevertheless, I say to you, hereafter you shall see the Son of Man sitting on the right hand of the power of God, and coming in the clouds of heaven." Then the high-priest rent his garments, saying: "He hath blasphemed, what further need have we of witnesses? behold, now you have heard the blasphemy." And all that were present said: "He is guilty of death."

From this simple narrative of St. Matthew, the immense injustice which was committed against Christ on this occasion can be recognized at a glance. So far from seeking for those who would give the Saviour a fair trial, men burning with hatred judged our persecuted Lord. *The testimony of hired witnesses*, who disagreed with one another was heard, and without further inquiry, the testimony which he had given to truth was declared blasphemy. He who had never ceased his efforts for the honor of God, and who had so often repeated that he was not seeking his own honor; he who knew that it was no robbery to call himself the Son of God, was branded as a blasphemer. The wicked judge refused to believe his word; ah! why did he not believe his works? Did they not speak for him? Far louder than words did his works confirm his truth. Behold! the blind upon whose darkened vision he had let in the glad, free light of day. Look at the lame whose helpless limbs had at his word assumed full vigor. Did not the dumb to whom he gave the power of speech, the sick whom, from a bed of pain, he had raised up to health, and the dead whom he had called from death's cold embrace, bear testimony, alike, to his truth? These miracles had not been wrought in closets or retired places. They had been the wonder of Judea and Galilee. And this his wicked judges knew full well, but every feeling of justice and humanity being extinguished in their hearts, their malice dared to call him a balsphemer. O! what inexpressible pain it must have caused our dear Saviour to stand before the people of Jerusalem branded as a blasphemer. Had only one of the many who had heard his doctrine, witnessed his miracles, partaken of his benefits, had only one, I say, indignant at the falsehood, defended him from their malice, it would have been a sweet solace to his desolate heart. But no one spoke in his favor. He who had ever befriended all, stood alone. His disciples forsook him, even Peter, who had so publicly vaunted his courage swore that he did not even know him, thus verifying what the prophet said in his name: "I am a worm, and no man, the reproach of men and the outcast of the people."

It remained, therefore, decreed in the council of these wicked maligners, that Jesus was guilty of death. This was the sure prelude to his sentence, and the soldiers regarding him as a legitimate object of sport, treated him most cruelly all through the long weary hours of the following night. Some spat in his face and buffeted him, others struck him with the palm of their hands, saying in derision: "Prophesy unto us, Christ, who it was that struck thee?" The King of kings, the Lord of lords, suffered all this for an ungrateful world. Spitting in the face was considered by the Jews so disgraceful, that if a father spat upon the face of his daughter, she was to be ashamed for seven days at least.—Num. 12 : 14. How great must have been the shame of Christ, when a set of the vilest and basest ruffians dared to defile his holy face with their spittle. The contumely and disgrace he suffered that night were so great that he was filled with humiliation. He, before whom the powers of heaven and earth tremble, whose very name causes the demons in hell to shudder with horror, became a subject of laughter for malicious men, so that he could most justly exclaim: "I am a worm, and no man, the reproach of men, and the outcast of the people."

The night had passed, the terrible night which held such bitter sorrow in its depths, the most memorable day in the history of the world began to dawn, and behold! the high-priest and the ancients of the people assembled again, and took council against Christ, as they had done the day before in the house of Caiphas, that they might put him to death. But for the execution of that sentence the approbation of Pilate, who, under the Roman Emperor, was then governor of Judea, was required. The Jews brought him bound to Pontius Pilate, that he might condemn him to be crucified, and now fresh disgrace confronts our suffering Redeemer—insult and outrage are cast in his path at every step—his sacred hands are tied, no covering on his head except his waving locks, his countenance pale and dejected, and his entire mien expressive of the deepest sorrow. Looked upon as a malefactor, he is led through the streets of Jerusalem. The curious gaze upon him from the windows, the rabble gather to see him, and instead of sympathizing with him, they overwhelm him with mockery and abuse. Arrived at the governor's palace, the chief-priest delivered him to Pilate. Pilate, seeing him in such a pitiable condition, turned to the multitude saying: What accusation do you bring against him. In the most insolent manner came the answer: "*If he were no malefactor we would not have delivered him to thee. We have found him perverting our nation and forbidding to give tribute to Cæsar and saying that he is Christ the*

Son of God." Pilate asked him : Art thou the king of the Jews? He answered and said : Thou sayest *it.* And Pilate said to the chief-priest and the multitude : I find no cause in him. He hesitated to pronounce the sentence which the cruel Jews desired, being not entirely blinded by the envy and hatred that corroded their hearts, he wished to let the law take its course, and to give the accused a fair trial. Having examined the case with the prudence and circumspection of an impartial judge, he could find nothing but innocence in Christ, and malice, envy, and hatred in his accusers ; hence, he proclaimed aloud that he could find no cause in him to put him to death. Now the Jews, growing desperate, lest their prey should escape, cried out : *He stirs up the people throughout Judea and Galilee.* Pilate hearing them speak of Galilee, asked them if the man was from Galilee. He seized this opportunity to be freed from the persistence of the Jews, who would compel him to condemn an innocent man to death. Hearing that Christ was from Galilee, which belonged to Herod's jurisdiction, he sent him to Herod, who was in Jerusalem at that time, and was, at the same time, enabled to become reconciled to Herod, without compromising his dignity. They had been at variance for some time, and this would be an overture for friendship. Thus our Lord was compelled to go from Pilate to Herod, and at every step of the long and painful walk he was exposed to new insults from the clamorous crowd. Herod was exceedingly gratified to behold Jesus, he had long wished to see him, having heard that he wrought great wonders and he hoped to see him perform some of those marvellous works. He questioned him in many words, to all of which he answered not a word. And, therefore, Herod and his men mocked him, putting on him a white garment, to indicate that Christ was a fool, and sent him back to Pilate. What shame, what confusion, must have covered the face of Christ, when he was thus inconsiderately forced to retrace his steps and appear in the streets of Jerusalem in that disgraceful garment, and to appear before Pilate in this humiliating attire. Pilate convinced of the innocence of Christ, called the high-priest, the Pharisees, and Scribes together, and said to them : " You have presented this man to me, as one who perverts the people : I have examined him in your presence, and find no cause in the man in those things wherein you accuse him : no, nor has Herod, for I sent him to him, and behold, nothing worthy of death is done to him. I will chastise him, therefore, and release him." The furious Jews, gnashed their teeth, demanding his death. Now upon the solemn day of the Passover, the governor was accustomed to release a prisoner, whom they would, and he had a notorious prisoner, who was called Barabbas. They, therefore, being gathered together, Pilate said : Whom will you that I release to you, Barabbas, or Jesus that is called Christ? for he knew that out of envy and malice they had delivered him up. O ! what horror overwhelms us to see the Most Holy One compared with the leader of robbers and murderers. But terrible as it is, that is not all.

The chief-priests and the ancients persuaded the people that they should ask Barabbas, and make away with Jesus. The governor, answering, said to them: Which will you have of the two to be released unto you? But they said: Barabbas. Pilate said to them: What shall I do with Jesus, that is called Christ? They all said: Let him be crucified: The governor said to them: Why, what evil hath he done? But they cried out the more, saying: Let him be crucified. And Pilate seeing that he prevailed nothing, but that rather a tumult was made, having taken water, washed his hands before the people, saying: I am innocent of the blood of this just man, look you to it. And all the people answering, said: His blood be upon us, and upon our children. Then he released to them Barabbas, and having scourged Jesus, delivered him to them to be crucified.

You now perceive how far man can wander into devious paths when he takes passion along as his guide. It was envy that corroded the hearts of the Scribes and Pharisees, when they saw the favorable impression made by the words and works of Jesus upon the people. They feared that by those words and works they would lose their coveted sway over them, and lose, too, some of the golden tribute which they paid. Envy and hatred made them petition for the life of Barabbas rather than that of our suffering Lord. Filled with the most intense hatred towards Christ, they began to caluminate him, and not content with this, they proceeded openly to persecute him. Closing their eyes against the light of truth which was confirmed by so many miracles, they were daring enough to resist Pilate who declared Christ innocent, and demanded the freedom of a murderer, that they might have the satisfaction of witnessing the murder of Christ. You shudder with indignation and cannot help execrating the injustice and wickedness of these Jews, but my brethren, turn your anger against yourselves, for not *once* have you committed that glaring act of injustice; O! Christians, but over and over again. As often as you have committed a mortal sin, what else have you done than preferred Barabbas to Jesus? How often have you preferred a temporal advantage to him? Behold the lesson which even the Jews can teach. The great aberration of which they made themselves guilty furnishes us with an opportunity of entering into ourselves and of considering how often we have renewed, by our sins, the injury, mockery, and unparalleled humiliation with which they insulted our Saviour but *once*. O, the black ingratitude! Let us learn to overcome our passions in the beginning; for if they are not eradicated in the very beginning, they will grow and acquire new strength every day, until they darken the understanding of man, and corrupt his heart and soul until he reaches the summit of wickedness and malice, and places the Lord of the universe far below the creation of his hands. And how is it possible that a Christian, after having seriously reflected on the outrages and humiliations which the Son of God endured for us, should not be ashamed of his pride, ambition, and haughtiness. Jesus Christ who was the holy, the stainless one, upon whose lips was found no guile, is treated as a malefactor, whilst mortal man, who is so full of sins and imperfections, and whose crimes and iniquities are, we may say without any exaggeration, more numerous than the hairs of his head—mortal man would have every one to praise his conduct and seeks the honor and respect of his friends. He to whom the highest honor is due, is despised, and man who is nothing but a handful of dust and ashes, desires to be honored. Jesus Christ, the Judge of the living and the death, is set below a murderer, and weak, impotent man desires to rule, and refuses to subject himself even to the authorities that are of God.

Let us renounce those inordinate desires for honors, dignities, and preferment. Let us be humble in spirit and understanding, and in heart and will, for humility is the road to heaven. Let us humble ourselves before God, before men and before ourselves, and on this way of humility, which Jesus pointed out to us by his holy example, we shall arrive one day at the house of our Father, wherein are many mansions, each one of which is an abode of perfect and perpetual bliss.

SERMON IV.

THE DENIAL OF PETER.

"*Before the cock crow twice, thou shalt deny me thrice.*"—*Mark 14: 72.*

Who can comprehend the greatness of the sufferings into which our divine Lord was plunged, during that terrible night which preceded the most terrible day of his crucifixion? What tortures had he not to endure before Annas, where he was abandoned to the ill-treatment of an obsequious servant, and where a troop of rude soldiers heaped the most insulting outrages upon his head. And yet, *all* the insults which those base creatures flung at our Lord did not affect him so deeply as did the conduct of one of his Apostles—the prince—the chief amongst them all. The men who abused and insulted, Jesus knew him not, they were men of the lowest class, but Peter had accompanied him during the whole course of his ministry. Peter knew him; for, a short time before, he had made that sublime profession of faith in his divinity: "Thou art Christ, the Son of the living God." Considering these circumstances, I ask again: Which grieved our Saviour more, the blow, given him in the face by a hireling, or the deliberate denial of the first of his Apostles on entering the palace of the high-priest, at the question of a poor weak servant-maid: "Art thou not also one of his disciples?" she asked. O, my brethren, though many hundred years have passed since the event transpired, the narration of St. Peter's defection sends a thrill of sorrow through every feeling heart, and, were it not that four Evangelists relate it, I could scarcely accord my belief to the tale. That Judas could betray his Master is more within the sphere of the possible; his thirst for money, the thefts he had committed, and the frequent and forcibly repeated warnings before his treason, without the slightest protest on the part of the traitor, except in the feeble words: "Lord, is it I?" all this tells us, that Judas came slowly but deliberately, and with premeditation, to his terrible crime. It was not so with Peter. Two hours before his denial he was the most zealous defender of his Lord, and, on a sudden, he falls. And this fall of St. Peter is, on account of these circumstances, deserving of our serious reflection, for what happened to St. Peter, has happened already to thousands upon thousands, and may also happen to us. *The sudden and deep fall of St. Peter, shall then be the subject of our meditation to-day.*

So far from having any idea of *denying* his Lord and Master, it is beyond question that nothing was more remote from his mind. He went into the palace of the high-priest, not with the intention of denying, but, if necessary, to die with him, for he had said a few hours before: "I will follow thee, even unto death." This, we may well believe, was his firm determination when the gate keeper refused to let him enter. He was most anxious to get inside, to watch his dear Lord, and to be there at the end. It is very probable that, while he was standing outside, he resolved, if he would be permitted to enter, to wait there for the end in the strictest incognito. He wished not to be known, and thought the less perplexity he would show the more easily he would succeed in remaining without difficulty to the end of the trial. Not the faintest shadow of a thought that he might possibly deny his Saviour arose within him. No matter what aspersions they might cast upon Jesus, he would not speak, so he said within himself; and surely his intentions were good. He resolved to conceal himself, as it were, amongst the crowd, that his presence might remain unnoticed, and that he might not attract the attention of others to himself. Faithful to his plans, we see him sitting at the fire with the people, mingling among them as if he were one of them, and as if their company were agreeable to him. Peter had formed his plans with the greatest confidence, and with the self-same confidence he endeavored to bring about their realization. But alas! he suffered a most deplorable shipwreck. The good disciple had determined to wait quietly, and in strict silence for the end; but he forgot what would in all probability come to pass. They might speak to him, though he should not speak to them; they might ask him questions, though he should not put one single question to any one of the crowd. Should he pass without being recognized or interrogated all would have been well. He wished it to be so, but the event proved far otherwise than he had hoped. By the intercession of John, Peter obtained permission to go into the palace of the high-priest. He had scarcely crossed the threshold, when a servant-maid said to him: "Art thou not also one of his disciples?" This question struck him, but thinking not to exchange many words with the woman, he gave her a short answer, saying: "I am not." Inside the court, he thought, amidst such a vast throng, no one will molest me with questions, the gate-keeper must remain at her post, and all the people are not so inquisitive as this woman. Having answered her, "I am not," he hastened from her, and went to the fire to warm himself. Behold his first downward step,—he had denied Jesus by a lie. O, what mistaken kindness in John! what a perilous favor did he not gain for his fellow-apostle, when, through his intercession, he obtained admittance for Peter! Had he foreseen the consequences, he would surely have refused the request. When the woman thus confronted him, had he wished to rescue himself, he could have done so by returning instantly without making any answer. This question was a warning for him. He wished to be unknown, but on entering the hall he was to hear that he was known. I say, this was a warning that he would come into the temptation of denying the Lord, but Peter understood it not. His overweening confidence made him perfectly blind; he denied his Lord at the first question, and, hoping this would be the last, he mingled with the crowd. And thus the first step was followed by another, and again another. In the whirl and confusion two hours flew swiftly by, yet in that little while Peter fell from lofty heights to the deepest of depths. Alas! he denied his Lord and Master! Believing that naught could weaken his strength, he recklessly courts the danger—and falls. With the greatest self-confidence, and the sure hope that he could remain there unknown, he had crossed the threshold of the palace of the high-priest. No sooner was this accomplished, than the gate-keeper recognized him, and the question of the servant-maid embarrassed him. Vain all his hopes of remaining unknown and unnoticed! O! foolish apostle to think that such hopes could be realized! Entirely confused, without one moment's thought on the words he would utter, he replied: "I am not." Instead of evading the question of the gate-keeper and returning, he denied his Lord, whom he certainly loved more than his life. Having denied him, he turned, scarce knowing what he did, in the maze of confusion which enveloped him, and which he vainly attempted to conceal. He went to the fire and sat down. The strange, exciting trial so engrossed the minds of those who were sitting by the fire, that they had no words for aught else, and some time elapsed before they took note of the unhappy apostle. But in a little while another maid-servant saw him, and having looked at him closely, she pointed at him with her finger, saying : "This man was also with him." When the gate-keeper, who had questioned him face to face, had annoyed him, we may easily imagine what confusion overspread his face when this woman drew a "sea of eyes" upon him, angry, inquisitive, threatening eyes. There he had been silently sitting at the fire, in order to remain unknown, and she pointed with her finger to him, saying : "This man was also with him." This unexpected occurrence made him lose all control over himself; from silence he fell so far as to lie ; for, in presence of those who had heard the woman say : "This man was also with him," he said in a loud voice: "Woman, you are mistaken, I know him not." With this direct falsehood on his lips he hurriedly left, and presently the shrill crow of the cock rang out on the air. Peter did not hear it, however ; he was so confused that he seemed to be utterly oblivious of the enormity which characterized the sin he was committing. He left the place, after extricating himself from the difficulty by a lie, but he had scarcely gone forth when again the maid-servant said to the bystanders : "This is one of them :" but he denied it again, and swore that he knew not the man. They molested him no longer, and seemed to believe his oath. Who could credit the fact, that after the lapse of a whole hour, and after he had so directly attracted the attention of all towards himself that their glances seemed to burn into his very soul, we find Peter still lingering there ? Yes ! he was entangled in a maze of confusion, from which he could scarcely emerge ; he dared not stay, he feared to go ! He feared that his flight might be interpreted as cowardice, and that not only his connection with Jesus might be discovered, but also his faithlessness toward him ; he would not go away, hoping they would now leave him in peace. Peter permitted the time, in which he might have left a place which had proved so fatal to him, to pass ; he lingered there, and alas ! he fell into a still deeper abyss ! About the space of an hour afterwards, as St. Luke relates, a man said to Peter : "Surely this man was also with him, for he is also a Galilean ; his very speech betrays him."

The two maid-servants who had asserted, "This also is one of them," could advance nothing to substantiate their assertion, but here is one who is able to prove what he says. Peter, to demonstrate that he was entirely fearless in the matter, had, we may conclude, asked those who were sitting at the fire with him several questions during the hour, and thereby had betrayed his Galilean accent, which is broader and flatter than that of the other provinces of Judea. This naturally elicited the remark, "You may say what you please, you can never deny that you are a Galilean, for your very speech betrays you." But Peter cursed and swore that he knew not the man of whom they were speaking. How, said another, can you deny it? Yes, you are one of his disciples; did I not see you in the garden with him? The speaker was a kinsman of Malchus, whose ear Peter had cut off with his sword. There was an eye-witness standing before him, who named the place where he had seen him with Jesus, namely, the garden of Olives. Nothing was wanting to complete the measure, but to brand him as having contemplated the assassination of his kinsman. Who can conceive the anguish and perplexity of the faithless apostle, when they assailed him with proofs? He knew not what to do to escape from the net in which he had ensnared himself; he stood amid a throng, while from lip to lip passed the telling words: "Your very speech betrays you." Now he began to curse and to swear: I know not this man of whom you speak, I know not what you say; and a second time came the warning crow of the cock. Thus a very brief space of time witnessed not only the first, but the second swift and deep fall of a disciple who had been the loudest in professions to Jesus. And perhaps he would have denied his Lord and Master oftener still, had not the scene between him and the crowd been brought to a close by Christ being led out of the house of Annas. All were too much engrossed to speak to Peter; with one accord they all followed in the train, and so did he, but how did the unhappy apostle leave? As a saint he had entered; as a sinner he went out. The cock had not crowed twice before he had already thrice denied his Lord. How short the time which beheld the chief of the Apostles changed into a great sinner. The first step was to deny his Lord with a lie; the second time, with an oath, and the third time, he employed even cursing and swearing to strengthen his word. From this sudden fall of St. Peter, the Prince of the Apostles, you see what can happen to man, even the best and holiest, in a short space of time. Who should not tremble? The downfall of Peter made even the Saints tremble. Who could rely on his own strength after this? Peter fell; he, who a few hours ago, had declared, in a solemn manner, that if all should be scandalized in him, he should never be scandalized in him. Now he is a reprobate; three times he denied his Lord and Master. It needs but a moment, one little moment, to transform a just man into a reprobate. If, relying on himself, and not supported by grace, he is left to his own weakness and to the powers of darkness, more swift than the lightning's flash will be his downward plunge. Yes, the powers of hell hold the proud man in thrall: this we see in the strange concatenation of circumstances which resulted in a tornado, and laid prostrate the stately oak. St. John, certainly with a good intention, had interceded for Peter, and obtained permission for him to enter the fatal house that caused his ruin. St. John stood under higher protection, because he was humble, but Peter was destitute of that protection because of his overweening confidence in himself. The spirit of darkness embraced the opportunity to sift him as wheat; at the very entrance into the court, a maid-servant confused him, he denied his Lord; he was scarce inside, when another woman looked at him and increased his confusion. He is now eager to leave, but on reaching the gate, the keeper said again: This is also one of them. This prevents him, he resolves not to run off like a coward: he remains, he draws the attention of the crowd upon himself; one asks him this, another that question: they surround him, and prove that he is, indeed, a disciple of Christ. He denies it by cursing and swearing—thus falling again and again, and each time into a lower abyss. It is thus the devil knows how to lay snares, and to prepare one opportunity of sin after the other. Many wish to return after the first false step, but there is a difficulty, and that difficulty becomes the opportunity of committing new sins. How true it is, that, if a man, after the first wrong step, does not return immediately, a second, and a third will follow in quick succession. Many a sinner would return, but he is held captive—a willing captive by sin; he longs to go, and goes not; he wishes to be constant, but alas! is constant only in sin and dies given over to a reprobate sense. Many wish to repent after having repeatedly denied the Lord, but what would the world say, what would the companions at the fire say, if they should renounce their evil ways and openly confess Christ? The world would say: "You are also one of his disciples." These words confuse them, and they say: "I am not, I know not this man."

Learn from the history of Peter's downfall that, besides his presumptuous confidence, the house into which he went, added to his sudden and deplorable fall. Peter wished not to be known as a disciple of Christ, he went into the midst of his enemies, hoping neither to be put to the necessity of confessing, nor the sin of denying him. But he soon experienced that from false shame and human respect, man easily adopts the maxims of those into whose society he is thrown. He that a few hours ago was with the Lamb, is now howling with the wolves, that he might remain unmolested, and not be overwhelmed with confusion in the face of that curious crowd. He denied Christ three times with cursing and swearing, so as not to displease his companions. whom he had met at the fire. O, how often is this repeated! How many go into societies and houses, the maxims of which they know to be dangerous to faith and morals. They go in, and while they do not think of *confessing* Christ, certainly nothing is more remote from their minds than to *deny* him, they only wish to see and to hear. They hope that no harm will result, Alas! many thousands have already denied Christ in this way who now acknowledge him and tremble, but in hell. From fear and shame they adopted the maxims of man; maxims which were at first utterly abhorrent to their souls. He that a few hours ago confessed Jesus with his heart and mouth, tacitly listens to blasphemies, then he makes another step and says: "I know not this man,

I am not one of his disciples;" at length, he blasphemes himself, and thus in a little while hell claims that wretched youth as its child. Of course his comrades will leave no effort untried for his ruin. The gate-keeper is there, he is the first that confuses and upbraids him for being so foolish as to be one of his disciples. The name of that gate-keeper is vanity; then comes another maid-servant whose glance at the face of the perplexed and embarassed man, confuses him still more, and this is concupiscence of the flesh. He will deny Jesus, not only once or twice, but numberless times, and the more abominable and infamous his denial is, the more his comrades will rejoice at it: the devil has made a new acquisition. In vain the cock will crow; in vain, the voice of conscience will speak; as Peter was deaf to its warning cry, so the deluded victim will not hear the cock's crow of his conscience, unless a look of Jesus, a saving ray of grace, fall into the heart and melt it into true sorrow for his sins. For this reason let us praise St. Peter, for having obtained that grace of repentance. This gracious look of Jesus, the bitter grief and life-long repentance of St. Peter after his fall, shall be the subject of our next meditation.

SERMON V.

THE REPENTANCE OF PETER.

"*And Peter went out, and wept bitterly.*"—Luke 22 : 62.

The cock crows the second time, but Peter is too thoroughly engrossed in cursing and swearing and denying his persecuted Lord and Saviour. He is speaking to the men who surround him at the fire, endeavoring to defend himself against their accusations. St. Luke says: "Whilst Peter was yet speaking, the cock crew." From this it is manifest that the voice of conscience, alone, is not able to arouse man from the sleep of sin. When the darkness of midnight envelopes the world, as well as when the bright sun at noonday illumines it, the cock of conscience may crow, the sinner hears it not, and will not hear it. And when that cock can no longer crow, but only gasp and flutter in the clutch of death; when the sinner trembling at the thought of death, and writhing in his agony, collects in one great effort his last remaining powers, even then the crow of the cock of conscience falls on unheeding ears. Wonderful and terrible at the same time! The power of sin is appalling, it deprives man of reason and understanding, and renders him totally blind. But there is little cause for wonder that the sinner hears not the cock of his conscience, when he does not regard the appalling thunderbolts of the judgments of God. Noah was a hundred years in building the ark; every stroke of the hammer was as so many crowings of the cock for that sinful generation, but of what use was the warning? They continued their feasting and revelry until the deluge was upon them and the waters submerged them in its pitiless depths. And when Pharaoh heard the threatenings and saw the judgments of God which came upon him and the land of Egypt, did he heed the warning which each successive calamity so impressively uttered? Ah! no; he was hopelessly deaf. Sin had deprived him of his senses. And, as it was in the time of Noah, so shall it be at the day of final doom, when in all his power and majesty, the Lord shall come to judge the living and the dead. Neither the voice of conscience, nor the sweet, inviting tones of prosperity, nor the crushing blows of adversity, are able of themselves to draw man out of his degradation, and rouse him from his legthargic slumber of sin, without the grace of God. Had not those merciful eyes looked graciously on Peter he would have been lost like Judas; but it was this pleading look that raised him from his fall; now, he remembered what his Lord had foretold him: "This night, before the cock crow twice, thou shalt deny me thrice." He went out and wept bitterly. I have now arrived at the point which I intend to make the subject of our meditation to-day, namely:

I. The gracious look of Jesus, and
II. The repentance of St. Peter.

Peter is yet speaking, curses and blasphemies tremble on his lips, he wishes that all evil may come upon him if he knows the man who is with Annas in the palace; when behold, the doors fly open, and the Man whom Peter pretends not to know, enters the hall where Peter stands shrinkingly at the fire, and this man is borne along by the crowd that surrounded the faithless apostle. The quarrel is at once ended, the eyes of all are turned towards Christ, and Peter likewise looks at the man, whom but a little while before he would not know. Jesus looks around in search of him, and having found him who had denied him, fixes his eyes upon him without speaking a word, but this *one look* was enough. Was it a look of destruction? Was it the look of a judge? No, it was the look of a merciful Redeemer who was come, not to judge, but to seek and save that which was lost. The Lord looked at Peter but was silent, except for that eloquent glance which said: Peter, what hast thou done? Where is thy faith, thy love, thy gratitude, thy word which thou hast pledged me? My enemies torment my body, but thou, my friend, dost torment my soul. Return, trust in my goodness, all shall be forgiven. Who does not admire the uspeakable mercy of the Good Shepherd? Though maltreated, abused and insulted, disfigured and so prostrated that, for utter weariness, his failing strength could scarcely guide his faltering footsteps, he remembered his poor, weak apostle. Yes, when he might well have been wholly occupied with himself—with his own misery, he disregarded it all, and forgot self to seek the guilty disciple. Ah! yes: faithless and treacherous, Peter now needs his aid more than ever. To snatch the stray sheep from despair and the jaws of the hellish wolf, he looks at him mercifully, and this look piercing Peter's heart, overwhelmed him with the bitterest shame. The hands of Jesus were bound, but his heart was ready to forgive, his eye ready to show mercy. He could only look at Peter, he could not go after the lost sheep, for his feet henceforth would go no more in the service of one, but for the salvation and redemption of all mankind. For this reason he sought the lost one with his eye, he pursued that erring soul with a look, to snatch it from the devil who had already seized hold of it as his prey. How consoling to us is this look of Jesus, which, with its stern reproof of sin, mingles love and welcome for the penitent sinner. We, too, will find him a good shepherd, whose glance at all times regards the erring with tenderest compassion and love. His look meets us frequently immediately after the commission of sin, as it met the treacherous disciple immediately after his denial. How often have we offended the Lord and at the same moment in which we fear the avenging hand of divine justice, we are met by the mildly reproving, merciful look of our Saviour. Unfortunate Christian! Year after year rolls by, and each one, perhaps, finds you in thought, word, and deed, treading the path with those who deny our dear Lord. You wonder, yourself, that nothing terrible has overtaken you, that God has not punished you; you must confess that the mercy of God has most graciously spared you, but not so his justice; he calls you, he invites you to penance, he turns full upon you his eyes of mercy, he looks at you with pitying eyes. Oh! that we all might avail ourselves of this merciful glance of the Redeemer, that we may not be annihilated one day by his look of wrath as a Judge. Let us cry out to him now: Look down upon me, O Lord, with eyes of mercy, as thou hast looked at Peter, that at the aspect of thy wrathful eyes, when thou shalt come as Judge, we may not be compelled to say: "Fall upon us ye mountains, and ye hills cover us." Woe to us if the eyes of the world can make an impression us, and not the merciful eye of Jesus. O! believe me, the day will dawn, and for many who now hear my words, its aurora has already appeared, when those eyes of men, whose look has power to turn your hearts from God, and whose scornful glances can lure your allegiance from him will be of no avail, when the inexorable look of Jesus will cast you to the ground. Christ has looked down upon thousands already with eyes of mercy, but they were entirely fascinated with the world and its pleasures, they had no time to turn their eyes towards him, they were riveted upon the perishable goods of this world; the hour of death came, they sought the merciful look of Jesus, but they could see nothing but the terrible eye of the Judge. They sought him too late: they sought him not whilst he could be found. *Judas was one of these.* When in the garden of Olives he approached his Lord to give him the treacherous kiss, Christ with eyes of mercy, looked at him, at the very time he was committing the greatest crime, but afterwards when bitter remorse took possession of him, he sought that merciful eye, but in vain—he despaired. Too long, too presumptiously had he trampled on the goodness of his God. Too deliberately had he despised the gracious look of Jesus. With unprecedented coolness of mind, he had planned his treason; with fiendish malice and a boldness which, for audcaity was unequalled. he perpetrated it. The measure was full; he became a suicide. *But it was not so with Peter.* He also had been forewarned like Judas, but whilst Judas opposed to the warnings a malicious silence, and had even the assurance, though conscious of his guilt, to ask: Lord, is it I ? Peter, in his love and enthusiasm for his Lord and Master, considered the caution superfluous, for he could not think it possible that he ever would be scandalized in him. " Lord, if all shall be scandalized in thee, I shall never be scandalized." And yet poor Peter *was* scandalized, thrice he fell, thrice he declared that he knew not his persecuted Lord ! His lips denied what his heart professed, he spoke in anguish and confusion, he wished to go away when confusion had forced from him the first denial; but it was far otherwise with the treacherous Judas. No one had asked him any questions; his being in the company of the high-priests was not accidental, no, he had sought them of his own accord, with the horrible intention of selling his Lord, he himself made this shameless offer: "What will you give me, and I will betray him." Judas was already a thief a year before the actual treason took place. He fell slowly, with premeditation; Peter, suddenly, and without a moment's reflection on what he was saying. The sin into which Peter fell was certainly great, he denied his Lord before servants who annoyed and besieged him with questions; but his sin was one of weakness, no malice intermingled therewith; he had not the boldness to say: When that man comes out, I shall stand before him face to face, and prove to you that I know him not. Judas, however, did so, and his sin was so grievous that the measure was full. Whilst committing the sin of treason, he received the last grace, for Christ said: Friend, why art thou come hither? He could have returned then, but he did not; he kissed his Lord and the time of grace was over; he went out and hanged himself. For this reason Christ said: "It were better for him had he never been born." Peter also went out after denying Jesus, but how ? Not like Judas, whose remorse drove him to despair, but he went out and wept bitterly.

II. Peter observing the look of Jesus remembered the words: "This night before the cock crow twice, thou shalt deny me thrice." And he went out and wept bitterly. This gracious look of Jesus had the desired effect, because Peter co-operated with the grace extended to him. We cannot form even a faint idea of Peter's feelings when he remembered his promise: "If all shall be scandalized in thee, I shall never be scandalized," and how did not his former profession, "Thou art Christ the Son of the Living God: to whom shall we go: Thou hast the words of eternal life," appear, compared to his last expression: "I know not that man, I know not what you are saying." And, as to the sorrow which wrung his inmost heart at his denial of Jesus, we can not even imagine its extent. The Sacred Scripture relates the repentance of Peter in these few words: *he went out and wept bitterly*. But we are not to understand that his weeping, sorrow and grief were confined to that moment: no, his fall was ever afterwards a source of the deepest grief, each successive day was a renewal of the last, and until the hour of his death his sin never failed to bring to his eyes penitential tears. Until God called him from earth he never heard a cock crow without weeping bitterly at the remembrance of his sin. The Holy Fathers relate that when preaching the Gospel, he frequently mentioned his own fall, and expressly desired St. Mark to give a description of his denial. He wished thus to humble himself and to do penance. The fall of this great Apostle awoke within him so watchful a spirit that his life was marked with an unwavering faithfulness, which he finally sealed with his blood. God deigned to look with such benignity on his repentance that Christ being risen from the dead, he appeared first to St. Peter, before he manifested himself to any other of his disciples. Poor Peter! How must he have trembled, what shame and confusion must have rushed over his soul when he beheld Jesus whom three days before he had so persistently denied! We do not read, however, that Jesus reproached him, no, he only appeared to him in order to sustain and comfort him, for he knew well that the poor Apostle needed some solacing words. We wonder when we read that he appeared first to St. Peter, and that the angel at the sepulchre told the women, "You seek Jesus of Nazareth, he is risen, he is not here, go and tell his disciples, *and Peter*, that he goes before you into Galilee, there you shall see him as he told you." But it admits of a ready solution: Peter denied Christ three times, therefore he might have considered himself unworthy of the apostleship and might have refrained from going to the sepulchre with the other Apostles, if he had not been specially named. The Lord prayed for Peter: he was confirmed: and he strengthened his brethren, for he gave testimony of Christ before the high council of Jerusalem: "God is to be obeyed before man."

Let it be our aim to imitate Peter in his repentance, since we have followed him in sin. But let us never forget that we cannot repent without the grace of God, for grace is the beginning of our conversion. We may resist this grace, we may regard it with an indifferent heart: the grace of

God does not force us to be good, we have our own free will; we must co-operate with the grace of God which is never wanting to us. We must look at Jesus when he looks at us; we must go out like Peter and weep tears of sorrow and penitent love. If our hand or foot scandalize us we must cut it off and cast it from us, for it is better for us with one foot or one hand to enter into life, than, having two hands or two feet to be cast into hell-fire, and if the eye scandalize us, we must pluck it out and cast it from us, for it is better for us having one eye to enter into life, than, having two eyes to be cast into hell-fire: this alone is true Gospel repentance. Peter went out and wept bitterly. Oh! let us weep for our sins, we have often wept for our passions, for the world, and the things of this world; but alas! we have no tears for our God, though they readily flow for everything else. O! folly, nay worse than folly. Glance over the world and consider the many trials to be found therein. They naturally cause tears, but they are neither so just, nor of such avail, nor so essential as the tears which should be shed for our sins. Christ shed his blood for us, and we, ungrateful beings that we are, will not shed a single tear for him who suffered and died for us. What can we look upon that does not revive the remembrance of our sins? Can we contemplate the beauty of the skies, and gaze in spirit beyond to the City of God without weeping at the sight of that glorious kingdom which we so basely renounced? Can we enjoy the light, and not bewail the dark spiritual night in which we remain? Can we observe the regular movement of the stars, and the obedience of all creatures to their Creator's laws, and not shed bitter tears that we so often rebel against God? He that weeps for his sins cannot be lost; the Good Shepherd will find him and bear him, rejoicing, again to the flock. The Angels in heaven were jubilant at the repentance of Peter when he went out and wept bitterly. O let your tears flow, weep for your sins, you have reason to weep, for you have denied Jesus more frequently than Peter. Oh! happy tears which dare not ask pardon, but nevertheless obtain it. And we who have followed Peter in his denial of Christ, O! let us resolve, like him, to atone for our sins; the Angels will be glad at our repentance. And if our penance be persevering to the end, if we be faithful followers of Jesus on earth, our penance will be rewarded with an immortal crown of glory in heaven.

SERMON VI.

THE SCOURGING AT THE PILLAR, THE CROWNING WITH THORNS, AND THE CRUCIFIXION OF CHRIST.

"They have dug my hands and feet, they have numbered all my bones."—
Ps. 21: 17.

We have, in a previous lecture, meditated on the interior anguish which our divine Saviour endured ; to-day we will let his corporal sufferings form the subject of our pious reflection. That we may obtain an adequate idea of the multitude and severity of his pains, let us consider for our edification the cruel scourging at the pillar, the crowning with thorns, and his crucifixion. Is there, amongst those who hear my words, one whose heart will not be moved at the consideration of sorrows so stupendous? Is there one who, after reflecting that the Son of God suffered so much in his body in order to redeem and save us from sin and hell, will not feel himself strengthened and encouraged to suffer patiently that which God sends in his way, and to do some penance for his sins? When Pilate, hearing the cries of an angry populace which clamored for the release of Barabbas and the condemnation of Jesus, could not resolve to doom an innocent man to death, he endeavored to extricate himself from the difficulty in another way. Although a heathen he understood very well that to condemn an innocent man is to act contrary to the light of reason, the laws of justice, and the dictates of conscience. He endeavored to release Christ. Hoping that the satanical rage of the furious mob would be softened were he to afford them some satisfaction, he commanded the soldiers to scourge him. The Evangelists pass over the special details of this scourging, saying nothing but that Jesus was scourged.

We may well imagine, however, that this unjust order was executed with the greatest possible cruelty; for when a common soldier dared to strike him before the eyes of the high-priest who had asked concerning his doctrine and his disciples, and when the guards that watched him in the house of Caiphas presumed to treat him most cruelly, we may also conceive in what manner they gave vent to their rage, after they had obtained orders from the governor to scourge him. Have you ever observed how dogs act when the prey is held back for awhile? They make a thousand attempts to seize the victim, and when the hunter yields the poor creature to their fury they rush upon the prey with haste and rage, stupefy it by their wild howling, force their sharp teeth into its flesh, and thus, inch by inch, slowly put it to death. Christ compared his enemies to a set of savage and blood-thirsty dogs, when he said by the mouth of the royal prophet that many dogs had encompassed him.—*Ps. 21.* As long as they were held restrained by the governor, and could not give full vent to their rage, they barked at him, ridiculed and mocked him, but after Pilate had sentenced him to be scourged they had no mercy, no compassion for him. They seized him, rudely tore off his clothing, bound him fast to a pillar, and tortured his sacred flesh with an almost incalculable number of strokes. By this stripes were formed which burst open, and the blood flowed from all parts of his body, without exciting the least feeling of compassion in the hearts of those monsters. Some writers hesitate not to say that three sets of executioners performed the cruel task. The first had knotty rods, the second, thick ropes, and the third, iron chains. The number of strokes was also not limited to forty, the usual number prescribed by law of Moses. To conceive some idea of the pains which Christ endured, when he was scourged, it suffices to take into consideration the natural barbarity of the soldiers, the delicate sensibility of the tender body of Christ, and the multitude and heaviness of the strokes. The heartless executioners found it a welcome task to maltreat those who were sentenced to death and to spill their blood. What recked they if their victims quivered beneath the lash! What heavy strokes, then, must they have heaped upon him, when there was a rivalry among them to please the Scribes and Pharisees, by whom they had probably been bribed. Jesus was of the most sensitive constitution, his body was the most perfect of all that were ever produced, being formed from the pure blood of Mary by the agency of the Holy Ghost. How agonizing must have been to Christ a punishment which even forced bitter tears from the eyes of slaves. And, as the punishment was to correspond to the guilt, according to what is written in Deuteronomy, chap. 25, "the number of strokes shall be according to the measure of sins," we must suppose that the sufferings which Christ endured in that scourging attained the highest degree, because the sins for which he rendered satisfaction to the divine Majesty were as great as they were numerous. The prophet Isaias compares him to a leper, and presents him to us so disfigured by strokes, that he was not like another man, and says that he was lacerated on account of our sins, wherefore, he calls himself the *Man of Sorrows.* He bore all this base treatment with indescribable patience; his mouth remained closed but he said in his heart: "I am ready for scourges."—*Ps. 37.* He was weary, well nigh unto death, almost prostrated by those heavy strokes, but at the same time he thought of us. He prayed for us to his Eternal Father; he offered for us, and for all sinful men, those merciless strokes as an expiation. For love of you, dear souls, thus thought our dear Saviour: It is for love of all souls that my hands are tied, my shoulders stricken without mercy, and my whole body one mass of bleeding wounds. I am suffering the most excruciating pains and torments, in order that you, seeing what I endure for you, may make the resolution to correspond to my love! Oh! my brethren! how much do we not owe to our divine Redeemer! He has done penance for our sins, and submitted to the punishment which should have fallen upon us. We are the criminals, and it is we who should have writhed under the terrible pain of the lash, but Christ bent his own shoulders to the blows that we might be free from the punishment which the divine justice had decreed against us. Who could be so callous as not to weep bitter tears of compassion, and to feel his heart almost breaking with love and gratitude at the pitiful sight of that disfigured countenance, that lacerated form, that innocent lamb covered with wounds, and blood streaming unheeded to the ground. But alas! how many there are among us who remain indifferent, hard and ungrateful! Though we know that our God has deigned to do such great penance for us, our hearts are so little moved, that we even dare to continue our wicked life, and commit the same sins almost daily. O! God grant that none of us may ever cause such sorrow to our amiable Redeemer, but that the sight of his scourged body, may implant in each heart the sentiments of King David: It is I that have sinned.—II. Kings, ch. 24. I have sinned by calumniating my neighbor; I have sinned by persecuting and hating those who offend me; I have sinned by intemperance and by blindly following my predominant passions; I am, therefore, to be punished. O! that each and every one of us, animated by the example of Christ, would begin to do penance for his sins, instead of enjoying the pleasures and amusements of this world! Let us pursue the history of the Passion of Christ, and each page will produce new and stronger proofs of our ingratitude and delinquencies.

After the executioners were wearied of scourging him, they loosed him from the pillar, and though the long and severe chastisement had almost exhausted his small remnant of strength, no one could be found to do him a favor, as was usual on such occasions; no one to dress his wounds or hold a cooling draught to his fevered lips. He complained thereof himself by the prophet Isaias: "I looked about and there was none to help, I sought and there was none to give aid." Ah? had their rage only been soothed by this scourging! but the pitiful state in which they beheld him inflamed, instead of softening their hatred, as Pilate vainly hoped. The sight of the innocent blood which should have awakened feelings of compassion, only increased their rage to maltreat and abuse him still more. It occurred to their minds that he had aspired to royal dignity, because he had said before Pilate; that he was King of the Jews. They accordingly invented a new kind of torture. After conducting him into the hall of the court, they gathered together unto him the whole band, and having violently torn off his clothing, they put a scarlet cloak about him, and platting a crown of thorns they put it upon his head, and a reed into his right hand, and bowing the knee before him, they mocked him, saying: "Hail! King of the Jews." And not content with having treated him with such contumely, they united cruelty with mockery, pressing the crown of thorns more deeply into his head, and thus making him the man of sorrows. I leave you to judge what great pains Christ must have endured, when the thorns pierced his adorable head, the most sensitive part of his body. Every thorn left a wound; some pierced his veins, whence the blood ran down his forehead and disfigured his countenance; others penetrated his nerves and caused the most violent convulsions. A slight headache often appears to us intolerable; what great anguish must our Redeemer have endured from so many thorns! If a single thorn in the hand or foot hurts us, what violent pains must not so many sharp thorns have caused? And those heartless, cruel men could find it in their hearts to mock the Saviour while in that pitiable state: "Hail!" said they, bending their knees in derision: "Hail! King of the Jews," and spitting upon him they took the reed out of his hand and struck his head so that the pains were renewed and the thorns thrust in still deeper with every stroke. When those wicked men had gratified their savage insolence, they presented him before Pilate, who beholding his sad condition, was moved to compassion, and bringing him forth from the palace, showed him to the assembled populace, saying: "*Ecce homo*"—"Behold the man," as if he would say, behold the the miserable state to which your cruelty has reduced him; behold a being who has the same nature as yourselves; behold how his face is swollen, his head pierced with thorns, and how the blood flows down from his forehead! He is not like to another man, let this suffice now, do not demand his death. The imprudent judge hoped to release Christ, but he was greatly deceived, for his language served only to heighten the fury and rage of the excited populace. The Scribes and Pharisees cried out: Crucify him, crucify him. Pilate said they might crucify him if they wished, but that he would not condemn a man to death, in whom he could find no cause. The Jews answered: We have a law, and according to that law, he ought to die, because he called himself the Son of God. When Pilate heard this he feared the more. He entered into the hall again, saying to Christ: Whence art thou? But he gave him no answer. Pilate, therefore, said to him: Speakest thou not to me? knowest thou not that I have power to crucify thee, and I have power to release thee. Jesus answered: Thou wouldst not have power against me, unless it was given thee from above. He, therefore, who has delivered me to thee has the greater sin. From henceforth Pilate sought to release him, but the Jews cried out, saying: If thou release this man thou art not Cæsar's friend; for whomsoever maketh himself a king, speaketh against Cæsar. When

Pilate had heard this he feared for the friendship of Cæsar, his self-love and human respect conquered his better nature, and he yielded to their demands. Fearing to lose the favor of his earthly master, he sacrificed the precious life of God-man. Woe to the man who suffers himself to be governed by passion. He is capable of doing anything. Avarice that ruled Judas, enticed him to sell his Master; envy and hatred that had taken possession of the hearts of the high-priest and the Pharisees made them petition for the death of Christ. Self-love, human fear, and worldly advantage were the predominant passions in the heart of Pilate, that urged him to pronounce sentence against Christ. These examples should teach us how necessary it is to eradicate passions in time, lest we should, if they acquire too much strength, be plunged into a thousand difficulties.

III. After the governor had pronounced the unjust sentence, the savages conducted Christ, without any further delay, to Mount Calvary, and eager to render his passage to the mount a "dolorous way" in every sense of the term, they compelled him to carry the cross on his own shoulders. Then it was fulfilled, what so many centuries before had been prefigured in the person of the innocent Isaac, who carried the wood for the holocaust, and in the ram, which, laden with all the sins and iniquities of the people, the high-priest sent into the wilderness. O! Christians! has earth ever witnessed a spectacle more fitted to excite compassion than that of the Son of God in the midst of a troop of rough and savage soldiers, going between two malefactors who were sentenced to death with him, and carrying the instrument of his death on his own shoulders! Weakened by the cruel treatment he had received, his head crowned with thorns, his whole body full of wounds caused by the scourging at the pillar; he walked, sighing under the heavy load of the cross, and overcome by the pains he endured; cold sweat ran down his face; he could endure it no longer, but fell with his face to the earth. When the women of Jerusalem, who followed him, saw this they wept over him. But, turning to them, he said: Daughters of Jerusalem, weep not over me, but weep for yourselves and your children. The soldiers, fearing that he would die under the weight of the cross, took it from him, and compelled a man from Cyrene, named Simon, to carry it. When they had come to the place that is called Calvary, they stripped him, and told him to stretch himself on the cross. Christ considered it as the altar, on which he was going to offer to God the most perfect and acceptable sacrifice that had ever been offered to him. He laid himself upon it, and lifting up his eyes to heaven, he adored the will of his Eternal Father, becoming obedient unto death, even unto the death of the cross. And offering himself as an expiation for our sins, he voluntarily laid his holy, innocent, and undefiled body upon the hard wood, saying: Sacrifices, oblations, and holocausts thou wouldst not, neither are they pleasing to thee, which are offered to thee, according to the law ; behold, I come to do thy will, O God.—Heb. 10: 8, 9. Immediately they perforated his hands and feet with large nails, and by the repeated strokes of a heavy hammer nailed him to the cross. The painful convulsions which this cruel treatment produced in all parts of his body plunged him into a sea of sorrows, and thus was fulfilled what had been foretold by the royal prophet of the Redeemer : "They have dug my hands and feet, they have numbered all my bones."—Ps. 21 : 17.

The pain which thrilled through every nerve of our Saviour whilst this cruel torture was in progress may be better imagined than described. Present, however, to your mind a man sick of the palsy. Such intense anguish racks his frame that his moans are the wails of one on the point of despair. And yet all that love can do is done in his behalf. His limbs take what repose they can, upon a soft easy bed, and his only pains are those caused by a few drops of biting substance which seize the nerves in the joints of the hands and feet with its itching parts. Now reflect what excessive pains Jesus must have endured. He was lying on the hard bed of the cross, whilst not only a few drops of a biting substance touched his nerves, but large rough nails were driven through his hands and feet. They thrust the sinews asunder, dislocated the small joints, and injured his nerves, of which the tenderest parts of the body are formed and composed. And how fearfully were not these pains aggravated, when the soldiers lifted up the cross on which he was nailed, and planted it in the hole already prepared for it, thus presenting to the vulgar gaze of the mob our dear Saviour and Lord. O ! God, what pain to sustain the whole weight of the body by the hands that were pierced through by nails! What agony to hang upon that instrument of death in a way, which allowed not the faintest hope that the torment would cease. What dislocation of the bones, what extension of the wounds, what great convulsions. When he wished to rest his head, his only pillow was the hard rough wood of the cross, which increased his pains, because the thorns were hereby pressed in the deeper. When he wished to support the weight of his body on his hands, the wounds were distended aud the pain became more violent; and when he wished to rest his hands, his feet were obliged to bear the whole weight of his body, and thus the pains grew more intense from moment to moment, and became almost unendurable, and yet he lived in this state whilst three long hours dragged their slow length along. Let us pause a moment, and at the foot of the cross of our Redeemer, ask ourselves how many drops of that precious blood we have forced from his body by our sins. Yes, my brethren, it was my sins, it was your sins, that made him fall under the weight of the cross, and that nailed him to it. Our sins were the thorns and nails that caused him unspeakable pains. We read in the book of Josue that when the wretched Achan was condemned to death, nine hundred thousand persons were engaged in executing the sentence, and of all that vast multitude there was not one woman or child that did not go in turn, to cast stones at that miserable being, and with every one thrown they hurled a curse at his head. It was not only nine hundred thousand persons, but the whole of Adam's posterity that overwhelmed Jesus with curses and insults, and we, we also, wretched beings, that we are, have nailed Jesus Christ, to the cross, and have, if I may so express it, inflicted on him as many mortal blows, as we have committed sins during our life-time. Oh? that never again might our offenses force blood from the veins of our Lord! But we continue ever to renew and increase this suffering by our sins. Yes, sinners, you renew, as far as it is in your power, the grief and anguish of your compassionate Saviour, by the malice of the numberless sins which you daily commit. Oh! the blindness and ingratitude of man! Where is our compassion? Has every feeling of humanity forsaken our hearts? We shed tears at the sight of the miseries of our fellow-men, and we make every effort to alleviate their sufferings; but when we see our divine Saviour crowned with thorns, falling under the cross, and crucified, where is our compassion? Judge now whether his sufferings can be compared to the sufferings of another. From this you will also recognize the fatal delusion of those who flatter themselves that the pathway to heaven is bordered with roses, or that they can reach its portals save by treading on thorns. Penance alone can win eternal life, Jesus Christ has shown us this by walking first in the way of the cross.

We are called to sufferings and trials, says St. Peter, because Christ also suffered for us, leaving us an example that we might imitate it. He is the model of all that are predestined, says St. Paul, and according to his life and virtues we must regulate our life. If the Father find in us no resemblance to his crucified Son, he will not admit us into the number of the blessed, for he will not acknowledge as children of election those who are not in some respects like his Son.—He will make partakers of his glory, only those who are formed according to the head of all the elect, for the disciple is no better than his master, and the servant cannot have a preference before his Lord. Does our life correspond to the life of Christ crucified? The life of Christ was one continued series of sufferings; the life of the generality of Christians is only a series of distractions and amusements. The innocent flesh of Christ was pierced by thorns, perforated by nails, but the criminal flesh of many Christians will relish nothing but pleasures, and will not endure the most trifling mortification. Undeceive yourselves for once. A life of excessive fondness for pleasures and amusements is not the proper life of a Christian. Read the Gospel, and then tell me, do you find anything else preached and inculcated in it, than self-denial, mortification, works of penance, and conforming ourselves to the will of God? If any man will come after me, says Jesus, let him deny himself, take up his cross daily, and follow me. If any man come to me, and not hate his father and mother, his wife and children, his brethren and sisters, yea, and his own life, he cannot be my disciple. Consider Jesus, in any condition of life you will, did he ever allow himself the slightest deviation from this rule? Poverty, nakedness, hunger, persecution, sorrows and desolation marked every hour of his life upon earth. Look at Christ crucified. Could he suffer anything more painful? Christ has suffered, so must we, if we wish to be counted among his followers, for those are Christ's, who have crucified their flesh with their vices and concupiscences.

Let us, at the foot of the cross, make the promise to our crucified Redeemer, to offend him no more, and to amend our lives. He suffered so much for us, let us imitate his example, and bear with patience and resignation to the will of God whatsoever afflictions he may send us, since it is for our good. The example of Jesus will console us in the troubles and difficulties of this life, it will comfort us in the hour of trial, and will make penance sweet and light.

SERMON VII.

THE SEVEN LAST WORDS OF CHRIST ON THE CROSS.

"*He that hath ears to hear, let him hear.—Matt. 11: 15.*"

We are assembled to-day, to hear repeated the oft-repeated narrative of the Passion and death of Jesus Christ, the Son of God, and Redeemer of the world. Represent to yourselves our Redeemer hanging on the cross, manifesting his ineffable love for mankind to the last moment of his existence. Great are the pains he suffers, yet he murmurs not against his Father in heaven, nor does he pronounce judgment on his murderers on earth. When he stood before Pilate, he opened not his mouth, and now, like a lamb in the hands of those who wait to slay it, he utters not a word on the cross. But as a tender father, about to depart this life, seeing his children gathered around his death-bed, opens his eyes again and whispers his last parting words, so our blessed Lord opens his eyes, his pallid lips part and his last precious words are given to mankind. We generally try to catch with the greatest eagerness the words of a dying friend, and a word coming from the pale lips of a father or mother makes such a deep and lasting impression upon even thoughtless and frivolous children, that you can hear them say, long after their parent's death: My dying father, or, my dying mother, told me this or that on their death-bed. I shall never forget it. But is not our dying Redeemer more to us than father or mother? To them we owe our corporal life, but to him, our spiritual life. Nothing, therefore, should excite within our hearts more ardent love and veneration than his last words. There is something so holy and majestic in them, that our whole being is thereby stirred to its very depths. Let us then listen to the last words of our Saviour and "he that hath ears to hear, let him hear."

1. We cannot look at the Redeemer hanging on the cross without reverence and awe, for there never was such a master of virtue, such an unerring leader to heaven, such a man mighty in word and deed, before God and men; Ah! we will never, again, behold such perfection on earth! Was this acknowledged when he was hanging on the cross?. No, he was treated with the utmost contempt. The people shook their heads and said to him : " Vah, thou who destroyest the temple of God and in three days buildest it up again, save thyself; if thou be the Son of God, come down from the cross. He saved others, himself he cannot save." If he be the king of Israel, let him come down from the cross and we will believe in him. He trusted in God, let him deliver him now, if he will have him, for he said : I am the Son of God, Even one of the Roman soldiers mocked him, saying : If thou be the king and Saviour of Israel, save thyself; and to complete the measure, one of the thieves who were crucified with him, said blasphemingly : " If thou be Christ save thyself and us." We must confess that the Redeemer could not be treated with greater contempt, nor offended and insulted in a more insolent manner. And what is his conduct under such humiliations? He looks down from the cross with eyes of mercy and compassion upon his enemies. He looks into the dark future where all the evils that will fall upon them are vividly before his eyes. These evils grieve him more than all his sufferings ; and he gathers his remaining strength and prays to his father—"he that hath ears to hear, let him hear "—he prays for his enemies.

"*Father forgive them, for they know not what they do.*" His doctrine was : Love your enemies, do good to those that hate you, pray for those who persecute and calumniate you, that you may be children of your Father who is in heaven. Here we see him put his doctrine into practice, and seal it with his own example. His enemies reviled him, and only blessings are heard from his lips ; they hate and persecute him, and he strews benefits untold in their path. Whilst they rage with the utmost fury, he prays : Father, forgive them ; he even excuses their blind zeal : "for they know not what they do." O ! the burning disgrace for us, if the example of Christ does not so touch our hearts that we will most readily pardon our enemies. You bear, perhaps, for years, hatred in your hearts, and your self-love is ingenious enough to exculpate you by many shallow excuses.

You say: he has grievously offended me, therefore, it is impossible to forgive. Are you more innocent than Jesus, who challenged his enemies to convince him of sin, which they could not? If the most innocent and holy One can pardon his enemies, why will you not forgive yours? Examine your conscience; ask yourself impartially: Do I entertain hatred against any one of my fellow-men? If its unerring verdict answers *yes*, lull it not to sleep by vain excuses, for this very night God may call you before his tribunal, and would you not shrink from appearing before him with hatred in your heart against your neighbor? He is love itself, and has forgiven a world of enemies. You do not know at what time God will call you. You have time for reconciliation, perhaps this year, perhaps this month, perhaps only this day; for you are like flowers which bloom in the morning but wither and decay at eve. Therefore, forgive now, and go not from the cross of your merciful Redeemer, before you have, like him, forgiven all your enemies from your heart.

2. When the Saviour was conducted to the place of execution, his disciples fled, overwhelmed with apprehension for their own safety, and their courage vanished before the perilous journey to the Mount. Yet, there was one who, in the face of every danger, had followed his Lord into the palace of the high-priest, and whom nothing could deter from accompanying him to the scene of his death. He placed himself near the cross so as not to lose the last breath from his beloved Master's quivering lips. This intrepid and fearless disciple was the faithful, noble-hearted John. Mary, the Mother of Jesus stood near him. While Mary and John, plunged in the deepest grief, look up to the cross they meet those dear eyes, over which the film of death is beginning to steal. They brighten like the departing day in the western horizon; for these are the Saviour's truly beloved friends whom he cannot forget even in the agony of death. He was fully aware, how deeply sorrow and grief, like a two-edged sword, was piercing his mother's heart; he knew what she was suffering; her heart was broken and in his last hour he provided for her, at the same time consoling and blessing his beloved disciple. Opening his mouth, he publishes his last will and testament; he speaks only a few words; he will not increase the grief of his dear ones by a long farewell. Only a few holy words, which I will repeat, "he that hath ears to hear, let him hear," he says with a dying voice: "*Woman, behold thy son.*" Whilst saying this he looked at John, who was to be the friend and protector of his sorrowing mother. And again he says: "*Son, behold thy mother,*" pointing with his eyes to Mary. By this he called upon John to interest himself in behalf of his poor mother; to console and comfort her, to assist her in every necessity, to be to her for the remainder of her life, what he himself had been to her. St. John provided for her as if she were his own mother until her assumption into heaven.

Children, engrave deeply on your minds what Christ did for his mother. As, during life, he recompensed her tender love by the greatest gratitude, so he remained a good son to the very last moment of his life. In like manner, do not forget the obligations you are under to your parents. *Children, look back.* From whom have you your being? Whose bread did you eat? What would have become of you, if your parents had not taken so great care of you? *Children, look back.* You were helpless, insensible, imprudent, thoughtless, like all children. Who watched over you with careful anxiety? You were exposed to a thousand dangers which threatened to destroy sometimes your health, sometimes your life; who watched over you, who protected you, who prayed to God for your temporal and spiritual welfare? *Children, look back.* You were ignorant, you knew neither God nor you destiny; who taught you to make the sign of the cross, who made you acquainted with the life and sufferings of Christ, who taught you to bend your knees, to lift up your hands and pray to God? In later years, when wicked inclinations crept into your hearts, who first observed them, who restrained them, who wept over them, who kept you from doing wrong? Was it not your parents? And in your sickness, who watched by your side during sleepless nights? Did not your parents do all this? And can you be so cruel as to be angry at the weakness and frailty of their age? Can you treat them rudely and unkindly when they require your assistance? Can you have the hardness of heart to embitter their old age, which is undoubtedly bitter enough, and to draw tears from the very eyes which wept so often for you? If you can do this, then you, once good children, smiling in loving glee upon your parents, have become ingratitude itself, and I should certainly pronounce it unparalleled audacity in you, to place yourselves to-day with the Blessed Virgin and St. John at the cross of the Redeemer, who loved his mother so dearly, that she was the object of his care and solicitude to the last. Our dying Redeemer provided for his mother, that after his death she might not suffer want, and can you, in the possession of temporal goods, see your parents suffer hunger? You eat and drink and enjoy yourselves, whilst the authors of your existence want for even a morsel of bread to appease their hunger. Children, by such conduct you commit an unnatural crime, which your Father in Heaven will not allow to pass with impunity, for he has given the commandment: "Honor thy father and thy mother."

3. For greater ignominy, two malefactors were conducted with Christ to Calvary, to be crucified with him, one on his right hand, the other on his left. In the wicked heart of the wretch who was hanging on his left side, every feeling of humanity seemed to be extinct, for in the hour of his death he was malicious enough to blaspheme Jesus, with his sepulchral voice, saying: "If thou be Christ, help thyself and us." Far otherwise was it with the criminal at the right of our Lord. He had long realized,

with inexpressible grief, that he was treading the path to perdition. Now on the brink of eternity, he sees the precipice, to which his crimes have brought him. Remorse of conscience tortures him more than his bodily pains, and the thought: what will become of me in the other world; in a few moments I must appear before the judgment-seat of God, torments him beyond description. He looks at the dying Jesus, observes in his countenance a divine majesty, and in his patience a calmness which only can come from above, and arrives at the conviction that Jesus is God; that he suffers for no crime, and will die an innocent death. He confesses his conviction immediately with a loud voice, saying: "We suffer indeed, justly, for we receive the due reward of our deeds, but this man has done no evil." Then he rebuked his companion for blaspheming Jesus, saying: "Neither dost thou fear God, because thou blasphemest this man." The forgiving love which Jesus had shown his enemies, and the tender care with which he had provided for his mother, inspire him with great confidence and courage to address Jesus, thus: "Lord, remember me, when thou shalt come into thy kingdom." Jesus hears the prayer of the repenting sinner who had gone astray, but who had returned with an humble and contrite heart, looks at him compassionately and mercifully, and forgetting his own pains, speaks to him the words of life: "*Amen, I say to thee, this day thou shalt be with me in paradise.*"

Such a reply certainly far exceeded the anticipations of the poor sinner. He received a greater grace than he could expect, and his last hour was rendered happy by the gracious words of Christ. A multitude of sinners, encouraged by this promise of Jesus, to do penance, enjoy now the greatest felicity in heaven. Even to our own hearts, wounded as they are by sin, these words by which Jesus promised grace and everlasting life to the penitent thief, are a salutary balm. If you have not lived heretofore as you should have, think not that there is no remedy for you, but raise your eyes to the cross—to your Saviour, who promises forgiveness and eternal life to the repentant sinner. Rise from the sleep of sin, return to God, your Father, who, in his boundless love and mercy, stretches out his arms to receive you. With God is mercy; he says: "As I live, I desire not the death of a sinner, but that he turn from his evil ways and live." Knowing this consoling truth, heap not sin upon sin, otherwise you will be unworthy of his mercy. Do not linger on your return, do not delay your conversion until the moment God calls you from this world. The Scriptures give only one example of a death-bed conversion, and from it you cannot draw the conclusion that God will be merciful to every one who returns to him at his last hour. Do you hold the hands of time, that you can lengthen your days as you please? Are you sure that you will not die without a moment's warning? And assuming that you will not die suddenly, but after a lingering illness, your conversion will be a difficult task, for, knowing that death is approaching, you will forsake sin, when you are no longer able to commit it. And do you call that a true conversion, if you forsake sin, only when sin has forsaken you? O! how seldom is a deathbed conversion a true conversion? A true conversion must originate from a real detestation of sin, and from the love of God. The fear of death, and of the judgment to come, are the cause of the conversion of many a sinner. If you desert God in life, he will desert you in death. Lull not your conscience to sleep by vain and deceitful excuses, and delay not what alone can make you happy, namely: a true conversion, lest the proverb might be realized in you: "As a man lives so he, dies."

4. Whilst Jesus was hanging on the cross his blood flowed in torrents from his open wounds, and by the loss of it his pains became more violent, and his lassitude more apparent. At length, feeling the bitterness of death, he lifted up his eyes to heaven in the anguish of his heart, and opening his mouth, he presented his afflictions to his eternal Father. "He that hath ears to hear, let him hear," for he says with a faltering voice: "*My God, my God, why hast thou forsaken me?*"

This plaintive cry shows us the depth of his anguish, and tells how deeply the terrors of death affected his soul. But he clings to his Father with a firm confidence, calls him his God in his bitterest hour, and suffers with perfect conformity to his will. My brethren, our pathway through life is full of briars and thorns, and at the end of it, death is awaiting us. Blessed are we if we live in innocence and virtue, for then, if we are overwhelmed with suffering, our conscience will not reproach us as having caused it ourselves. We can rest assured, that God who holds our fate in his fatherly hand, has destined them for us. If you have to suffer much in this world, believe firmly that you are a favorite of heaven, for God chastises whom he loves. These trials and crosses are proofs of his love for you, by which you should become better and more worthy of heavenly bliss, for God says: "He that is just, let him be justified still, and be that is holy, let him be sanctified still." In prosperity, you have, perhaps, forgotten your destiny: perhaps you have not seriously reflected upon your obligation to aspire to perfection. But since God has sent you crosses and afflictions you cling to him more closely, and study to lead a good life. Punishment without doubt is painful; but, if you bear it patiently, you will reap sweet and imperishable fruits. Banish every useless grief from your soul, do not murmur and complain of your sufferings, but consider and use them as means which God offers you to exercise you in patience and meekness. Say with your Lord and Saviour, in the hour of trial: Lord, thy will be done.

But, if you have chosen the way of sin, if it has rendered you miserable, you have every reason for sorrow, for you suffer justly, and receive the due reward for your sins. You should feel that contrition for your sins, which David felt, when he said: "I know my iniqnity, and my sin is always before me. Cast me not away from thy face; and take not thy holy spirit from me. A sacrifice to God is an afflicted spirit; a contrite and humble heart, O God, thou wilt not despise." If sinners feel the consequences of sin, let them not dare to say: I suffer innocently, but say to themselves, what the prophet said to the children of Israel: Thy own wickedness shall reprove thee, and thy own apostasy shall rebuke thee; know thou and see, that it is an evil thing to have left the Lord. Reflect that you can remove many of your sufferings, by removing sin, which is their cause. To-day, then, hearing his voice, do not harden your hearts.

5. Jesus is exhausted from his pains and the loss of blood, his lips are parched. One prophecy concerning him was yet to be fulfilled: "I have labored with crying: my jaws are becoming hoarse: my eyes have failed, whilst I hope in my God. They are multiplied above the hairs of my head, who hate me without cause. And I looked for one who would grieve together with me, and there was none, and for one that would comfort me, and I found none, and they gave me gall for my food, and in my thirst they gave me vinegar to drink," Jesus, tormented by a burning thirst, says: "*I thirst.*"

Jesus who had given food to thousands, had not wherewith to quench his thirst in his dying hour. While living, he was the comfort of the unfortunate, and dying, he finds no refreshment; he never permitted any one to go from him without his blessing, and he himself finds none to comfort him in this, his hour of trial. Would to God we had been present at the crucifixion of our Lord! How cheerfully we would have quenched his thirst. And if he now sojourned visibly among us and would say: I am hungry, I am thirsty; O! how gladly you would share with him the last morsel of bread. But he is no longer visibly in our midst, and therefore, we can give him nothing to eat and drink, but he assures us that he will accept what we do to the least of our brethren, as done to himself, for he says: "He that shall receive one such little child in my name, receives me." And, after relating the parable of the generous and charitable Samaritan, he added: "Go, and do thou in like manner."—Luke 10: 37. Go, and do in like manner, I also say to you who have received from God the means to be useful to your fellow-men, in what manner soever it may be. Take the Samaritan for your model, and do as he did. Look at Jesus, and help your fellow-men in his name. Here you see a hungry man, let him not go hungry away. There you see a stranger, destitute of means to pay for his lodging, God places him before your eyes, take him into your house in the name of Jesus, and you will receive Jesus in him. Again, persecuted innocence implores your aid; it is the most precious moment of your life; use it well, deliver the innocent, before the poor soul hastens to perdition. It may cause you some expense, but what of that? Do it cheerfully, as if you were serving your Redeemer, who says: "By this shall all men know you are my disciples, if you love one another." And suppose that those whom you help, prove ungrateful. Oh! think of your Redeemer who forgave his murderers, for if you love only those who love you, what reward shall you have? Do not even the publicans do the same? Therefore be merciful and charitable. And at your last moment, when you stand at the gate of eternity, Oh! what bliss will be yours, if, in answer to your knock, heaven's portals unclose, and you hear the words: Come, ye blessed of my father, take possession of the kingdom prepared for you, from the foundation of the world; for I was hungry, and you gave me to eat; I was thirsty, and you gave me to drink; I was naked, and you clothed me; I was a stranger and you took me in; sick, and you visited me. Amen, I say to you, as long as you did it to one of these, my least brethren, you did it to me.

6. Jesus is hanging on the cross between heaven and earth; nature itself revolts at such cruelty; the sun refuses his light, for the space of three hours an impenetrabe darkness overspreads the whole earth. The end of his sufferings is at hand. He beholds the fruition of his labors, the redemption of mankind is accomplished. He raises his eyes to heaven, and says, with feelings of triumph and joy, "*It is consummated.*"

No one could affirm this but Jesus, for, from his first entrance into the world to his last hour, he did the will of his Father. His maxim was: "I must do the will of him, that sent me." No labor fatigued him, no humiliation lessened his courage. He had been sent by his Father, to free us from ignorance and sin, and in a measure most superabundant he has done it. Well for us, if we can say, with equal truth, in our dying hour: "it is consummated." If we have carefully performed our duties, we can appear before God with joy and confidence; nothing will trouble us; it is consummated. That we may be able to say so when death calls us away, let us follow the example of our Master, let us scrupulously fulfil our duties, let us not waste our precious time in idleness, for the night will come when no one can work. *Husbands and wives,* walk diligently now in the ways of the Lord, comfort each other in afflictions, spend daily some time in prayer, that God may give you his grace, to fulfil faithfully what you promised with a solemn oath, at the altar of God: Then you may say when the last dread summons comes: "It is consummated." *Parents,* be careful of the salvation of your children, teach them by word and example, have them instructed in religion in early youth; see that they learn something by which they can earn their bread in honesty: then, if departing hence you see that your children are beloved by God and men, you can say with a good conscience: "It is consummated." *Children*, obey the commandment of God: honor thy father and thy mother, that thou mayest live long on earth; never be wiser than your parents, do not slight them nor their commands. Be thankful to them for all they have done and suffered for you. Then, whether you die young or old, you can say: "It is consummated." *Suffering friends*, imitate your Lord and Master, suffer with patience if you cannot with joy. Sufferings endure but a little while; they open for you a pathway into heaven. If you bear with patience what little afflictions fall to your lot in this world, under the hand of God's mercy, you will escape those far greater ones which the souls detained in the prison of purgatory are suffering under the hands of his justice, and you can say in your dying hour: "It is consummated."

7. Paleness has covered the Redeemer's face. He seems to have expired, but no; once more he opens his eyes, and looking up to heaven with confidence, raises his voice for the last time: "He that hath ears to hear, let him hear" the dying words of the Redeemer: "*Father, into thy hands, I commend my spirit.*"

The hour of separation of the soul from the body will also come for us. That hour will be decisive for all eternity, and the end we shall make, will be of the greatest importance. If we ponder seriously on the termination of our life, a torturing anguish overpowers and takes possession of us. What anguish would seize us if the moment were really now at hand in which our summons would come to give up our spirit into the hands of the living God. All the good we have neglected, all the evil we have done, and of which have been the cause, will then come to our recollection, and and stare us in the face. *Proud men*, whose thoughts are concentrated upon your elegant attire, your worldly possessions, the honors that attend you; who think yourselves superior to others, who despise your poor neighbors, what anguish will befall you, when you shall be compelled to surrender your souls into the hands of God, *who resists the proud and gives his grace to the humble*. *You, who are unjust in your dealings with others*, who destroy the prosperity of your fellow-men, and build on the ruins of their fortune, your own, what anguish will seize you, when you must surrender your souls into the hands of him who has said: "*The unjust and covetous shall not possess the kingdom of God.*" You, *unmerciful men*, who close your ears to the entreaties of the poor, who ridicule the tears of the afflicted and oppressed, what anguish will befall you, when you must yield your souls into the hands of him, *who will pass judgment without mercy, on all those that show no mercy.* You, *sensual and effeminate men*, who seduce innocence by sweet flattery and flippant promises, who heap crimes upon crimes, scandals upon scandals, who have no perception of what is right and good, how will you feel when you surrender your souls into the hands of him who has said, that: "*Neither fornicators nor adulterers shall possess the kingdom of God.*" Parents, who introduce your children to the follies and crimes of the world before they have power and understanding to resist them, who for want of watching over them, give them to perdition, what anguish will befall you, when you surrender your souls into the hands of him who has said: "*If a man have not care of his own, and especially of those of his own house, he has denied the faith, and is worse than an infidel.*" Children, who disobey and dishonor your parents, what shame and confusion will overwhelm you, when you must approach the judgment-seat of God, who has said: "*Honor thy father and thy mother.*"

These are the seven words of our Lord, spoken on the cross for our instruction. The first word: "*Father, forgive them, for they know not what they do,*" teaches us to forgive our enemies from our hearts. The second word: "*Woman behold thy son, Son, behold thy mother,*" admonishes us to love, honor, and obey our parents. The third word: "*This day thou shalt be with me in paradise,*" exhorts us to do penance for our sins. The fourth: "*My God, my God, why hast thou forsaken me,*" bids us cling to God in times of adversity. The fifth: "*I thirst,*" tells us that in the persons of the poor we help and assist Christ himself. The sixth: "*It is consummated,*" encourages us to be zealous and faithful in the performance of our duties; and the seventh: "*Father, into thy hands I commend my spirit,*" reminds us that we should walk in the presence of God, and commend our souls now, and at all times, into his hands. Let us at the foot of the cross, promise to God, henceforth to comply with all this. Let us act resolutely and fulfil what we have promised. Then when the final hour comes, and life is closing for us, let us turn our dying eyes to Jesus, and remember that he is the Eternal Light. When the film of death darkens our vision, and the world is fading from our view let us think that Jesus is *our* light and our exceeding great reward. Oh! let us ever be faithful to the good resolutions which we have to-day written down upon our hearts. Amen.

LENTEN SERMONS.

FOURTH COURSE.

SEVEN SERMONS.

HOMILY I.

THE WASHING OF THE FEET, PETER, JUDAS, AND THE QUESTIONS OF THE DISCIPLES.

"*O all ye that pass by the way, attend and see if there be any sorrow like to my sorrow ; for he hath made a vintage of me, as the Lord spoke in the day of his fierce anger.*"—*Lam.* 1 : 12.

These words clearly indicate the subject I have selected for our Lenten meditations. It is the Passion and death of Jesus Christ who has redeemed us from sin and hell. We will consider not so much *sin in itself* as *the Victim for sin*. What atonement does sin demand? You are fully aware that sin is an infinite evil, and that for its atonement an infinite sacrifice is required. Hence God himself is and must be the victim. The question is : Has God made this sacrifice ? Did he permit his love to reach such lofty heights that it led him to offer himself in expiation for those who offended him by their crimes? Our holy faith answers this important question : Yes, ye poor miserable sinners, God himself became the sacrifice for your sins. The omnipotent Father spared not his only-begotten Son, but sacrificed him for the sins of the world. Look up to Calvary and behold the Lamb of God who taketh away the sins of the world, crying out : "It is consummated."

The victim dies. Who is it that dies? The holy, the spotless Son of God. But oh! eternal Father; he is thy only-begotten Son! He is the light and life of the world—and he dies! Must he die? And the Father replies : *He dies, and die he must.* But why must he die? Because of sin. Of sin! And whence comes sin? Sin is the work of man. And for it, thy Son must die? How my, brethren, is it for me, for you, for all the sinners of the world, the Son of God must die? The innocent Jesus for guilty sinners, the Creator for the creature, the God of holiness for fallen sinful man ? Ah ! who could believe this, if our holy faith did not assure us, saying : The infinite God alone can make an infinite sacrifice ; without this sacrifice, sin remains—without this sacrifice, there is no redemption. Truly, sin must be something terrible, something awful, since it demands so enormous a sacrifice. If we bestow due consideration and attention on its magnitude, we will be forced to exclaim with St. Thomas of Villanova : "My Lord and my God, you carried your love to too great an extent.

With fear and trembling I must confess that you transgressed the limits of justice, and whilst wishing to be just, you were overjust. Your love of justice renders you unjust; for what kind of justice is it, that requires your Son to die for a servant; the innocent for the guilty? Is not the reparation you demand greater than the loss sustained?" Indeed, a single drop of the precious blood of Christ would have more than sufficed to accomplish the redemption of mankind, but the justice of God demanded it even to the very last drop.

The manner of the offering should also correspond *with the greatness of the sacrifice*. It was to be offered in the most *painful, ignominious*, and *cruel manner*. Whatever the martyrs suffered, they suffered in body, but in Christ were united the bitterest mental and bodily pains, for which reason he is called the *Man of Sorrows*. The martyrs even in the midst of their tortures could rejoice, because they knew that they would possess him for whom they gave their life, but Christ knew that he would never win all for whom he was shedding his blood; he knew that the greater part of mankind would be lost, notwithstanding his Passion and death, as Isaias had foretold: "In vain have I labored, in vain have I exhausted my strength." Whatever the martyrs suffered, they suffered at the hands of men, their equals, but the Son of God was smitten and wounded by his creatures, and by the hand of God, as the prophet says: "We hold him for a leper, whom the Lord has stricken and humbled." *The cause of his death is as astonishing as the manner in which it was inflicted.* Jesus is innocent before his Father in heaven, the devil has no part in him. Jesus, therefore defrayed a debt which he did not owe. The Father himself acknowledged him as innocent, speaking from heaven. "This is my beloved Son, in whom I am well pleased." *His enemies* confessed his innocence, for no one could convince him of sin. *The wife of Pilate* affirmed his innocence, saying to Pilate: "Have thou nothing to do with this just man." *Pilate* himself declared: "I find no cause in him." The traitor Judas confessed: "I have betrayed innocent blood," and at the foot of the cross, the *Roman centurion*, striking his breast, cried out: "Truly this man is just and the Son of God." *All the witnesses say:* "The victim is innocent," but the justice of God demanded that the innocent should die for the guilty.—Venerable Bede relates that the stone, on which our Saviour prayed to his heavenly Father in the garden of Gethsemane, became so soft that the impression of his knees remained thereon. Are our hearts harder than a rock? The sun was darkened, the earth trembled, the rocks were rent, the heart of Mary was pierced by a two-edged sword, when sin demanded this sacrifice. Can we remain cold and insensible, unmoved, when it is for us this sacrifice is offered? Ah no! I know that the suffering and dying Redeemer is your hope, your refuge, your love. I know that Christ crucified is neither the history of an idle tale nor a stumbling block to you, but that he is your adorable Redeemer. I know that you look up with a heart full of love and hope to the Lamb on the altar of the cross, and for this reason our suffering and dying Redeemer shall be the subject of our meditations during the holy season of Lent.

1. The bitter Passion of our Lord was preluded by a sign of love so unprecedented that all heaven and earth looked with amazement upon the scene,. When Christ had eaten with his Apostles the Paschal lamb, he arose, laid aside his garments, and having taken a towel, he girded himself, poured water into a basin, and began to wash the feet of his disciples. Of all the Evangelists, St. John alone mentions this wonderful action of Jesus, and he describes it in a remarkable manner, in order to arouse our admiration. He begins his description by an introduction, in which he points out to us the *Omniscience, Love,* and *Divinity* of Jesus Christ. His words are: "Before the festival of the pasch, Jesus, knowing that his hour was come, that he should pass out of this world to the Father, having loved his own, he loved them to the end. These words; "*knowing that his hour was come,*" signify his omniscience; "*that he should pass to the Father,*" signify *his Divinity ;* and "*he loved his own to the end his,*" signify his *Love.* Jesus, the only-begotten of the Father, and co-equal to him in all things, prostrates himself like a menial at the feet of poor fishermen. Abigail washed the feet of the servants of David. Abraham washed those of the three Angels who went to Sodom. Mary Magdalene washed those of Jesus with her tears, but the humility of all these loses its lustre before that which prompted our divine Saviour. The Apostles were astonished when they saw their Master pour water into the basin and perform before their eyes a work of such great love and self-abnegation. They had frequently witnessed the greatest miracles wrought by their Master, but never had they beheld anything like this. The Lord of heaven and earth to wash the feet of his disciples! In the Red Sea the Lord performed marvelous works, for there he manifested the omnipotence of his arm, when he cast the proud and obdurate Pharoah with his whole army into the depths of the sea, but he appears more wonderful with the basin of water at the feet of his disciples, for therein *he drowns the pride and haughtiness of the world.* Truly, as long as the world exists men will never be able to comprehend what the Son of God in his profound humility accomplished at the feet of his disciples. What a picture! Jesus kneels at the feet of the Apostles, the maker of the universe bends low in the dust, the Creator prostrates himself before the work of his hands to perform the office of a servant, to wash the feet of his disciples! Admire your humble Jesus, who, kneeling in the dust, cries out: "Learn of me, because I am meek and humble of heart." When the Lord approached Peter to wash his feet, Peter said: *Lord, dost thou wash my feet ?*

St. Augustine, explaining this passage, says: When Peter saw the Son of God kneel before him, he grew pale, trembled, and in his astonishment cried out: *Lord, dost thou wash my feet? No, thou shalt never wash my feet.* Peter was terrified by the incomprehensible self-abasement of his Master, and in his consternation asked him: Lord, dost thou wash my feet? As if he would say: Lord, thou wilt not wash my hands, my head, but my feet, the lowest and most insignificant part of my body, with those hands which have made heaven and earth, fed the hungry, cleansed the lepers, and raised the dead to life. When St. John the Baptist, who, according to thy own testimony, was the greatest among those born of women, deemed himself far too unworthy to loose the latchet of thy shoe, how can I, without making myself guilty of culpable pride, suffer thy adorable hands to wash my unclean feet! How can I suffer thee to humble thyself so far as to kneel before me. No, sweet Lord, Son of the living God, thou shalt never wash them: it is my duty, sinner that I am, to prostrate myself before thee in the dust and to serve thee. O Christians, who call this humble Jesus your God, your Master, your Teacher, fix your eyes upon this divine marvel, and contemplate it with tenderness and affection; then look into your own heart which is puffed up with intolerable pride and ambition. Where is your conformity to your divine Master? The God of glory did not hesitate to wash the feet of sinful men, that he might destroy your vanity, confound your pride, and teach you humility.

Jesus, seeing Peter so persistently resist his love and humility, said: "Peter, if I wash thee not, thou shalt have no part with me." The apostle, hearing this, exclaimed: "Lord, wash not only my feet, but also my hands and head." These words of our Lord: "If I wash thee not, thou shalt not have part in me," concern us also. We, too, must be washed by Christ, otherwise we can have no part with him, for who can cleanse us, who have been conceived and born in sin, but he who washed the feet of his disciples? But, indeed, we all have been washed by Jesus Christ, it being Christ, not man, that baptizes. We have been cleansed, but who has preserved untarnished the white robe of innocence with which he was invested at his baptism? Alas! if we look around and examine all the stages and conditions of life from youth to old age, we can scarcely go beyond the limits of childhood and find one who has retained his nuptial garment pure and undefiled. We need a second purification, a new bath, to restore the pristine brightness, with which Christ adorned our hearts. Behold, the Lord himself goes to prepare for us a new bath in his precious blood, wherein alone our purification can be accomplished, and it is Christ only that can effect it. To him we must cry with the prophet: "Wash me yet more from my iniquity, and cleanse me from my sin. Wash, O Lord, the garment which thou gavest us in Baptism, for we have defiled it by sin; wash it in thy blood. In the blood of thy sacred head wash our pride; in the blood of thy adorable heart wash our envy; in the blood of thy holy hands wash our wicked and sinful deeds; in the blood of thy wounded feet wash our sloth and negligence in the affair of salvation. Wash us, O Jesus, in thy blood, that we may appear before thy judgment-seat, clothed in the nuptial garment of innocence." It is the opinion of St. John Chrysostom that the Lord commenced the washing of the feet with Judas. He says: "I think, Jesus washed first the feet of the traitor," and St. Thomas of Aquin asserts that the washing of the feet was done by the Lord principally for the sake of Judas, in order to humble him and to cause him to desist from his diabolical design.

2. St. John was struck with amazement when in his revelations, he saw a woman girded with the sun, having the moon under her feet, and he exclaimed: "*A great sign appeared in heaven.*" But oh! beloved disciple of Jesus, what seals your lips when you see your Lord and God kneel at the feet of this wretched, miserable Judas? Why do you not now exclaim: "*A great sign appeared on earth.*" Behold the eternal Son of God at the feet of a man who is surrounded not by light but by infernal darkness! Behold, holiness kneels before crime; justice, before iniquity; love, before malice; God himself kneeling in the dust before a servant of the devil. When Simon the Pharisee saw Mary Magdalene fall down at the feet of Jesus and bathe them with her tears, he could not comprehend why the Lord permitted himself to be touched by a woman who was known by all to be a public sinner, therefore he presumed to pass a rash judgment: "If we were a prophet, he would certainly know what kind of woman that is, who touches him," he would know that she is a public sinner. O sinner, if it were but vouchsafed you to behold the Lord himself at the feet of Judas, you could say with greater justice: "If he were a prophet; he could easily measure the depths of that guilty heart, and, knowing before whom he kneels, and whose feet he washes, would know that he kneels before his own betrayer. And yet he is a prophet and more than a prophet, being King of the Prophets, whose all-seeing eye perceived what was passing in the heart of Judas, who knew that he prostrated himself before a devil, as St. John says: "*The devil had given it into the heart of Judas to betray Jesus.*

When Satan tempted Jesus in the desert and showed him all the kingdoms of the world and the glory thereof, and promised to give him all these if, falling down, he would adore him, Jesus, full of indignation, said to him: *Begone, Satan!* and *here he kneels before him.* And why? In the first instance the salvation of no soul was imperiled, but in the latter case the Lord sees the soul of Judas in imminent danger. Christ hereby teaches us, that a soul is of more value than all the kingdoms of the world, as he afterwards said: What does it profit a man if he gain the whole world and lose his own soul? In order to wrest this unhappy soul from the abyss into which it had plunged, Jesus refuses not to kneel before Judas. But neither his humility nor his love and tears could soften that hardened heart.

3. Seeing this, Jesus decreed to wash him in his most precious blood. For shortly after washing the feet of his disciples, he instituted the most holy Sacrament of the Altar. Under the appearance of bread and wine he gave to his Apostles his body and blood, to Judas, too, whom he placed *near himself*, that he might keep him *far from evil*. But as the humility of the kneeling Jesus was powerless to move the heart of the traitor, so his love in the Blessed Sacrament produced no effect on him. Judas was the first that received Communion unworthily. The deepest sadness overwhelmed the spirit of Jesus, and he said: "*Amen, amen, I say to you, one of you shall betray me.*" Seeing that all his exertions to save Judas were unavailing, and that he persevered in his diabolical project, profound sorrow and dejection seized the sacred heart of our Lord. He trembled for the soul of Judas, which he wished to save, and he made one more effort to move the wretched apostle to repentance, by *warning him publicly*. All the other Apostles were touched, only one remained unmoved—Judas—for spiritual blindness, alas! is the consequence of an unworthy Communion. The Apostles, desponding and sorrowful, asked their Master: Is it I, Lord, am I the traitor, Peter taking the lead; whereupon St. John Chrysostom addresses him in these words: O great apostle, your conscience bears your testimony that you have never offended your divine Master, that you always loved him, why, then, do you ask: Is it I? Oh Lord! No, you never can betray him whom you confessed to be the Son of the living God. And you, St. John, beloved disciple of the Lord, your soul is so pure, your heart without guile, your love so great, why do you ask: Is it I? Oh Lord! Am I the traitor? Why do all the other Apostles ask this question? This is a certain characteristic of pious souls; they always live in holy fear. Those who love God sincerely always tremble lest they may lose him, and, although their conscience does not reproach them, they are aware and convinced of their weakness, and in holy humility fear lest they commit sin. This also proves that, without a special revelation from above, no one knows, whether he is worthy of love or hatred.

4. But who, finally, draws near to his Saviour, his whole mien expressive of tenderest love, and his heart, apparently full of sympathy for his sorrowing Lord? Who asks: Master, is it I, am I the traitor? Full of indignation St. Augustine explains: "Judas, whom do you ask: Is it I? Master! do you not know that he is omniscient? He knows and sees that you are the unfortunate wretch, of whom the Scripture says: *He that eats bread with me raises his heel against me*. Give heed then, Judas, your Master answers your question in plain and simple words: *Yes,*

it is you that will betray me." O Judas, how is it possible that your heart is not shaken to its inmost depths with contrition. Wherefore do you not fling your treachery to hell whence it came? When Saul persecuted David, Jonathan said to the king : Sin not, my lord, against thy servant David, for he has not sinned against thee. His works to thee are good, and he has placed his soul in thy hands, he has slain the Philistines and has saved Israel. Why will you shed innocent blood? Why will you kill David, who has done no evil? When Saul heard these words of his son, he was pacified and said : "As the Lord liveth' he shall not die." With the words of Jonathan, I will address Judas : Sin not against your God, for he has not offended you, he has done great things for you, he has placed his body and soul in your hands. Why will you betray innocent blood? Oh, say with Saul : As the Lord liveth, he shall not die, I will not betray him. Ask no longer: Is it I? O Lord! but cast yourself at the feet of your Lord, confess your guilt and say with an humble heart: Yes, O Lord, it is I.

Oh, what joy Christ would have experienced if Judas had acknowledged his fault, if he had humbly said : "Lord, I have sinned against thee, but behold, here I am at thy feet. Pardon me, Oh Lord! thy loving heart went out to Magdalene in grace and mercy when fainting beneath the weight of her sins; she cast herself at thy feet, be thou also a God of mercy to me. With tears of bitterness and compunction, I will bewail my sin, which thy mercy surpasses by far. Pardon me." Had Judas done this, his salvation would have been secured, for Christ came into the world to seek and to save that which was lost. He is the incarnate mildness, his heart is overflowing with mercy, he welcomes all who return to him from their evil ways. Had Judas struck his breast with sorrow, Christ would not have rejected him, he would have received him, embraced him, and one throb of his sacred heart would have cast the demon from his tempted soul. He would have rejoiced, because that soul was snatched from perdition ; like the good shepherd, he would have brought the lost sheep back to the fold, like that tender father mentioned in the Gospel, he would have exclaimed : Let us rejoice : Because this my son was dead, and is come to life again : he was lost, and is found. But, alas! Judas remained hardened, obdurate, and persevered in sin. O, the hardness of heart, *God kneels before Judas,* and Judas remains hardened, *Jesus washes and kisses his feet,* and Judas remains hardened, *Jesus gives him his body and blood,* and Judas remains hardened, *Jesus is troubled and trembles,* and Judas remains hardened, *Jesus lays open the secrets of his heart,* and Judas remains hardened, *the Apostles in their turn ask :* Is it I? O Lord, and Judas remains hardened, *he himself asks this question,* and his Lord and God says, yes, it is you, still Judas remains hardened. All our Saviour's anguish seems forgotten—yes, even his Passion and death sink into oblivion. He, the betrayed, mourns over the traitor, but in vain, for Judas remains hardened and perseveres in sin. Oh, how terrible are the effects of an unworthy Communion!

PERORATION.

God grant that the history of the wretched Judas may not prove unavailing for us! Truly, Jesus embraces us with the same love, he enriches us with the same graces, and invites us with the same tenderness to return from the way of sin, he has cleansed us in the bath of regeneration, received us into the number of his friends and disciples, he nourishes our souls with his own flesh and blood, he evinces nothing towards us but the tenderest love. But if we look into our hearts, if we examine ourselves, can we say with the other Apostles, Lord, is it I? without fearing to hear the answer: Yes, *it is you that have betrayed me.* My brethren, what testimony does your conscience give you? How is it in regard to your profession of faith, your fervor and fidelity in the observance of the commandments of God? What is the object of your care and anxiety upon earth? To what does your soul cling? What does your heart love? Is it your God, your Saviour? Is it he alone, or have you become traitors, and again enlisted under the banner of sin? Ah, our life, our conscience bears testimony against us, that we are traitors to Christ and false to his holy cause. *But although our sins be great and numerous,* let us take to heart this consoling truth that the mercy of God is still greater. The sacred heart of Jesus should inspire us with confidence, courage and love. Judas did not acknowledge his guilt; oh, let us not walk in his footsteps. Christ trembles not only for his soul, but also for yours and mine. Without asking, Lord, is it I? let us at once confess: Lord, it is I. I acknowledge my injustice, and my sins are continually before my eyes. Against thee, I have sinned and done evil before thee. It is I, O Lord, who betrayed thee for the miserable price of sin. It is I who slighted thy warnings, who abused thy mercy, and who transgressed thy divine precepts and laws. Lord, I know and acknowledge my guilt; I am sorry for it from the deepest depths of my heart. Pardon my sin, rescue me from perdition, wash my soul in thy blood. O, sacred heart of Jesus, I beseech thee, not only for myself, but for all sinners, for all hardened hearts. For the love thou has wasted in vain to soften the heart of Judas and to save his soul, I humbly beg thee, to infuse thy love into the hearts of all assembled here, that in holy repentance they may seek pardon from thee who goest forth to death, that sinners may live. Suffer not, O merciful Jesus, one of these to become a second Judas.

HOMILY II.

THE GARDEN OF GETHSEMANE, THE PRAYER, THE AGONY AND THE BLOODY SWEAT OF CHRIST, AND THE COMING OF THE ANGEL.

"O all ye that pass by the way, attend and see if there be any sorrow like to my sorrow; for he hath made a vintage of me, as the Lord spoke in the day of his fierce anger."—Lam. 1 : 12.

"My soul is sorrowful even unto death :" (Matt. 26 : 28), thus the Lord said to his disciples. Jesus is not sorrowful *on account of death* but *unto death.* Should you ask the reason why he was sorrowful unto death, I answer: The Eternal Father wished his only-begotten Son to atone not only for original sin, but also for all actual sins, mortal and venial, which have been and will be committed from the beginning of the world until time shall be no more. For this reason the pure and spotless soul of Christ was filled with pain and sorrow. According to the law of God, without penance there is unquestionably no salvation for those who, having passed the innocent years of childhood, have stained their soul with sin! Christ says: "Unless you do penance you shall all likewise perish."—Luke 13 : 5. No forgiveness for them till they have trodden the dolorous way of the cross.

Not every kind of penance, however, effaces sin. *King Saul* wept and did penance, and yet he was rejected by the Lord. *Antiochus* was sorry for the sacrilege he had committed—yet there was no pardon for him. The unfortunate *Judas* repented. Oh, how deep was his sorrow! The Scripture tells us: He brought back the pieces of silver, and cried aloud to the chief priests and all who were present : "I have sinned in betraying innocent blood."—Matt. 27 : 4. They replied : "What is that to us? Look you to it." St. Matthew tells us that casting down the pieces of silver in the temple, he departed and went and hanged himself with a halter. In order to efface sin, a repentance corresponding with the greatness of the guilt is required, which will lead the soul—not to despair like Judas, but to the love of God. Man of himself being powerless to excite such a sorrow, the soul of Jesus became sorrowful in order to give to the Sacrament of Penance the virtue and efficacy which are necessary for the forgiveness of sin ; therefore, Christ supplied by his God-like sorrow what was wanting to our sorrow.

1. Behold, O Christian, the soul of our Redeemer is sorrowful unto death, because he no longer sees in your soul, *the image and likeness of God.* Christ's holy soul is filled with sorrow because your soul grieves not at having lost God in the devious paths of sin where you stray with such joy. *His holy soul is sorrowful* even unto death, because *your soul is defiled by sin* unto death. If you lose a child, a father, a mother, a wife, or husband, nay, even an unimportant law-suit, you exclaim: "My soul is sorrowful unto death." But when you lose the grace of God, innocence, heaven, even your immortal soul, you cease not for one moment to enjoy the pleasures of life. My soul is sorrowful, says our divine Redeemer, for whilst I pledge my soul for you, you turn from me, lest the sight of my anguish compel you to forsake those sins which are the cause of my sorrow. The number of sinners is great, yet how few, how very few! have a heart-felt sorrow for sin! If the forgiveness of sin depended on man alone, very few would obtain it; for this reason Christ took upon himself our sins, that the merit and efficacy of his sorrow might supply the deficiency of ours; his sorrow extended to all sin, hence: "*My soul is sorrowful even unto death.*"

Whence cometh this excessive anguish? Jesus sees himself condemned to death by the Holy Ghost who is Charity; he turns to his heavenly Father who has no solace, no comfort for him; the sins of the whole world crush him down, whilst his coming tortures rise vividly before him. He knows that one of his chosen twelve will basely barter away his life. Oh! how deep must have been his grief, knowing, as he did, by his omniscience that the Holy Ghost had decreed that he should die. The Holy Spirit is Charity and knows not how to punish, but gives life to all, yet in regard to Christ who is fully equal to him, he seems to forget his attribute, prophesying by the mouth of Caiphas, the high-priest: "It is expedient that one man should die for the people, and that the whole nation perish not."—John 11: 50. The words: "for the people," signify the love and mercy of the Holy Ghost who condemned the innocent Jesus to death in order to show mercy to sinners. To be punished by the hand which in its very essence is charity, which in its infinite mercy spares sinners, caused Christ's sorrow on Mount Olivet, and for this reason he exclaimed: "My soul is sorrowful even unto death." With a touching appeal from this sentence of the Holy Ghost, he turns to his heavenly Father, and prays: "Father, if it be possible, let his chalice pass from me." The hope of being heard seems to strengthen him, for the loving Father must hear the prayer of his innocent, well-beloved Son. The Son turns to the Father, he knows him to be the Father of mercy and the God of consolation. To him plead not only his anguish and innocence, but also the punishments and sufferings which all unmerited though they be, are pitilessly waiting for him. Surely his Father will not be deaf to his prayer. In this hope, he says: Father, let this chalice pass from me, have compassion on me. Behold, I have announced thy holy will to the children of men. I have always fulfilled thy holy will, oh, let this bitter chalice pass from me. But his heavenly Father hears him not, for although he is the Father of mercy and God of consolation, he is also the God of justice, and, as an offended Judge, will not change the sentence of the Holy Ghost. God spared not his only-begotten Son, but gave him for us all. Not to be heard by his Father, but to be condemned to death, notwithstanding his innocence, this caused Christ's bitter grief on Mount Olivet, and forced from him the cry: "My soul is sorrowful even unto death."

The prophet Isaiah (53: 6) says, "*The Lord hath laid on him the iniquity of us all.* We also read, that when Achan was stoned at the command of Josue, all Israel participated. "Every one cast a stone at him."—Josue 7: 2. What was done to Achan by the Jews was done to Christ in the garden of Gethsemane by all men of whole world. All Israel stoned him, *i. e.*, all men who lived from the beginning of the world and who shall live to the end of time cast the stones of their sins upon the innocent Jesus, and he assumed the enormous weight in order to satisfy his offended Father. Oh, what ignominy overwhelmed our Saviour when, borne down with this burden of guilt, he could cry out with Esdras: "My God, I am confounded and ashamed to lift up my face to thee, for our iniquities have multiplied over our heads, and our sins are grown up even into heaven."—2. Esdras 9: 6. One sin is more abominable in the sight of God than the rotteness of all wounds, more abominable than the putridness of all carcasses. We can scarcely imagine the confusion of our dear Lord, when this envenomed mass of sin —the sins of the whole world—fell upon him. This is what made Jesus exclaim: "My soul is sorrowful even unto death."

Indeed, his sorrow and confusion reached such a climax that he dared not lift up his face, as St. Matthews says, but, "*fell on his face*" (26: 39). St. John Chrysostom remarks: "Ah, he who is higher than the heavens is bowed to the ground, and lies on his face." But why is he prostrate on his face? Why is he ashamed? We are the sinners, not he; we are the culprits, not he. Our presumption permits us to raise our eyes, and thou, O divine Redeemer, why dost thou cast thine own upon the ground? His infinite love gives answer. He falls on his face in order to raise our eyes to heaven, and to fill us with shame and confusion on account of our sins. Our iniquities are gone over his head, and as a heavy burden have weighed him to the earth. O Christians, my astonishment ceases that it was sin which hurled the third part of the Angels from the joys of heaven into that abyss, whose flames were enkindled by the wrath of God. Can we marvel thereat since it laid prostrate the Lord of heaven into the dust of the earth. I no longer wonder that sin casts a soul into perdition, since it cast the spotless Lamb of God upon his face. No, I wonder not at that, but I admire the love of Christ, because by its excess he lies in the dust and voluntarily bears the infinite load, the guilt of mankind. I admire and adore the loving heart of Jesus, which is sorrowful even unto death on account of my sins, yours, and those of the whole world. There, in the garden of Olives my sins, yours, and the sins of all men, have cried out to our Lord: "Bow down, that we may trample upon thee, lay thy body on the ground as a way for us over which to pass." There in the garden of Olives the *concupiscence of the flesh*, with all its train of wicked thoughts, carnal desires, immodest language and songs, impudent looks, criminal and shameless touches, impurities, adulteries, incests, sacrileges, all these cry out: Bow down, spotless Lamb of God, let thy body be the path for our feet. The *concupiscence of the eyes*, theft, fraud, usury, bribery, envy, avarice, and every kind of injustice, cry out: Prostrate thyself on the ground, we too require thy body for a path. The *pride of life*, anger, revenge, vanity, ambition, pride, and cruelty, cry out: Bow down, O Jesus, detain us not—we must trample thee down! And what did Jesus do? He bowed down his head, prostrated himself on the ground, and buried his face in the dust, that the long, repulsive train might go over. O Christians, give heed, and never forget that our sins cast Christ to the ground, on account of their weight he lies in the dust. Let your hearts be touched by this spectacle of love, and make the solemn promise to your sorrowful Saviour never to offend him again.

2. Whilst our Saviour was lying on his face, the justice of the Father presented before his soul, in vivid colors, the tortures of the coming night and the following day, in consequence of which, his soul was tormented with such anguish that his sweat became blood and in great drops rolled down upon the ground. Drops of blood? What is this? Who moistens the arid soil of that garden with his blood? I see no scourges that tear his body, no thorns that wound his head, no nails that pierce his hands and feet. But woe! woe! I see there my sins, your sins, and the sins of the whole world. These are the scourges that tear his body, these are the thorns that wound his heart, these are the heavy burden which he cannot bear without sweating blood. How could it be otherwise than that he should sweat blood, he thought of the sins of all, he was penetrated with sorrow and sadness for all sins, as if he had committed them himself. His sorrow and contrition was of infinite strength, because being an infinite God, he comprehended the infinite malice of sin. On account of this infinite sorrow, he is called the Man of Sorrows. Being filled with bitterness and grief, he exclaimed: My soul is sorrowful even unto death. Jesus wept when he stood at the grave of Lazarus whom he loved, he wept over the inhabitants of Jerusalem, because in the blindness and hardness of their hearts they had rejected his love, mercy, and grace; how, then, can we wonder that he shed tears of blood seeing that thousands upon

thousands of souls created for eternal life, live and die in sin, and are buried in hell? How can we wonder that the anguish of his soul was so great that his sweat fell in drops of blood from his whole body.

When the wrath of God burst forth over Egypt for the sins she had committed against Israel, the chastisements commenced and ended with the death of the first-born. Will, then, the bloody sweat of Christ be the beginning and his death the end, since he is the first-born of the Father, and since in him all the sons of mankind will be punished? Indeed, each one of the signs foreshadows this terrible conclusion. It is a law of nature that the blood suddenly flows to the heart when it is seized with anguish and perturbation. But with the Redeemer, it is the very reverse. His heart is oppressed, and his soul sorrowful unto death, yet his blood flows not from the members of his body to the heart. In direct violation of nature's law, it forces its way in great drops thick and fast from every pore, that his heart, destitute of all solace, might feel the keener anguish and pain for our sins. The two eyes with which nature has provided man to express his emotions by tears sufficed not our Saviour, who shed tears of blood from every pore, *and all for us!* Would it not seem as if the innocent Jesus had sinned more greviously than Adam, since he is punished more severely than our progenitor? I grant that the penalties meted out to Adam for his great disobedience by the offended majesty of God were severe, but the chastisement was tempered by mercy and by the circumstance of its being divided between Adam and Eve. God said to Adam: "In the sweat of thy brow thou shalt eat thy bread," and to Eve: "In labor, thou shalt bring forth children." Both punishments, however, are inflicted on Christ, namely: labor and sweat; labor, when the dark waves of trouble encompassed his soul; sweat, when, in the garden of Olives, the perspiration flowed like blood to the ground, and when, bathed in tears of blood, he exclaimed: "Oh all ye that pass by the way, attend and see if there is any grief like to my grief. My soul is sorrowful, even unto death." But what was the cause of this bloody sweat? Alas! my brethren, as in all the other tortures of Jesus, when we ask the cause, the horrible echo: sin, sin, reverberates with painful force. Yes, Christians, seek no other reason than this, and learn from this the greviousness of sin and the ineffable love of Jesus, which, with his bloody sweat, will blot out the guilt of our souls and inflame our hearts with love. Oh, because of the sadness of Jesus, open your eyes and hearts to know the evil you have done in committing sin, and for the love of Christ, who falls on his face, fall down upon your knees and bewail your sins with tears of sorrow.

The prophet Isaias says: (49: 1. 4) "*Give ear, ye islands, and hearken, ye people from afar. I said: I have labored in vain, in vain have I exhausted my strength.*" When I represent to my mind the Son of God on Mount

Olivet, when I see his soul sorrowful unto death, his trembling lips move in prayer for sinners, and his blood flow to the ground, and when from this awe-inspiring spectacle I turn my eyes upon the world and behold the hearts of men so cold, so hardened, and insensible, it is to me as if I heard the Son of God call heaven and earth to be witnesses of his love and his blood. "Give ear, ye islands, and hearken, ye people from afar. I said: I have labored in vain, in vain have I exhausted my strength. Of what use is the blood I am going to shed, when men will not purify their souls therein, when it will not induce them to renounce Satan, when they will not forsake their evil ways, but continue to sin? Of what use is my blood, when they abuse my Sacraments, my doctrine, my grace and love; when, in spite of my labor to rescue their souls from perdition, they rush headlong into hell?" The thought that, notwithstanding his infinite love, so many souls would perish, was one of the chief tortures of the Lord in the garden of Olives. My brethren, do not merely say: Ah yes, there are many hardened sinners, many who go on the broad road of perdition. This would be an idle, useless reflection; on the contrary, give heed to my admonitions. The Son of God speaks to each one of you individually: Of what use will my blood be to you, if you rise not from your sin, if you delay your conversion from day to day, from year to year, if you do not avoid the occasions of sin? At the sight of your obdurate heart, the Lord must exclaim: "I have labored for you in vain, in vain have I exhausted my strength." I wished to cleanse and purify you, I wished to save your soul, but you resisted my grace and inspirations. O, all ye who call yourselves disciples of Jesus, if the benefits of God seem to you too insignificant, if the omnipotence of God has for you no power to arouse you from the sleep of sin, if heaven appears to you too insignificant a prize to contend for, and hell wears so fair an aspect that you choose the pathway which leads to its gates, if the curse of God on sin can not move you to renounce it, and if nothing else is able to touch and move you, Oh! I beseech you, let your hearts be softened by the blood of the Son of God. Through love for the blood which Christ shed abandon sin; for love of that precious blood, give up your evil habits, that your merciful Redeemer may not be compelled to say: Woe! woe! for you, also, I have shed my blood in vain, in vain have I labored, in vain have I exhausted my strength.

3. An angel descended from heaven to console Jesus in his agony. He was comforted and strengthened by the heavenly spirit, but his sorrow was not thereby diminished, but rather increased. What astonishment must have seized the angel of the Lord, on beholding the Son of God in such an agony approaching even to death, his whole body bathed in a bloody sweat. When holy Job, stricken by the hand of the Lord, and sitting on a dunghill, broke out into bitter complaints because of his pains and misfortunes,

his friends came to comfort him; but when they saw him, covering their faces, they dared not address the sufferer, but mourned with him for seven days and seven nights. Why should not the angel grow dumb, seeing the Son of God in agony, covered with blood, and lying on the ground? The prophet Jeremiah wept when he saw the women of Jerusalem pale with hunger, but what should the angel say to the Son of God, whose face he saw covered with blood? When Jacob saw the bloody, stained coat of Joseph, full of grief and sadness, he exclaimed: "This is my son's coat, grief will kill me, and I will go down into the grave." The angel came to comfort Jesus, a creature to comfort the Creator! With what comfort could he strengthen and console the anguish of the Sacred Heart? Pious souls, who have made the Passion of Christ their study, suppose the angel to have said: "O divine Redeemer of the world, I adore thee as my Lord and God. Thy heavenly Father wishes to see all the types and figures of the Old Law fulfilled on the day before Easter. This day *the Church* shall be formed of the tree of life of the New Testament, on the cross, out of thy opened side, as under the tree of paradise the *mother of all the living* was formed out of Adam's side. As innocent Abel was slain by his brother Cain *out in the field*, so thou shalt be slaughtered by the Jewish people, thy brethren, and chosen nation, *outside of Jerusalem;* like the patriarch Isaac, thou shalt be loaded with the *wood of the Cross*, be led to Mount Moria and offered to thy Father as a victim; thou shalt be sold, like Joseph, and like a highway robber be declared guilty of death. As water came forth from the *rock* which *Moses* struck with his rod, so *water and blood* will issue from thy opened side, with the blood thou shalt redeem mankind, and with the water cleanse them from every stain; thou wilt be exalted on the cross like the *brazen serpent* of Moses, and thou wilt restore to all who have been bitten by the serpent life and health, if they look up to thee. Like Samson, thou wilt lose thy life, but dying, thou wilt conquer more enemies than during thy life. Like David, thou wilt wound unto death the *giant* on his forehead, and at the same time *deliver mankind* from the power of *its greatest enemy*. Thou shalt raise *thy cross* as formerly thou didst set thy *rainbow*, as a sign of reconciliation and peace between heaven and earth, and, like the dove of Noe, bring to the true ark of the Church, that olive branch which loudly proclaims that there is peace, a holy, happy, heavenly, and eternal peace, established between God and man, between the Father and his children. Such is the will of thy heavenly Father. O Redeemer of mankind, the heavenly spirits long for this hour of fulfillment, the fathers in Limbo sigh for it, the whole world awaits it with an impatient desire, for it yearns to be released from the slavery of Satan and sin. Go, therefore, whither *thy love leads* thee, whither *thy Father calls* thee, whither the *salvation of the world invites* thee, *accept the chalice*, the *sentence is irrevocable*, the *means painful*, the *end glorious*, the *price*, *thy blood*, the *recompense*, the *redemption of mankind*, and *thy eternal victory.* Thou must die on the cross, but dying thou wilt give life. Accept, then, the chalice which thy Father offers thee; it is expedient that thou drink it, for thereby thou reconcilest thy Father, redeemest the world, and sweetenest all the bitterness of this life." To this Jesus answered: "O Eternal Father, not my will, but thine be done. I am ready to do thy holy will, to drink the chalice; I am ready to die, that thy children may live."

PERORATION.

And he rises to enter on the bloody way of his Passion, to tread the way of the cross, to consummate the sacrifice. What sacrifice? The sacrifice for the sins of the world. Oh! turn your eyes once more upon the Victim, and learn what sin is; learn the infinite love of your Redeemer, who, to snatch you from hell's fearful torments, paid for your sins the price of his blood; learn, and strive to fathom the incomprehensible hardness of man, who, after all these sufferings, can yet offend so good and merciful a God. Penetrated with a lively faith, and full of sorrow and contrition for your past sins, with a resolution not to sin any more, cast yourselves at his feet and pray: Lord Jesus, Son of God, "have mercy on us, according to thy great mercy, and according to the multitude of thy tender mercies, blot out my iniquities." Amen.

HOMILY III.

JUDAS IN THE GARDEN, THE APPREHENSION OF CHRIST, ANNAS, THE BLOW, CAIPHAS.

"O all ye that pass by the way, attend and see if there be any sorrow like to my sorrow; for he hath made a vintage of me, as the Lord spoke in the day of his fierce anger."—Lam. I: 12.

1. The angel of light who descended to comfort Jesus in his agony had scarce returned to heaven, when the angel of darkness came to perform the mission of darkness. Judas, one of the twelve, who sold his Master now shows the way to those whom the Scribes and Pharisees had sent to apprehend Christ; he had promised to give them a sign, namely, to kiss the victim of his treason. "Whomsoever I shall kiss, that is the man." What must have been the feelings of our Lord, when he saw his disciple lead on

his implacable foes. What excessive sorrow must have filled his soul, when one of his chosen ones, one of those whom he loved, whom he had made bishops of his Church, and princes of his kingdom, when one of these sold him for the paltry sum of thirty pieces of silver, about eighteen dollars of our money. What pain must have pierced the heart of our Saviour when he saw his apostle fall into such a terrible abyss. Truly, this was a new sorrow for his soul. The earth had been bedewed with his bloody sweat, and heaven was witness that the Son of God, of his own free will, had resolved to drink the bitter chalice which the world had prepared and his Father offered him. He was bound and dragged to death by a troop of ruffians, as if he would fain have escaped. To prove that he was dying voluntarily, and out of love for us, he had foretold his Passion and death, and now he flees not before his enemies, but approaches them with courage, dignity, and majesty, first of all addressing Judas: "Friend, whereto art thou come."—Matt. 26: 50. As if he would say, was it necessary to come in such a manner, with such instruments, with robes, swords, and clubs. All this is needless, for I am willing to die. No other cords could be so strong as those by which I am already bound, the cords of love. Judas, approaching the Lord, saluted him: "Hail, Master," and kissed him. The Lord replied: "Friend, why art thou come hither? Judas, why dost thou betray the Son of Man with a kiss?" O, the mild, meek Jesus rejects not that wolf in sheep's clothing, that hypocrite who approaches him with a kiss, but offers his lips whereon truth sits enthroned to those of Judas, overflowing with venom and hate. But even this is an effect of his love and mercy. He would exhaust all means to soften that hardened heart. "Friend, why art thou come hither? Judas, why dost thou betray the Son of Man with a kiss?" Who can behold Jesus, without sympathy and admiration? He, the omniscient God, penetrates with his all-piercing eye to the deepest recesses of that wicked, godless heart, and yet he calls him *friend*. He is the holy, spotless Lamb of God, to whom the sight of iniquity is abhorrent, yet he refrains from addressing that black heart with well-merited words of reproach. He threatens him not with his anger; he hurls not at him the destroying thunderbolt of his justice, no, for this day is not *a day of justice and wrath, but of mercy and love;* for this reason he asks him: "Friend, why art thou come hither?" As if he would say: Judas, my friend, behold, how unjustly you act in making yourself the instrument of so heinous a crime? Have you forgotten my friendship, my love, and the benefits I lavished upon you? Have you forgotten that I am the Son of God? Judas, dost thou betray the Son of Man with a kiss? What cruelty to betray the Son of Man with that sacred sign of friendship and love.

But alas! the Lord bestows the priceless gift of his love, in vain, and all vainly does he strive to win him by the sweet name of friend. In vain he reminds him of his sin, in vain he calls him familiarly by his own name, Judas; Satan has already taken possession of his soul, the prince of darkness dwells in his heart and clutches it so tightly in his terrible grasp, that the gracious voice of mercy and love cannot pierce the coat of mail that surrounds it. St. Chrysostom says: The Lord called Judas by his name because he mourned over him and wished not to punish him, but to recall him from his evil way, for he did not say: Why dost thou betray thy Lord and Master, the God? but, why dost thou betray the Son of Man, namely, him who is meek and humble of heart, him who did not deserve to be betrayed were he even not your Lord and God. You betray the Son of Man who for the salvation of men and your own, descended from heaven upon earth. O Judas, if you come as my enemy, why do you salute me? why do you kiss me? and if you come as my friend, why do you betray me?

Judas was the first that touched the blood of Jesus Christ; the precious drops which trickled down his face, were not yet dried when Judas, with his sacrilegious lips, kissed him. But even the blood of Christ failed to bring one throb of pity to that sinner's heart. Oh! when the demons of hell gain the mastery over a heart, its hardness becomes fearful, and the blindness in which the wretched soul gropes does not admit one ray of light. Judas is a terrible example in this regard. He forgot the love and benefits of his Master, the sinner too casts off all sense of gratitude for the love and benefits of God. Judas forgot the holy doctrines and the glorious miracles of his Master, the sinner closes his ears to the word of God. Judas forgot his dignity, vocation and election, and where is the sinner who remembers his dignity, as one whom God has received into the number of his friends, as one whose soul is destined for salvation, for a happy eternity. Ah! when the prince of darkness has made of a man's heart his dwelling place he becomes another Judas, a betrayer of his God and Redeemer, a betrayer of the sacred blood of Jesus, of his own soul and salvation. The more grace is offered the less he perceives it, the nearer Christ is to him, the greater stranger is his Saviour to him. Behold in Judas the blindness of the sinner! To commit a mortal sin is to betray God. Friend, why art thou come hither? is the question which Christ asks Judas, and which he asks every one of us. Behold, Christian, you are his friend, he has imprinted on your soul the seal of his friendship, in the Sacrament of Baptism, he has received you into the number of his elect, he has destined you to participate in his happiness, he has enriched you with his graces and nourished you with the heavenly manna, behold, the benefits with which God has enriched you! and he asks you: Friend, why art thou come hither? Have you come to commit sin? Will you betray your soul? Will you cast off my sweet yoke and once more range yourself under the banner of Satan? O Christians, answer these questions, and rejoice if you can say: Lord, I have never deserted thy standard, never betrayed thee, and I shall never betray thee. But if you cannot say this, fall, at least, on your knees with the penitent prayer: "Many times have I deserted thee and betrayed thee to sin, but O Lord, I return to thee, I bewail my sins, my infidelity, my treason from the very depths of my heart, and I firmly promise, with thy holy grace, never more to desert and betray thee."

2. After the treacherous kiss had accomplished the base purpose, Jesus, the betrayed victim of Judas, moved towards the troop of soldiers, to show that he was delivering himself voluntarily and that nothing on earth could have power over him if he did not so will it. He asked the soldiers: "Whom seek ye?" They answered: "Jesus of Nazareth." He said: "I am he," and immediately "they went backward and fell to the ground."—John 18 : 6. The Lord said : "I am he," and his word strikes the wicked crowd to the ground. Jesus had, as it were, only breathed upon them, and the breath of his Divinity would have blasted them had he not immediately concealed it. O! terrible will that day surely be when he shall come in the full splendor of his power and majesty *to judge*, when he thus manifests his power, when he goes to *be judged!* What will he do when *reigning in heaven*, when he does such things when about *to die on earth?* With what weapon does the Lord strike his enemies? With his word only; he speaks and the mountains tremble. What power is there in these little words: *I am he*. A vast army of "strong men armed" has less strength. Gaze upon the majestic countenance of the speaker and learn the power of these words, *I am he*. I am he whose garment is omnipotence, I am he who is eternal, who has neither beginning nor end, the only-begotten of the Father, and equal to him. I am he, your Lord and your God. "I am who I am." Omnipotence speaks, dust trembles; the Creator speaks, the creature recoils; God speaks, his enemies are confounded.

What will he do when he shall come to judge, when he does such things when he goes to be judged? Let us be candid and sincere. Let us reason like men of common sense. Either there is an eternity, or we have been constantly deceived or deluded. If there is an eternity, there is a God, and if there is a God, there will be a retribution. But if there is no eternity, no God, no retribution, then preaching should be cast aside as a folly, then truth finds no place in our hearts, We may leave the Church, we need no longer confine ourselves within such narrow limits to participate in all possible pleasures, every moment that is not enjoyed is an irreparable loss, for the hours to the grave are whirling on with incredible speed. We live only once, and after this life we shall be as if we had not been. But if there is an eternity, a God, and a retribution, what will take place when the Almighty with fire in his eyes and anger in his countenance shall say to his enemies : *I am he*. Impiety in our days treads the way of darkness, uses the weapons of darkness, and the arrows of sin, in order to extinguish the light of faith upon earth, but what will take place when the Lord shall rise in judgment and say : I am the Lord, your God? He will send all those who love darkness to hell. What way do you walk? Whom do you seek? Is it Jesus of Nazareth, and him alone? If so, why do you stand on the side of his enemies? Hear what Christ says : *I am the Lord, your God*, why do you persecute me? I am your *Lawgiver*, why do you rebel against me? I am your *Creator, Benefactor*, and *Redeemer*, why are you my enemy, for "he that is not with me is against me, and he that gathereth not with me scattereth." If you wish to be a friend and disciple of Christ, come forth from the enemies' camp, return from your evil ways, for woe, eternal woe, when he shall say to his enemies on the day of judgment : I am he. They shall fall to the ground, never to rise again!

When the terrible effects of their fright had partially passed away Jesus asked them again : "Whom seek ye," and having received the same answer, he said to them : "If you seek me, let these go their way." By these words, he saved the life and liberty of his disciples. Then he said : "You are come out as against a robber with swords and clubs to apprehend me. I sat daily with you teaching in the temple : and you laid not hands on me."—Matt. 26 : 55. Then he delivered himself into their hands : "They took Jesus, and bound him."—John 18 : 12. He makes no resistance, he says no more : I am he ; he keeps silence and patiently endures all as if all strength had left him like Samson when Delila had cut his hair and cried out : Samson, the Philistines are upon thee. The work of darkness is accomplished, the victim is bound, and his captors are guarding him well. Judas, thou fallen apostle, betrayer of thy Lord and God, behold, he stands before thee like a criminal. Judas, thou hast given the advice to apprehend him, to bind him, and to conduct him safely, behold the culmination of thy diabolical malice. Judas, rejoice at thy success, rejoice at thy treason, count thy money, the price of blood, the noble captive is well worth thirty pieces of silver. But let us leave that child of perdition to his master, the devil, at whose instigation he committed that wicked deed, for "the devil gave it into his heart to betray Jesus."

3. **The Son of God is brought into the city handcuffed.** Oh, how the faces of his enemies must have been irradiated with sinister joy. Oh what must have been his sufferings on this painful journey, when, like a highwayman, he was conducted through the principal streets of Jerusalem! They stopped at the house of Annas who had been high-priest the year before. He asked Jesus of his doctrines and disciples, but our divine Lord made no answer concerning his disciples for they had fled. In re-

gard to his doctrines, he said: "I have spoken openly to the world: I have always taught in the synagogue, and in the temple, whither all the Jews resort, and in private I have spoken nothing. Why askest thou me? Ask them who have heard what I have spoken to them; behold, they know what things I have said."—John 18 : 20. And one of the soldiers standing by gave Jesus a blow, saying: "Answerest thou thou the high-priest so?" I tremble with indignation when I consider that the Creator receives a blow from his creature. No more scathing insult can be offered to a respectable man than to strike him in the face, and one thus offended will resent the insult with the sword, his blood, and his life. We can scarcely conceive then the extent of the insult here offered to Jesus. Should a subject treat his sovereign in such a manner, he would pay the penalty with his life. What then is due him who strikes the King of kings in the face? Jeremiah exclaims: Be astonished, O ye heavens, for the majesty of your God is violated, innocence is struck in the face. Oh! my Redeemer, why do you suffer this ignominy? Why does not that arm wither which raises itself against you, and dares to strike your holy face? Oh the incomprehensible magnanimity of Christ has no other chastisement for this cruel treatment than the question of love: "Why strikest thou me?"

As page after page of the history of the Passion opens before us, we do not find that any complaint ever issued from our persecuted Lord. He was scourged and he complained not; the thorns wounded his head and he said nothing; the nails perforated his hands and feet and he kept silence; but when he received that blow he remonstrated, saying: "Why do you strike me?" And why did he complain on this occasion? Because in this blow was contained an infinity of malice. Which must astonish us more, the wickedness of the soldier, or the love of Jesus? I believe he asked not in vain: Why strikest thou me? His motive was to confound and move the wretch to repentance, as well as to confound and move to repentance those who, like that wicked soldier, strike their Redeemer in the face. Yes, Christ is struck in the face by every Christian who commits a grievous sin. Oh Christians, hear the Son of God complain: Son, daughter, behold, I teach daily from the pulpits, that you should lead a Christian life, that you should not love the world and the things of the world, that you should mortify your flesh, resist your inordinate desires; and you obey me not, but by your sinful passions and inclinations, you strike me in the face and reject my holy doctrines. Behold, I teach: he that wishes to be my disciple let him deny himself, take up his cross and follow me, but you say: "Come let us enjoy the things that are present."—Wisd. 2 : 6. O. Christian, answerest thou the high-priest so? Behold, I teach openly to the world: "Blessed are the clean of heart for they shall see God," but you say: Life is fleeting, time is short, man must enjoy of it as much as he can. Answerest thou the high-priest so? Behold I teach openly to the world: "Unless you do penance, you shall all likewise perish." But you say: "Let us crown ourselves with roses before they are withered, let none of us go without his part in luxury, let us everywhere leave tokens of joy, for this is our portion, this is *our lot.*"—Wisd. 2:8, 9. Answerest thou the high-priest so? You hear my voice, you know my doctrine, but you raise your hand against me, like that cruel soldier. Why do you strike me? What evil have I done to you? Have I offended you? Behold, I have sacrificed my life for you, I have created you for an eternity of bliss, I have sought you during my whole life upon earth, I have redeemed you with my blood and opened for you the portals of heaven, What evil have I done? If I have done no evil, why do you strike me? We are justly enraged at the cruelty of this wicked soldier who struck the Redeemer in the face, but let us rather turn our indignation against ourselves who strike Jesus in the face by our sins.

4. When Annas had derided Jesus to the full extent of his malicious will and found no fault in him, he sent him to Caiphas, his son-in-law, who was high-priest that year. The Saviour was led into the inner court. Here the high-priest was sitting on a throne surrounded by the ancients of the people, the Scribes and Pharisees. Jesus stands handcuffed before him. Witnesses are brought in to bear testimony against him. They say: "He cast out devils by Beelzebub, the prince of devils, he violated the Sabbath, he broke the fast, he does not allow his disciples to wash their hands before meals, he calls the Pharisees wolves in sheep's clothing, associates with sinners and publicans, introduces a new doctrine, says that his flesh is meat and his blood drink, that no one, unless he eat his flesh, and drink his blood, shall be saved, he asserts that he is older than Abraham, and that he is one with the Father." But the witnesses contradicted one another and even their malice could allege nothing that could doom him to death. And last of all there came in two false witnesses and they said: This man said: I am able to destroy the temple of God, and in three days to rebuild it. And the high-priest rising up, said to him: Answerest thou nothing to the things which these witness against thee? Jesus held his peace.—Matt. 26. It is a natural right to defend one's self. Why does he not assert and prove his innocence? He needs no defense, the witnesses have contradicted one another. Full of indignation the high-priest rises from his seat, the witnesses move back, the eyes of all are turned upon him, profound silence reigns throughout the hall. All are in suspense and expectation. And Caiphas, vested in his high-priestly vestments, raises his right hand to heaven, and says with a loud voice: "I adjure thee by the living God, that thou tell us if thou be the Christ, the Son of God." That is, I the high-priest, am the voice of God on earth. By virtue of this office

with which I am invested by God, whom I call to witness what you say, I command and adjure you, that you tell us if you be the Christ, the Son of God. Jesus answered: "Thou hast said it. Nevertheless I say to you: Hereafter you shall see the Son of Man sitting on the right hand of the power of God, and coming in the clouds of heaven." The high-priest rent his garments, saying: He has blasphemed; what further need have we of witnesses? The trial is over, the crime proved, what think you, what is your opinion, O ancients of Israel. And they answering, said: "He is guilty of death." Oh heavenly Father, Eternal God, thou hast been called as witness, and hast confirmed the truth that Jesus Christ is truly thy Son. Hear it, Caiphas, the living God bears testimony against you, he declares to you from Mount Thabor: "This is my beloved Son, in whom I am well pleased." Lazarus, the son of the widow, and the daughter of the Ruler, bear testimony against you. He made the blind see, the deaf hear, the lame walk—all bear testimony against you. Wicked judge, the wind and storm, land and sea, men and beasts, heaven and earth, Angels and devils, rise up in testimony against you. Call these as witnesses, and with a unanimous voice they will proclaim his Divinity and say: Jesus of Nazareth is truly the Son of God. O! wretched judge, you have blasphemed and not Christ, you are guilty of death not Christ, because you have sinned against the Son of the Most High God and against the Holy Ghost.

PERORATION.

Oh adorable Jesus, we confess and are ready to seal our confession with our blood, that thou art Christ, the Son of the living God. What ignominy, what disgrace for the Son of God to appear before judges who are at the same time his accusers, who, contrary to law and justice say: He is guilty of death! What is his crime? Why must he die? Ah, it is the judgment of the Father. Christ must suffer death that sinners may live. It is for our sins that Jesus dies. Ah, cry out from the inmost recesses of your heart, with sorrow and contrition for your sins, Oh Jesus, Lord and Saviour, thou art innocent, thou shalt not die, but live, sin shall die in us, yes, grace shall destroy sin in our hearts, that Jesus may live and reign therein now and for ever. Amen.

HOMILY IV.

THE INTERIOR SUFFERINGS OF CHRIST, THE DENIAL OF PETER, PILATE, THE DESPAIR OF JUDAS, HEROD, BARABBAS.

"O, all ye that pass by the way, attend and see if there be any sorrow like to my sorrow; for he hath made a vintage of me, as the Lord spoke in the day of his fierce anger."—Lam. I : 12.

1. The high-priest and the judges had retired to rest that they might finish their cruel work on the following morning. Christ remained in the hands of the soldiers. The Evangelists do not tell us all he suffered during that terrible night, they mention only a few incidents : *they spat in his face and buffeted him ; others struck his face with the palms of their hands, saying:* "*Prophesy unto us, O Christ, who is it that struck thee?*" Of what value our souls must be in the sight of God, who, to save them endured such disgrace! Where is our gratitude, where our love toward our suffering Redeemer? Nothing wounded our Lord more deeply than the denial of Peter. Peter had solemnly promised and sworn : "Though I should die with thee, I will not deny thee." When Christ was apprehended in the garden, his disciples all fled ; Peter alone followed, but from afar. Oh, that he had fled with the rest, then surely he would have been saved from his terrible fall. While he stood with the soldiers at the fire, a servant said to him : "Art thou not also one of this man's disciples." And he answered: I am not. O Peter, are you ashamed of your Lord? Are you afraid to profess Jesus before a menial ? What is this? You tremble before a servant, at the question of a maid you deny that you are a disciple of Christ? Have you not left all to follow him? Have you not confessed him to be the Son of the living God? Have you not said : "Lord, I shall never leave thee, for to whom shall we go, thou alone hast the words of eternal life. And now, chosen disciple, Prince of the Apostles, you shrink from confessing your Lord and Master before a menial? you tell a lie, saying : "I am not," Perhaps that servant addressed him too harshly? By no means. She said not : art thou not also a disciple of that blasphemous teacher, but said : "*of this man,*" as if she were commiserating him. She speaks of Christ not with bitterness and contempt, but with a feeling of compassion, as if she would say : Ah, how much does this man, whom they call Christ, suffer, how they abuse and maltreat him ! Art thou not

also one of his disciples? She says: Art thou *not also one*, because St. John, whom she knew to be one of his disciples, and at whose request she admitted Peter was close by. Art thou not also one of this man's disciples, as St. John is? Peter tells a lie the second time to another servant, and a third time before soldiers, who asked him the same question. These successive questions so intensified his confusion that cursing and swearing he says: I know not this man, I know not what you say.

These curses, lies and imprecations fell upon the ear of Christ who turned his eyes towards his faithless apostle. Their glance said: Peter, where is the promise you made in so solemn a manner at the last supper. I have made you the rock, the foundation of my Church. You hold from me the keys of my kingdom, I have made you my vicar on earth, and behold, you are ashamed of me, you deny me. You say that you do not know me? How will you profess my name before the princes of the earth, when you deny me before a menial, when before soldiers you affirm upon an oath: "I know not the man." Christians permit me to ask you *one* question: *Are you not also one of this man's disciples?* I am sure you will not say with Peter: "I am not," for by Baptism you have been made one of their number. But tell me, why do you forget the covenant which you have made with your Redeemer? You have solemnly promised to renounce the devil and all his works and pomps, but listen to the voice of conscience which reminds you of your sins and reproaches you with your infidelity. Do you realize what you have done? You have said with Peter: I know not the man. *Are you not also one of this man's disciples?* Yes, but tell me, why do you heed the voice of the tempter and stifle the admonitions of your conscience? Behold, you say with Peter: "I know not the man." *Are you not also one of this man's disciples?* Yes, but why do you forget the love of your Redeemer, who became man for you, who prayed, suffered, and died for your salvation? Why do you seek your chief joy in creatures, and not in the Creator? How is it possible that, believing what you believe, you can forget the love of Jesus and afflict his heart by sin? Each one of your sins cries out with Peter: "I know not the man." Not to know him is not to know your *friend*, not to know your *benefactor*, not to know your *Lord and God*. Oh, let us renew our promise, let us again renounce the devil with all his works and pomps, let us say to them: Begone, Satan, and let our constant and universal practice be to confess by word and deed, that we know this man, Christ Jesus.

The cock crows, the Lord turns round and looks at Peter, over whom rushes the memory of what his Master had said: "Amen, I say to thee, that in this night before the cock crow, thou wilt deny me thrice." And going out he wept bitterly. Let this prompt repentance of Peter teach us to bewail our sins. Peter sinned, but out of weakness and by surprise; he did not persevere in sin, but speedily returned to the way of salvation, he fled from the place which had alas! proved so fatal, left the wicked company into which he had come, and hastened where, apart from the crowd, he could give full vent to his grief and remorse, to wash away his sins by tears of love, and going out he wept bitterly. Behold, O Christian, your soul is perhaps for years, yes even from the time of childhood, defiled by sin, sin has become to you a second nature, it may be that the day does not dawn upon which you do not deny your Lord and God. But where is your repentance? Where is your flight from sinful company and the proximate occasions of sin? Where is your sorrow? Where are your tears? Alas, you scarcely understand and feel what sin really means, you act as if it were nothing, you continue to associate with your companions of sin, to frequent the place of your fall, and you go so far as to commit new sins instead of bewailing those of your past life. O unfortunate sinner, what will become of you? Peter received pardon, because he wept bitter tears of repentance, how can you expect forgiveness when you will not shed one penitential tear? Your state is truly deplorable.

2. The sun had scarce begun to gild the eastern hills, when the members of the council reassembled and summoning their Divine Victim asked him, if he were Christ the Son of God. Receiving the same answer the same sentence is pronounced: "He is guilty of death." Then he is conducted to Pontius Pilate, the Roman Governor of Judea, that he might ratify the sentence of death, in order that Jesus might be executed. Pilate begins the trial by asking the accusers: "What accusation bring you against this man?" They answer: "If he were not a malefactor we would not have delivered him up to thee." As judge, Pilate could pronounce no sentence upon this general accusation, he desired to be informed as to what crime Christ had committed. As the Jews had violated truth before the spiritual court of Caiphas, so they repeat their false testimony at the temporal court of Pilate. Knowing well, however, that before this tribunal accusations concerning religion would avail nothing, they cunningly devised something new, Pilate was a pagan and cared little for religion, therefore they changed their accusation and made Christ a political culprit, a demagogue, a rebel, saying: "We have found this man perverting our nation and forbidding to give tribute Cæsar and saying that he is Christ the king." Pilate was astonished that to all these accusations, Christ answered not a word and did not defend himself. Christians, behold what contumelies are uttered against your Saviour, but with divine patience he suffers it all. Jesus, to whom the highest honor is due in heaven and on earth, endures all for your sake, and you who deserve all for your sins, resent with anger the least appearance of neglect, your blood boils and you meditate revenge when others speak ill of you.

3. During the progress of the trial a new wound pierced the most sacred heart of our Lord. St. Matthew relates: Judas, who had betrayed him, *seeing* that he was condemned, repenting himself brought back the thirty pieces of silver to the chief-priests and ancients, saying: I have sinned in betraying innocent blood. The Evangelist says well: Then Judas seeing. Was he blind before? Not in body, but in spirit, like unto those of whom Sophonias says : "They who sin against the Lord walk like the blind." The eyes of Judas were opened and he saw his crime. When the devil lures man on to sin he darkens his vision, that, like one deprived of sight, he may not perceive the enormity of sin, but when he has yielded to the tempter he opens the sinner's eyes, that he may be overwhelmed with despair. This was the case with Judas; he despaired, went out, and hanged himself with a halter. When Christ at his last supper said : "One of you shall betray me," the Evangelist adds : "He was troubled in spirit," he was troubled in spirit not for his own sake, but for the near perdition of Judas. When David received the terrible news that his son Absalom, suspended by his hair on a tree, had been killed by three lances he was troubled and wept, and in the bitterness of his soul wandered about mourning and saying : "My son, Absalom, Absalom, my son, who would grant me, that I might die for thee." When he heard that Saul had taken his own life on Mount Gelboe, he wept bitterly and bewailed his death. But why did David weep over his criminal son Absalom whom the just punishment of God had overtaken? Why did he grieve for the suicide of Saul? He wept and mourned for both because they had died *in their sins.* How much greater must have been the grief of the Holy of Holies at the despair of Judas, for whose salvation he had done so much? Indeed, the wicked end of Judas grieved him more than all his other sufferings.

Let us pause for a moment beneath that tree on which Judas hangs, whilst we ask : who is it that hangs here dead by suicide? One of the twelve, one of the chosen ones. There is no security on earth, since Judas was lost in the school of Jesus Christ. Oh, that his sad fate might inspire us with a holy fear. Oh, that of us may never be uttered those awful words : one of them a traitor and damned. But shall we all be saved? shall none perish? will there not be a child of perdition among us? I know not, such knowledge is given to God alone. But thus far I know : if we do not do penance for our sins, if we do not abandon our sinful ways, if we persevere in lukewarmness and indifference, more than one out of twelve will perish.

4. Pilate, perceiving that the Jews had delivered Jesus up out of envy and that he was perfectly innocent, sent him to Herod who was a Galilean. Herod who had for a long time been desirous of seeing Jesus, eagerly availed himself of this first opportunity, for the story of his marvelous deeds

had reached his ears, and he hoped that now he would see some miracle wrought by him. Herod awarded him no higher rank than that of a strolling magician, and overwhelmed him with questions: Are you not the same who deceived my father when he ordered the children of Bethlehem to be slain? How did you succeed in evading his wrath? Are you not he of whom it is related that wise men from the East visited and laid rare offerings before you? Are you not he of whom John the Baptist spoke so much? Are you not he of whom it is related that he made the blind see, the lame walk, and raised Lazarus and the widow's son to life? If so, give some manifestation of your power, work some miracles, change water into wine, or stones into bread that I may see them. Suppose Jesus had performed miracles before the very eyes of Herod, would he have believed in him? No, Christ, therefore, remained silent, answering not a single question. This silence exasperated Herod, he and his soldiers despised and mocked our Saviour, and putting on him a white garment, sent him back, declaring him to be a fool!

Our divine Redeemer suffered himself to be treated by Herod as a fool, that he might confound the folly of men who for the love of earth, lose heaven. The white garment with which he was clothed, how many mysteries does it not contain! Adam had lost two garments in paradise, the garment of innocence which is white, and the garment of immortality which is purple. That both might be restored to man, the love of the heavenly Father wished that his beloved Son should assume the white garment in the court of Herod, and the purple garment in the tribunal of Pilate— pause a moment and reflect. Behold, Herod rejoiced when he saw Jesus, in whom he did not believe; and you offend him in whom you believe. You also have heard much of Christ and his holy doctrine, but have you imitated his holy example? With what eagerness do you not seek the pleasures of the world, with what carelessness do you not exchange the treasures of heavenly wisdom for the wretchedness of worldly wisdom. But my brethren, there is an hour in our life, when all illusion vanishes, when the world no longer dazzles, when gold no longer glitters, when the tempting cup no longer invites, when beauty and youth lose their charms, and this is the hour of our death. Then repentance or innocence will alone be of value, then that wisdom which the world rejects will be of worth. Therefore let us learn of our Redeemer to be fools among men, that in our dying hour we may be found truly wise in Christ.

5. Pilate was convinced that Christ was innocent, and that envy alone had instigated the Jews in their cruel persecution. A feeling of sympathy seizes him and he conceives the idea of setting him free. To accomplish his design he makes use of a means which was an ordinary custom among the Jews. It is your privilege, said he to the Jews, on the festival of the pasch

to liberate one prisoner. You know we have in prison the notorious Barabbas whose name alone spreads fear and terror throughout the land. Whom will you that I release unto you, Barabbas or Jesus who is called Christ? Pilate placed a malefactor, a murderer in the same category with Jesus, convinced that they would choose Jesus. He could not believe that even their malice would reach the height of preferring Barabbas to Jesus, but he was greatly mistaken, for in their rage and blindness, they would have set free all the malefactors of the world rather than Jesus. How painful must have been this comparison to the Lord? And indeed he was not only compared to a malefactor, but placed below him. My brethren, if it were painful to Christ to be ranked below Barabbas by the Jews, it must be more painful to him to be despised by those who pretend to be his disciples, to such a degree that they put him not only below Barabbas but below the very devil himself. There is a war between Christ and the devil. Each wishes to possess you. The devil is planning the ruin and damnation of your souls, for he goes about like a roaring lion seeking whom he may devour; Christ wishes to possess your souls, to save them for eternal life. Now, to whom do you wish to belong? To the devil or to Christ? I hear you say: We give ourselves to Christ, we will follow and serve him. But do you not prefer Barabbas to Jesus when you commit a mortal sin? As much as is in your power you wish the life of the creature and the death of your Saviour in your heart. Christ recommends to you humility, meekness, love, peace, and every virtue. Satan, on the contrary, suggests pride, anger, revenge, hatred, and every vice, and as often as you sin you cry with the Jews: Give us Barabbas. Which prevails? the spirit, or the flesh; concupiscence or reason; heaven or earth; Christ, or the devil. Examine your conscience and you will find that you frequently say: Give us Barabbas.

PERORATION.

Oh, bend your knees before that Jesus whom you have so often crucified by your sins, and cry out: It is I, Lord, who have despised thee, I am the miserable and ungrateful sinner who have listened to the suggestions of the devil, I have chosen to be his servant rather than a child of God. Merciful Redeemer, look down upon us with eyes of mercy, pardon our past offences. We choose thee for our leader and guide, thou shalt be our portion and inheritance for time and eternity. Amen.

HOMILY V.

THE SCOURGING, THE CROWNING WITH THORNS, AND THE DERISION.

"O all ye that pass by the way, attend and see if there be any sorrow like to my sorrow; for he hath made a vintage of me, as the Lord spoke in the day of his fierce anger."—Lam. 1 : 12.

Barabbas had been released at the request of the populace. Pilate had again and again loudly reiterated that Jesus was innocent of the crimes, alleged against him. He says again: "You have brought this man to me, as one that perverteth the people: and behold, I, having examined him before you, find no cause in this man touching those things wherein you accuse him; no, nor yet Herod," (Luke 23: 14, 15); yet the fury of the Jews gained the ascendency. Pilate lacked the determination requisite to refuse their unjust demands, and sentenced Christ to an ignominious punishment, as if he had really found him guilty. "Then, therefore, Pilate took Jesus and scourged him."—John 19: 1. "I will chastise him, therefore, and release him."—Luke 23: 16.

1. Scourging was a punishment which the ingenuity of the Romans had specially marked out for their slaves; it was, in fact, the most agonizing torture that could be inflicted upon a malefactor; and was almost equal to capital punishment, for many who were sentenced to be scourged, expired in the hands of the torturers. Perhaps our Saviour, whose innocence Pilate had solemnly declared, will protest against such an unjust and cruel punishment. Perhaps he will not recognize this unjust court but appeal to a higher tribunal, wherein he may find justice. To whom can he appeal? Is not Pilate the representative of the Roman emperor, the highest judiciary in the land? But Pilate, forgetful of the duties of a judge, bade them scourge him, of whose innocence he was convinced and in whom he could find no cause. Is Christ to appeal, as St. Paul did, from the governor to the Roman emperor himself in Rome? He has no right to do this not being a Roman citizen. Why does he not appeal to the highest spiritual court in the land, the high-priest? The high-priest, on the testimony of false witnesses, had already judged him guilty of death. Can he not appeal to his own people, who had been the recipients of his benefits, and who had been witnesses of his miracles and of his innocence? His own people had rejected him and set him aside for one whose soul was steeped in the blackest of guilt. Why does he not appeal

to his heavenly Father, the God of justice, who rewards the good and punishes the wicked. O ! surely he, at last, will gladly rise to protect his innocent Son and ward off the tortures decreed for him ? No, the Father bade him drain the bitter chalice to the dregs, his love and mercy for sinners had decreed that the body of his Son should be torn by scourges. Men eagerly hasten to protect the criminal, but Jesus finds none to take his part. Heaven and earth have forsaken him. What will he do ? With one effort of his omnipotence, will he not burst asunder the cords with which he is bound, like another Samson, and make of them a scourge to drive away his executioners, as he once banished from the temple the buyers and sellers, because they had made the house of prayer a den of thieves ? No, Jesus is the obedient Son of God, who does the will of the Father, saying : "Father, not my will, but thine, be done." And thus humbly and without a murmur he submits to the order of divine justice, saying with meek obedience : O my Father, I am ready to receive the scourge from whatever hand thou art pleased to ordain.

Scarce had the soldiers heard the command of Pilate, than with rude haste they tore the clothing from Jesus to begin the cruel scourging. Jacob, the patriarch, gave Joseph a coat of many colors, because he loved him, but his brothers, envying him, took his coat and sold him to the Ismaelites. It pained Joseph to see himself deprived of the coat, which he had received from his loving father, but what grief must it have caused the Son of God, to see himself stripped of his garments while the rabble gazed curiously at the sight. But his denudation contains a profound mystery of wisdom, love, and mercy of the Lord towards us sinners. True, the God of all justice and purity could have stricken those blasphemers with blindness, as he formerly did the licentious inhabitants of Sodom, who were given to uncleanness and were about to abuse the guests of Lot ; but our Saviour submitted to this confusion, because Adam had stripped himself and his posterity of the garment of innocence ; the Lord submitted to this confusion, because so many Christians strip themselves of the garment of grace and pass years, yes, too often their whole lives in this nakedness ; the Lord submitted to this confusion, because he wished to atone for those unspeakable sins of shamelessness by which his children lose the garment of innocence, Ah, how many could we address with these words of the Sacred Scripture : "Thou sayest : I am rich and made wealthy, and I have need of nothing, but thou knowest not that thou art wretched, and miserable, and poor, and naked, and blind," for your elegant apparel serves only to cover a soul and body that are stripped of all virtue. When Adam by sin had lost the garment of sanctity and justice, of innocence and grace, so intense was his confusion that he hid himself, and when God called him, he said : "I heard thy voice in paradise, and I was afraid, because I was naked," as if he would say: O, God of holiness and justice, my whole being trembles in thy presence, because I have lost that garment of sanctity and grace, which would make me worthy of appearing before thy eyes; I have become naked by sin. And yet Christians who have become adorned by him in Baptism with the garment of innocence are not ashamed to trail its whiteness through the mire of sin, and appear before the all-seeing eye of their divine Judge in the miserable nakedness of their souls. O, lift up your eyes to your Redeemer and be witnesses of his anguish when thus exposed naked to the gaze of a rude soldiery, and tell me: Are you still clothed with that precious garment with which his love clothed you, or have you cast it from you by sin. If you are naked, that is, in the state of sin, oh, clothe yourself, at least, with the garment of penance, bewail your misfortune and your sins, otherwise the eye of Jesus offended by your nakedness, will turn in anger away. If you cannot appear before the Lord in the garment of innocence, appear before him in the garment of penance lest you find not mercy but justice at his hands.

2. When God commanded Abraham to sacrifice his only son Isaac, he bound him, before he laid him on the altar. Isaac bound is a figure of Christ, who was bound not so much by the soldiers as by his Eternal Father, who not sparing his Son, but delivering him up for us, held, as it were, the hands of Jesus, that he might be tied to the pillar, for if the Father had not previously bound him, and if Jesus had not given his consent, neither Jews nor Gentiles nor the powers of darkness could have tied the Almighty Son of God to that pillar. There Christ said with the prophet: "I am ready for scourges," thy offended majesty, O Father, demands for the injuries, by which it was blasphemed, a corresponding atonement, thy justice demands a perfect satisfaction, behold, here I stand as a victim for all mankind, I assume the whole crushing burden of guilt, I will pay for it, let justice have its sway, O Father, I am ready for scourges.

Pilate ordered Christ to be scourged as if he had really found him guilty. With frantic haste rushed the guards, not one of their number stayed back —and the barbarous sentence was executed on him with the most merciless and unfeeling cruelty. His whole body becomes one wound, and the blood flows in torrents from all his members, whilst the frightful stripes he has received, so shockingly distort his divine countenance, that he appears as a leper and as a man stricken by God in the excess of his wrath. Truly, he has borne our infirmities, and has carried our sorrows. Behold, then, how your Saviour is stricken, contemplate his open wounds, see how his flesh is lacerated to the very bones, how the crimson tide of his blood causes the very earth to blush for the cruelty of man, see how he trembles and writhes under the tortures, consider all this, and read in his gaping wounds that boundless mercy which is ready to give even sinners a refuge therein. Read in his blood, the barbarous cruelty of sin for which it is shed, read in the sweet heart of your suffering Saviour, the fervor of a love, which did not hesitate to include all sinners, even the most guilty, in its embrace. To thoroughly convince you of the great magnitude and cruelty of sin, I will cease to direct your attention to the immensity, omnipotence, and greatness of God, I will not say : sin is a rebellion against the infinite majesty of God, I will remind you no more of our first parents who, laden with a curse, were driven out of paradise; I will no longer present for your consideration the deluge, by which the God of justice drowned a wicked generation, I will remind you no more of the sad fate of Sodom and Gomorrah whose sins called down a fire from heaven which consumed them, I will lead you no longer in spirit to the abyss of hell, to show you those Angels and men to whom God said : Depart from me, ye cursed, into everlasting fire ; no, no, I will lead you to the suffering Jesus at the pillar, show you the mangled, bleeding, dying Lamb of God and tell you: Behold, sinner, the work of sin, sin has done this! O sinners who in your blindness never reflect upon the crime which you commit, when, transgressing the law of your God, you throw yourself into the arms of sin, *behold your Redeemer in his blood!*

We find in the Sacred Scripture many examples of people who had to suffer much, but even the most unfortunate had some consolation in the midst of their sufferings. Job fell from the pinnacle of happiness into the deepest misery, and suffered the most excruciating pains in his whole body, so that, in the bitterness of his soul he exclaimed : he has torn me with wound upon wound ; but sympathizing friends came to console him. St. Paul and Silas his companion were scourged and cast into prison, but the keeper had compassion on them and dressed their wounds. That unfortunate man, who, in his way from Jerusalem to Jericho, fell among robbers, was robbed of all he had and left half-dead on the road, but a merciful Samaritan, coming the same way, was touched with pity for his sad state, bathed his wounds, poured wine and oil into them and carried him to an inn. The Son of God who, for us sinners, went from Jerusalem to Calvary, has also fallen among robbers, is stripped of his clothes, is wounded to his very bones and is at the point of death; but no friend approaches him to sympathize with him or to console him, no merciful Samaritan comes to dress his wounds; his executioners rage with diabolical malice and cruelty against the divine Victim. Yet, one of them was moved by the cruelty of the tortures, to cut the cords with which he was tied to the pillar, who cried out to the rest : Will you kill him who is not condemned to death? The cords are cut, the victim can no longer stand on his feet, his strength is exhausted, he faints, falls, and lies in his blood. Yet those monsters cease not to maltreat him, they strike him with their scourges, and kick him with their sacrilegious feet. Then it was that the Son of God prayed in these words: "Have mercy on them, O God, for man hath trodden me under foot; my enemies have trodden on me all day long; for they are many who make war against me."—Ps. 55:2, 3. O all ye that pass by the way, attend and see if there be any sorrow like to my sorrow. The Father in heaven hears him not, for he hath made a vintage of him, as he spoke in the day of his fierce anger; he hears him not, for he punishes in him the sins of the whole world, which are laid upon him.

Mourn, O ye heavens, and divest yourselves of your beauty and glory, for he is without beauty and form, who called you out of nothing; behold the Lamb of God in his blood. Mourn, oh earth, crumble into nothingness beneath the curse laid upon thee, for thou hast drunk in the blood of thy God. Mourn, O ye Angels, and cover your faces with your wings; at the birth of Jesus you chanted canticles of joy and announced to the world the happy tidings of the Saviour's birth; O come now, and weep bitter tears of sorrow, for the world has wounded the Saviour and bathed him in his blood. O sinners, come, also, and gaze on your Saviour prostrate on the ground bathed in his sacred blood. Does not this sight move you? do not these wounds soften your callous, stony hearts? does not the cry of his blood pierce your soul? Hear what Isaiah says to you: "He has been wounded for our sins." Behold, the unjust have sinned and the just one is punished; the guilty have erred and the guiltless is stricken, the good man endures what the sinner has deserved, and God expiates the sins which man has committed, God is scourged that he might save us from the scourges of hell, behold your suffering Redeemer, and recognize his ineffable love towards you, consider the greatness and cruelty of sin and the inestimable value of your soul. If you are Christians in reality and not so only in name, if you believe that the Son of God submitted to such intense tortures, *all for you*, that he accepted this barbarous treatment to pay your debt; if you believe all this why do you not cast yourselves at his feet, ask forgiveness for your sins, and offer him a heart full of love and gratitude, cying out: O Jesus, eternal love, I love thee above all things.

When the patriarch Jacob saw the coat of his beloved son saturated with blood, he rent his garments, girded himself with a rope, bewailing the fate of his son and sighing continually: "A wild beast has devoured him."—Gen. 37. But you, sinners, seeing not only man but the Son of God without a garment, covered with wounds and lying at the foot of the pillar in his blood, rend the garment of sin, and cry with Jacob: A wild beast, sin, has lacerated my Saviour. When the high-priest Mathathias beheld the temple of God demolished by the enemy he wept and moaned, saying: Behold our sanctuary, our beauty and glory is laid waste, and the Gentiles have defiled it; to what end then should we live any longer? But you, sinners, seeing not only the Sanctuary of our Lord, but the Holy of Holies in his blood, can you turn away your eyes and say: Let the blood flow from my Saviour if I only can live in the full gratification of my passions. Will you have the temerity to inflict new wounds on Jesus by your sins? No, I do not think you capable of this, your hearts are not of adamant, they are human, they feel the infinite love of Jesus, and pierced with sorrow and grief, they must cry out: O amiable Jesus, have mercy on us.

3. Pilate intended to scourge Christ and then release him. But his enemies thirst, like wild beasts, for more blood, and meditate new tortures. "Platting a crown of thorns, they put it upon his head."—John 19 : 2. This was a new punishment, a new device of those monsters, of which no tyrant had ever made use. Behold your Saviour, lying on the earth, bathed in his blood, and crowned with thorns. Now are fulfilled the words of the prophet: "From the crown of the head to the sole of the foot there is no sound part in him," the blood gushed forth from his ears, nose and eyes, that he might shed blood of tears for our sins. But that you may the more thoroughly comprehend the love of God in the crowning with thorns, meditate on the words of the Apostle: "What man sows he shall also reap." This is the rule, but it was far otherwise with our dear Lord; he has sown wheat, but his harvest is thorns. He has strewn the good seed of the doctrine of his heavenly Father, he has strengthened the hearts of his hearers with truth and enlightened them with wisdom everywhere; he has scattered benefits, and yet from his labors he reaps but thorns, What have we sown? What do men sow? Sin, murder, impurity, fornication, adultery, incest, sacrilege, theft, robbery, usury, oppression of the orphans, the widows, and the poor. pride, envy, revenge, hatred, wickedness, and iniquity of every description. This is what men sow, and the fruit thereof they must reap, namely: sorrow, for he that sows sorrow shall reap sorrow. The thorns of sorrow are justly our due, and we richly merit their sharpest sting, yet our merciful Redeemer wished to reap our thorns and save us therefrom. He wished to be crowned with thorns that we might be crowned with glory.

After they had, with cruel force, pressed down his painful diadem the torturers arrayed him in a purple cloak, put a reed in his right hand, and bending their knees, said: "Hail, King of the Jews." They struck his head with the reed, dared even to spit upon him, and as though the scourging were not enough they still give him blows. What royal insignia? crown, sceptre, purple, what sublime homage, Hail King, but also what contumely for the King of kings! They clothe him in purple, not to do him honor, but to make him an object of scorn. In heaven the Seraphim tremble before him and adore him, the ancients prostrate themselves and lay their crowns at his feet, acknowledging him King of eternity, and here, by way of derision, he is called king, as if he had usurped the title, and yet in heaven he is adored King of Kings and Lord of Hosts.

Job, that admirable model of patience, endured all losses and afflictions without a murmur or complaint, but when his acquaintances came and ridiculed him, he complained, saying: "Now they, younger in time, scorn me."—Job. 30: 1. Samson bore hard labor and the plucking out of his eyes with fortitude, but when the Philistines mocked him he tore up the pillars of the house, preferring to be buried alive, than to be scoffed at and derided. David said, if an enemy had done this I would verily have borne with it, but thou, my friend and my companion. Saul, having lost a battle, said to his armor-bearer: "Draw thy sword and kill me, lest these uncircumcised come and slay and mock me." Yet Jesus was silent and did not open his mouth, although he was overwhelmed with contumely and derision.

PERORATION.

Dear Christians, you also acknowledge the Son of God as your King and your Lord, you also bend your knees before him to adore him, but tell me, why do you so often act in direct violation of his law? If he is your king, then you are his subjects, if he is your Lord and Master, then you are his servants, and no power can dispense you from fulfilling his holy will. But unhappily the majority of Christians profess Jesus with their lips, but deny him by their whole manner of living, they pray to him as their God, but treat him as though he were their bitterest foe. Are you of this class of Christians? Do you treat your Saviour in so contemptible a manner? No. I cannot believe it, for I know you love him. Therefore, kneel down to adore him, to honor him, who stands before you with purple, sceptre, and crown, and cry out: Hail, Jesus, King of our souls, rule, thou, over us for time and eternity.

HOMILY VI.

ECCE HOMO, THE CONDEMNATION, THE WAY OF THE CROSS FROM JERUSALEM TO MOUNT CALVARY.

"*O all ye that pass by the way, attend and see if there be any sorrow like to my sorrow; for he hath made a vintage of me, as the Lord spoke in the day of his fierce anger.*"—*Lam. 1: 12.*

The soldiers had so successfully accomplished their nefarious designs that even Pilate could not restrain his expressions of pity when he came out and saw Jesus so unmercifully abused, covered with wounds, and lacerated, that he had no longer the appearance of a man. This frightful spectacle inspired him with the hope, that, could they see the pitiable form of Jesus, the Jews who demanded his death would be overwhelmed with compunction, and that he might, in consequence, have an opportunity to set him free. Accordingly he brought him out before the populace, and said: "Behold the man," "Ecce homo," that is, behold the remnant of a man whom your rage, madness, and cruelty, have almost destroyed. Tell me, has he not suffered enough? What more do you desire? Have pity on him who is no longer a man, but has only the appearance of a man, release him now, do not demand his death, he cannot recover from his wounds, death is inevitable. *Behold the man!* He has restored sight to many of your blind, has healed your sick, has lavished on many of you his love and benefits, and now like a leper from the crown of his head to the sole of his foot there is no form nor beauty in him, therefore have pity, and grant him at least the boon of life. *Behold the man!* Ah, he no longer appears to be that *great prophet*, whom you yourselves have acknowledged, nor that enthusiast, so terrible in his wrath at the temple, before whose scourges you have fled; nor like that *Omnipotence*, whose miracles struck you dumb; nor like that *Son of God* whom some of you proclaimed him to be, but like a *lamb* prepared for sacrifice; like a *culprit* who bleeds to death from the wounds inflicted by wild beasts; like one from whose pale lips will soon issue the last breath; have pity on him and do not demand his death. Your rage should be satiated; for even though he has erred, "he has been punished above measure." Ah! the sufferings and pains of the divine Redeemer moved the heart of the heathen, but the hearts of the chosen people of God were harder than adamant and the glittering ice was less cold, for the air rang with the wild cry of this ungrateful degenerate people: "Away with him, away with him; crucify him."—John 19: 15.

1. I have frequently remarked and I repeat it, that in the Passion of our amiable Jesus, there is not a single circumstance that does not contain profound mysteries. Thus in this public presentation, or rather exhibition of our Lord by Pilate before the Jews and Gentiles, before the highest temporal and spiritual authorities; before the priests and the people, in fact, before all mankind there represented, there is a great mystery. Pilate exhibited the suffering Son of God before the people. Now, this presents itself to me under the following aspect: It is not so much Pilate, as the heavenly Father himself, who exhibited his only-begotten Son before all mankind in their representatives, in these words: *Ecce homo*, behold the man. As if he would say: this is my beloved Son in whom I am well pleased; he is God and man, your Creator and Redeemer. He created you out of love and his love now completes the work of your redemption, behold the man, and in him, the price with which he ransoms you from your captivity. He is truly both God and man, but he might be more appropriately called neither, for his humility is so great that no one judges him rightly, that scarcely one looks upon him as God. Behold the man, who is my beloved Son, he has become a frightful spectacle to the world, to men, and to angels; behold the man who bears within him the likeness of the invisible God, but here it is disfigured and dishonored, the first-born of all creation has become the outcast of men, and the reproach of the people; behold the man, in whom the fullness of the God-head dwells corporally, treated as a malefactor; he has committed no sin, no guilt has been found upon his lips, but behold he is stricken and wounded for the sins and iniquities of my people. This is my only-begotten Son, whom I have not spared, but given up for the salvation of mankind. Behold the man, behold your Redeemer, behold the ransom he pays for you ! Whilst Pilate presents Jesus to the gaze of the populace I seem to hear the Son of God say to his Father: Oh Eternal Father, thou hast said once by the mouth of the prophet Ezechiel: "I have sought among them for a man that might set up a hedge and stand in the gap before me in favor of the land, that I might not destroy it, and I found none," behold I am the man that will set up a hedge between thee and the land, between thee and fallen mankind, that you mayest not destroy them, behold I will deliver man from thy just anger, and for this reason wear a crown of thorns on my head; behold I will restore man, disfigured by sin, to his former beauty and sanctity, and for this reason I am so disfigured that I have lost even the appearance of a man. Behold, O just Father, behold a man who suffers innocently for the guilty. I have become a living leper, that thou mayest not pour out thy indignation upon those who thus outrage and maltreat me. Behold, O Father, a man who is ready to suffer, ready to die, to redeem sinners, to reconcile them with thee, and to conduct them to the kingdom of glory. And now I would hold him up to view before heaven and earth, but not with the words of Pilate: "Behold the man," but

with the words that correspond to his nature: *Behold God!* Oh ye Angels, lift up your eyes to this Jesus, for he is your God, before whom you prostrate yourselves and whom you adore; he is your God, whose lightest word you obey. What do you say of your God, thus covered with wounds and blood? What do you think of him? Ah! the Angels answer with the Prophets: "We have seen him without figure, without form, without beauty." All the celestial spirits mourn and lament at the sight of their God thus abused, and exclaim: "Woe, woe, they have blasphemed the Holy of Israel." You also my brethren, behold your suffering God whom Pilate exhibits with the words: *behold the man*, and whom I place before you with the words: *behold God!* Behold God, who for love of you left heaven and the glory he shared with the Father, who for love of you descended from his throne of majesty to a bed of straw in the crib, who strove for thirty-three years in toil, tears, and sweat for your salvation; behold, this amiable God suffered all the shame and confusion of this exhibition for your sake. Behold God, who offers himself as an expiation for your sins, who with his holy blood will redeem your soul, who in his blood and wounds reveals the excess of his love for you. Oh! consider him from the top of his head to the sole of his foot and see if he is not worthy of all your love, compassion, and tears. Behold those open, bleeding wounds; behold the crown of thorns; behold the purple garment; that disgraceful reed in his hand; behold those instruments of torture; all these pains he suffers of his own free will because he loves you, because he wishes to snatch you from the fiery prison of hell. Behold, he chooses a crown of thorns that he might crown you with a crown of glory; he endures those frightful scourges to free you from the scourge of damnation; he permits himself to be spit upon and mocked that he may restore beauty and holiness to your souls and prepare them for heavenly joys, for Jesus does all this for you, reflect upon it, and tell me: is not this merciful loving, suffering, and bleeding God worthy of all your love, all your compassion, all your tears! O Christians, O sinners, behold your Jesus who is presented before you with the words: *behold the man ; behold God*, and tell me: do you really and firmly believe that this suffering Jesus is your Lord and God? Do you really and firmly believe that he suffers all this for your sake? Do you really and firmly believe that he gives his precious blood for your sins? You answer, yes, I believe that Jesus is my Lord and my God. In is sufferings, his pains and his blood, I behold the rich guerdon he gives for my soul. Believing this, how can you behold him without sentiments of the deepest sorrow and contrition for your sins, through which all his wounds bleed afresh. How can you see your merciful Jesus suffer all this and yet turn coldly away, and return to your sins? Can your heart be really so hard? Ah, if I speak in vain to your heart and soul, if I labor in vain to excite in you reciprocal love for your Redeemer, and contrition for your sins, I will turn to those who do not yet know their God, upon whose ear the name of Christ has never fallen, who know naught of his love and sufferings, the Gentiles shall be the judges between you and your amiable Redeemer.

"Hear, then, ye isles, and hearken, ye people from afar, ye, who inhabit the uttermost parts of the world, come, see, and judge." *Behold a man. Behold your God.* Know then, he who suffers is not only man, but also God. He is the Lord of heaven and earth, legions of Angels and all creatures obey his commands. Do you know why the omnipotent God suffers, and for whom he suffers all those tortures? Hear! he suffers for those who are here assembled, he suffers for their brothers and sisters, he suffers for all men, in order to deliver them from eternal sufferings, he suffers to pay their penalty, he suffers to show them in his wounds his ineffable love. What, O Gentiles, do you think of this God of love and of mankind for whom he suffers! Tell me, is it not the duty of all to love that God with all their heart, with all their soul, and with all their strength? But listen and wonder, they love him but little, they forget his love, even despise him, alas! they repeat the very thing for which he suffers. And what is worse, O Gentiles, this God is utterly prostrated by his sufferings and his pains, but, to pursue the mad whirl of their joys, those who call themselves his followers turn away from him. This God has shed *all his blood* for them, and they will *not shed a tear*, this God is *meek, patient,* and *humble of heart*; they suffer themselves to be carried away by *anger*, they are inflated with *pride*, and *for days the fire of impatience, anger and enmity* flames up in their hearts. Tell me, O Gentiles, what think you of this amiable God, and these hard-hearted people, who call themselves Christians? Ah! they must say: these people, whom you call Christians, have no faith, for if they did believe this sufferer is their God, that he suffers for them and their sins, that he suffers to redeem their souls for heaven, they would shed tears for their sins, they would be filled with gratitude and love for this good God; they would sacrifice all they possess, even their life rather than offend by a single sin this God who has manifested such love towards them.

And now, I turn to you and appeal to your own hearts, O Christians. *Behold the man* whom God presents to you as his only-begotten, well-beloved Son, behold the man, who offers himself to pay the penalty of your sins, behold the man at the sight of whom the heavenly spirits mourn, *behold your God* who moves even the Gentiles to compassion, will you alone remain hard, cold and insensible at such a sight; will you alone turn your eyes from this God and Redeemer; will you alone refuse to acknowledge the love of this God and the enormity of sin? Oh, say, who has inflicted on the Son of God these deep and mortal wounds, if not sin, of which you have contributed your share. Who has torn and mangled his body, who has crowned his head with thorns, if not sin, in which you have participated. Judge yourselves; is not this God worthy of all your love, compassion, and tears? Or will you with the Jews fill the measure to overflowing? Will you join with them in the cruel cry "away with him, away with him, crucify him, crucify him?" If there be such a one amongst you, I will ask him: Oh flinty heart, destitute of feeling and love, what evil has Jesus done? Why should he be crucified? Is it because he is innocent, because he is holy? Is it because he has done so much good to you? Hear, then, his judge declares: *I find no cause in him.* Great God, if in this congregation one soul should be found wicked enough to pronounce the words: "crucify him," I am innocent of the blood of this just man, which will be lost on that soul. But no, O Lord, the hearts of thy children are not so wicked, so diabolical; they indeed suffer themselves to be carried away by surprise, by inadvertence, by temptations and passions, to offend thee, but even the most obdurate will tremble and will never say: *his blood be upon us and upon our children.* Oh! heavenly Father, behold, we all are moved and penetrated with sorrow, we all with a contrite heart look up to thy Son, who stands all wounded and bleeding, before our eyes. O most loving Jesus, I address thee with the most humble petition, not however in the sense of the Jews: *Lord, thy blood be upon us and upon our children.* Our souls have been bought by the price of thy blood, in thy blood alone is our strength, our hope, confidence, and salvation. O Jesus let thy blood come upon us, let its crimson tide enter and inflame them with the fire of thy love.

2. Pilate, seeing, at last, that his efforts to release Jesus were in vain, and that his enemies, lashed on to wild fury, still fiercely cried: crucify him; and hearing their threat: if you set him free *you are not Caesar's friend,* delivered him to them to be crucified. Pilate, the representative of the Emperor, to whom, above all others, it has been given to preserve and cherish right and justice. Pilate shrinks from the wrath of an excited populace. He has not the courage to defend right and to oppose injustice, but suffers himself to become guilty of injustice in order to ingratiate himself with that wicked rabble. He is convinced of the innocence of the accused, he himself had confessed Christ's innocence, he knows they have delivered him up out of envy, he knows that all their accusations are groundless and false, he has already heard that Judas confessed his crime of treason, and in despair hanged himself; his wife has warned him to have nothing to do with that just man; he is fully aware of all this and yet he condemns him to death, he condemns him to be crucified like a malefactor between two thieves. You may wash your hands a hundred times and say: "I am innocent of the blood of this just man, the water will neither wash

your hands nor cleanse your soul, they are defiled and stained with the blood of God.

To the ocean of torments in which he suffers, is to be added the bitter and ignominious death on the cross. *He is to be crucified.* But, *Oh, heavenly Father,* will you forsake the eternal Word, will you permit your only-begotten, well-beloved Son to be crucified? The Father answers: he is to be crucified. But why? Christ is innocent. The Father answers: So much I have loved the world as to give my only-begotten Son for its redemption, But, *Oh Angels,* what do you say to this last, this unprecedented condemnation of your God? They answer: *he is to be crucified.* But wherefore; of what evil has he been guilty? Of no evil whatever, but he must die, that the mansions of heaven, once the abode of those Angels who are now burning in hell, may be peopled with men, ransomed by the precious blood he will shed. And you, *O Adam,* can you find words where with to pronounce upon him this sentence? *He is to be crucified,* he must die on the wood that he may redeem thereon my children whom I lost by the wood. And you, weeping and most afflicted *Mother of Jesus,* will you not raise your hands to heaven, will not your powerful prayers penetrate the clouds. You have found grace with God, will you not pray that he be delivered from this ignominy and death? Ah! no, such is not her prayer; she says: Knowing it is the will of God, that my Son should die for the sins of the world, his will be done, *he is to be crucified.* And *you, O! Christian,* who have frequently defiled your soul by sin, *give your verdict on the fate of your Saviour.* Oh, I hear you also cry out: *he is to be crucified,* if he die not, I must be lost. But for you I have only one word: Say: *he is to be crucified,* but he shall be crucified in my heart, he shall be fastened therein with three nails, that I may never lose him again, and upon these three nails their names: Faith, Hope and Charity, are inscribed.

3. The sentence is passed, everything is ready, the vast crowd moves from the house of Pilate, out of the city, up to Calvary's heights. What a sight All Israel is assembled, they follow him who carries the cross, as they followed him once before, when in a column of fire he went before them. A curious multitude accompany him; a crowd of wicked boys surround him, mocking and blaspheming him; soldiers walk in front and on both sides, as if a criminal were being led to the place of execution; behind him two thieves, who are also condemned to death. St. Augustine, representing to his mind the Son of God walking through the streets of Jerusalem with the heavy load of the cross on his shoulders, says: "If faith beholds him, what a magnificent spectacle, but if impiety, what mockery; what a great mystery to piety, what horrible contumely to impiety. To see the Holy of Holies, like the chief of a band of robbers, led to death, what contumely; but to see the Son of God carrying the cross that on it he might conquer the invisible

enemy who once conquered mankind on the wood, what a profound mystery!"

But behold, his strength fails, his tortures have already brought him nigh to death, he can scarcely move beneath the heavy load, he is exhausted, he falls. They drag him up and compel him to continue his journey. No one pities him, no one sympathizes with him, his enemies are jubilant, his friends have abandoned him. O yes, there are tears flowing, but they are no consolation. "Weep not for me," said he to the women of Jerusalem, "but for yourselves, and for your children." Ah! here at last is one soul that loves him, one heart that feels for him, his holy mother, What a meeting! What pains for these two loving souls! Ah it was no consolation, but a bitter pain, for this mutual pain was to be measured by their mutual love.

Jesus falls again beneath the cross, he can carry it no longer. For this reason, and not through compassion, but, apprehensive that he might die before reaching Calvary, they compelled Simon of Cyrene to help him carry his cross. Time does not allow me to lead you more deeply into the mystery of these sufferings. I will briefly point to you your Redeemer carrying his cross. Behold, with what joy he embraces the cross and lays it on his shoulders, to redeem you, whereas your chief aim is to have the cross rather beneath your feet than on your shoulders. See, your Redeemer faints under the heavy load, and no friend approaches to speak one kind word or to divide with him its weight, he is surrounded by enemies on all sides, and you sigh and murmur when God sends you some little mortification. Your Redeemer carries the cross and cries out to you: "If any man wishes to follow me, let him deny himself, take up his cross and follow me," again, "he that will not carry his cross, cannot be my disciple and is not worthy of me." Separate yourselves therefore from those who carry crosses, even great ones, not for Jesus' sake, but for the world.

And now they have reached Calvary's summit, where, urged on by malice and hate, they complete the preparations for the consummation of the sentence. They tear off his garments. At the scourging, Jesus was exposed naked to the soldiers, here on Calvary, to the whole world. What shame and confusion must have overwhelmed the sensitive heart of our Saviour. How intense must have been his anguish, when his clothes being torn off his wounds began to bleed afresh. Thus he has to endure the gaze of a vile rabble. I represent him to my mind as crying out in the words of which the Church makes use in these days: "O my people, what have I done, whereby have I offended you? Out of love for you, I struck Egypt with many plagues, but you have stricken me from the crown of my head to the sole of my foot. I delivered you from the oppression of

Egypt, but you have delivered me to my enemies; I brought you out of the land of bondage, but you have dragged me out of Jerusalem to crucify me; I slew the first-born of Egypt, and you are going to kill the only-begotten Son of God. To save you from the fury of Pharaoh, I divided the red sea for you to pass through, but you have torn my body with scourges; I fed you with manna, in the desert, and you give me vinegar and gall. On Mount Sinai I gave you the law of life and you pronounce the sentence of death upon me. I gave you Moses and Aaron as leaders, and you give me two malefactors as companions."

PERORATION.

Would to God that our Saviour were not obliged to renew these complaints! Alas! their echo comes clearly through the corridors of time. From Calvary's mount, Jesus cries out: Christian people, that the perfidious Jews should treat me thus was no marvel, but that you, you, who by so many titles are my people, that you should prefer Barabbas to me, that you should betray me, that you should crucify me; Oh, this is the excess of ingratitude. O ye Christian people, whom I love above all the rest that inhabit the earth, whom I have redeemed with my blood, enriched with my graces, nourished with my flesh and blood, in what have I offended you? Answer if you can. Because I was bathed in my own blood in the garden through love for you, you daily betray me like Judas and crucify me with the Jews. Hear, the Jews preferred Barabbas to me, and he was a man, but you prefer sin to me; Judas betrayed me to the Jews, and they were men, you betray me to the devil. What have I done to you, in what have I offended you, that you love me so little? Oh, love me, as I love you. But if you wish to love me, hate sin, love virtue, keep my commandments. Ah, for the love of Jesus remember and repeat daily to the end of your lives those sweet and beautiful words of St. Theresa: "Oh, Jesus, my love, I will love thee for ever, Oh Jesus, from this moment I will sin no more, no, never, never.

HOMILY VII.

THE CRUCIFIXION, THE SEVEN WORDS AND THE DEATH OF CHRIST.

"*O all ye that pass by the way, attend and see if there be any sorrow like to my sorrow; for he hath made a vintage of me, as the Lord spoke in the day of his fierce anger.*"—*Lam. 1 : 12*

In narrating the other sufferings of Christ the Evangelists give either a detailed account of them, or the one supplies what the other omits. But here they all declare as with one voice: *They crucified him.* In the contemplation of the incomprehensible depth of this mystery revealed to them from the cross, in contemplating the numberless pains and the great ignominy which Jesus suffered, and in dwelling on the ineffable love, with which the divine God-man offered his hands and feet to be pierced through with great nails— the pen falls, as it were, powerless from their hands. In vain they seek for words to express in fitting terms the unprecedented cruelty on the one hand, and the unspeakable love, with which, on the other, such great blessings have accrued to poor fallen man at this stage of our Blessed Redeemer's sacred Passion. The Evangelists say: "they crucified him;" they seem not to have the courage to mention his adorable name, they merely sum it up thus: they crucified him.

1. Would you understand the manner of this cruel and painful crucifixion? Then, in fancy vividly place before your minds Mount Calvary as the great theatre of the inexorable justice of God, and represent to your mind the Eternal Father addressing his Son in the following words: My well-beloved Son, whom I have begotten before the morning star from eternity, you have through infinite love and mercy offered yourself as the Redeemer of of fallen man. Behold the time, the hour is at hand, when the promised debt must be paid, behold the place where the sacrifice is to be consummated, behold the altar on which the victim is to be immolated. This is the cross on which you are to die, you have carried it to Calvary's heights, but this carrying alone will not be sufficient, you must be nailed to it and upon it must you die. Jesus replies: "Father, thou hast prepared a body for me, behold, I am ready, I come to die, that I may satisfy thy justice, and reconcile mankind with thee, that those may live whom my soul loves. O cross, on thee I will lay my lacerated, pierced head and wearied limbs, on thee I will keep my second Sabbath rest from work which will be com-

pleted to-day. Thou, O cross, wilt be that *wonderful rod*, which destroys the venomous serpent of sin, thou art that *mysterious rod*, with which the Red Sea of my blood will be divided, through which my people will be conducted into the Land of Promise; thou art the *scales*, on which the price of my blood will be weighed; thou art the *bank*, to which I will pay my people's debt until the very last farthing; thou art *the ladder*, on which men will ascend with me to the mansions of bliss; thou art the *holy tree*, from which the Redeemer will gather the fruits of immortality; thou art the *invincible sword* stronger than that of David, which slew Goliath, with which I will slay the giant of hell; thou art the *golden key* which will open the gates of paradise, for so long fast closed against fallen man; thou, O cross will be the *weapon* of my Apostles, the *shield* of my confessors, the *consolation* of the afflicted, the *refuge* of sinners, the *staff* of the poor, the *glory* of the rich, the *teacher* of the ignorant, the *hope* of the dying, the *terror* of hell, the *redeemer* of the world, the *delight* of heaven, and the *sign* of the last judgment. Therefore I take possession of thee, O glorious cross, I embrace thee, I salute thee, I kiss thee with the lips of my soul. On thee I will rest and die, and dying I will conquer hell, gain heaven and redeem man.

Such were the thoughts of Jesus. He stretched out his hands on the cross to satisfy for wicked deeds, murders, adultery, fornication, and injustice; in like manner he offered his feet to satisfy the criminal ways of mankind. The soldiers apply the nails to the hands and feet, stroke follows stroke, the wailing sound re-echoes far o'er the blood-stained mount, penetrate the highest heavens, and ascend to the throne of the Almighty. O God, what a spectacle! Murderous iron pierces those hands which laid the foundation of the world, barbarous nails fasten him to the stake of ignominy, the blood flows in torrents from his pierced hands and feet to saturate and wash the curse-laden earth which thirsts for redemption. There he hangs between heaven and earth. Look up to the cross, those nails and hammer will speak to you, they will cry out to you with more emphasis and vigor than I can: O man, perceive the malice of sin, which cries to heaven for vengeance, which is punished in the innocent, those pierced hands and feet announce to you more eloquently than I can, the punishment due to sin. The sacred blood which reddens the cross and the earth speaks louder and more eloquently than I can of that love with which the suffering Jesus embraces you. Look into those wounds and read therein that which the Son of God has inscribed in them: O man, I love thee, and for love of thee I die.

At what time was Christ crucified? On the day of preparation before Easter. About the sixth hour. Again a great mystery. About the sixth hour the first Adam sinned by the tree of knowledge in paradise when he ate the forbidden fruit; about the sixth hour the second Adam satisfied for this sin of disobedience by his death on the cross. The first Adam contracted the debt about the sixth hour, and the second Adam to pay that debt shed his blood about the sixth hour. Thus the time of redemption corresponded to the time of sin, as the wood of sin corresponded to the wood of redemption. But to have crucified Jesus was not sufficient for the malice and hate of the Jews. They crucified with him two thieves, one on the right and the other on the left with Jesus in the middle. O! what an outrage to inflict upon him! No tongue can express, no pen can describe an ignominy so great that it overwhelmed our Lord with the deepest confusion. The Jews did this to show their intense hatred and utter contempt for Jesus, that punished with thieves and robbers he might be regarded by all as a malefactor. What is more like than these three crosses, and what more widely different than those who are suspended thereupon! Truly the Just, Holy, and Innocent hangs between thieves, as if he were the chief among robbers and the wretch who incited them to every crime. Again a great mystery. The Son of God is everywhere in the middle, he worked out our redemption in the middle of the earth. *On Mount Thabor* he was between *Moses and Elias*, between the law and the Prophets, announced by both, adored by both; in *the crib* he lay on straw between *Angels and men;* in the temple he was found in the *midst of doctors;* in the midst of the Apostles he gave the divine revelations; on Calvary he hangs as mediator between heaven and earth, between two robbers. The Lord hanging between two robbers, rejected the one and saved the other. Raise up your eyes to your Mediator, for he has fallen among robbers. As I must be brief, I have but one word to say, remember it and engrave it indelibly upon your hearts: When this same Jesus comes into your hearts may he never find a place among robbers, when in the Blessed Sacrament he descends from Jerusalem to Jericho, when he comes to dwell in you, may he never fall among robbers, namely, sins.

Pilate in the meantime had written the inscription and ordered it to be put on the cross. It reads: Jesus of Nazareth, King of the Jews. This excited the anger of the Jews. Lest it should be generally believed that the crucified was really king and that they were guilty of regicide, they said to Pilate: Write not king of the Jews, but that he said: I am king of the Jews. But Pilate answered: "What I have written, I have written." What moved the governor to place this glorious title on the cross of Jesus whom he had suffered to be crucified between two malefactors. This was not his work so much as an ordinance of God. Those hands, wounded, pierced and held fast by cruel nails to the cross, directed the hand of Pilate to write the truth. The title was to remain unchanged because the word of God is unchangeable. While Jesus hangs on the cross and the glorious inscription glitters above his head raise up your eyes and consider the image and inscription.

2. Whose image and inscription is it? I hear you answer: the image is that of a poor, suffering and dying man, but the inscription is that of Jesus Christ, the Redeemer of the world; the image is that of a wounded, lacerated man, who has become the reproach of men and the outcast of the people, but the inscription is that of the Son of God; the image is that of a sinner, of a criminal, but the inscription is that of a just man; the image is that of a tortured slave, but the inscription, it must be a mighty prince who is suffering there, the image is that of a punished blasphemer, of a scoffer and transgressor of the commandments of the Most High, but the inscription is that of a confessor, of one who nobly defends the divine truth. Behold the image of sufferings and the title of salvation, the image of death and the title of life and triumph; the divinity and humanity of Jesus Christ, for Christ needed both to *conquer hell.* Oh that this glorious title might be written in our hearts: "Jesus of Nazareth, King of the Jews. Give heed, O Christians, in you also there is an image and an inscription. The image is that of God, for you are created according to the image of God, but the inscription, which not Pilate but the Church has imprinted on your forehead with indelible characters, reads: this is a Christian, a follower of Christ. Glance from the image and inscription on the cross to the image and inscription within you and see if they correspond. Examine your conscience and ask yourselves whose image is this? O! can you deny that the image holds up to view a vile sinner, a violator of the commandments of God, but the inscription belongs to a Christian called to sanctify his immortal soul. Must you not say: the image is that of a man who has forgotten his Redeemer and denied him by his works, but the inscription is that of a Christian who should live and die with his crucified God. Oh! take courage and firmly determine that henceforth your works shall correspond to the glorious title of a disciple of Christ.

Jesus is nailed to the cross, the cross is raised, he hangs between heaven and earth, praying to his heavenly Father: "*Father forgive them, for they know not what they do.*" Oh that word of sweetness and love, of patience and forbearance. As once from his divine lips came the words: "*a new commandment* I give you," so he can now say: a *new example* I give you. Scourged and crowned with thorns, nailed to the cross, a frightful spectacle to the whole world he forgets his own pains and prays: *Father, forgive them.* He once gave the precept: pray for those that persecute and calumniate you; he is the first to teach the observance of this precept by his own example. David had prophesied: "Instead of loving me, they calumniated me but I prayed." Here you see the fulfillment of the prophecy. Such infinite love deems it so light a sacrifice to bear the sins of the world and to die for men, that Jesus even prays for his murderers; he demands no revenge but pleadingly cries mercy. *O! Father, forgive them.*

The blood of Abel cried to God from the earth for vengeance against his brother Cain, but my blood cries to thee, Oh God, for mercy and pardon: *Father, forgive them.* The thorns on my head, the nails in my hands and feet, the wounds of my body, the pains of my soul cry out : *Father, forgive them.* Offering to thee my tears, my blood, and my life, I pray, *Father, forgive them.* Let my blood, which these people have called upon themselves and their children, be more efficacious than that with which the Israelites sprinkled their door-posts, let it cause their purification, I ask no vengeance but mercy, I suffer all those things out of love for them. To-day is the day of pardon, the hour of superabundant redemption : *Father, forgive them.*

Who can fully comprehend this mercy, grace, and ineffable love? Forgotten is their hard-heartedness, their obstinacy and cruelty; forgotten their denial and ingratitude; nothing but love and mercy for those wretches breathes forth from their crucified Lord. O amiable Jesus, how adorable art thou in this love. O Jesus, as thou dost pray, behold around thy cross are assembled not only those who pierced thy hands and feet, but also those who love thee, who confess and adore thee as their Lord and God. O Jesus! I recommend them and myself to thy prayer, Oh, pray for us to thy heavenly Father : Father, forgive them. I know sweet Jesus that, not the Jews, but the sins of the world have crucified thee, I know that of thy own free will, through love of us, thou hast offered thyself to death, I know that thou hast shed thy blood for me and for all those that hear me ; O Jesus, I recommend myself and them to thy prayer, Oh, pray for us : Father, forgive them. Open, O sinners ! your hearts and ears, and hear the voice of your dying Redeemer praying for you : Father, forgive them.

If the suffering, bleeding, crucified, and dying Son of God has no power to touch your hearts, if you can look into his dim and dying eyes without exclaiming : O Jesus, my love, I will show you the *praying Jesus*, who, lifting his pierced hands to heaven, prays for you with the voice of his lips, his heart, his wounds, and blood : Father, forgive them. Oh, be moved by the immensity of his love, love your Saviour, he merits your most devoted and unselfish love, he has exhausted his love for you. Oh, that this divine prayer might exercise its holy influence over your hearts, that it might conquer and compel them to love ; Oh! that in the conversion of your hearts it might celebrate a triumph as on Calvary, for there it gained salvation for one of the thieves, who from his Saviour heard the gracious words : "*This day thou shalt be with me in paradise.*" There it opened heaven to the Centurion and many of the Jews, who, with humility and contrition, struck their breasts and acknowledged him whom they had crucified to be their Redeemer, their Lord, and God, crying out : "Truly, this man was just and the Son of God." There on Calvary, it prepared the hearts of thousands, who shortly after, by the Sacrament of Baptism, from children of darkness became children of God. O Christians, your Redeemer from the cross bids you come that he may pardon your sins; were they even so great as to reach to the clouds, your Saviour has mercy on you; were they even so abominable as to cry to heaven for vengeance, his forgiveness will feelingly be given. Therefore, do not harden your hearts this day, which is the day of mercy, but pray with the thief: Lord, remember me when thou shalt come into thy kingdom.

3. There were some women present at the crucifixion. Mary Magdalene, Mary the mother of James and Salome, who witnessed the crucifixion from afar. Beneath the cross I see the mother of Jesus, and the disciple whom he loved, to his mother he said: "*Woman, behold thy son,*" and to the disciple: "*Son, behold thy mother.*" Christ prayed first for his enemies; then he spoke to the penitent thief and assured him of redemption, the fruit of his sufferings, and his admission into heaven; only then had he a word for his afflicted mother, who, with a bleeding heart, stood beneath the cross. Ah! it seems that his enemies meet with more favor than his friends; the heart of the *Redeemer* is quicker and more deeply moved by the humble confession of the sinner than the heart of the *Son* by the unutterable sorrow of his afflicted mother. St. Augustine remarks: he indeed preferred his mother to all others, but he wished to show the world how solicitous he was for the salvation of sinners, for this reason he addressed them first and then his mother. What did he say to her? "Woman, behold thy son." At this word a pang keener than a two-edged sword pierced her sensitive suffering heart. Her Son calls her no more by that *sweet name of Mother*, which belongs to her by nature. He no longer addresses her with the angel *Mother of God*, but simply *woman*. Why does our Saviour use this expression? What had she done that she should forfeit the title of mother. Is Jesus ashamed of his mother? Ah, no, but his motive was to guard against increasing her grief by that sweetest of names. Another reason why he thus spoke to her was: because he had declared with a solemn oath, "I am Christ, the Son of the living God." His enemies cried out to him: "If thou be the Son of God come down from the cross." To prove that he was the Son of God he said to his mother: "Woman, behold thy son." This was the moment in which the prophecy of the venerable Simeon was fulfilled: "a sword shall pierce thy soul." But oh! Mother of God, what an exchange, John is given to you in place of Jesus; the disciple, for the master, the servant, for the Lord; a mere man, for the true God. This was a great affliction for her maternal heart, for although John was holy and innocent, he was only a creature, whom she was to take in place of her Son, who was born of her, and who was God.

"*Son behold thy mother,*" these words are of the deepest significance not only to John, but to us all, for she is given to us all as our mother, as irrevocably as if the Lord had said: until now thou wert my mother exclusively, but henceforth thou shalt be the mother of all. As my mission was to die for all men, so shall yours be to live for their sake. O Holy Virgin, happy the hour in which your Son gave you to us for our mother, so that we can say, we are children of your grief. Your Son called you woman, that you might become our mother, and whilst he has become our Father of mercy and the God of consolation, you become our mother of mercy, our hope and our consolation. But where do you see this loving mother? She stands beneath the cross. The world has never seen more perfect beings than *Jesus and Mary*. He, the King of Kings, the Lord of Hosts; she, the Queen of heaven; he the *Son of God*, and she his holy *Mother;* he, *on the cross*, and she under its shadow, but neither *without the weight of the cross*. And why? To teach us that in the cross, alone, there is salvation. Jesus suffered to enter into his glory; Mary, the Immaculate, suffered to enter into the kingdom of God, and both, *without guilt and sin*, and you who are conceived and born in sin, who yourselves have committed sin, and spent the greater part of your life in sin, you wish to be without a cross? Or will you, who are enemies of the cross, who do not look up to your suffering and dying Redeemer—but to sin—will you be able to ascend from earth to heaven without the cross? Do you think you can obtain salvation without the cross of self-denial and penance. Have you forgotten those menacing words of the Law: "the measure of punishment will be according to the measure of sin." Therefore, O man, O sinner, here on Calvary, in sight of your Redeemer, in his pain on the cross, and with the pitiful spectacle of the divine Mother, the mother of mercy beneath it, but one choice is left to you, a choice on which depends your salvation or your damnation. Choose either with Jesus to carry the cross and enter into life eternal, or without the cross to be cast into the terrible fire of hell.

4. A great darkness covered the earth which lasted from the sixth to the ninth hour, and about the ninth hour Jesus cried out with a loud voice: "*My God, my God, why hast thou forsaken me?*" Knowing that all was fulfilled, he said: "*I thirst.*" One of the soldiers, taking a sponge, filled it with vinegar and gall, and gave him to drink. What father, at the sight of his son suffering and appealing to him for help, does not haste to his assistance? That father mentioned in the Gospel, went to meet his prodigal son who had wasted his paternal substance, he kissed him, and was rejoiced at his return. Yet the heavenly Father forsakes his Son, who, in his sufferings on the cross, struggles with death. Well could he say with the Psalmist: "O my God, I shall cry by day and thou wilt not hear, and by night, and it shall be reputed as folly in me." In the garden I called

at night, and thou heardest me not, now I cry by day, and thou forsakest me. Joseph prayed in the well, and God moved the hearts of his brethren to release him. Daniel prayed, when cast amid furious and raging lions, and God delivered him ; the three young men prayed in the fiery furnace of Babylon, and God made the flames gently fan them like soft cool breezes. Jesus prays and God hears him not, his enemies surround him like lions, he is devoured by pains, he is rejected by his people, sold by his brethren, deprived of life by those whom he loved, and is also forsaken by his Father. "My God, my God, why hast thou forsaken me?"

The great pain of desolation was increased by a burning thirst. He had patiently endured everything, and now he complains of thirst. He suffered intensely from a double thirst, a spiritual and a natural thirst. The natural thirst has its cause in the great loss of blood. Consider how much blood he lost in the garden of Olives, at his scourging, at the crowning with thorns, and by the crucifixion. His word, "*I thirst,*" signifies also his interior spiritual thirst. O heavenly Father, when the Israelites thirsted in the desert, thou didst open a rock and give them water, thou didst send an angel to Hagar to show her a fountain, thou didst cause water to come forth from the tooth of animal for Samson, thou hast given David to drink out of a cistern at Bethlehem, and behold, for more than three hours, thy Son must endure an intolerable thirst. Oh, let his mother dip the tip of her finger in water to quench his burning thirst, for he suffers the most terrible pains. But the Father refuses his Son this refreshment, not one little drop of water shall moisten his fevered lips, gall and vinegar are given to him to drink. Do you wish to know the true cause of our Redeemer's thirst? Hear, then, St. Augustine, who says in the person of the Lord : "My thirst is your salvation, my thirst is your redemption, I thirst for your faith and for your souls. The thirst for your souls torments me more than the thirst of my body." These words of St. Augustine should sink deeply into our souls since they reveal to us the ineffable love of our Saviour. Christians could quench that thirst of their Redeemer by dedicating themselves to his service, by thirsting for his justice, but with the Psalmist I will and must complain : They thirst, but do not thirst for God." One thirsts for money ; another for honors; another for power, and scarcely one can be found who can truly say : my soul thirsts for God.

Having taken the vinegar and gall he said : *It is consummated*, and once more cried out with a loud voice : *Father, into thy hands I commend my spirit*, and bowing down his head he gave up the ghost.—Luke 23 : 46. When the priest at the altar offers to God the same sacrifice which the Son of God offered on the cross of Calvary, namely, the holy Sacrifice of the Mass, he says at the offertory : "Accept, O holy Father, this unspotted

Host, which I, thy unworthy servant offer thee, my living and true God for my numberless sins, offences and negligences, for all here present and for all faithful Christians, living and dead, that it may avail me and them to life everlasting." Having offered this sacrifice, he turns to the people and says: "*Ite missa est,*" go, the sacrifice is offered, it is consummated. Jesus said this offertory in the sacrifice which he celebrated on the cross, when he prayed to his Father: Father, forgive them, accept this sacrifice as an expiation for the sins of the world," and the "*Ite missa est,*" he sang when he said, "It is consummated."

O the great and consoling words: It is consummated. But what is consummated? The sacrifice of *atonement,* the sacrifice of *salvation,* the sacrifice of *redemption.* Mankind is saved, unbarred are the portals of heaven, and closed is the prison of hell. Sin is atoned for, the victim has vanquished. It is consummated, hear it, O ye heavens, and give ear, O earth. Heavenly Father, the holy sacrifice is consummated which appeases thy anger, satisfies thy justice, and completes thy plan with the world. Thy creatures are ransomed, thy honor restored, peace established between heaven and earth. Now on Calvary, as once on Bethlehem's plains may radiant spirits chant: *Gloria in excelsis.* It is consummated. From henceforth the mansions of bliss rendered vacant by the fall of the apostate angels, will be the happy abode of men rescued from the power of Satan. It is consummated, hear it, O man, your debt is cancelled, the curse is effectually taken away, God is again your father and friend, heaven your inheritance, the devil can no longer harm you, you are delivered from eternal death. It is consummated, namely, the work which the Prophets had foretold, which the Patriarchs had foreshadowed, for behold here the *true Abel,* who by his brethren is led out to the field and cruelly deprived of his innocent life; behold here the *true Noe,* who is mocked by his sons in his nakedness; behold here the *true Joseph* with his coat dipped in the *blood of his humanity;* behold here the *true Isaac,* who not only carried on his shoulders the wood for the sacrifice, but who is also the victim on the wood; *behold the brazen serpent of Moses,* by whom every one that looks up is saved; behold here the *true Moses,* the Mediator between God and his people; the true *High-priest Aaron,* who offers himself; behold the *Lamb of God,* that taketh away the sins of the world. It is consummated, what thy eternal wisdom had decreed, what thy divine justice had demanded; what the mercy of Jesus had promised; the Angels rejoice, the Patriarchs exult in their prison house, and hell trembles, the prince of this world is defeated, he skulks back to his dismal abode, and ransomed humanity triumphs.

But scarce has the world received these joyful tidings: It is consummated, when a heart-rending voice is heard from the cross: *Father, into thy hands I commend my spirit.* But why? Oh may that sun over whose shining face a sombre shadow has fallen tell you why. May the rocks that are rent, as it were, out of compassion, may the earth which is moved to its very depths with pity, may the dead who come forth from the narrow prison house of the tomb, may the veil of the temple which is rent from the top to the bottom, may the most afflicted Virgin Mother tell you the reason. Oh Mother of God, why has thy Son cried out in so doleful a manner. Alas, exclaims this weeping mother, he has died the bitter death of the cross, died for all, bowing down his head, he gave up the ghost. Thus our Lord died on the cross. Mourn, O sun, for the *Sun of Justice* has died, be extinguished, O light of heaven, for the *divine Light* is extinguished, tremble, O earth, for thy Lord and God has returned his soul into the hands of his Father.

PERORATION.

You know why he died? He died for the sins of the world. Do you not yet understand the enormity and grievousness of sin? When, if not at present, will you learn to loathe and abhor your sins which have crucified Jesus. When our Saviour died, rocks were rent and the people returned to Jerusalem striking their breasts. Will you alone remain unmoved? Look at the wounded body of Jesus, the Lord has made a vintage of him, as he said in the day of his fierce anger. What more could the Son of God do for you, that he has not done? You deserved death, but he died for you, that you may live. Does he not merit your undivided love and affection? Oh love this sweet Jesus with your whole heart and soul, renounce sin, fall on your knees and pray: Sweet Jesus from the depth of our misery we sinners cry to thee, Lord hear our supplication for mercy and grace. We hate and detest, we bewail and lament our sins. In thee, O crucified Jesus, we place all our hope and confidence, for with thee is redemption; thou hast redeemed Jacob, and Israel is glorified. Lord Jesus, save us, strengthen our faith, and inflame us with the fire of charity, that we may live and die in thy love. Amen.

The Seven Last Words of Jesus on the Cross.

(SKELETON SERMONS.)

FIFTH COURSE.

SEVEN SERMONS.

LENTEN (SKELETON) SERMONS.

The Seven Last Words On The Cross.

THE FIRST WORD.

"Father, forgive them, for they know not what they do." Luke 23 : 24.

"Hear ye him" (Mt. 17 : 5), said a voice out of the cloud at the transfiguration of Jesus Christ. "One is your Master, Christ," declared Jesus of himself.—Mt. 23 : 10. As our master and teacher he still addresses salutary words to our hearts from the cross, the first of which is: "*Father, forgive them, for they know not what they do.*" This first word of our Saviour contains :

I. A PETITION.

1. To whom did Jesus address this petition? To his *heavenly Father*. This is an example for us: Do we act in a like manner? As a general rule, God is the last being, whose help we implore, and, then, not before we have sought it from men in vain.—Only in the Holy Ghost can we call God our Father. "You have received the spirit of adoption of sons, whereby we cry: "Abba (Father)."—Rom. 4 : 6. "Because you are sons, God has sent the Spirit of his Son into your hearts, crying : "Abba, Father."—Gal. 4 : 6. We have God for our Father, inasmuch as we have the Holy Ghost in our hearts. The Holy Ghost abiding in our hearts manifests itself by holy deeds. "For whosoever are led by the Spirit of God (to perform good works), they are the sons of God."—Rom. 8 : 14. "But the fruit of the Spirit (the works to the performing of which he leads) is charity, joy, peace, patience, benignity, goodness, longanimity, mildness, continency, chastity."—Gal. 5 : 22. Is this fruit of the Holy Ghost in our hearts? If not, are we children of God?

2. For what did Jesus pray? To obtain *forgiveness for his enemies.* Let us meditate.

(*a*) On the *incomprehensible charity* of Jesus toward his enemies. He prays in the extremity of suffering for the salvation of those who are intent only on increasing his sufferings. He prays, before the mouths of the blasphemers are silenced, and before he addresses his Blessed Mother and his beloved disciple in their grief. His word is a word of reconciliation.

(*b*) *On our duty to follow* his example. All men, especially those "who will live piously in Christ Jesus" (1. Tim. 3 : 12) have their enemies. Respecting them we received the precept of Jesus Christ: "Love your enemies; do good to them that hate you; and pray for them that persecute and calumniate you."—Mt. 5 : 44. According to this rule we are obliged to forsake all hatred and indignation, and to wish our enemies good from our hearts; to manifest by our actions this sentiment of benevolence, and to pray for our enemies. Have you, heretofore, acted toward your enemies in this manner?

(*c*) On the *severity* with which the love of our enemies has been inculcated on us. Call to mind the parable of the unmerciful servant, with the concluding sentence: "So also shall my heavenly Father do to you, if you forgive not every one his brother from your hearts." —Mt. 18 : 35.

(*d*) On the grand *promise* connected with fulfillment of this command. "That you may be the children of your Father, who is in heaven: who maketh the sun rise upon the good, and the bad, and raineth upon the just and the unjust."—Mt. 5 : 45.

(*e*) On the great *meritoriousness* of loving our enemies. It is a work of penance and self-denial, more generous and meritorious than the severest discipline and fasting.

3. *For whom did Jesus pray?* For his enemies and tormentors.

(*a*) For all those who assisted in crucifying him and for those who calumniated and blasphemed him. He hastened to be their intercessor to hinder the punishment due for such a wicked deed.

(*b*) For us, also, who by our sins crucify again the Son of God, and make a mockery of him.—Heb. 6 : 6. Let us repent of our sins as being the cause of his crucifixion; let us implore his intercession with the Father.

II. AN EXCUSE.

"*They know not what they do.*" Why did Jesus add these words to his petition?

1. To inspire us with great *confidence* in his mercy. Jesus on the cross excuses the sinner before his heavenly Father. How great a consolation in the depressing remembrance of our past sins! "Who is he that shall condemn? Christ Jesus who died, yea, who rose also again, who is at the right hand of God, who also maketh intercession for us."—Rom. 8 : 34. "If any man sin, we have an advocate with the Father, Jesus Christ the just."—1. John 2 : 1. Let us always remember the charity of Jesus to us poor sinners. He does not remind his heavenly Father of our wickedness, but makes excuses for our frailty and ignorance. Let us thank him for his exuberant charity. Far be it from us to excuse ourselves before God! Let us implore Jesus to do it for us.

2. *To set a good example.* Behold the meekness and patience of Jesus, who at least excuses what he cannot deny. Let us resolve to follow him in this regard, for which purpose the following considerations may serve :

1. Few are those Christians who follow Jesus in this regard, excusing those who have trespassed against them. How have you borne offences heretofore? You make a great deal of talk about them, and are too ready to charge your neighbor with malice. Repent of this weakness.

2. Such conduct is a proof of your imperfection and sinfulness. "Charity thinketh no evil."—1. Cor. 13 : 5. A heart so prone to think evil must be void of charity.

3. It is generous and salutary to excuse to ourselves all offences inflicted on us. "With what judgment you have judged, you shall be judged ; and with what measure you have measured, it shall be measured to you again."—Mt. 7 : 2.

PERORATION.

Let us ponder on the first word upon the cross. It makes known to us the charity of Christ, which surpasseth knowledge (Eph. 3 : 19) that charity which "many waters cannot quench ; neither can the floods drown it."—Cant. 8 : 7. It inculcates on our minds the love of our enemies : "Love your enemies: do good to them that hate you ; and pray for them that persecute and calumniate you."—Mt. 5 : 44. Our crucified Master was not like those "who have sat in the chair of Moses, and say, and do not," (Mt. 23 : 2, 3); but "he hath prayed for the transgressor."—Is. 53 : 12. The efficacy of this prayer is apparent by the conversion of many of the bystanders, by the centurion confessing : "Indeed this man was the Son of God," (Mk. 15 : 39); by the multitude striking their breasts (Lk. 23 : 48), and by three thousand souls being added on the day of Pentecost—Apoc. 2 : 41. Verily our High-Priest "in the days of his flesh, offering up prayers and supplications, with a strong cry and tears, to him that was able to save him from death, was heard for his reverence." —Heb. 5 : 7.

II.

THE SECOND WORD.

"Amen, I say to thee, this day thou shalt be with me in paradise." Luke 23 : 34.

"He was reputed with the wicked," said the evangelist of the Old Testament; (Is. 53 : 12), and Mark the evangelist, (15 : 28), when mentioning that they crucified two thieves with him, refers expressly to the fulfillment of the above prophecy. Whilst one of them reviled the Saviour, the other, repenting of his crimes, addressed Jesus, whom he acknowledged to be the Messias, in the following words: *"Lord, remember me, when thou shalt come into thy kingdom;"* whereupon the Saviour of all men opened his mouth saying: *"Amen I say to thee, this day thou shalt be with me in paradise."* What a consoling promise, worthy indeed of being the object of our meditation!

I. WHAT WAS PROMISED IN THESE WORDS?

1. *The kingdom of heaven.* Jesus promises the thief to take him into paradise, i. e., to grant him the vision of God. To all of us the same promise was then made, if we not only say, Lord, Lord, but if we do the will of the Father who is in heaven (Mt. 7 : 21); for this is the will of God, your sanctification. "We are not to partake of great rewards but by great efforts." St Gregory. From this it is evident that

(*a*) *We must comply with the condition;* sanctifying ourselves by avoiding sin and the proximate occasions of sin, and by performing good works, particularly by fulfilling the duties of our state of life. How have you complied with this condition heretofore? How will you comply with it for the future?

(*b*) *We must not allow this our hope of heaven to degenerate into presumption.* Baptism alone will not save you, nor the recitation of certain prayers, nor a so-called honest life not contaminated with public crimes; but, seriously intent upon our sanctification, "we must work our salvation with fear and trembling."—Phil. 2 : 12.

2. *The companionship of Jesus.* "Thou shalt be *with me* in Paradise." He promises the thief not only heaven, but the most intimate union with himself: As thou art now with me on the cross, so thou shalt be with me

this day in my own joy. All of us are destined for the same divine union. "Where I am, there also shall my ministers be."—John 12 : 26. "In my Father's house there are many mansions. * * I go to prepare a place for you. And if I shall go and prepare a place for you, I will come again, and will take you to myself; that where I am, you also may be."—John 14 : 2. Reflect.

(a) *How exceedingly glorious and consoling is this our destiny!* To be with Jesus in the enjoyment of his tender affections and friendship; to partake of his glory; to behold Jesus in his incomprehensible beauty; to know him, and to be known by him.

(b) *The condition of this future union.* To be with Jesus in our temporal life, to concentrate our thoughts on him, to keep his commandments, to imitate his example, to devote ourselves entirely to him. Have we complied with this condition in our past life? Contrition. Implore his grace, that by being here with him, you may be found worthy of being with him hereafter.

3. *This kingdom and companionship of Jesus will come to us very soon.*— "This day thou shalt be with me in paradise." We all have to appear before Jesus our Judge, if not this day, at least so soon that it seems to be this day. This consideration may inculcate on our mind three rules full of wisdom:—

(a) *Flee all sins without delay*, and defer not your repentance. "Delay not to be converted to the Lord, and defer it not from day to day."—Eccles. 5 : 8. For how many years have you been buried in the mire of sin? "To-day if you shall hear his voice, harden not your hearts."—Ps. 94 : 8.

(b) *Bear all afflictions with patience.* "For our present tribulation which is momentary and light, worketh for us above measure exceedingly an eternal weight of glory."—2 Cor. 4 : 17. *This day* the thief entered from the torments of the cross into the joys of paradise. Oh! that we were ashamed of our pusillanimity!

(c) *Make conscientious use of your time.* "The night cometh, when no man can work."—John 9, 4. And how have you employed your time? How many days of your life without fruit, without a good work for heaven! How many days and years spent in sin! Let us amend our lives!

II. WHO MADE THIS PROMISE?

Jesus on the Cross, when being reviled and blasphemed. Hence you become more convinced :—

1. *Of his infinite love towards sinners.* He does not think of his own unspeakable sufferings, when the salvation of one penitent sinner is at stake. We, on the contrary, shun small efforts and inconveniences, when our neighbor is in distress. Let us make the firm resolution to assist our fellow-man in his needs.

2. *Of his divine omnipotence.* A thief becomes so great a penitent that Jesus promises him that "this day" he shall be with him in paradise. "This is the change of the right hand of the Most High."—Ps. 76 : 11. This omnipotence is manifested when Jesus appears in his deepest debasement. Nailed to the cross and being at the brink of death, he shows his divine power by the conversion of this sinner. How great is the virtue of the cross! Let us embrace it with faithful confidence, that we also may experience its virtue.

III. TO WHOM WAS THIS PROMISE MADE?

1. *Truly, to a great sinner.*—No one need despair of divine grace and mercy. God is the Father who sees the returning son, when he is yet a great way off, and embraces him—Luke 15: 20. He is the good Shepherd who goes after the lost sheep, and lays it upon his shoulders, rejoicing.—5 : 4. It is he who "desireth not the death of the wicked, but that the wicked turn from his way and live" (Ezech. 33 : 11); who says : "God so loved the world, as to give his only-begotten Son, that whosoever believeth in him may not perish, but may have life everlasting. For God sent not his son into the world, to judge the world, but that the world may be saved by him."—John 3 : 16.

Do we entertain a great confidence in the Lord? Or do we think with Cain : "My iniquity is greater than that I may deserve pardon?"—Gen. 4 : 13. Or are we to despair with Judas? Trust in Jesus. One drop of his precious blood would have been sufficient to take away the sins of the whole world; and now he has poured out all his blood.

2. *But to a sincere penitent also.* He was deeply grieved over his sins which he publicly confesses : "We receive the due reward of our deeds." —Luke 23 : 41. He puts his confidence in Jesus whom he addresses without delay as his Lord. He suffers the rest of his time with the patience and resignation of a penitent. Such is the efficacy of penance

based on our confidence in Jesus. The thief obtains remission of all sins and of all punishment due for them, and even the joys and happiness of paradise. Let us also do penance, and turn our mind from evil to good.

PERORATION.

"Only remember me, when it shall be well with thee, and do me this kindness; to put Pharao in mind to take me out of this prison," said Joseph to the chief butler."—Gen. 40 : 14. "But the chief butler, when things prospered with him, forgot his interpreter."—40. 5 : 23. Not so Jesus, who made and kept a consoling promise to a malefactor, a great sinner, and sincere penitent, and so encouraged our hope and confidence. "The Lord taketh pleasure in them that hope in his mercy."— Ps. 146 : 11.

III.

THE THIRD WORD.

"*Behold thy son! Behold thy mother!*" *John 19: 26, 27.*

"Now there stood by the cross of Jesus, his mother and his mother's sister, Mary of Cleophas, and Mary Magdalene."—John 19 : 25. The greater the love of a soul to Jesus, the nearer she is to his Cross. Accordingly his Blessed Mother stood the nearest to the Cross, her heroic soul not fearing offences and insults,—the leader of souls, loving God. "When Jesus, therefore, saw his mother, and the disciple standing, whom he loved, he saith to his mother : Woman, behold thy son ! After that, he saith to the disciple : Behold thy mother !"—John 19 : 26. This is the third word of Jesus upon the Cross, the last will and testament of our dying Saviour. Let this third word be the subject of our meditation.

PART I.

THE WORDS ADDRESSED TO MARY.

"*Woman, behold thy son!*"—

1. Consider first the inner sentiment expressed by these words : *A sentiment of compassion for his Mother*, who stood by the Cross, the grief of her heart being great as the sea. "To what shall I compare thee, or to what shall I liken thee, O daughter of Jerusalem ? For great as the sea is thy desolation."—Lam. 2 : 13. Like Jesus we should come to the assistance of the suffering. Or have we no consoling word for the afflicted, no soothing word

for the dejected? If you have been wanting in this regard, repent of your hard-heartedness, and make firm resolutions for the future. How good and salutary is compassion for our neighbor's grief! It is one of the principal virtues. Its reward is heaven. Call to mind the sentence at the Last Judgment.

2. *A sentiment of filial love and gratitude.* His grateful heart could not forget what she had been to him for thirty-three years, what she had suffered for his sake: Joseph's uneasiness; the journey into Bethlehem; the disdain in the city of David; the flight into Egypt; the three day's searching. With filial solicitude he confides her to his disciple whom he loves, being of all the most qualified to replace him, and to make the grief for her exceedingly great loss more bearable.

Your conduct toward your parents, ye children, should be similar. Acknowledge what they are to you. Rejoice their hearts. Support and console them in sickness, and in old age, on their death bed. Have you no reason to reproach yourselves in this regard?

2. Consider the meaning of these words. "*Woman,*" not "*mother,*" that by this sweet name he may not increase her grief. So tender is true love, as to cause no unnecessary pain. How many occasions have been offered to us to appease our neighbor's wrath, to sooth his afflictions! And we have made no use of them.

"*Behold thy son!*" Jesus whom she had carried in her womb with indescribable delight, who, when a bright boy, had been smiling at her with the sweet smile of a child; who, being the best of sons, had rejoiced his mother's heart; now suffering unspeakable agony on the Cross.—John henceforth her son instead of Jesus; the son of the poor fisherman instead of the Son of God; the disciple instead of the Master; a subject instead of the King; a servant instead of the Lord; a feeble man instead of the Almighty.

When God deprived you of what was the dearest to your heart, did you resign yourself to the adorable will of God? Perhaps your heart was distracted from God. Jacob, the Patriarch was separated from his son Joseph, because he loved him above all of his sons, and more than he ought to have done in justice to his other children.

Part II.

THE WORDS OF JESUS ADDRESSED TO JOHN.

"*Behold thy mother!*" These words contain:

1. A sweet consolation for St. John. The more he loved his divine Master, the deeper was his grief at his loss. Jesus seeing his great sorrow, says to him: "Behold thy mother!" i. e., I know the torments of love

in thy heart. Thou art in need of consolation after my departure. So let my Mother be thy mother, she will console and encourage thee.

For *all pious Christians*. The word addressed to John is addressed to them also. He represented to them his own mother as their mother. When you are forsaken by men, depressed in consequence of great sufferings, when you are attacked by the enemy of mankind, when you struggle with death; raise up your eyes to Mary, your mother, who protects you and intercedes for you. Put a son's confidence in her, and commit yourself to her maternal care. When St. Therese, at the age of twelve years, was bereft of her mother, she implored in burning tears the Blessed Virgin to be henceforth her mother and protectress. And St. Therese experienced the special protection of the Blessed Virgin in all her needs.

2. A great commandment.

(*a*) St. John was by the words of Jesus obliged to regard Mary as his mother, to treat her as such, to obey and love her. He fulfilled the will of his Master, conscientiously, for "from that hour the disciple took her to his own."—John 19: 27.

(*b*) We are under the same obligation to regard Mary as our mother, to honor, love, and follow her. Have we been conscientious in complying with this demand of our Saviour? Let us repent of our carelessness in her service; let us make the firm resolution to perform a good work in her honor every day; as to recite the rosary, the Litany, or her office.

PERORATION.

Such is the last will and testament of our dying Saviour. Resigned to the divne will, his Virgin Mother accepted it as the handmaid of the Lord, unto whom it should be done according to his word. The disciple kept sacred his Master's will. Let us also regard Mary with reverence; let us trust in her protection in life and death.

IV.

THE FOURTH WORD.

> "*My God, my God, why hast thou forsaken me?*" Mt. 27: 46.

"Now from the sixth hour there was darkness over all the earth, until the ninth hour," (Mt. 27: 45), an extraordinary darkness, not caused by the course of nature by which God intended to manifest his indignation at the wicked deed, by which the Sun of Justice was darkened, and by which, at the same time, Jesus was to be glorified, the sun in the heavens bewailing his death, and communicating its mourning to all nature. Let us, in the shadow of this mysterious darkness. meditate on Jesus being forsaken of his Father, when about the ninth hour he cried with a loud voice, saying: "Eli, Eli, lamma sabacthani?" that is, "*My God, my God, why hast thou forsaken me?*"—Mt. 27: 46. If we inquire after the causes which occasioned this great sadness in the soul of Jesus, they are the following:

I. HIS INEFFABLE BODILY PAINS WITHOUT ANY RELIEF.

His head crowned with thorns. He cannot lean it againt the Cross without increasing its pains.—*His wounds on his hands and feet expand more and more.* His wounds are his only support.—*His body is bruised and fatigued.* "Despised, and the most abject of men, a man of sorrows and acquainted with infirmity. We have thought him, as it were, a leper."—Is. 53: 3, 4.

His exclamation. My God, my God, why hast thou forsaken me? is not so much a lamentation, as a prayer and necessary utterance of his excruciating pains, by which he intended to manifest his being true man capable of suffering. Besides, he called attention to Psalm 21, wherein the Passion of the Messias is described, the beginning of which he recites: "O God, my God; look upon me: why hast thou forsaken me?" Let us also pray, when we are visited with sufferings and afflictions. "Is any one of you sad? Let him pray."—James 5: 13.

II. ABSENCE OF CONSOLATION HIS SOUL.

Jesus wanted to be "tempted in all things, like as we are," (Hebr. 4: 15). "For in that, wherein he himself hath suffered and been tempted, he is able to succour those also, who are tempted,"—Hebr. 2: 18. Therefore he was willing to be bereft of all consolation. Consider:

1. *The greatness of this suffering.* On earth he sees no one to speak comfort to him. No angel descends from heaven to console and strengthen him.

2. *The end to be obtained.*

(*a*) It is an atonement for our unfaithfulnes to God ;

In *general* for all mankind. "They are all gone aside, they are become unprofitable together : there is none that doeth good, no not one."—Ps. 13 : 3. "They turned away, and kept not the covenant."—Ps. 77 : 57. "These men have not known my ways : so I swore in my wrath that they shall not enter into my rest."—Ps. 94 : 11.

In *particular* for your unfaithfulness. How many times have you promised to serve God only, and yet you turned your affections to the creature again ; to serve him only, and yet you offended him again. How often have you sworn to shun the familiar occasions of sin, and yet have returned to them? Thank Jesus for his atonement ; repent and amend.

(*b*) It is a model for us when we are in a similar condition. This kind of suffering is the prerogative of pious souls. In this state were St. Francis of Assisi during the three years preceding his death, St. Catharine of Siena, St. Francis of Sales, St. Therese and many others. In this state the soul finds no consolation, no delight in prayer and devout exercises ; she thinks herself forsaken of God.

In this state of mind we should follow Jesus, who investigated into the course of it : "Why hast thou forsaken me?" It is either a gracious trial for the purpose of granting us more abundant graces ; or a deserved punishment for our unfaithfulness. Bear this state with patience. Jesus says not : My Father, but my God, to express clearly his resignation to the will of God. Let us not become despondent ; let us not give up our devout exercises. This resignation is acquired by prayer.

III. HIS BEING FORSAKEN BY HIS DISCIPLES.

1. By his Cross Jesus would draw all things to himself,—John 12 : 32. This desire was completely fulfilled.

(*a*) The by-standers are obdurate, or mock and blaspheme. His own disciples stand afar off.

(*b*) In all future times he sees the same continually repeated. He foresees thousands and millions apostates from his doctrine, innumerable Christians not living up to their faith : entire nations hostile to the Gospel.

(c) Have we not been also the cause of the sad disconsolate state of our Saviour on the Cross? We have sinned grievously and repeatedly, have refused to drink the cup of sorrow, have been so tardy in performing good actions, listening to the revilings of the world, the enemy of Jesus Christ. Let us repent of our ingratitude from the depth of our hearts.

PERORATION.

We all are to experience a similar state of despondency, to that experienced by Jesus who was forsaken by God and men. This anguish will befall us at the hour of death. Let us lift our eyes to Jesus who, by his forsakenness on the Cross, has diminished the terrors of death. Oh! let us cling to Jesus in good days, that he may not forsake us in the evil day. Let us often cry out to him: "When my strength shall fail, do not thou forsake me"—Ps. 70 : 8. And whenever we pray to the Mother of sorrows who stood by the Cross, being a witness of her Son's anguish, let us pray with devotion and fervor: "Pray for us now, and at the hour of our death, Amen."

V.

THE FIFTH WORD.

"I thirst." John 19 : 28.

The fifth word upon the Cross is another manifestation of the ineffable pains of Jesus. "Jesus knowing that all things were now accomplished, that the Scripture might be fulfilled, said: I thirst. Now there was a vessel set there full of vinegar. And they, putting a sponge full of vinegar about hyssop, offered it to his mouth."—John 19 : 28, 29. The fifth word upon the Cross admits of a literal, and of a mystical sense.

PART I.

THE LITERAL SENSE.

1. The *excruciating pain* of his thirst.

(a) Thirst in general is in itself a very excruciating pain, producing more tormenting effects upon body and mind than even hunger. It is still more vehement when produced in consequence of wounds, or in the last hours of the death struggle, when it is increased in consequence of internal fever.

(*b*) For special reasons the thirst of the Saviour must have been infinitely great, and more painful than it ever could be in the experience of man. Remember his Passion and loss of blood on Mount Olivet, at the scourging, crowning with thorns, at the carrying of the Cross, during the three hours of unutterable torments on the Cross; his anguish of soul. "My strength is dried up like a potsherd, and my tongue hath cleaved to my jaws; and thou hast brought me down into the dust of death."—Ps. 21 : 16.

(*c*) Let us have compassion on the Saviour in his burning thirst, and reflect on the anguish of the Mother of Sorrows who, at the lamentation of her Son, suffered incomparably more than Hagar, who could not see her child dying with thirst.

2. The *motives* inducing our Saviour to suffer this thirst :

(*a*) That the *Scripture* might be fulfilled. All prophecies were fulfilled but one : "In my thirst they gave me vinegar to drink."—Ps. 68 : 22. How unlike are we to him! He is so anxious to fulfill the will of his heavenly Father, and we are so tardy in complying with our most important duties.

(*b*) That he might atone for our sins of the *palate*. Men sin in many ways by eating and drinking. The greatest sinners among them are the drunkards, "they that pass their time in wine, and study to drink off their cups."—Prov. 23 : 30. The time will come, when in hell they will long for one drop of water, but in vain.

3. The wording itself teaches us in what manner we should make our sufferings *known* to others :

(*a*) He discovers his burning thirst at the last moment. He has compassion on others, before he provides for himself.

(*b*) He does not use many words, nor does he lament, whilst we relate our sufferings with minuteness and exaggeration.

Part II.

The Mystical Sense.

Greater still 'was 'the spritual thirst of Jesus. He was more anxious to have it stilled, than to have his mouth moistened. To what was the desire of the thirsting Saviour directed?

1. To *fulfill the will of his heavenly Father*. What was his food in his lifetime is changed into thirst on the Cross; as if he would say: "I long to do the will of him that sent me, that I may perfect his works."—John 4: 34.

(*a*) How great was the virtue of *obedience*! His whole life from the first moment of becoming a man to the last, when he gave up the ghost, was an uninterrupted, perfect sacrifice of obedience, in order to redeem us poor children of Adam from the sin and punishment of disobedience.—Rom. 5: 19; Philip 2: 8, 9. For the sake of obedience he even did the will of his tormentors.—Luke 2: 21. Isa. 50: 5, 6.

(*b*) Our hearts should be actuated with a similar readiness to execute the will of God. Blessed are they that hunger and thirst after justice for they shall be filled."—Mt. 5: 6. But how little inclined are men, especially young people, to subject themselves to proper authority.

2. *To suffer for us.* By sufferings our Lord sought what was lost; hence this thirst for more pains, that all men might partake of everlasting joys.

(*a*) This manifests the abundance of his *charity* towards us. One drop of his blood, one tear of his divine eyes, one prayer from his lips, would have been sufficient to redeem the whole world, nay, thousands of worlds. Yet he is willing to drink more bitterness, if it contributes to our salvation.

(*b*) We should have a similar desire, we whose inheritance, is suffering. If the Lord desires affliction, why not his servants? If the innocent, why not the guilty? The Christian heroes and heroines were very desirous of suffering, as St. Francis of Assisi, St. Pius V, St. Therese, St. Magdalene of Pazzi, Aut pati, aut mori.

3. *To save all men.* He came into the world, that all might be saved; and from his Cross he would draw all things to himself. Now the time had arrived, when all mankind were to be drawn to the Crucified.

(*a*) The *sinner*, that he may be converted, and live. The Saviour on the Cross cries out: I thirst for thy tears of repentance, O impenitent sinner! For thy fear of God, O frivolous sinner! For thy modesty, O shameless sinner! For thy humility, O proud sinner!

(*b*) The *just* that they may be justified the more. He thirsted for their increase in virtue, for their perfection and zeal in performing good works. He thirsted for the obedience of good children, the solicitude of parents, the peace of families.

(c) *All human hearts*, that, thirsting after truth and salvation, they may come to him and drink out of the fountain of living waters (John 7 : 37), that by faith and charity they may belong to him who "also hath loved us, and hath delivered himself for us, an oblation and a sacrifice to God, for an odor of sweetness."—Eph. 5 : 2 ; and that they may say in truth : "As the hart panteth after the fountains of waters ; so my soul panteth after thee, O God."—Ps. 47 : 2.

Where is our zeal of penance and virtue ? Where are our works for the honor of Jesus, for our salvation and the salvation of our neighbor? "One pants after silver and gold, another after a rich inheritance, a third after honors, and scarcely one is found who can say : My soul panteth after thee, O Lord! They pant, but not after God."—St. Augustine.

PERORATION.

Let us implore the Mother of Sorrows in consideration of her grief at seeing "vinegar offered to her Son's mouth " (John 19 : 29) to obtain for us the gift of tears, so that we may shed tears of penance for our sins, and tears of gratitude and love for our Saviour ; and so by quenching his thirst, we may on the Day of Judgment hear the consoling sentence : "I was thirsty and you gave me to drink."

VI.

THE SIXTH WORD.

"It is consummated."
—*John* 19: 30.

"When Jesus, therefore, had taken the vinegar, he said: "It is consummated," a very important and instructive word out of the mouth of our dying Saviour.

Part I.

WHAT JESUS HAS CONSUMATED.

1. *The Scripture.* In its *prophecies* concerning him, particularly his sufferings:

(*a*) His seizure and the flight of the disciples. "Christ the Lord is taken in our sins."—Lam. 4: 20. "Strike the shepherd, and the sheep shall be scattered."—Zach. 13: 7.

(*b*) The betrayal by Judas. "Even the man of my peace, in whom I trusted, who ate my bread, hath greatly supplanted me."—Ps. 40: 10. "And they weighed for my wages thirty pieces of silver."—Zach. 11: 12.

(*c*) His flagellation, derision and crucifixion. "We have thought him as it were a leper, and as one struck by God and afflicted. But he was wounded for our iniquities, he was bruised for our sins: the chastisement of our peace was upon him, and by his bruises we are healed."—Isai. 53: 4. "I am a worm, and no man, the reproach of men and the outcast of the people. All that saw me have laughed me to scorn; they have spoken with the lips, and wagged the head. * * They have dug my hands and feet. They have numbered all my bones. * * * They parted my garments amongst them; and upon my vesture they cast lots."—Ps. 21: 7.

In its *types* of the Messias:
Isaac carrying on his shoulders the wood for the sacrifice.—Gen. 22: 6.
Joseph being sold by his brethren.—Gen. 37: 28.
The Brazen Serpent in the desert.—Numb. 21: 8.
The Paschal Lamb.—Exod. 12: 5.

2. All is consumated:
His *vocation* of being the Good Shepherd.

He procured for his flock the best pasture by his doctrine, example and grace, by his precious blood and the institution of his Church.

Let us learn from him to be faithful in performing the duties of our vocation, so that at the end of our lives we may say also:—It is consummated. Reflect:

(*a*) On the stern *obligations* of fulfilling the duties of our state of life, as it is set forth in the parable on the talents."—Mt. 35 : 14.

(*b*) On the *solicitude* required. We should fulfill our duties perfectly (not indifferently or inadvertently) and for the promotion of God's glory.

(*c*) On the *reward* : Peace of heart, God's complacency, heavenly glory. "Well done, thou good and faithful servant; because thou hast been faithful over a few things, I will set thee over many things; enter thou into the joy of the Lord,"—Mt. 25 : 21. Oh that we might have cause to say at the close of each day : It is consummated! Contrition. Good resolutions.

3. *His life.* Now was the moment when Jesus was to give his life for our salvation, after he had fulfilled the Scripture and the task of his life.

The hour will, sooner or later, come for us also, when "it is consummated," when life is over.

(*a*) The *sinner* will pronounce this word in great anguish, at the sight of his many sins and vices. "It is consummated!"—a life destitute of virtue, of sincere conversion, full of vanity and sins. The transient joys, perishable riches, and vain honors, are past. The time for salvation is past; the measure of sins is full to the brim; an everlasting life commences—in hell. Have we no reason to fear the fate of a sinner? Let us do penance without delay. Let us implore God for his grace and assistance.

(*b*) The *sincere* Christian will pronounce it in sacred joy and with a cheerful heart. "It is consummated"—a life of grace well employed, a holy life, acceptable in the sight of God. The afflictions, sufferings, and severities of penance are over. The combat against world, flesh and devil is fought. Revilings and calumnies are no more. The life of an innocent or penitent soul is consummated. "I have fought a good fight; I have finished my course; I have kept the faith. For the rest there is laid up for me the crown of justice, which the Lord the just judge will render to me at that day."—2. Tim. 4 : 7. Have we any claim to this consolation? Let us decide at once for a short penance, for the narrow road. Let us pray for divine grace, especially for the grace of perseverance.

Part II.

HOW MUCH JESUS HAD TO SUFFER BEFORE HE COULD SAY: "IT IS CONSUMMATED."

1. His *entire life* was an uninterrupted suffering.

(*a*) In his earliest *childhood*, suffering was the share of his inheritance. The stable at Bethlehem. The persecution by Herod. The flight into Egypt.

(*b*) His *hidden life* at Nazareth was a life of poverty, want, and hard work.

(*c*) His *public life* was full of hardships, perils, and persecutions.

(*d*) At the evening of his life his sufferings were completed on the mount of Olivet, up to Calvary, till he could say at last: "It is consummated!"

2. Therefrom we draw the following conclusions:

(*a*) Afflictions and sufferings are necessary for man, as sequels of sin. "Cursed is the earth in thy work; with labor and toil shalt thou eat thereof all the days of thy life."—Gen 3 : 17.

(*b*) As tests of our virtue. "As gold in the furnace he hath proved them; and as a victim of a holocaust he hath received them."—Wisd. 3 : 6. "Tribulation worketh patience, and patience trial."—Rom. 5 : 3. Joseph's virtue was tested and proved in Egypt, and in the prison; Tobias's virtue was tested by blindness.

(*c*) As an indispensable condition for the kingdom of God. "Ought not Christ to have suffered these things, and so to enter into his glory?" —Luke 24: 56. "Through many tribulations we must enter into the kingdom of God."—Act. 14: 21. "Abraham said to Dives in hell: "Son, remember that thou didst receive good things in thy lifetime, but now thou art tormented."—Luke 16: 25. Let us, therfore, when we are afflicted, praise divine Providence.

3. Sufferings and afflictions are profitable.

(*a*) They afford us an opportunity of showing our confidence in divine Providence. The greater the storm, the deeper does the tree take root. The firmness of faith shone the brightest in the martyrs and confessors.

(*b*) They detach our hearts from earthly things. Our heart is more or less alienated from God by terrestrial things. "Where thy treasure is, there is thy heart also."—Mt. 6 : 21. Afflictions are the cutting-knife in the hands of the heavenly physician.

(*c*) They are a suitable means of mortification. Man is not inclined to mortify himself, and when he mortifies himself, he is often partly led by self-love.

4. We profit by sufferings and afflictions, if we

(*a*) Accept them in faith, by being convinced that divine Providence has sent them. "A hair of your head shall not perish."—Luke 21 : 18. "The Lord gave, and the Lord hath taken away. Blessed be the name of the Lord."—Job. 1 : 21. " Blessed are they that mourn."—Mt. 5 : 5.

(*b*) Bear them with patience. "In your patience you shall possess your souls."—Luke 16 : 19. "Patience is necessary for you; that, doing the will of God, you may receive the promise."—Hebr. 10 : 36. Make good resolutions.

PERORATION.

"It is consummated!" a sweet word after an innocent or penitent life. Oh! that we might be able to repeat the word at the hour of our death! To obtain this grace, let us, during this short space of our time, persevere in patience and firmness.

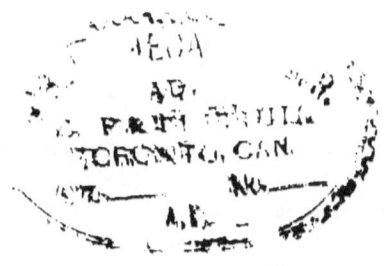

VII.

THE SEVENTH WORD.

"Father, into thy hands I commend my spirit." Luke 23: 46.

One act was yet to be performed, which was the most painful to our Saviour, the most profitable to us, and the most ardently desired by the world. The Lord of whose greatness there is no end (Ps. 144 : 3) "crying with a loud voice, said : Father, into thy hands I commend my spirit." —Luke 23 : 46. Let us meditate on the following circumstances :

1. "He cried with a loud voice," to intimate that he gave his life willfully.

(*a*) At the approach of death the human voice fails. Jesus crys with a loud voice as a proof how right he was in saying : "No man taketh away my life from me ; but I lay it down of myself; and I have power to lay it down ; and I have power to take it up again."—John 10 : 18.

(*b*) Infinite was the charity of Jesus, inducing him to give himself voluntarily to death, to take away the sting of death. "Greater love than this no man hath, that a man lay down his life for his friends."—John 15 : 13. And we have repaid him with ingratitude, by loving sin, though he died to deliver us from the death of sin. Let us repent of the past, and amend for the future !

2. That he was subject to the natural agony caused by the separation of body and soul.

(*a*) Every soul is in great anguish at the separation from her body. Jesus was to make known to us that he went through the same struggle, wherefore he said with a loud voice.

(*b*) With Jesus the agony was the greater, because his body had been the most faithful companion to him for thirty-three years, and because his Godhead was united with his body as well as with his soul. O dearest Jesus, vouchsafe, we pray, through thine agony to mitigate our anguish at the hour of our death!

2. Meaning of this word. He addressed his heavenly Father, to teach us :

(a) That he has been sent into this world, to give testimony to the truth, in confirmation of which mission his last word is an address to God, his Father.

(b) That in all our tribulations we should find consolation in the thought of God being our Father. God knows what I suffer; he takes care of me. Have you acted according to this truth heretofore?

2. Jesus recommended his *spirit*, the noblest part of his humanity, reminding us of our obligation to provide in life and death for the welfare of our soul. "For what doth it profit a man, if he gain the whole world, and lose his own soul?"—Mt. 16 : 26. It is a lamentable fact that we neglect the salvation of our soul, amidst the cares of life. Jesus inculcates on our mind that we can do nothing better than recommend ourselves and all that belongs to us into the hands of our heavenly Father. "Thou openest thy hand and fillest with blessing every living creature."—Ps. 144 : 16. "Behold, the hand of the Lord is not shortened, that it cannot save."—Isa. 59 : 1. "No man can snatch them (whom the Father has given me) out of the hand of my Father."—John 10 : 29. Let us then often recommend ourselves into the hands of God, especially at the close of each day. Let us belong to him alone. "I am thine, save thou me."—Ps. 118 : 94.

3. This last word must be applied to us also. We should recommend ourselves every day into the hands of God, by performing good works. "Therefore, also they, who suffer according to the will of God, let them commend their souls in good deeds to the faithful Creator."—1 Pet. 4 : 19. By wicked deeds we deliver our soul into the hands of Satan. "Whosoever committeth sin is the servant of sin."—John 8 : 34. To whom have you given preference in your past life, to God or Satan? Contrition; amendment. At the hour of death, the same word should proceed from our lips. We cannot, however, repeat it with confidence at that dreadful hour, unless our lives were lives of penance. "Unless you do penance, you shall all likewise perish."—Luke 13 : 5. As to this penitent spirit let me remark:

(a) It must come from the Holy Ghost. Penance is not a work of our nature; on the contrary the concupiscence of the flesh, and the concupiscence of the eyes, and the pride of life protest against penance. The penitential spirit, as every best gift, and every perfect gift, is from above, coming down from the Father of lights (James 1 : 17), and Jesus himself was led by the spirit into the desert.—Mt. 4 : 1.

(b) This repentance of the Christian is manifested by pious exercises, zeal of prayer, to which penitent souls devote much time; by love of silence, contrite Christians preferring to converse with God ; by patience in the daily hardships of life ; and by voluntary works of penance.

Such penitent souls will be allowed to say with the dying Saviour : "Father, into thy hands I commend my spirit." Do you see the above indications of penance in your own life? If not, commence a penitent life without further delay, and implore divine grace.

PERORATION.

When Jesus had said this word, bowing his head, he gave up the ghost. This Sun of Justice who is a bridegroom coming out of his bride-chamber, hath rejoiced as a giant to run the way, whose going out is from the end of heaven, and his circuit even to the end thereof, (Ps. 18 : 6) had set in the most painful death. In the words of David his ancestor, Jesus could say after the finishing of his sufferings : "In peace in the self-same I will sleep, and I will rest."—Ps. 4 : 9. How painful must have been the sentiments of the Virgin, the Mother of God, when her divine Son, bowing his head, gave up the ghost; the sentiments of her who desired to die with him, or in his stead! Oh! that she would protect my soul in death "lest my enemy say : I have prevailed against him."—Ps. 19 : 5.

From Mount Olivet to Mount Calvary.

SIXTH COURSE.

SEVEN SERMONS.

From Mount Olivet to Mount Calvary.

I.

JESUS ON MOUNT OLIVET.

His sweat became as drops of blood trickling down upon the ground.—Luke 32: 44.

On Ash Wednesday morning, my dear Christians, when you entered this temple of God, called hither by the voice of our Holy Mother the Church, you could not fail to be immediately impressed by the atmosphere of penance and mourning which pervaded its walls, and whispered in solemn tones, that the ecclesiastical year had led us on, until we stood upon the very threshold of this penitential season. Vested in the robes of penance and mourning, she renews the commemoration of the Passion and death of our Redeemer,—a remembrance which, while it fills the eye with tears of sorrow and compassion, imparts to the heart heavenly consolation and peace. She initiated us into this salutary season by the solemn remembrance of death, and how? By the ashes which her minister placed on your foreheads, this wise and loving Mother wished to remind you that the day will come when an empty hearse will stand at your door waiting to receive the casket which contains your lifeless form on its way to the silent city of the dead—where it will be laid in its "narrow house" there to remain until the Resurrection morn. She admonished you to descend in spirit into that grave whilst you strive to realize what will most certainly befall the body upon which you now lavish such excessive solicitude. The worms, although satiated with the rich banquet of corruption afforded them by the decaying corpse which lies beneath that stately monument close at hand, will, in a brief space of time, drag their slimy length eagerly to yours, and feast upon its already decomposing parts. Yes! hideous, creeping, crawling things will riot upon the lifeless tenant of every grave, until the flesh, which, O! Christian people, it will be well for you, if you have not pampered during life, will drop from the bones, and finally all will turn to the dust of which you were so forcibly reminded at the beginning of this holy season of Lent. To celebrate in sorrow and contrition, and with grateful, loving hearts, this solemn remembrance of the greatest and most touching truths of our holy religion, I behold you assembled in this sacred edifice. And how could I better correspond with the wish of the Church than by preaching to you—*Christ crucified!*—how more effectually gratify your own pious desires than by placing before you the sufferings of him whom, as the tiny babe of Bethlehem, you loved and welcomed, at the joyous Christmas time to your purified hearts! For this purpose let us transport ourselves in spirit to those places sanctified by these precious sufferings, to those hallowed spots, towards which every Christian heart turns in pious longing; thrice valued monuments of our redemption as they are, and even at the present day, visited by many devout pilgrims and watered by their tears. Let us, then, during the holy season of Lent, accompany our Redeemer from Mount Olivet to Mount Calvary, not as heartless spectators, but with eyes filled with tears, and hearts full of compunction, gratitude and love, because of the sufferings *which for our peace are laid upon him*

Behold! The day preceding the night, which was never, never to be erased from the annals of the world, had passed, and the dark shadows of that memorable night now wrapped the earth in their sombre gloom. It was the night upon which the fallen apostle, Judas, had yielded to the whisperings of the demon of avarice, and determined to betray his divine Saviour; it was the night upon which his merciless foes took counsel, each with the other, that they might device the most cruel means to torture the Son of God, and take his life; it was the night when they, perhaps, even framed the cross whereon he was to atone for our sins, and to suffer for the transgressions of the entire human race. Ah! yes, my brethren, it was a memorable night—a fearful one for those wretched creatures who harden their hearts and refuse to repent, but a blessed one for all who will, with me, follow Jesus in his anguish, and try to gather some drops of his precious blood, as it falls unheaded to the earth. It was upon this eventful night that our divine Lord, in the cenaculum at Jerusalem, having washed the feet of his disciples with a humility, so profound that any attempt to form even a faint idea of its extent would be vain indeed, having spoken to them words of instruction and consolation, and instituted the most holy Sacrament of his love—arose, saying these solemn words: "*The world may know that I love the Father, and as the Father hath given me commandment, so do I. Arise, let us go hence.*—John 14: 31. O! the love of this dear Saviour for man! He loves us far more than we, poor sinful beings, can love ourselves. Forth he went with his eleven disciples —Judas no longer being with them—out of Jerusalem to his favorite spot, the Garden of Olives. The way thither led through the dark valley of Josophat, whose stately cedar trees cast their shadows on the graves of the Prophets, whom Jerusalem had put to death—over the brook Cedron, deeply dyed by the blood of sacrificial animals—to the Garden of Gethsemane. At the entrance he bade eight of the Apostles to be seated, and took the three who had been witnesses of his transfiguration on Mount Thabor, with him further into the garden. Fear, anguish, and sadness now seized upon his soul, he began to tremble, he abandoned himself to an inward desolation *far, far* more bitter than any of his exterior pains, he experienced a deadly sadness and a dereliction of spirit so overwhelming that it forced from him the plaintive cry : "*My soul is sorrowful even unto death : stay you here and watch with me.*" And withdrawing from them a stone's cast, he fell upon his face and prayed : "*O my Father, if it is possible, let this chalice pass from me. Nevertheless, not as I will, but as thou wilt.*" Matt 26 : 38, 39. He prayed three times, each time more imploringly, whilst through the horrors of death's agony his blood pressed through the pores of his body, and, mingled with water, fell in great drops to the earth, which hard and arid as it was through very pity for him, became moist and soft with this most precious blood. Yes, thick and fast came these sacred drops till the raiment of our dear Lord was saturated with the flow, while the herbs and plants, and even the very stones became red as if in anger at this night's most fearful work.

Let us fix our eyes upon our Saviour in his agony, and let us at the same time ask ourselves, for our spiritual benefit, the cause of his inexpressible sadness of soul. The cause is threefold :

I. *The sins of the world.*
II. *The foreknowledge of his sufferings.* And
III. *The knowledge of how profitless his sufferings would be to many.*

Part I.

Jesus, the strength of martyrs and the comfort of the sorrowful, is himself weak and sorrowful unto death. And why ? Christ is sad for the sins of all men, and his sadness surpasses all human sorrow, because his pain extends over all sins, as the Scripture says : "*He has borne our infirmities, and carried our sorrows.*" Sin, therefore, which we have committed and still commit with such levity and frivolity, perhaps even in laughter and gayety, the sins of all, yes, the immense guilt of the millions of sinners of the whole world, beginning with the first in the Garden of Paradise, to the last until the end of time, in their immense number, atrocity and malice, pressed heavily upon our innocent Lord, with their fearful consequences and terrible forms. This awful guilt, which had accumulated in the long course of centuries, and came, not from one place alone, but loomed up darkly from all the regions of the world he is about to atone for. From this we may infer how great was the grief of the soul of our Saviour, who is eternal sanctity and justice ! "*The Lord,*" says the prophet, "*has laid upon him the iniquity of us all.*"—*Isai* 53 : 6. Let us endeavor to form some faint idea of the enormous weight which caused the Lord of heaven such inexpressible anguish of soul. Alas ! I fear that to count the sands which strew the shores of the mighty deep would be an easier task, or that we might far more readily compute the number of the glittering stars which so beautifully adorn the azure sky. Not only were the sins committed in the past, with all the revolting circumstances attendant upon them clearly present before the divine victim, but all those of which every human being until "time shall be no more" would be guilty, were visible to his all-seeing eye. You all know very well that one mortal sin alone is an outrage to the majesty of God so heinous that an entire lifetime is passed in doing penance for it, should be deemed a small return for its forgiveness through his mercy and love. Imagine, then, if you can see the vast throng of human beings who have existed from the beginning of the world, and picture to yourselves those who will yet be born. Think of the many, many sins committed and never repented of, which crushed down our poor, fainting Lord, and tell me, do you wonder that their weight forced the crimson tide of agony from the innocent Lamb of God.

Now let us ask ourselves how much our sins have contributed to this sad and painful scene? Our heart, beating with emotion and compunction, answers this question : may our divine Saviour, however, deign to grant us the grace that we may draw from the ocean of his grief tears to bewail our sins, to blot them out during this holy season by a good confession, in order to avoid becoming suddenly a prey to that fearful, eternal, fruitless grief, of which it is said : *"Their worm shall not die-"*—*Isai* 66 : 24.

Part II.

The second cause of this unparalleled agony and sadness in which our Saviour laments : "*My soul is sorrowful even unto death,*"—was the foreknowledge of his innumerable torments and painful death.

Christ whom we behold prostrate on his face on Mount Olivet, bathed in a bloody sweat, and whom we hear pray so beseechingly "*with a strong cry and tears.*" "*Father, if it is possible, let this chalice pass from me. Nevertheless, not as I will, but as thou wilt,*" is on the point of offering himself as an expiation for all, and he voluntarily offers to drain to the very last drop the chalice of suffering for the best work of his divine hands, for his masterpiece, for mankind, whom he so tenderly loved. And, knowing all things as he does, there arises a terribly vivid picture of the torments he must undergo. He beholds the sharp nails with which his sacred body will be pierced, he sees the long, stinging, prickling thorns which will press deep into his holy head, and he already seems to feel the lash of his cruel executioners descend heavily upon his quivering flesh. O! Christians, he sees too that in spite of all he is so willing to suffer for us that, upon innumerable souls, his anguish will be utterly fruitless, and his precious blood will be rejected with indifference, and even trampled upon with fiendish malice and hate.

Tell me has some vague, indefinable presentiment of evil ever caused your heart to beat in wild unrest? Has the very air seemed heavy with the weight of some coming sorrow, coming, too, you could not tell how or whence? If so, then, you can, in a very remote degree, realize the interior dereliction which rent the heart and soul of our suffering Lord. You can form at least a faint idea of the agony of your suffering Saviour. A faint one, indeed, it will be for it was *no vague apprehension of evil*, which haunted his beautiful soul. He, in his omniscience, had a perfect and definite view of the excruciating anguish which was so soon to overwhelm him, and all, that he might deliver us from the greatest, the most horrible, the most protracted woes that could come upon the children of men. And what were these woes? The misery of sin, the just anger of an offended God, endless persecutions of infernal fiends, and the perpetual loss of God. O! what sufferings! Alas! what pains! Like mocking demons came, one by one, these various torments, and taunted their victim until he writhed in indescribable pain. Yes! he saw the scourge, the painful crown, and the mantle of derision about his shoulders, He beheld the heavy, hard cross, the long sharp nails, the death agony upon the cross, endured amid the scoffs and jeers of the crowd, and borne without one kindly word or friendly glance. And beneath the cross!—alas!—beneath the cross he saw his dearest Mother in grief, too deep for words as she stood close to the Sacred Rood.

O! my Redeemer! "*Great as the sea is thy pain.*" Vast as the mighty ocean is its extent. And not only did his own sufferings present themselves before him, on the lonely mount, but those of obdurate Israel, of his Apostles, martyrs, and confessors rose up clearly and distinctly to his view—the sufferings of his Church caused by Judaism and heathenism, by infidelity, heresy, and superstition, by political power and revolution throughout all future ages. He also saw how tyrants would strive by every means in their power to lure his faithful servants from their allegiance to the true religion, and, when their glittering stores and worldly honors could not make those noble souls swerve one instant from the path of right, he foresaw the tortures and persecutions which won for them eternal bliss. It was thus that Jesus "*took upon himself our infirmities and bore our diseases.*"

If, therefore, our Saviour gives vent to his feelings through the lips of the prophet, saying: *O! all ye that pass by the way, attend and see if there be any sorrow like to my sorrow*," Lament, 1: 12. There is one question which confronts us with a significance which we can not and must not ignore. Look into the fathomless depths of this vast ocean of suffering, and reflect: "How many drops of pain have my sins poured therein?" O! how many! how many! But we have one great consolation when ever the weight of the cross seems to press too heavily for our poor weak human nature to endure. We can look at our divine Exemplar, our model in suffering, and rejoice that he took all our infirmities and pains upon himself. When anxiety knocks at our portals, or poverty stalks, gaunt and wretched, in our houses—when illness casts its withering blight upon our lives, or death robs us of those we most cherish upon earth, we can nail our grief to the cross, and remember that Jesus died there for our sake. Hence it has ever been that truly noble and magnanimous souls, in their afflictions have, with the Saviour, prayed that sublime prayer: "*Not my will but thine be done,*" and with St. Philip Neri have exclaimed, "*More crosses, but also more patience, O! Lord.*" Sufferings or death was the watchword of St. Theresa and her devoted clients. "Yet more, O! Lord, yet more," was the constant cry of the ardent St. Francis Xavier, and innumerable fervent souls unite with him in the heroic prayer.

Hence it is that so many have followed, with Christian heroism, the glorious standard of victory, the Cross, to the lonely desolate mount of Olives, to the Calvary of suffering for Christ's dear sake. With the triumphant palm branch in their hands, they now stand around the throne of God, their countenances radiant with the joy of eternal safety, their hearts exultant with a bliss which will endure forever, ever more. Backward they glance upon their temptations, their sufferings, their trials, their fidelity to grace, whereby they have gathered the priceless guerdon of a happiness which the eye is not capable of beholding, the ear is not attuned to hearing, and which is too perfect for the mind to conceive: the possession of the Creator, of God himself, and in him, of all other joys.

Part III.

"*My soul is sorrowful even unto death.*" Let us briefly consider what our Saviour wished to convey to us by this most touching plaint. Was he indeed sad and apprehensive, he who was the light of the world and the joy of all faithful hearts? Was he, the very essence of fortitude, appalled; could he, who holds heaven and earth in the hollow of his hand, fear and tremble? He tells us through the lips of the prophet: "*I have labored in vain: I have spent my strength in vain.*" He complains with the Psalmist: "*What profit is there in my blood?*" Yes, my dear Christians, our Saviour in his omniscience foresaw that his bitter Passion and his fearful death would be for many a scandal, a folly. With the eye of his soul he beheld the ruling infidelity and heresy over a great part of mankind, despite his Passion and death ; he heard the blasphemous insult of a certain infidel : "If we wrest the halo of divinity from the head of Christ, he will, nevertheless, always be entitled to an honorable place in the temple of genius and humanity as a recognition of his lofty morality in which he had no peer. He foresaw the black ingratitude and atrocity of so many who despite his sufferings and death serve the lust of the eyes, the flesh and the pride of life, and give themselves over to the malice of sin ; he saw the many relapses into sin, and with it, the ease with which so many neglect the fountains of grace, the holy Sacraments, frequently for a whole year, nay, for years, or do not approach them at all, and others who approach unworthily. " *What profit is there in my blood?*" He saw the scorn for the Gospel of the Cross, the contempt for the holy sacrifice of the Mass, in which is represented in an unbloody manner the great work on Calvary, or saw the contempt of the graces so dearly purchased, and that final ruin of millions of sinners whom on the day of judgment he must, notwithstanding his sufferings and death, condemn to hell on account of their having died in their sins. " *What profit is there in my blood?*" No wonder that our Saviour is sorrowful unto death. No one ever loved man more than Christ ; no one ever understood better than he the misfortune that arises from sin. O my dear Christians, our Redeemer on Mount Olivet directed his sorrowful glance also upon this congregation, looked at every one of us. It seems that I behold the innocent Redeemer turning his tearful eyes upon each one of us, with the sad reproach : O Christian, of what benefit is my blood for you ? Who can be so obdurate as to resist this look of our Saviour, who so deaf as not to listen to this gentle reproach ! Oh, then, let us behold our Saviour on Mount Olivet with tears of compunction, of gratitude and love, and with the firm determination to enter upon a new life ; for we, too, by our offences, have saddened still more his already sorrowful heart. Our sins and ingratitude have wounded him unto death and forced that painful sweat of blood from his pores. Let us look at him in the hour of temptation when the world, the flesh and the devil let loose against us their infernal machinations, in the hour of suffering when we shrink from the chalice of pain, and in the last supreme hour of our lives when death, our sins, and the judgment of God overwhelm with fear our departing soul.

PERORATION.

May the image of our divine Saviour, so pathetic in his hour of agony, be imprinted upon our hearts. May the thought of incarnate Innocence, fainting beneath the guilt of a sinful world in Gethsemane's lonely garden, prevent us from adding to his already overcharged heart, and inspire us to follow his footsteps on his dolorous way to Calvary. May we be thus aided in temptation, assisted in suffering, and sustained when the angel of death covers us with his sombre pinions, and we stand, *alone*, before the Judge of the living and the dead. Amen.

II.

JESUS BETRAYED BY JUDAS, APPREHENDED, AND ABANDONED BY HIS DISCIPLES.

"And he that betrayed him, gave them a sign, saying: Whomsoever I shall kiss, that is he, hold him fast."—Matt. 26: 48.

In our former meditation I presented for your consideration a subject so intensely pathetic that it could not fail to make an impression even upon the most indifferent heart. I endeavored to depict in as vivid a manner as could be done, how your dear Saviour, and mine, was so overcome by his interior desolation, that his precious blood, instead of water, streamed forth from every pore, and, although my picture must needs fall far short of the terrible reality, I feel assured that the divine Redeemer would graciously bless my efforts in your behalf. I will lead you this evening again into that ever memorable spot, that secluded grove upon the summit of the bleak desolate mountain where, beneath the gloomy skies which seemed to mourn for their Creator's sorrow, the Redeemer began the sacrifice of atonement for sin; for that sin which, in the lovely garden of Eden, bright with the rarest and most fragrant flowers, was first committed by man.

Alas! for the millions and millions of unborn human beings against whom the portals of heaven were instantly barred! But the loving heart of our divine Redeemer found the key to open those massive gates. This key, my dear Christians, was—*suffering*, and the victim, the voluntary victim—to endure the suffering was *himself*, the second person of Blessed Trinity, who has loved each one of you with an everlasting love.

Was it the breeze faintly stirring the foliage of the olive trees, as it was wafted from the Tiberian lake that broke in upon the deep silence of the grove? Ah! no! On golden pinions, which moved lightly on the evening air, a radiant angel left his heavenly home, and, with reverent tenderness, ministered to his dear Lord, who thus strengthened, became fully resigned to the will of his Father in heaven. Nay, in view of the honor of his Father, the joy of the Angels, and the redemption of mankind as being the fruits of his Passion and death our Saviour was even consoled, and, as he rose from his touching prayer, awakened his slumbering disciples, for the hour had come. "*The hour is come: behold, the Son of man shall be betrayed into the hands of sinners. Rise up; let us go. Behold he that will betray me is at hand.*"—Mark 11: 41, 42.

And now the sombre shadows of night began to fall over the brook Cedron, and all grew still and dark, whilst the measured tread of a numerous band came nearer and nearer—then suddenly stopped. Loud and angry words were heard, for a dispute had arisen between the leader of the band and his adherents. Ah, well might that hypocritical traitor hesitate to approach Jesus in such company! The band consisted of the soldiers sent to apprehend him, and the servants of the high-priests, bearing lanterns, torches, clubs, swords, spears, chains, and ropes, but the malice and hate of all combined failed to equal the diabolical venom which consumed the black heart of the wretched fallen apostle, Judas. Our dear Lord awaited them with a divine willingness to suffer death, a celestial light in his beautiful face. Alas! my brethren, how soon was that majestic countenance to be disfigured and defiled! Behold, how the arch-traitor, at last, approaches and, falling upon the neck of his Lord, gave him the treacherous kiss agreed upon, and the salutation: *"Hail Rabbi!"* which delivered him into the hands of the blood-thirsty crowd. But how does our Saviour receive him? Once more, once more! Yes, but for the very last time he looks sorrowfully at the lost apostle, and says: *"Friend, whereto art thou come? Judas, dost thou betray the Son of man with a kiss?"* With a majesty and diginity that *emanated from his divinity*, he went towards the impious band, and, having proved it by those all powerful and annihilating words, *"I am He,"* he manifested his love by the miraculous cure of Malchus, and then willingly delivered himself to chains and bonds. The sanguinary wretches rudely seize his holy hands, and bind them fast till the cords discolor and lacerate the tender flesh, and then cast ropes about his virginal body, as though he would attempt to escape!

And now he stands, deserted by those who should have clung to him with steadfast love. All his disciples, even the ardent Peter, even John the disciple of love, take to flight and abandon their Lord and God. If we devote a brief space of time to an earnest consideration of this picture of the Passion which I have endeavored to delineate for you, three significant features will stand vividly forth as most fitting subjects for our meditation this evening,

> *I. The malice of Judas,*
> *II. The actrocity of our Saviour's enemies,*
> *III. The weakness of his disciples.*

Part I.

Judas, once an apostle, a companion of our Lord, an associate so intimate that he was a constant witness of the innocence and sanctity of his life; one who shortly before sat with him at table, has now become a monster of deceit, an accomplished hypocrite, a betrayer of innocent blood. With consummate malice he employs the most tender mark of friendship and love as a countersign for the most terrible crime. O! what deep grief this perfidious disciple caused his divine Lord who loved him and who during the three years of his public mission so often denounced hypocrisy, and branded those who practised it as "*whited sepulchers,*" as "*serpents,*" and as a "*generation of vipers.*"

When the Roman Senator, Julius Caesar, entered the Senate Chamber, he was suddenly attacked by a crowd of conspirators, one of whom who for a long time had been most bitterly inimical to him, stabbed him with his poniard, yet not a word of surprise escaped his lips. When, however, he beheld Brutus, his adopted son, who had for so long been the object of his devoted love and kindness, among the murderers, his heart broke, and in the deep anguish of his soul he cried out: "*Thou too, my son Brutus!*" Then he wrapped himself in his toga, and, without a struggle, resigned himself to his fate. The sight of his son with the murderers was too much. It proved the death stroke to his overcharged heart.

But his was a light grief compared to that which pierced the heart of our Redeemer when he beheld Judas, the recipient of so many favors, coming at the head of his murderers as his betrayer. Although our Lord knew that the same lips which now greet him with a kiss had, a few hours ago, said to the Pharisees with most unblushing perfidy: "*What will you give me, and I will deliver him unto you?*" although, with a breath, he could have hurled him to the depths of a never-ending hell, he had only words of the gentlest and mildest reproach. O! the heart of Judas should have been rent in twain at these loving words, tears of penitence should have moistened his eyes, and, at the feet of the All-merciful he should have knelt to implore pardon and grace. You, my dear Christians, can learn from this terrible example the end of the man who rejects and abuses the good and gentle Saviour's warnings, and the grace offered him by the Almighty God.

But, what can we expect from one who after receiving holy Communion, left the table of the Lord to claim the money for which he betrayed Jesus! And now he hastens from the fearful scene. Remorse, it is true, has taken possession of him, but it is remorse without a ray of hope, remorse which looks into the black gulf of despair wherein the light of mercy does not shine, and recklessly plunges him in. Back to the Synedrium is he driven where he confesses that he has sinned in betraying innocent blood; then, in a frenzy he hurls the thirty pieces of silver away, and in frantic haste, rushes through the city gates till he reaches a solitary wood. See the fugitive fleeing down the steep sides of the mountain, then, to the Synedrium, and thence, after his fearful confession, through the crowded streets, his hair tossed about in wild confusion, his eyes burning with a lurid light caught from the fire of hell which will so soon receive his guilty soul, and his form flitting like an evil shadow to the wood. There he loosens the rope from his mantle, fastens it to a branch of the tree nearest him, and hangs himself thereupon. In the fearful death struggle he wrenches himself asunder, his entrails protrude and hang down to the ground below, a terrible end! What a terrible end! And his soul? *Alas, his soul!* The words of our dear Lord sufficiently indicate his fate: "It were better for him had he never been born."

But has this terrible example the effect for which we would most certainly look. *Alas, no.* The base conduct of this fallen disciple is constantly bearing repetition, and truly, at the present day, its frequent occurrence is most alarming Every hypocritical act, every unworthy communion, every perjury for gain is a deed similar to that perpetrated by Judas,— Every connection with secret impious societies, or lodges, every betrayal of innocence, every desecration of God's holy days for gain is a deed worthy of the wretched apostle. Woe to those, especially, whose hearts are consumed with the greed of gold.

"Three vices" in particular "plunge man into eternal ruin : *Pride Impurity*, and *Avarice* ; if, of one hundred proud persons fifty are saved by the Sacrament of Penance, of one hundred impure, thirty, of one hundred avaricious there will be scarcely three." In truth, man is open to conviction in regard to his pride, and the impure one cannot fail to know the wickedness of his ways, but who can convince a man of his avarice ! And what does it avail, *O! what does it avail him* were he to gain all the gold on this earth? It is but dust, and death will not permit him to tarry for it to take with him to the other world. Arise and come with me, death will cry, "and wait not to gather thy golden store. Thou art going into the house of thy eternity, and O! man *there* will riches be of no value for thy soul. Leave the gold for which thou hast forgotten thy God, to heirs who will squander it, and let thy memory die, and come with me to meet thy unrelenting judge." O! my dear Christians, let our Redeemer be our wealth, our only treasure, our joy and the object of all our desires! "*What shall it profit a man, if he gain the whole world and lose his own soul?*"

Part II.

A frantic, infuriated mob of Jews and heathens now rush upon the innocent Lamb of God, cast ropes around his neck, bind his holy hands, and drag him away, insulting him at every step! They treat him as if he were the vilest of criminals. But a few moments have elapsed since by one stroke of his omnipotence they were hurled, all helpless, to the earth, prostrated by him who was the supreme Ruler of men and Angels, and yet they dared to seize him as a victim, and to bind him fast with ropes and cords. Alas! the passion of man! Behold how it impels those who yield to its promptings to cast aside every fear, and scorn the perils which encompass their path. But when this victim is the Son of God, Word of God, the Father by whom all things were made, when he could command legions of Angels to obey him, why did he not punish those insolent wretches? Why did he not bid the earth to open and take them, alive, into its depths? Did he not by that simple word, "*I am He,*" smite that impious crowd to the ground? Why, then, does he allow himself to be deprived of his freedom? Why are his limbs bound by ropes? He answers by the lips of the Psalmist, "*The cords of the wicked have encompassed me.*" "*The cords of the wicked.*" Yes, Christians, our sins have twined those ropes wherewith his enemies bind the hands of our dear Saviour, our suffering Lord.

Careless, negligent Christians, who look upon venial sin as a trifling wrong, you have multiplied cord upon cord, they have been firmly twined together, until at last by "contemning small things," you have fallen into greater and mortal sin, with you, becomes not an unfrequent occurrence. O! you have, indeed, of cords twined the ropes; you have greatly augmented our Saviour's pain, and added to his woe. And in his love for us he suffers it, in order, as he promised by the prophet to redeem the captives, to deliver those who were in bondage, and sever the shameful ties which held man chained to the triumphal chariot of hell. And yet many voluntarily and repeatedly exchange the precious liberty of the children of God for the humiliating shackles of sin. O! that during this penitential time the image of our fettered Saviour might be constantly and vividly present to the spiritual vision of those who are enthralled by the glamour of some sinful association, and that they would see in his manacled hands a tender appeal to seek, in the Sacrament of Penance, a sure means of freeing themselves from those sinful bonds.

But it is as inexplicable as it is sad that many drag along from Easter to Easter, nay, for years and years, enchained in the fetters of Satan, although our Saviour never ceases to offer them the precious boon of liberty and the peace "which the world cannot give." Borne down by the heavy chains of sin, they are like prisoners, sitting in the dungeon of spiritual darkness, and deserving eternal death, and they refuse pardon, liberty, eternal bliss. O! Christian people, are they not mad, beyond all idea and conception, *insane?* How can a Christian, a Catholic, who knows that one mortal sin places him in a state of damnation, who knows, besides, that at any moment death may call him, and that he may have neither time nor grace to make an act of perfect contrition, live for weeks and months, for a year, nay for years, in that terrible state? What terror for them if the thread of their life be cut short, and without preparation they are called to stand before an avenging Judge! *"Having bound his hands and feet, cast him into exterior darkness. There shall be weeping and gnashing of teeth.."*

Part III.

The third significant feature in the picture which I have presented for your consideration is the *weakness of the disciples,* who, because they forgot the divine admonition: *" Watch and pray,"* fled, thus forsaking their Lord and Master in his hour of need. Even the prince of the Apostles who had feared not death, even St. John, the glorious disciple of love, who, at the Last Supper, was so favored as to repose on the Sacred Heart, and James, who with those two had witnessed the transfiguration of our Lord —all, all, overcome with terror, rushed from the spot. O! surely such timidity and weakness must have caused an additional pang to our Lord. Still they were not as yet fortified by the gifts and power of the Holy Spirit, and there was something which grieved him in an uncomparably greater degree than this desertion of his poor timid disciples. In his omniscience he foresaw how many Christians would, notwithstanding the loving inspirations with which that divine spirit is ever seeking to recall his wayward children, in spite of the graces received through the Holy Ghost, in spite of the blessings contained in the the treasury of the Church, and the graces she has always the means of dispensing to those who accept them, abandon him and his Church during the years which would follow, and join in the conflict against him. He foresaw how, for the sake of earthly interests and low, sordid motives, they would join the ranks of infidelity and heresy, and strive to destroy, if that were possible, the end for which his bitter Passion and ignominious death were endured. I can almost hear the plaintive tones of our dearest Saviour ask us, as on that memorable eve he asked his Apostles: *" Will you also go away?"* Will you also leave the Church where Christ lives, the only saving vessel which has valiantly breasted the storms of almost two thousand years, the Church which has a sure anchor to which she can cling, O! how securely, in the most violent tempests of life, and which will land her safely with her children upon the eternal shore, the haven of everlasting bliss! Daily, thousands of shipwrecked mariners are seeking refuge beneath her sails. They dread the storms which surround them. They discover in the Catholic Church a higher mission, a divine power, the life of the God-man and the work of her divine Founder. No, we shall not go away. We shall answer with St.

Peter: *Lord, to whom shall we go? Thou hast the words of eternal life. And we have believed, and have known that thou art the Christ, the Son of God."* —John 6 : 68 : 70.

PERORATION.

Let us once more cast a glance at our dear Redeemer who is betrayed, in chains, and abandoned, and let us promise him that never, never will we act the part of Judas, the base, the treacherous friend; that we will endeavor to cast of the fetters of sin, and that we will ever love his Church and cling to it with a fidelity that naught can change. May our beloved Saviour by his blessing strengthen and confirm this resolution in each one of our hearts. Amen.

III.

JESUS BEFORE THE HIGH COUNCIL OF THE JEWS.

"Now the chief priests and the whole council sought false witnesses against Jesus, that they might put him to death.—Matt 26 : 59.

In our preceding meditation I directed your attention to the anguish which overwhelmed the divine Sufferer upon that ever memorable evening when he was plunged into an ocean of desolation, the depths of which could never, never be sounded by man. And this desolation was not merely a sharp, passing, fleeting affliction, for it began when the shadows of evening first fell over the earth, and lasted until the midnight hour proclaimed that a most memorable day was about to dawn upon the children of men. We have seen the meek and innocent Lamb of God proceed, with his three favored disciples, to the scene of his agony. St. Peter, to whom he entrusted the keys of his heavenly kingdom, St. John, whom at the Last Supper, he had permitted to repose upon his breast in such intimate union that he could even feel the throbbing of the Sacred Heart, and St. James, who had, with these two, been allowed to witness his glorious transfiguration, followed him reverently to the garden of Olives. There we have witnessed our Saviour praying in the deepest sorrow, we have seen the arch traitor Judas give him into the hands of a sanguinary band, and we have also been touched to the quick to see that even those three chosen companions of our Lord have weakly fled when the enemy drew nigh. We have watched with indignation and horror the base act of the infamous Judas and the sacriligious deed of the soldiers who seized and bound the Lord of heaven and earth, and I feel very sure that many a loving soul in this assemblage has inwardly breathed in ready sympathy the ardent wish : O! that I had been called to accompany our dearest Lord, how gladly would I have remained with "him to the last." Dear, faithful souls, you *have* been called ; our Saviour during these days of grace entreats you to accompany him from Gethsemane to Calvary, and eagerly heeding the divine petitioner, let us accompany him, step by step, upon his path of sufferings, through the long hours of the weary night. He does not ask you to suffer the torments which he endured, he requires nothing beyond your strength, but every sacrifice you offer up for him he will reward you a thousandfold. As, with the deepest interest, we walk from midnight to early dawn with our dear Redeemer, we observe that his being led away by those merciless captors, his trial, which was characterized by the most flagrant injustice, his preliminary condemnation, which was an outrage upon every preconceived idea of right, the denial of Peter, which so cruelly wounded his sensitive heart, and the tortures inflicted upon him by his inhuman enemies, during that most painful night, offer two points worthy of our present meditation. And these points are :

I. *The affliction of the divine Sufferer.* And
II. *The love of our merciful Redeemer.*

Part I.

Our divine Lord suffered himself to be bound, and bore his chains for love of us. The cruel crowd, having bound him, moved on, and Jesus was led to Annas, who was formerly high-priest and the father-in-law of the present high-priest, Caiphas. On the way from Mount Olivet he endured indignities so great that each new insult appeared to surpass the preceding one in malignity and extent. The very devils of hell seemed to have taken possession of that frantic, howling mob, and, indeed, they acted more like demons than human beings, as they gloated over the sufferings which they had caused. Would that we could realize the love which, after the mandate of the Eternal Father had gone forth, depriving our first parents, with their hapless posterity, of their heritage of celestial bliss, could leave the joys of heaven and accept such treatment, all to unbar for us those massive gates and win for us the right to strive for and gain unending happiness. Would that we could realize even in a faint degree that mighty love, and return it at least, so fully as is consistent with these poor, weak, ungrateful, miserable, earthly hearts of ours. Endeavor, my dear Christians, as we leave Gethsemane, to excite in your hearts an ardent love for Jesus, for his love contains treasures far exceeding any joys the world can give. To love him is to have all and possess all ; not to love him is to lose all ! Without his precious love there is nothing left but sin, and the terrible punishment which its wilful commission merits and receives from a God who will not be angry nor threaten forever, and into whose hands it is terrible for the unrepentant sinner to fall.

The creature before whom our divine Lord was arraigned was Annas, whose ruling passion was ambition, and whose proud arrogance beheld here an opportunity to display his judicial knowledge, and to crush to the earth, to humble to the very dust him who was so infinitely greater than the brightest angel in the heaven which was the work of his own hands. Having assumed an appearance of official wisdom, he presumed to enact the part of judge to eternal Innocence and Sanctity by questioning our Redeemer concerning his doctrine and his disciples. Alas! my dear Saviour, what a humiliation to atone for our pride! But still more does he desire to humble himself; for when he replied to Annas: "*I have spoken openly to the world: I have always taught in the synagogue, and in the temple, whither all the Jews resort, and in private I have spoken nothing. . . . Ask them who have heard what I have spoken to them: behold, they know what things I have said,*" a servant was guilty of an outrage so terrible that we shudder at the mere recital of the deed. He dared to raise his unholy hand and to give our Lord a blow on the cheek, saying: "*Answerest thou the high-priest so?*" Oh, just God, the Lord of Hosts receives a blow from a vile menial—the Creator receives a blow in the face from that hand that he created; the Ruler of the Universe receives a blow in that countenance which the Angels venture to behold only when they sing the "Holy, holy, holy!" Who does not feel the most intense indignation at such an atrocious deed! But behold the wonderful humility and meekness of the Son of God! Our Saviour who could have caused that insolent arm to fall powerless and rigid, and that vicious hand to wither, reproaches the sacrilegious deed only with composure and dignified earnestness. That cruel deed, because of sin, is also our deed, and alas! is only too frequently repeated by cursing, blaspheming and impure language. Oh! let us learn from this humility and meekness to annihilate our pride and anger and avoid everything which might prove a new blow to our suffering Lord.

But the divine Sufferer was to endure still more painful cruelties! From Annas that impious band led him, all the time heaping upon him inexpressible abuse and cruelties, into the court-yard of Caiphas. There the high-priest is seated, as one on a throne, surrounded by the scribes and elders of the people. There the Son of God, chained and bound, in the midst of a crowd of rude soldiers, is placed before the bar of an unjust tribunal, False witnesses, bribed to act their part, men without honor or conscience, come forward with their lies and deceitfulness against Eternal Innocence. They become hopelessly involved in a labyrinth of contradictions, they distort the truth, and the innocence of our divine Saviour penetrates the dark tissue of their calumnies and equivocations, and, to the grievous disappointment of his prejudiced enemies, stands forth brilliant and clear as the sun in a cloudless sky. The sapient judges cannot conceal their perplexity, and Caiphas, who took precedence over the rest, then asks our divine Saviour: "*Answerest thou nothing to the things which these witness against thee?*" But Jesus answered not. This behavior of our Saviour incensed the high-priest, he rises suddenly, and whilst all eyes are turned upon him in breathless anticipation, raises his hand to heaven and conjures our Saviour, saying: "*I adjure thee by the living God, that thou tell us if thou be the Christ the Son of God.*" And our Redeemer, adjured by the judge by the living God, in view of the most terrible death, answers: "*Thou hast said it,*" and he adds: "*Hereafter you shall see the Son of man sitting on the right hand of the power of God, and coming in the clouds of heaven.*" One would think, my dear brethren, that this solemn assurance from the lips of our divine Lord would have overwhelmed the high-priest and his companions with awe, and that, in view of that terrible second advent of the Son of man, they would have fallen, in penitence, at his feet. But, alas! their hearts were so defiled with sin, filled with malice, inflated with pride and corroded with the venom of self-love, that they were hardened against all the inspirations of divine grace. Their vile deceitful hearts were more adamantine than the hardest rocks, and they assumed that the Saviour's words were false, in their dread that he might escape from the death which they so ardently wished to see inflicted upon him.

That which the truthful lips of our humble Saviour here asserted under such significant circumstances, and which he even condescended to render more momentous by uniting to his affirmation a solemn oath, the Prophets bore witness to throughout many preceding centuries. The voice of the heavenly Father, that voice which resounded at the river Jordan, the life, doctrine, miracles and prophecies of Jesus confirmed his word, the elements which obeyed, the sickness which departed when he came, the dead who at his word rose to life, nay, even the evil spirits, acknowledged that Jesus was the Son of God. Nevertheless, the hypocritical high-priest rends his garment and with an insolent affection of uprightness cries out: "*He hath blasphemed: what further need have we of witnesses? what think you?*" And all cry with one voice: "*He is guilty of death!*" Unjust sentence! Yet Christ, the Eternal Innocence, suffers this sentence to be pronounced upon him. Why? He desires to die that we sinners may be converted and live. Who is it, therefore, properly speaking, that has rendered this awful verdict? Alas! let us acknowledge it—we sinners have rendered the sentence. This thought should touch our heart, fill us with sadness and urge us to avoid sin, on account of which our Saviour suffered so much, cost what it will! It is not for any fault or imperfection of his own that he chooses to suffer. Ah no! he, the infinite sanctity, he before whom the Angels veil their faces with their shining wings, does not suffer for any offence of his own: One drop of his precious blood would have more than sufficed for the redemption of a thousand worlds, and yet he permits it to pour forth in a plenteous tide from his sacred wounds. All this he does for love of us, and so magnanimous is that love that, no matter how great the tortures he would be called upon to endure, no matter how protracted they might become, they would still be far from equaling the extent of his feeling for us.

The trial is concluded, the verdict rendered, and our Redeemer is delivered into the hands of the rude servants who glory in the office assigned them, that of keeping guard over him, in as much as they can torment him as they see fit. The wicked judges, well satisfied with their success, have left the spot. It was the hour of midnight; a dismal darkness, broken only by torch-lights and watch-fires in the court-yard, reigned over all. Oh! fearful night! during which indescribable pain alternates with the greatest ignominy! These inhuman wretches fall like fiends upon the Saviour, a shower of spittle, a storm of blows and stripes with rods, rage around him; one pushes, another kicks, and another strikes him. "*I have given my body*," our Saviour complains through the prophet, "*to the strikers, and my cheeks to them that plucked them: I have not turned away my face from them that rebuked me, and spit upon me.*" Still this was not enough for their insatiable fury. They ridicule his prophetic dignity, cover his countenance with rags and striking his head, say in mockery: "*Prophesy unto us, O Christ, who is it that struck thee?*" O Father in heaven! why dost thou not transfigure thy Son as thou didst on Mount Thabor! Alas! our sins answer: Our Saviour desired to atone for the lust of our eyes, the lust of the flesh, the pride of life and the numberless sins committed by the tongue of man. He wishes to satisfy the justice of the Eternal Father for those unchaste ones who wound his adorable heart by their despicable sins, for those proud and arrogant ones who turn heedlessly away from the lessons of humility he has taught, and for those evil minded ones who over and over offend against the virtue of charity, all forgetful that he is the God of infinite love. Curse not, therefore, this impious band of Jews and heathens, but beg with contrite hearts, from your Saviour, forgiveness of sin. Oh! if your heart is not colder and harder than a rock it will be moved to compassion, and with tears and sorrow you will vow never to renew those sufferings of our dear Redeemer; for every unjust deed, of which you are guilty, is another blow upon his holy face, and every irreverence towards sacred things flings a new mockery upon your Lord. Every time you forget that upon you rests the all seeing eye of divine Omniscience you again blindfold the Son of God.

Part II.

Whilst on the one hand this dark night of suffering permits us to behold the pain of the divine Sufferer, we, on the other hand, gain an insight into the infinite love of our merciful Redeemer, which appears all the more resplendently in view of the striking contrast presented by their bitter malice and deep seated hate. And this happy insight is an insight into the mercy of Jesus, which bears with the sinner; an insight into the amiability of Jesus, which calls the sinner to repentance; and an insight into the love of Jesus, which celebrates in the penitent sinner a magnificent triumph of grace.

At the time when Christ was tried, he was three times denied by Peter in the court-yard. Peter, who was to be the Prince of the Apostles, the rock of the Church and the bearer of the keys of the kingdom of heaven, three times denies his Lord and Master, to whom he had made professions of fidelity that naught could change. He was not "standing a-far off" from our Saviour. Ah, no! he was within reach of his divine and adorable presence, and he had but a little while before affirmed that though all should be scandalized in him, he would never be scandalized, and yet he fell. He was not content with a simple assertion that he did not know Jesus, with oaths and imprecations he interspersed his denial. Alas! the depths to which even the just man can fall while the tempter can assail him in the land of his exile! And why did Peter fall so deeply? Because he trusted in his own fortitude, and felt himself stronger than the other Apostles; because of his vain glorious assurance: "*Though all men shall be scandalized in thee, I will never be scandalized;*" because despite the exhortation of our Lord: "*Watch and pray!*" he watched not, neither did he pray; because he followed his Master, as do the luke-warm of the present day, from a distance, and imprudently went into dangerous society. O Peter! Peter! teach us all the dangers of sin and obtain for us humility, watchfulnes, devotion and the grace to flee from these occasions, which we know are replete with peril for our eternal salvation. But teach us also to weep after our fall hot tears of repentance and then to live for our Redeemer, to labor, and, if necessary, to die for his sake!

When Peter had, for the third time, denied our Lord, the cock crowed the second time. "*And the Lord, turning, looked on Peter. And Peter remembered the words of the Lord, how he had said: 'Before the cock crow, thou shalt deny me thrice,' and Peter went out and wept bitterly.*" Christ, my dear brethren, who does not break the bent reed, nor extinguish the glimmering spark, Christ, who as the Good Shepherd, seeks the lost sheep in the midst of his sufferings turns upon the weak apostle a look of mercy and love, exhorting him to repentance, a look which Peter understood, for "*He went out and wept bitterly*," wept tears of repentance which were to flow anew as often as by the crowing of a cock he was reminded of his fall. "O humble tear!" exclaims St. Jerome, "thine is the power, thine the dominion. Thou art not afraid of the judge; thou wilt silence every accuser; thou hast everywhere access. If thou approach alone, thou wilt not return void; thou dost torment the devil more than hell does. Still more! Thou dost conquer the unconquerable, thou dost subdue the Almighty!" Blessed tears of the penitent! O! what nobleness of soul, what grandeur characterizes the repentance of St. Peter! All through his subsequent life he wept openly for a sin committed more through weakness than malice. We are told that he even desired the details thereof to be proclaimed aloud until "time shall be no more," as a warning to all in that Church, of which he was the chief upon earth. We must humbly bow before Peter, forgetting the great sinner, admiring and honoring the truly penitent apostle, who never again lost Christ, but lived for him and for him alone, laboring for his Master with a love that made him rejoice to die upon the cross, a devoted love which is now gloriously rewarded in heaven and on earth. Let us reflect well upon the important fact, and take it deeply to heart, my dear brehren, that if Peter had resisted that first ray of grace, he would perhaps never have received a second, but would, like the unfortunate Judas, have been lost. If, therefore, we have fallen, let us rise at the first call of grace.

PERORATION.

My dear brethren, whenever we have listened to the tempter, and sinned grievously, we have denied Christ. We have denied him who, from the manger to the tomb, from Bethlehem to Calvary, spent every moment of his life in suffering for our sins. Let us, therefore, like Peter, weep tears of sorrow, whereby to purify our heart. Such tears rejoice the triune God and the Saints in heaven; such tears reconcile heaven, no matter how many and how grievous the sins may be. One glance at Christ crucified will produce such tears. He was, ere yet the ignominy of his bitter Passion, hung, like a dark pall, over his fainting soul, designated as the most beautiful of all the children of men. His eyes were of a color which it were difficult to describe, lovely in shape, but a world of tender sadness seemed ever to dwell in their luminous depths. His mouth was exceedingly beautiful, his nose straight, his forehead broad and high, whilst his fine and waving locks often caught the sun light as he walked majestically forth on some mission of mercy to man. But O! how changed was our dear Lord after our sins had nailed him fast to the cross! Oh! behold him now covered with wounds; behold his head crowned with thorns, his outstretched arms, his hands and feet bound fast to the wood of the cross; look at his pierced heart; behold the Lamb of God which bleeds for you, poor sinners! Can you do otherwise than shed tears of sorrow, which will be carried by the Angels to the throne of the All-merciful Love? And when you have again received the white robe of innocence, then work out your salvation by watching and praying, with fear and trembling, and be faithful disciples of Christ in the midst of a time in which infidelity and impiety have reached their culmination. Such true penance is a sweet satisfaction for our divine Saviour in his painful sufferings, and for us the key to the heavenly Paradise. That celestial garden where the foul miasma of sin never scatters its poison through groves fragrant with the thousand flowers of virtue, for sin has ceased, and sinful weakness is no longer known. May the great penitent, Peter, obtain for us in this gracious season a repentance like unto his, and may the great Sufferer, Christ Jesus, in his mercy, grant us this grace for the sake of that dreadful night of sufferings. Amen.

IV.

JESUS BEFORE PILATE AND HEROD.

THE FLAGELLATION, CROWNING WITH THORNS, AND MOCKERY.

" Pilate took Jesus and scourged him. And the soldiers, platting a crown of thorns, put it upon his head ; and about him they put a purple garment, and they came to him and said : " Hail, king of the Jews ; and they gave him blows."---John ,19 1. 3.

You have not forgotten, my brethren, how, when on a previous occasion, we assembled for the purpose of earnestly reflecting upon our dear Saviour's sorrows during the last few eventful days of his life upon earth, we followed him in spirit through every phase of his bitter pain. From the midnight hour when the powers of darkness were let loose upon the world until the first faint roseate tinge of dawn caused the eastern hills to blush for the outrages committed against their Creator, we walked by his side, and mourned at the sufferings he so meekly bore. We witnessed his trial, heard his unjust sentence, knew of St. Peter's denial, and beheld the indignities he had to undergo. O! the agony that was crowded into that little space of time, those few short hours from midnight to early dawn. It was, we may well believe, a night of the most intense pain and anguish ever known in the history of mankind.

One that suffers counts the hours, minutes and seconds of a night of affliction, and longs for the friendly light of day to come with its cheerful glow, but alas! for our dear Lord, his most painful and ignominious sufferings were to commence in the morning, and Jerusalem would be there to witness his shame. With his hands tied upon his back, our Saviour, a heart-rending picture of suffering, was dragged like a criminal, in wild triumph, surrounded by a blaspheming raging rabble, through the streets of ungrateful Jerusalem—to the judgment-hall of the unjust and cowardly Pilate. As governor and judge, Pilate was to pronounce sentence upon our dear Lord in the name of the Roman emperor, the supreme ruler of Judea. Pilate, although a heathen, despite the tissue of lies and false accusations, does not find even a shadow of guilt in Jesus of Nazareth. Nevertheless he again delivers him into the hands of his enemies to be conducted to Herod. This miserable man, who likewise finds no guilt in him, treats him like a fool, by having him clothed in a long, white robe, and then sends our Redeemer again to Pilate, where, to gratify the blood-thirsty people, our Saviour is scourged, crowned with thorns and ignominiously mocked and derided.

In all these sufferings of Christ we find three special points for our present meditation :
I. *The justice of the Eternal Judge.*
II. *The patience of our Redeemer.* And
III. *The ingratitude of those for whom he suffered so much.*

PART I.

God is just and must, therefore, punish sin unrelentingly. But what punishment does this justice demand? I will not speak of the fall of the Angels, that fall whereby legions of radiant spirits were in one instant hurled to the depths of a newly-made hell, and doomed to dwell forever amid the tormenting flames kindled by the wrath of an angry God. I will not dwell upon the fatal banishment of our first parents from the beautiful garden, where the divine Goodness had placed them, into a world which is most fittingly known as a valley of tears, nor linger upon the hours of that deluge, in whose surging waters the entire race of man, with a few exceptions, found one grave—one mighty grave. I will briefly mention that terrible visitation which overwhelmed Sodom and Gomorrah, that fire from heaven which sent the sinful creatures to the tortures of a never-ending fire in hell, and tell you of something far more dreadful than all those evidences of God's justice combined in one fearful group.

Let us look in spirit upon the pillar to which our Lord permitted himself to be bound and torn with stripes for our salvation. The sufferings of the preceding night, great as they were, failed to satisfy him who has loved man, *O! how dearly*, from all eternity, and who would suffer still more for his sake. Place yourself in spirit, my dear Christian, in the court-yard of Pilate, so that you may the better depict this terrible tragedy to your mind. There you see him who clothes all creation in wondrous splendor, deprived of his garments, bound to the pillar like a criminal, to be scourged. His impious tormentors fall like wild beasts upon their prey; a storm of stripes with rods, scourges, sinews and disciplines, to which hooks and pieces of metal were fastened, fall upon his sacred virginal body, which soon becomes one painful wound. Alas! words fail me to describe the rage of these inhuman wretches, the whizzing of the scourges, or the sound of the blows through the court-yard; words fail me to convey to your mind an adequate idea of how his tender body is so lacerated that pieces of his sacred flesh are strewed upon the ground, saturated with the same crimson tide. What heart could bear such a description, to say nothing of such a sight? His whole body, from the crown of his head to the sole of his foot is reduced to so terrible a state that the prophecy of Job: "*His flesh shall be consumed away, and his bones that were covered shall be made bare,*" was literally fulfilled. And nowhere, my dear Christians, nowhere, is a merciful Samaritan to be found to pour healing balsam into his wounds. O holy and just God! why does such unprecedented ignominy encompass the Son of man why do those livid stripes disfigure his virginal flesh? The justice of God, my dear Christians, gives the answer: "*He was wounded for our iniquities, he was bruised for our sins.*" Yes, to atone for our miserable pride and vanity in dress, our Saviour was deprived of his clothes, to atone for the sins of immodesty, he had to stand naked before the young and the old and suffer that cruel flagellation of his most holy body. And you, O, souls, for whom he endured all this, will you, nevertheless, in the face of all this, repeat those sins? If so, know then, you repeat the ignominy of your Saviour, and the blood of his scourging will cry louder to heaven for vengeance than the blood of Abel; it will call down upon you a fearful judgment, which this same Saviour will hold on the day of retribution— that same Saviour who was once so cruelly scourged for those sins!

Once more let us turn our eyes toward the court-yard of Pilate, where we behold Jesus liberated from the pillar, standing in the midst of the soldiers, trembling in every limb from excess of pain. O! what an object for our deepest compassion is our suffering Redeemer as he stands, without a friend, while the cruel tormentors rudely gaze at him, well satisfied with their fiendish work. What crime, my dearest brethren, brought upon him the excruciating scourge? O! perish the thought. He was infinitely holy, sanctity itself, incarnate Innocence, and it was for no sin or crime of his that those stripes cut into his quivering flesh. When the soldiers convinced themselves that their task had been well performed, they took a purple mantle from one of their number and threw it around the almost fainting form of our Lord; they bid him hold in his hand the reed which they scoffingly designated his scepter, and pressed the sharp thorns of the crown they had woven till they penetrated far into the holy head. O! should not our hearts break with sorrow, should not sighs of pity and compassion testify our feelings at this most pathetic sight?

Thus has been fulfilled the prophecy of Isaias: "*The whole head is sick, and the whole heart is sad."* "Who can fully comprehend," says St. Vincent Ferrier, "the pain that sacred head, pierced by so many thorns, must have felt, since we experience almost intolerable pain at the sting of a thorn !" And yet the degree of malice has fallen short of the requisite measure, a new indignity is offered to the Son of God. They lead him to an old broken, jagged column, and bid him to assume his rightful royal throne. They fall on their knees to deride and mock him, making his sacred countenance, his open mouth, the mark for their sacrilegious spittle. O dear friends, let us cover our face in the presence of such ignominy and such a scene ! But no ! Let us look at the fearful scene, yes, look closely— and tremble before divine Justice, which punishes him who clothed himself in the habiliments of sin in order to atone for the sins of human ambition. Let all our sentiments henceforth be characterized by humility, as were those of the heroic Godfrey of Bouillon, who, at the moment when his most ardent hopes were realized, and that too through his own undaunted bravery, manifested the virtue of humility in a very rare degree. He had taken Jerusalem, and when his followers desired to crown him with a precious diadem, he cried out : "I could never consent to wear a crown of gold in that city in which my Saviour wore a crown of thorns." Let us look upon our Saviour, in order that his sacred, thorn-crowned head may also, in the hour of temptation, be vividly before our mind ! Look upon him, sinner, and understand that sin, on account of which your Redeemer suffers so much, is no trifle, and, consequently, hell no fevered dream of some frenzied visionary, but rather the most stupendous, the most horrible evil that can be inflicted upon any human being, the most protracted punishment and intense pain that the most vivid imagination could conceive. In that cavernous pit, the depths of which it hath not been given to any one of the human race to sound, a fire, compared to which the lurid light of the fiercest earthly fires is but a painted picture, perpetually burns, without consuming, the wretched souls of the lost, and devils of the most hedious aspect go hither and thither, one demon for each particular sin. The never ending tortures are an unceasing reminder of the magnitude of the punishment which they are forced to acknowledge is just. O! sinnner, tremble. "It is a terrible thing to fall into the hands of the living God !"

Part II.

Behold the patience of our Redeemer ! He the most pure, the most holy, the most just that earth ever bore, the innocent Son of God, endured all these sufferings with a patience which alone was sufficient to prove his divinity. He objects not to the barbarous scourging, to the cruel crowning with thorns, to the ignominious mockery ; no sigh, no complaint, escapes his lips. "*My Father, not my will, but thine be done,*" are his words here also. "*When he was reviled, he did not revile; when he suffered, he threatened not.*" "*He was offered because it was his own will, and he opened not his mouth.*" "*He is led as a sheep to the slaughter, and is dumb as a lamb before his shearer.*"

By this incomparable patience Christ desired to become an example for us in the endurance of our sufferings. "*Christ also suffered for us, leaving you an example, that you should follow his steps,*" says St. Peter. And, indeed, if Christ, our Lord, has suffered so much, should then we, his unworthy servants, complain? What are all our sufferings in comparison to the sufferings of Christ? As a drop of water to the ocean, a grain of sand to a lofty mountain! If Jesus, the guiltless, was willing to drain the bitter chalice of suffering to the last drop, should we, guilty sinners, turn away with indifference, coldness, or alas! perhaps even deliberate malice from the chalice of atonement? Shall we go along carelessly treading that broad and pleasant road where flowers spring up at every step, sweet sounds delight the ear, and perfumed breezes cool the summer heat? When Christ, the King of Glory, chose the most sorrowful path, the royal way of the cross, to enter into his heavenly kingdom, is it fitting, O! souls redeemed by his sufferings, that we, his co-heirs by grace and mercy, should expect to follow him thither by a path of roses? Hence the apostle says: "*Let us look on Jesus, the author and finisher of faith, who having joy proposed unto him, underwent the cross, despising the shame, and sitteth on the right hand of the throne of God.*" Yes, in your sufferings, look on Jesus, your divine model. Are you poor? Jesus was poorer. Are you misunderstood by the world, calumniated and persecuted? So, too, was Jesus, but in an infinitely greater degree. Do you suffer pain? Is the ruddy glow of health a stranger to your cheek? Do your faltering steps almost refuse to bear your weight? Oh, how light are your afflictions in comparison with his ocean of sufferings! Yes, behold his cross, his patience, but also his glory!

Part III.

Alas! how great the ingratitude of so many who rebel at the lightest contradiction, whose lips cannot restrain the angry word, and who deem it a great cross to carry even a little cross with patience in loving union with their fainting Lord. How great the ingratitude of so many, who by sin renew the sufferings of Christ, Our Lord bore all that ignominy, pain and bitterness in the midst of his highly-favored and chosen people, whom he desired to redeem, sanctify, and endow with celestial bliss. Is it thus you repay the love of your Saviour? But if we revolt against this ingratitude, let us examine and see whether this reproach does recoil upon ourselves; whether our Saviour could not turn to us and cry: Foolish people, is it thus you reward my love? Might I not with equal reason cast aside your love when laid as a just tribute at my feet as I implore you, which I do in so many ways, to give it to me as if it were a precious boon? Or could our Lord not say to many of us in our days: I have innocently suffered so much for you, and you are not willing to suffer the least pain for my sake! I have endured all for your sins, and without the least feeling of compunction you plunge anew into the ocean of sin, and thereby remorselessly renew the cause of my pains! Clothed in the garments of derision, I was mocked and derided that I may atone for your proud and improper extravagance in dress; the toilet table is a far dearer shrine to you; thoughts of fashion come more readily than holy thoughts of prayer and meditation! I was cruelly beaten for your sins, your sensuality, your effeminacy; and you, nevertheless, seek the pleasure of this world, of sensuality and the lust of the flesh: For you I have borne, with ignominy and pain, the crown of thorns, and you sin grievously by cherishing a proud mind, as also by the ears, the tongue and the lips. I am derided and mocked for you and you mock me anew by your blasphemous and derisive utterances against religion; you read productions of a shameful and immoral literature which bears the stamp of impurity and blasphemy, and you pay the base disseminators of such literature for their blasphemies against God and his Church! Thus our Saviour could speak to the world in our times, and thus he will speak when he comes to judge the world. Oh! what will be the answer of the world when, arraigned at the bar of the Eternal Judge, there will be no avenue by which to escape, no hope of availing itself of those dazzling equivocations, whereby it so often deluded its poor foolish votaries. And, mark well the truth I tell you, that these accusations will fall with far more crushing force upon Christians than upon those who did not enjoy the happiness of knowing our beloved Lord. Alas for those worldlings who, while enrolled among the children of the one true Church, and professing to belong to "the household of faith," do not know the Saviour, and care neither for his knowledge or love. If they ever knew and loved him, that time has for so many years been hidden in the misty recesses of a vanished past, that they have utterly and entirely forgotten their Creator, their God. O, Christians, it is this forgetfulness of God, which is one of the prevailing errors of the present time. Do not you be of that ungrateful multitude who forget him. Love him, and he will repay you superabundantly. Labor for him, and you will be met by a gratitude so touching that there is no proportion whatever between its extent and the poor weak service we have offered his most sacred heart. Forget him, who during this most painful night even whilst he endured those cruel tortures, remembered you, and what will become of you when you shall be summoned to stand alone, with empty hands, before the Judge? Alas! you will learn that it is a hard and bitter thing to fall into the hands of an angry God, that it is a terrible fate to be sent into everlasting fire, and a just punishment to be sent to answer that question: "Who, O! my soul, can dwell with devouring fire?"

PERORATION.

Let us learn from the justice of the divine and inflexible Judge, the weight and the punishment of sin, and from the patience of our Redeemer, patience and resignation in our sufferings. Let us abhor the black crime of ingratitude towards our suffering Jesus. May our dear Saviour, in whose name these words have been spoken, and in whose name you have received them, render them so efficacious that they will, in a very great degree, promote the salvation of our souls, and aid us to enter the abode of everlasting happiness. Amen!

V.

JESUS SENTENCED TO BE CRUCIFIED.

"Take him you and crucify him: for I find no cause in him."—John 19: 6.

In our previous meditation we beheld our Redeemer cruelly scourged, crowned with thorns and shamefully mocked. Covered with wounds and blood, lacerated from the crown of his head to the sole of his foot, the God-man awakened, even in the heart of Pilate, a feeling of compassion and mercy. In the whole course of his life among all the criminals, who during his official career he had had occasion to observe, never had he witnessed such a picture of utter desolation as this. Not realizing, perhaps, the entire absence of all human feeling which characterized the persecutors of Jesus, the cowardly Judge thought that by presenting the pathetic Sufferer to their notice he might inspire them with the same merciful sentiments as himself. He, therefore, led the Saviour to the balcony of the forum. As the divine Victim with Barabbas and Pilate appeared before the people who had assembled about the palace, a fierce cry of insatiable fury rent the air. Almost fainting from the effects of the tortures which had been so wantonly inflicted upon him, a wave of sorrow seemed to sweep over the soul of our Lord, as he listened to the wild vociferations of ungovernable rage which burst forth from the mob, directed not against Barabbas, but himself. Behold him standing there, divested, indeed, of that wonderful beauty which had captivated the hearts of all who had ever come within its sphere, but clothed in a divine dignity, of which, despite the diabolical malice of his foes, he could never, never be deprived. He stands there in full view of the angry crowd, the fearful crown on his head, the reed in his hand and the cloak of derision clinging to his mangled shoulders. He stands there in deep sadness and infinite mildness, his sacred blood purling down from beneath the crown, his dim eyes, full of divine love, turned upon his unfortunate, ungrateful people. All eyes are rivited upon the balcony, in breathless expectation. At this moment Pilate steps forward, and, pointing to Jesus, exclaims in a loud voice: "*Ecce Homo!*" *Behold the man!* But a few more moments of quietude prevail when the blood-thirsty Jews, becoming more and more enraged, demand pardon for Barabbas, the infamous murderer and chief of robbers, and for our Saviour the death of the cross. As if drunk with the desire to murder, they cry out with one voice: "*Crucify him, crucify him!*" Pilate, recognizing the inutility of further efforts, became indignant at their obstinacy, yet as if one faint hope remained within his breast he assured the multitude "*that he found no cause in our Lord.*" Let us for one moment contemplate Barabbas, between whom and Jesus the choice remains. A noted criminal he stands beside Christ, a man, upon whose countenance every vile passion has left its trace, he dares to take his place beside the holy one. His unkempt hair and matted beard, his eyes glowing with an evil light, his lips parted with an expression of scorn, and his stalwart form full of an insolent strength, present a most striking contrast to the dear suffering Lamb of God by his side. He, too, surveys the crowd, as if he knew well what its verdict would be, and as they still cried out: "*Crucify him, crucify him: give us Barabbas,*" Pilate said: "*Take him you and crucify him: for I find no cause in him.*" What a judge! O! Christians, what a sentence! The long course of centuries which had, since the beginning of the world until now, vanished down "the corridor of time" most assuredly had witnessed many an act of flagrant injustice, many a verdict which trampled upon every principle of right, but alas! never any thing so glaringly wicked as this.

Not a murmur, not a remonstrance is heard from our Saviour who accepts the decision in silence, and bows to it with divine resignation. It may be that his adorable heart felt an added pang when he looked at the monster of depravity and felt that Barabbas had been preferred before him. It may be that he fully realized, at that painful moment, the ingratitude manifested towards him by mankind for whom he had done and suffered so much. Oh! how many tears had been shed for us by those sweet and merciful eyes, how many words of loving exhortation had come from those blessed lips! How many steps did he not take when, weary and footsore, he would gladly have rested. All to gain some way-ward soul for God! Oh! let us not marvel at the Redeemer's sorrow, but strive to learn.

I. What is the cause of this unjust sentence; and
II. The purpose.

Part I.

Who is he that is before the bar of the most unjust court, sentenced to the death of the cross, in ancient times the most ignominious death that could be inflicted upon man? It is eternal Sanctity, incarnate Innocence, in whom the searching eye of Roman justice could not detect even a shadow of guilt; it is he, the Holiest of the holy, who as the friend of sinners, of the sick and the poor of every kind, could call upon every deed of his to be witness of his noble career on earth, and could without hesitation ask: "*Which of you shall convince me of sin?*" It is he, the faultless one, of whom even Pilate, poor trembling craven though he was, declared to the people: "*I find no cause in him.*" Nevertheless, our Saviour is condemned to death. And why? Faith answers: He is our Redeemer, who as the representative of all mankind, ladened with the guilt of sin, as the Mediator between man and God, desires to be for all of us the immaculate Lamb of sacrifice, the reconciliation with divine justice, to atone on the tree of the cross for sin, which originated beneath the tree, in the garden of Paradise. Open your hearts, my brethren, to sentiments of the deepest sorrow, and resolve to abandon sin, for O! believe me, it was *sin, accursed sin,* your sins and mine, which caused the unjust sentence of death to be pronounced against Jesus. Who is it, therefore, that pronounced this deicidal verdict by the lips of Pilate? Oh! sorrowful answer but true! Listen, we must hear it, and repent until the very latest moment of our lives. We have pronounced it, we have all joined in the cruel cry: "*Crucify him! Crucify him!*" for we have all contributed to the common guilt of sin, on account of which our Saviour permitted so cruel a sentence to be pronounced upon him. Painful thought! But still more painful is the thought that we pronounce anew the sentence of blood, that we cry, as it were, anew: Crucify him, crucify him! as often as we repeat *the cause* of that sentence and of that cry, namely, *sin!* Will we continue to commit sin? O dear Christians, redeemed by Christ, consider, if infidels and heathens deserve hell on account of their sins, the Christian deserves it doubly, because he transgresses the law of God, knowing that the Son of God, for the sake of sin, was condemned to the death of the cross. And if on account of that unjust sentence streams of blood flowed through the streets of Jerusalem, by the avenging sword of the Romans, if Pilate, who preferred to sacrifice Christ rather than incur the displeasure of the emperor in whose royal favor he delighted to bask, was after all deprived of that fitful honor, an earthly monarch's notice, and died in a condition of misery that might well have touched the hardest heart, but which failed to elicit any compassion for *him,* what retribution shall be meted out to *us* if we continue to repeat, by our sinful lives, that cruel verdict? O! that my words could so effectually touch the heart of the impenitent sinner, if there be any such present here to-night, that the figure of his agonizing Redeemer would be ever more present before his eyes. I would wish that when he walks forth upon the broad road of sin, that alluring pathway where bloom the rarest flowers of forbidden pleasure, but which terminates in the firey prison of hell, that the pathetic figure of the Saviour would follow his footsteps. I would wish in the silent watches of the night, when, after the revolting delights of some bacchanalian revel, he throws himself upon his couch and loses himself in the inebriate's slumber, that in his troubled dreams he would behold the Saviour sentenced to death, the sad, sad eyes looking at him with sorrowful love. Yes, Christians, I hope that every impenitent sinner who listens to my voice, whether he is treading the broad road through the gates of pride, of avarice, of unchastity, of gluttony, of envy, of anger, or of sloth, will be followed at every step by the crucified Lord until, unable to resist the pleading glance of his loving eye, he will turn from the path of sin and repent. The sharp points of the thorns which encircle that aching head, the cloak clinging to the lacerated shoulders, the reed, that sign of derision, in his divine hand, and above all the tender, inviting look in the Saviour's eye, will certainly appeal to the most obdurate heart. O! that the cruel cry: "*Crucify him, Crucify him!*" would constantly and everywhere resound in his ears, until at last he begins to reflect, and from reflection to lead a penitent life; until he exclaims with St. Theresa: "O Jesus, my Love, I desire to love thee forever. O dear Redeemer, from henceforth no more sin, no! no sin!"

PART II.

Sin was the cause of Christ's condemnation to death; the purpose for which our dear Lord suffered this sentence to be pronounced upon him was: our reconciliation, sanctification and eternal happiness. Sin deprived man of the grace and friendship of God; all mankind languished under the sentence of eternal damnation; sin had, as it were, destroyed the bridge between heaven and earth, so that mankind beheld with terror the flames of hell below. In fear and trembling the human race stood upon the edge of that frightful abyss and gazed far into its yawning depths. They looked upon utter darkness, which even the lurid seething mass of molten fire failed to light, although it revealed the hideous, the shapeless forms of the infernal spirits, as they heaped tortures on the souls of the lost. O! how the more thoughtful shuddered and clung to the hope that a Redeemer would come to their aid. Here, indeed, our Redeemer intervened, in order to effect, through his death on the cross, perfect reconciliation between God and man, and to establish again between heaven and earth that connection which no man, nor angel could bring about. For that purpose he permitted this sentence of death to be passed upon him. But sin had caused discord also among mankind; the lust of the eyes, the lust of the flesh and the pride of life had made man an enemy to man; even the individual man was at war with himself; the storm of passions raged within him, and his heart was oppressed with the night-mare of a wicked conscience, and the terrifying aspect of hell surrounded him. Our Redeemer wished to establish harmony between man and man by the truth and grace of the Church, he desired, as the Apostle so beautifully says, "*through the blood of his cross to unite in peace the things that are on earth and the things that are in heaven.*" And, truly, the words which resounded above Bethlehem's crib : "*On earth peace to men of good will,*" have been verified since that other cry : "*Crucify him, cracify him !*" The sentence of death pronounced upon our Saviour was hell's last cry of victory ; whilst it is for all who are of good will, in heaven, the cry of reconciliation, and on earth, the watch-word of peace.

In connection with our reconciliation our Redeemer had in view our sanctification. He had promised : "*And I, if I be lifted*" (on the cross) "*from the earth, will draw all things to myself,*" like the eagle, in the prophetic picture, who, enticing her young to fly, hovering over them, spreads her wings to take them upon her shoulders and bear them aloft. And when the fulness of time had arrived the Creator of the world entered the world in order to redeem it. He entered it in an obscure grotto on the outskirts of a little town, he, the Lord of the universe, chose to come at midnight as a tiny babe. He came not as a mighty monarch. No, my brethren, he wished by his humility to attract the whole human family, so that when the time for his great suffering should have arrived he would win the children of men to accompany him on his sorrowful way to the cross. Mindful of his promise *to draw all things to himself*, our Redeemer to ensure its fulfilment, suffered himself to be tried, and accepted the condemnation to the Cross. He embraced the Cross, he welcomed its advent, he shrank not from its hard, rude, painful touch. All good things emanate from the cross. The sage finds his wisdom beneath its sheltering arms, and close by its protecting shadow the tempted soul finds strength. The saintly author of the "Imitation" had a perfect realization of this for he tells us : In the cross is salvation ; in the cross is life ; in the cross is protection from thy enemies; in the cross is infusion of heavenly sweetness; in the cross is perfect joy of spirit. . . . There is no health of the soul, nor hope of eternal life, but in the cross." Mankind, formerly deprived of truth and fortitude, now glories in the cross, wherein is wisdom and fortitude. Ask all the "men and women, Saints of God," whose virtues bloomed as so many miraculous flowers of sanctity in the garden of the Lord, whence did they receive strength and grace ? They will answer : From the cross. Ask the martyrs who have shed their blood for Christ, whence their fortitude and grace? They will answer : From the cross. Ask the daughters of Charity, whose heroism by the bed of pain and human misery is admired by physicians who have grown grey in their profession, whence their heroism? They will answer: From the cross! Ask the men and virgins in the lonely forests and arid deserts of distant countries, who, after having left all, served the Crucified, whence such self-denial? They will answer: From the cross of Christ! And at present, in our own country, behold the many who, though thrown among people who are ever ready to sneer at them for belonging to the household of the faith, nevertheless, adhere to and love that faith more than all the world; who, though in the midst of an immoral world would preserve their souls and bodies pure and holy; ask them, whence this fortitude and grace? And all, all will answer: From the cross of Christ!

Finally, our Saviour had in view our eternal happiness, in taking upon himself that cruel sentence of death. Heaven, which was closed by sin, was to be re-opened by the death of Innocence upon the cross. "*We have*," says the Apostle, "*a confidence in the entering into the sanctuary by the blood of Christ, a new and living way, which he hath dedicated for us.*" The grace from the cross, by which we are now united with God is the beginning of that eternal, happy union with him, in which all earthly woe and misery will cease, and in which a full, yea, an overflowing measure of joy and bliss will quicken us. With justice, therefore, St. Chrysostom calls the cross, "the hope of Christians and the key to Paradise." O! let us live, so that it will one day open the golden gates for us."

And now, my dear Christians, once more cast an eye upon our suffering Redeemer, as he stands before us beside Pilate in the face of his ungrateful people, bearing the crown of thorns upon his wounded head, the mantle of derision about his mangled shoulders, the reed in his hand, his eyes filled with sorrowful tears, and his heart filled with sadness and infinite love. Let us meanwhile hold fast to the truth that our sins also have condemned him to death, let us remember that to secure for us the great boon of reconciliation, and thus win, too, sanctification and eternal happiness for mankind, he suffered to be pronounced against him the sentence of condemnation to the painful and ignominious death of the cross. O! how God loved the world! Is there any one of us so dead in heart, so blighted in mind as not to be won by this stupendous love to a better life? O! from the deepest depths of our hearts let us mourn for our sins, let us detest them, let us ardently long that the purpose of all his agony may not be frustrated in our regard.

PERORATION.

In this frame of mind let us turn to the loving mediatrix of Christians, and implore her aid that the cross of her dear Son may indeed yield us salvation, and that in his Passion we may find a ready shield for every snare of our enemy, the prince of hell. Then when our earthly frame shall be laid in the silent grave, and all that is mortal of us is hidden forever from view, Eden's unfading joys will delight our ransomed souls, and we will be forever happy in the realms of perpetual bliss. Amen.

V.

JESUS CARRIES HIS CROSS AND IS CRUCIFIED.

"He delivered him to them to be crucified. And they took Jesus and led him forth. And bearing his cross, he went forth to that place which is called Calvary, but in Hebrew Golgotha, where they crucified him."—John 19 : 16-18.

I will, this evening, dear Christians, consider with you the final sufferings of our Redeemer. After our dear Saviour was, notwithstanding his innocence, condemned to death, he was delivered into the hands of his enemies, to carry on his wounded shoulders the heavy cross from the house of Pilate to Calvary, where he was nailed to it with a criminal on either side. This was that he might establish the new covenant of peace between God and man. An immense multitude of people thronged the streets of the city of Jerusalem, in the midst of them walks Jesus, the crown of thorns upon his head, the cross upon his shoulders. We have followed our Lord from the hour when he began to suffer so intensely, and we will cling to him with that great love which is born of sympathy on this, his last sad journey to the sacred Mount. But, first, my brethren, let us pause one moment and contemplate the wonderful love which could impel the Son of God, the perfect equal of his Eternal Father, the Lord, the King of Heaven, to voluntarily become the principal actor in such a wild tumultuous scene as this. We marvel anew as we meditate upon each added indignity, and behold each new torment heaped with such venom and hate upon his head, and we have ever to revert to the one reason, the only cause, and are lost in amazement to think that it is all through the excessive love of Jesus for us, poor erring children of men. It passes our comprehension, this almost piteous love of our Lord. It does not exclude sinners. Nay, they have ever been the dear objects of his most tender solicitude. Even whilst they deliberately turned away from that holy love and chose the lurid light of everlasting fire, our gracious Lord was ready, should they turn to him with repentant hearts, to forgive, and place them again on the way to eternal life.

O! then sinners! this season of grace is drawing to a close, and each hour bears away in its depths a portion of your life upon earth. Close not your hearts to my appeal. Join the Saviour on his way to Calvary, but join him with a firm resolution to kneel beneath the cross, there to enter a new and better life—a life for him! Let us meditate on this scene of the Passion to which my text refers, namely:

I. Christ carrying the cross. And
II. Christ crucified.

Part I.

After the sentence of death had been pronounced upon our dear Lord, the soldiers prepared to set forth to Calvary. They rudely tore from him the purple cloak, clothed him in his own garments and placed the heavy cross on his mangled shoulders. The signal to set out being given, the procession takes up its line of march. Alas! what a touching sight! Onr Saviour, pale and bent from pain and suffering, falters and sways beneath the heavy cross. Close to him walk the executioners and the soldiers; behind him follow the two thieves and a multitude of people, attracted by curiosity and a variety of causes, not one of which was compassion for the Saviour. No one pities him; mockery and words of derision are heard on all sides; his enemies rejoice over the victory; his friends have fled. But have not his unutterable sorrows called forth the tears of some pious women? Yes; but their tears afford no consolation for our Saviour. "*Weep not over me,*" he says, "*but weep for yourselves and for your children.*" Ah, surely upon his way to death, the heart that of all others in the world loved him most dearly, did not forsake him. Surely his afflicted mother was near at hand. Ah! yes, she who stood close by the cross, followed him to Calvary, but, thrust aside, and pushed hither and thither by the rude mob, she could not go near enough to her divine Son to perform those tender ministrations which a fond mother fain would lavish on a suffering child. And how painful, how weary and sad was the journey for Jesus! The way to Calvary is long, the cross of rough, unfinished wood and extremely hard to carry; our divine Saviour moves slowly along beneath the weighty burden. Every step is a new torment to him; for whilst the one end of the cross rests upon his shoulders, the other, dragging along the ground, knocking against stones and falling into cavities, causes his limbs, which are already covered with wounds, the most painful concussions. Exhausted by the loss of blood, he falls repeatedly beneath the cross to the ground, so that his wounds open and the blood—a crimson tide—streams forth. Here they compel Simon of Cyrene to assist Jesus in carrying the cross, not indeed through compassion for him, but that they may bring him alive to Calvary. It was the number of our sins, my dear Christians, which weighed so heavily upon him, that he fell beneath this burden of sin!

And now, my dear Christian, behold your Saviour carrying the cross! *"Now the King goeth before you!"* If Simon of Cyrene had known who Jesus was he would not have waited until *"forced"* to show the greatest honor and love to our blessed Saviour. Like St. Andrew, seeing his cross from a distance he would have rejoiced : " Hail, precious cross ! O good cross ? O holy cross !" Now, my dear friends, *we* know upon whose shoulders the heavy cross was laid, we know his words : *" If any man will come after me, let him deny himself, and take up his cross daily, and follow me."* Let us, then, not refuse to carry the cross which God places upon *our* shoulders. Each one knows well his own particular cross. It is, perchance, not so very oppressive. It may be some trial that, at times, threatens to crush you beneath its weight. It may be of recent date, or it may be that for years and years its shadow has embittered your life. Be it what it may, summon all your strength, and carry it after your Saviour with patience and resignation. It will be to your honor, your salvation, your eternal glory, your unutterable joy in heaven. Always bear in mind your Saviour ladened with the cross, that you may not faint and falter by the dreary wayside of a clouded life. Your Redeemer walked, as an example for you, the royal way of the cross ; he has invited you to his heavenly dwelling where crosses are changed to fragrant roses, and sufferings to glittering gems. Behold him at the end of his earthly pilgrimage ! Behold, also, his holy Mother, the Apostles, martyrs, confessors, and all his faithful followers of every rank and condition of life ! They all carried the cross after him and received for it a crown in heaven. If you desire to be crowned there, follow then your Saviour on the way of the cross. We may picture to ourselves the swiftly flying moments of time by comparing them to the never ceasing flow of an impetuous stream, hastening onward to the sea. Onward and ever onward rush its crystal waters, not one drop ever flows back whence it came. And when it reaches the vast ocean it is absorbed in its depths, and we see it no more. Thus it is with time. On, on, fly the passing moments seeking for the ocean of eternity, not one ever looks back, nor returns that it may be more fittingly employed. And when it finds the eternal waters it speeds towards them, to be absorbed in their unfathomable depths. Yes, time is short, man's life is but a span, but the reward is eternal and infinitely great.

But it is not sufficient that we carry the cross, that is, those sufferings which his love imposes upon us, we must also carry the cross of mortification and self-denial, which we must voluntarily take upon ourselves. If we desire to be his disciples we must deny ourselves. We must joyfully impose upon ourselves priviations and mortifications of body and soul in order to gain spiritual fruits. *" They who are Christ's have crucified their flesh, with the vices and concupiscences."*—Galat. 5 : 24. Follow the advice of St. Peter : " *Wherefore, having the loins of your mind girded, being sober, hope perfectly for that grace which is offered you at the revelation of Jesus Christ as children of obedience, not conformed to the former desires of your ignorance, but according to him who is holy, who hath called you; be you also holy, in all conversation,* . . . *converse in fear during the time of your sojourn here: knowing that you were not redeemed with corruptible gold or silver* . . . *but with the precious blood of Christ, as of the lamb unspotted and undefiled."*—1. Peter, 1 : 13.

Part II.

The procession has arrived on the heights of Calvary, and Christ desires just here, where repose, according to universal tradition, the ashes of Adam, the first sinner among men, to effect on the cross the redemption, salvation and eternal happiness of the world. On Calvary was committed the most atrocious crime ever perpetrated under the sun. "*They crucified him*"—three words only! but oh! what inexpressible woe! The executioners roughly seize our Saviour, tear his clothes, which adhere to his wounds, from his body, throw him naked upon the cross and then, driving heavy iron nails through his hands and feet, fasten him to the wood. The flesh of his sacred hands and feet are pierced by these cruel nails, the sinews and nerves severed, the veins torn, the bones wrenched asunder, and streams of blood flow from every wound, whilst mournful sighs betoken our dearest Redeemer's pain. The cross is raised and fastened in the earth. Thus he is suspended a most heart-rending spectacle, with arms outstretched, between heaven and earth, in the presence of a wild and infuriated multitude. For three hours, he hangs suffering the most excruciating torments. Turn wheresoever he will, he is immersed in a vast ocean of pain, he experiences only pain, nothing but the most excessive pain. If he looks up to heaven, he finds himself forsaken by his Father; if he looks around him he sees two thieves, one of them blasphemes him; if he looks down from the cross he sees his executioners, with hearts devoid of feeling, and—his holy Mother in tears for his sake. O! the abundance, the effrontery of sin which created for that tender mother a lifelong grief, as she wept there beneath the cross.

Let us, my dear Christians, remain still longer with this willing Victim of our sins, and let us read what is written there—the writing is large, engraved in characters of blood on the sacred body of our Redeemer! O sinner! sinner! "*If in the green wood they do these things, what shall be done in the dry?*" "*Unless you do penance, you shall all likewise perish.*" But the same aspect which fills the sinner's heart with terror, imparts hope, consolation and peace to the heart of the penitent Christian. Come, therefore, contrite souls, to the feet of your crucified Redeemer and let the bright sun of hope gild with its cheering ray the dense gloom of your desolate souls! Why should you feel discouraged? Is it on account of sins committed, but for which you have already done penance? Christ has atoned for them in an abundant measure, only do not fail to offer your penance in union with his sufferings to the heavenly Father. Or do you fear on account of your daily transgressions? Christ has by his death obtained for us those saving means which impart strength to resist the wiles of Satan, and fortitude to suffer with him in his hours of pain. Do you tremble on account of the constant temptations of the world, the flesh and the devil? Christ has, on the cross, conquered the world, gained the victory of the spirit over the flesh and crushed the head of the infernal serpent; his very name puts the devils to flight. Do you fear on account of the few merits you possess for heaven? Christ has gained for us on the cross infinite merits, as also sanctifying grace, which ennobles the most trifling act performed with a good intention, and renders it worthy of a great reward. Do you fear that the loving sorrow which overwhelms your hearts to-night will vanish with the morrow's dawn, or that struggling with passion's fierce assaults, you will for a few brief years still thread the narrow path, then falter on the way, and fail at last? Do you fear for your final perseverance? Christ has gained this grace on the cross for all who are of good will. Have confidence, therefore, penitents. Look to your Saviour; behold! his head is inclined to give you a kiss of peace; his arms are extended to draw us to his reconciled heart, which is open to show us his love. That adorable heart was opened then, a sure refuge for sinners. It is open to-night. It is the living and life giving fountain of eternal life, the glowing furnace of divine love, the infinite treasure of the Divinity! More than ever is it opened in our days, beloved Christians, since the Saviour himself declared that he reserved it as a last best gift to mankind "to win their love." His precious blood is flowing from his wounds to be balm for the wounds of the soul, and his suffering form proclaims in a loud voice, the consoling truth : *" I desire not the death of the wicked, but that the wicked turn from his way and live.*

PERORATION.

Come, therefore, penitent Christians! cast aside all fear, come with child-like confidence, with hearts burning with love for your crucified Saviour and an earnest determination to offend God no more. Approach him who so lovingly opens his arms to extend you forgiveness from the cross. Go to the foot of the cross, and in the precious blood streaming from the sacred wounds write the holy resolution to die to sin and to live by virtue for him who died to win for us eternal life. Amen.

VII.

GOOD FRIDAY.

"He said : It is consummated. And bowing his head he gave up the ghost."—JOHN 19 : 30.

This mournful day calls us beneath the cross of our Redeemer. Calvary stands before the eyes of our soul, and on its summit the cross of redemption, between two other similar instruments of torture. On this cross our Saviour hangs, from his gaping wounds the blood flows down in streams on Calvary's hallowed ground. On this cross Jesus, who was consumed with love for man, and scattered blessings whithersoever he went, hangs between heaven and earth, while the burning heat of the Palestine's sun pours down on his uncovered head. Beneath the cross stands Mary, his mother, with the other women and the disciple of love. Let us, dear Christians, join this sorrowful group and consider the last words of our dying Saviour, words of the greatest weight, which, summoning all his remaining strength he cries in his death agony : "*It is consummated!*" What is consummate

I. *The malice of man.*
II. *The justice of God,* and
III. *The love of Jesus.*

PART I.

The malice of man. When we look at that adorable head, and think how many times the Saviour had not, whereon to lay it: when we reflect how often he was exposed to drenching rains, to cutting winds, and to discomforts of every kind throughout his earthly life, we weep to see that, even in his dying hour, it must rest against the rough wood of the cross, and at the slightest movement feel the sharp sting of the crown of thorns. When we look at that face which in its divine beauty was so dear to his blessed Mother, but which now, all bruised as it is, and livid with the blow of a sacrilegious hand, is dearer and more precious far, we bow in profound adoration and mourn for the malice of man. When we behold those loving eyes, which were ever ready to shed tears of compassion for the afflicted, now almost closed, filled with the dust of the crowded streets, dim and well nigh sightless, we glance at the Queen of Martyrs and mingle our tears with hers. When we see those pallid lips which were ever the medium of all-holy and beautiful thoughts, now bereft even of a drop of water to assuage their burning thirst, we resolve that by a good Christian life we, at least, will be far removed from the diabolical malice of man. O! sacred hands, O! wounded feet that did so much, and took so many steps for love of us. Why do you permit this outrage, O! heavenly

Father, why are they fastened with cruel nails to the cross? Listen to the answer: "Jesus, for your salvation, accepts it all, and does not rebel at the malice of man. Finally the heart of the man-God, pierced, and shedding its blood for love of us, calls upon us to condemn and execrate the vile malice of man."

Yes, my brethren, we stand beneath the cross, on which is exhibited the masterpiece of man's malice, the murder of the Son of God before heaven and earth. If we consider the chain of impious deeds of which this murder is the last link,—O God, in what a light do we behold human malice! At first, our eye meets Judas, the so highly-favored, yet perfidious, disciple, who for thirty pieces of silver betrays his Lord and Master. Did avarice ever manifest itself in a more vividly detestable nature? Consider also attentively, the council of the high-priests and Pharisees, who decree the death of Christ for no other reason than because by the sanctity of his life, the power of his words, his many charitable acts he gained over the hearts of all who came within his sphere an ascendancy, which awoke their jealous rage. Where will you find envy in a more abominable, more malicious form? Listen how Peter, the rock, asserts with an oath that he knows not Christ, and see how all the Apostles have fled! Do you know of a more shameful example of human weakness, of human inconsistency? And when Herod rejoices to see Jesus, that he may demand from him, for the sake of mockery, a miracle, though our Saviour could have called upon hundreds of miracles as so many witnesses; is not thereby the entire spiritual emptiness and blindness of unbelief united with malice, laid bare to view; unbelief which, instead of blushing with shame, ventures even to boast of wisdom? But human malice goes still further! Pilate, in presence of the accusers and witnesses, who, by conflicting arguments and testimonies in which one word is but a falsification of the next, become hopelessly confused, is convinced of the innocence of Jesus, and publicly, with a loud voice, affirms it repeatedly, before all the people—but, nevertheless, has him scourged and condemns him to be crucified. Oh! the cowardice and malice of one who holds the office of a judge! Lacerated by the fearful scourging at the pillar, with the crown of thorns on his bleeding head, and the mantle of derision about his wounded shoulders, Jesus stands like a meek lamb full of divine benignity, before the assembled crowd. What feeling heart can bear to behold that bruised form? On the contrary, what heart does not turn with disgust from the dissolute appearance and the black heart of Barabbas? But the terrible barbarity of the inhuman rabble demands the release of Barabbas and the death of the Son of God, crying out: "*Crucify him, crucify him!*" And when, at last, hanging on the cross—when instead of words of compassion, which are offered to every sufferer, words of mockery, derision and blasphemy are heaped upon him—human malice has reached its climax. It is consummated!

Behold the malice to which man is led by sin. Oh! let us, therefore, kneel at the foot of the cross and renounce sin, which can transform us into such monsters of iniquity. Let us renounce sin, which had, on that terrible day on Calvary, which has to-day, and which will have always for its sure result, the dreadful punishment of an angry God. God is love, my dearest brethren, but he is the Eternal Justice too. His justice does not begin until we have slighted his love, and trampled upon his mercy, but O! it comes. He will cast his fiery bolts upon the sinner, and hurl him to the fathomless depths of hell, that burning abyss, from which the divine hand had striven to hold him by mercy and love. Yes, the amazing extent of that love, it would almost seem, strove to surpass the justice which could no longer save the sinner from his awful doom. Yes! the result of sin is the terrible, the never-ending punishment of an avenging God.

PART II.

This also we learn when looking at the cross, on which the justice of God is made manifest and consummated in its fulness. The Passion, my dear Christians, is the greatest manifestation of divine justice. Our Redeemer had taken upon himself the sins of all mankind. They weighed upon him in the garden of Gethsemane, while he was prostrated to the earth in a bloody sweat, and their punishment stood before him like a bitter chalice, which he must drain to the very dregs. His whole being trembled, and he prayed so beseechingly three times: "*O, my Father, if it be possible, let this chalice pass from me.*" But it was the will of his heavenly Father that he should drink the bitter cup. And although he had received from heaven the testimony: "*This is my beloved Son, in whom I am well pleased*"—he is, nevertheless, delivered up to cruelties, the most atrocious that can be conceived. Neither men nor all the Angels could make satisfaction to the justice of God for sin! On the cross, then, we hear this beloved Son lament: "*My God, my God, why hast thou forsaken me?*" But the Father seems not to hear his Son, all the rigor of divine justice falls upon him; he is plunged into an ocean of pain so great, that he complains with the prophet: "*O all ye that pass by the way, attend, and see if there be any sorrow like to my sorrow, for he hath made a vintage of me, as the Lord spoke in the day of his fierce anger.*—Lament 1-12. And although the earth trembled and the rocks were rent for excess of pain at the sufferings of the Lord; although the sun refused to be witness of his death and placed a dark veil between the world and his brilliant light, Christ must suffer and agonize to his last breath. No loving hand tenderly wipes the cold sweat of death from his brow; no one stays the flowing blood; no one pours healing balsam into his smarting wounds; no one alleviates his pain; no one whispers, in gentle accents, consoling, kindly words!

What then will be the fate of the sinner who falls into the hands of the just God, if the well-beloved, innocent Son of God had to endure such agony, such pain, such a death, for the sins which, alas were ours, not his! Truly, at the feet of the crucified Redeemer, we comprehend the weight of sin and the punishment thereof. Therefore, let us not be of the number to those who, devoid of feeling, trample continually on the blood of Christ! No! with a heart full of sorrow and eyes filled with tears let us kneel at the foot of the cross and vow : O my dear Saviour, never will we sin again, at least, never will we commit a wilful sin. If we make this vow in all earnestness and keep it during our life, then Golgotha will be to us the place where Jesus exhibits his love in all its divine completeness.

And as we approach the close of our last meditation for this Lent, concentrate your thoughts upon this mighty, this almost fabulous love. Think again of the accumulation of sin which our Saviour took upon himself, making it, as it were, almost his very own. In exchange he gave those sufferings which I have endeavored to portray for you, and paid his precious blood to ransom us from the debt into which we had so thoughtlessly—nay even willfully and wickedly rushed, all regardless of what might come. Yes, Christians, God loves us, he wishes our love, even the love of our poor miserable earthly hearts. You will not refuse him—you cannot. Oh! let us to-night lay the coveted gift at his sacred feet!

Part III.

During his whole earthly life our Redeemer manifested to sinful man his infinite love. Out of love for us he descended from the glory of heaven into a wretched stable; out of love for us he assumed the form of a servant, bearing for many years the labors and hardships of an earthly life; out of love for us no labor was too difficult for him, no sacrifice too great, no ingratitude so discouraging that it forced him to abandon his aim. With truly touching love he went as the Good Shepherd in search of the lost sheep. The towns and cities of Judea through which he traveled, the hungry he fed, the sorrowful whom he consoled, the sick whom he healed, all the miracles which he performed, every drop of sweat, the tears which so often bedewed his divine eyes,—are so many testimonies of his divine love. But at the close of his life this love manifests itself in the most perfect manner, in its completeness. For love of us he gave his tender body to be scourged at the pillar, and his head to be crowned with thorns; he suffered himself to be innocently condemned to death; for love of us he walked through the streets of Jerusalem with the heavy cross on his wounded shoulders, and although bending, even falling, to the ground, beneath its weight, he is determined to carry it to the end, to Mount Calvary, where he was to be nailed to it and suffer inexpressible torment.

And when his feet were fastened by cruel nails so that he could no longer walk about to do good, when his hands were nailed to the cross and he could no longer raise them to bless, when his head sank heavily on his breast and his eyes began to break—he had still a heart which was not pierced, and a tongue that he could use to manifest and express his love for us sinners." "*I thirst!*" he cries. For what? For the souls of sinners, for our souls. "*Father, forgive them, for they know not what they do;*" thus he prays for his enemies, for his murderers, for us. They knew, or, at least, they could have known, had they desired it, as many in our days know, or, at least, could know, but they harden their hearts and wilfully close their eyes to the truth. He gives his holy Mother to us as our Mother: "*Behold thy Mother!*" And when a poor sinner, at the last hour, implores his mercy, the Saviour speaks these words of consolation to him: "*Amen, I say to thee, this day thou shalt be with me in paradise.*" And now the sacred blood flows more slowly, it comes drop by drop from the almost empty veins; the Angels of peace veil their faces and weep bitter tears beside the dying Redeemer. Once more, he collects all his remaining strength, and raising his head, cries with a loud voice: "*It is consummated!*" It is consummated—the sacrifice of atonement, the sacrifice of redemption. These words are the great *Ite Missa est* of the high-priest Jesus, at the end of his sacrifice. Ite Missa est, Go, Mass is finished, says also the priest, having offered the sacrifice of the New Law.

PERORATION.

Yes, "*It is consummated.*" Mankind is saved, heaven is re-opened, the debt of sin is paid, death is conquered. "*It is consummated.*" The Angels bear the words on high, through the clouds, to the throne of eternal justice, and God looks down upon the great sacrifice of atonement on Calvary, with a reconciled countenance, the sword of vengeance drops from his hand, the wall of separation between heaven and earth is thrown down, and through heaven's vast expanse the Angels, exultingly cry out: "*It is consummated!*" And in the cross the sinner now finds grace, the afflicted, consolation, and all who desire it, heaven. This is the petition which to-day I lay at the feet of our crucified Redeemer. My dear Saviour, grace for the sinner, consolation for the sad and afflicted, and for all, who desire it, heaven! Amen.

THE SINNER'S RELATION TO GOD.

SEVENTH COURSE.

SEVEN SERMONS.

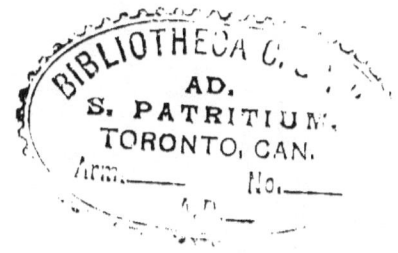

The sinner's relation to God.

I.

VENIAL SIN.

"Blessed is the man that always feareth sin."—Prov. 21.

Permit me, once more, my beloved brethren, at the opening of this holy season of Lent to direct your gaze to your holy Redeemer, suffering and dying for the sins of mankind.

"Behold," said he to his disciples, "we go up to Jerusalem, and all things shall be accomplished which were written by the Prophets concerning the Son of Man. For he shall be delivered to the gentiles, and shall be mocked and scourged and spit upon, and after they have scourged him they will put him to death."

With what meekness must our amiable Jesus have said this! With what grief and anguish must he have gone forth, beholding in anticipation all the horrible tortures which awaited him! See him, in spirit, sorrowful unto death in the garden of Gethsemane, agonizing in prayer, and bathed in a bloody sweat. Look upon that rabble, those frenzied executioners, who fetter him and drag him before his unjust judges. Hearken to those false accusations! Behold him after his cruel scourging! His head is crowned with thorns; he sinks to the earth under his heavy burden. Stretched out upon the cross, his hands and feet transpierced, listen to him, as he sways between heaven and earth, exclaiming in utter dereliction of spirit: "My God, my God, why hast thou forsaken me!"

My dear Christians, all that the entire human race has ever suffered collectively, the Redeemer of the world endured in his own person, in the way of the cross. Is it not, therefore, just and proper that, during this penitential season, we should accompany our Lord to Calvary, and, in the consideration of his Passion, suffer, as it were, with him? Is it not right that we should now gather round the cross by which we, delivered from sin and hell, and, ignoring, for the time being, all the joys and pleasures of life, endeavor by prayer, fasting, and penitential tears to make some satisfaction to our outraged God? Is it not meet that, clasping the crucifix, we should kiss the imprint of his sacred wounds, while we cry out: "Why, O blessed Saviour, why hast thou been immersed in this sea of bitterness?" And the pallid lips of the dying God-man will reply: "*Your* sins have caused all this!" My beloved friends, whenever we gaze upon the cross, we should call to mind with terror the words which our Saviour addressed to the pious women of Jerusalem who met him upon his sorrowful journey. "Weep not over me, but over Jerusalem and your children; *you* have been the cause of these torments, of this ignominious death! I die upon the cross, that I may blot out your sins!"

O dearly beloved, can we behold our Redeemer expiring upon the cruel Tree, and still continue ungratefully to offend him? Can we contemplate his bitter Passion, and go on sinning, go on renewing his agony by our transgressions? In this holy Lenten season, which sets before us in a special manner the tortures we have inflicted on him and the terrible expiation our sins demanded, what can we do more beneficial to our souls, than reflect upon the magnitude of sin, excite within ourselves an intense hatred for it, and exclaim from the bottom of our hearts: "From this day, O my God, no more sin!"

Let us, then, examining more closely into *the nature of sin and its relation to God;* consider:

I. The nature and gravity of *venial sin*, and how these slight faults lead one onto
II. *Mortal sin*, which when persevered in becomes
III. *Habitual grievous sin*, which begets
IV. *Obduracy and final impenitence;* the only means whereby to escape that terrible end, being, with God's help,
V. *To repent;* and finally,
VI. *To experience that mercy which is promised to the penitent sinner.*

Let us then consider, in the first place, *the nature and enormity of venial sin.* How true, my brethren, are the words of St. Augustine, when he says that we do not always weigh the malice of sin in the proper scales. There are many sins which we would be inclined to consider trifling, did not the Holy Scriptures assure us to the contrary. For example, if Jesus himself had not asserted it, who would venture to declare that the man who cries out angrily to his brother: "Thou fool!" commits a sin deserving of hell fire? In like manner many grievous offences are committed against God's law in the guise of petty faults and defects.

Venial sin is a transgression of a law slightly binding, or when the act is not committed with full advertance and consent of the will. He who, for instance, tells a lie in jest, or steals five cents, or indulges a self-complacent thoughts commits a venial sin, because there is no actual malice in these faults. Although offensive to the infinite sanctity of God, they proceed mainly from human frailty. It is also venial sin when a grave commandment of God or of his Church is broken, but without full knowledge and consent. Such sins appear as trifles; nevertheless, they stain the white robe of our innocence, grieve the heart of an all-holy God, and gradually lead to wilful mortal sin.

The enormity of venial sin may be better known from a contempaltion of *the temporal punishments* incurred by those who have committed it. When the Angels led forth Lot and his wife, from the judgment of fire and brimstone that was destroying Sodom and Gomorrah they were forbidden to look back at the doomed cities. Through curiosity, and perchance through pity for others Lot's wife disobeyed the divine command, and was immediately turned ino a pillar of salt. Behold, how dreadful the punishment of a fault committed without reflection! Moses, the faithful servant of God, for a single venial sin was excluded from the promised land, for which he had sighed for forty years. Yea, more, to add to his penance the Lord permitted him to see at a distance the delights of which he had been deprived. And what sin, think you, had he committed? Once, in the desert, the Lord commanded him to strike the rock that water might burst forth for the thirsting people. Moses *doubted* whether such a miracle could be granted to the ungrateful Jews. This was the sin for which he was so severely punished. David, we are told, once mustered his warriors through vanity, desiring to see how many valiant men he had in his army. This was, certainly, not a grievous sin, and yet, as the holy Scriptures tell us, God permitted seventy thousand of his men to perish in punishment of his vanity, God is just. He punishes no offence more severely than it deserves. What a dreadful evil, then, must even venial sin be in his eyes! Should we not tremble at the bare thought of it. If he punished with a like justice every curious glance, all indecorous behavior, all envy of the neighbor's good, and every idle word, how terribly will he not chastise us Christians for our vain thoughts, our pride in our perishable possessions, our exaggerations, and other glaring defects?

I must here refute an objection which is often heard. What harm is there in a careless word, a trifling lie, a profane expression that can really hurt no one? My Christian friends, I will answer you thus: What is it if we call our brother a fool? It can surely do our neighbor no harm, and yet our Lord threatens us with judgment and damnation for all such offences. Why? Because they injure your soul and offend God, being opposed to his holy commandments. The Saints realized this truth, hence their dread of venial sin. St. Jerome tells us: "All the sufferings of this world, war, famine, and pestilence do not injure mankind as much as a single voluntary venial sin offends God ; and if we could abolish all these evils by committing one sin, we dare not commit it." Yes, he even goes further : "If," he says to Christians, "if you were able to convert all the sinners of the universe by the commission of one venial sin, aye, even were you able thereby, to deliver all the holy souls from Purgatory, you dare not commit that sin."

Another reason why we should flee from this great evil of venial sin is, because *God will hereafter punish it so severely.*

Our Saviour, the Eternal Truth, once said : "And they shall render an account of every idle word." Idle, useless words are assuredly not mortal sins, and yet a severe reckoning awaits them after death. In the Psalms we read these words of the Lord : "I will judge justices." What does this mean? Surely not that Christ will judge mortal sins. Such grievous transgressions of the divine law cannot be called *justices.* To judge justises" will be to judge the defects even in our good works. Voluntary self-complacent thoughts, idle words, emotions of vanity, petty injustices,— these are the faults which Almighty God will severely chastise. And, in another portion of Holy Writ, we are warned that we shall not come forth from the prison of divine justice until we have paid the last farthing. What does *that* mean? Is it a grievous thing to steal a farthing ? Certainly not, but the justice of God demands satisfaction for even the smallest defect, and until satisfaction is made, the offender remains shut out in suffering from the unveiled glories of the Beatific Vision.

My dearly beloved brethren, behold the mercy of the Sovereign Judge as manifested in the doctrine of Purgatory ! God cannot forgive even the smallest sin unless it has been atoned for by penance ; hence, his love has provided a place of purgation for his elect, wherein they must be purified from the dross of failings before they can become the pure gold of life eternal, Yet, even this clearly shows the terrible light in which he regards venial sin. The most trifling fault must be expiated, the last farthing must be paid.

Turn to St. Paul, and you will find that he, too, tell us that the just shall be saved, "yet so as by fire ;" and, speaking of the torments of Purgatory, St. Augustine says : "The slightest pain *there* must be greater than all imaginable sufferings of this world taken together." How great, then, must be the evil, for which God has reserved these terrible tortures of purgatorial flames !

Finally, my dear Christians, consider that venial sin is to be avoided, because *it gradually leads to mortal sin.* We must be explicit. Venial sin in and of itself can never become mortal sin, but (and herein lies one of its chief dangers), it gradually disposes the soul to mortal sin. It weakens and decreases the love of God in our souls, and by causing us to offend him frequently and recklessly, implants in our hearts evil inclinations towards mortal sin.

St. Ambrose here makes use of a beautiful simile : Whence comes it, says the saint, that so many vessels are shipwrecked ? Is it always attributable to sudden and violent storms ? No, it is often caused by neglect of slight precautions. Perhaps the captain knew there was a tiny leak in his ship, but he thought it of no consequence. At the outset, it was so small it was scarcely noticed, but the opening grew larger ; the water began to creep in, then to fill the lower deck, and when the crew endeavored to stay its progress, it was too late, and the vessel sank. Thus, venial sin, which is so easily committed, leads almost imperceptibly to mortal sin. Another example will assist us in comprehending this. Tell me, pray, whence came it that Eve sinned so grievously in Paradise ? She sinned through curiosity in looking at the forbidden fruit. This was a venial sin, but it led her to delight in looking at the fruit, it filled her with a desire to possess it. These seemed like light offences, yet from them sprang the greed which prompted her to put forth her hand to touch, to taste, to eat,—in short, to commit mortal sin.

Had David, that man after God's own heart, when his gaze fell upon the wife of another, instantly turned away his eyes and banished the evil suggestion, he would never have yielded to temptation and become an adulterer. "He that despiseth small things shall fall by little and little."

Alas! we need not go to the buried ages to confirm our text. Let us simply look at our own lives. How is it, friend, that you have become a confirmed drunkard ? Is it not because you accustomed yourself by degrees to gratify your appetite for strong drink ? Whence comes it that yonder young man has become a profligate ? Because he did not carefully avoid sinful occasions, and guard sedulously his looks, thoughts, and words. Why have numbers perished in prison, or on the gallows, as thieves and murderers ? For the simple reason that they did not shun the very first suggestion of dishonesty, or of revenge. Thus, we see that, as one cannot attain Christian perfection at a single bound, so neither does he suddenly become proficient in evil. There is a gradual growth in all things. Venial sin disposes to mortal sin.

The Saints of God well understood this truth; hence, they fled from the smallest occasion of evil, and practised the most rigid austerities to atone for their little imperfections. We are told of St. Ignatius that, when a thoughtless boy, in company with other children, he once took some fruit from a neighbor's garden. This, assuredly, was not a mortal sin. But mark the penance! When he became a priest, remembering this fault of his youth, he once took occasion to preach upon the vice of theft. In the course of his sermon, he accused himself publicly of this sin, and seeing the owner of the fruit among his hearers, he besought him vehemently to pardon him, offering his entire fortune to be distributed to the poor in satisfaction for his fault. Think you, if he had overlooked his childish fault, and had persevered in committing others like it, he would ever have become the great Saint Ignatius? Certainly not. St. Aloysius, too, when but five years old, and in camp with his father not only stole some gunpowder from the soldiers' pouches, but also learned from them the use of certain profane expressions, his innocence preventing him from comprehending their malice. Nevertheless, in late years, he always spoke of these childish errors as his "two great crimes," and he never mentioned them without sobs and tears. We, my dear brethren, consider these, the scruples of an exaggerated piety, but would Aloysius have ever attained the pinnacle of his exalted sanctity, if he had made little of these early defects?

Let us compare ourselves with these saintly models. How easily we commit venial sin! Daily—may I not say hourly—we behold ourselves enraged at the slightest injury, impatient under trifling contradiction, finding fault with our neighbor's petty defects, whilst we ourselves commit much more serious offences! Do we not violate charity by equivocal expressions, resort to falsehood in small matters? Are we not habitually careless and distracted in prayer? Do we not often pronounce the holy name of God without due reverence? In short, are we not guilty of all the faults of which ever the just are obliged to accuse themselves, seven times a day? And what penance do we perform? We repent verbally to-day, and to-morrow, we repeat the same offences. Let us reflect upon the enormity of even one venial sin, on the temporal punishments which it deserves, on the severity of its judgment after death. Let us fully digest the terrible thought, that venial sin disposes the soul to mortal sin. The Saints have done the most rigid penance for it, and if we do not imitate their example, we cannot expect to succeed in the all-important affair of our eternal salvation. Either the Saints were foolish in thus chastising and mortifying themselves for light faults, or we are fools in making little of our venial sins. None will dare assert the former, and if we admit the truth of the latter, what remains for us to do?

II.

MORTAL SIN.

"Flee from sins as from the face of a serpent: for if thou comest near them, they will take hold of thee."—Sirach 21: 2.

We have learned in our previous meditation what a serious matter deliberate venial sin is, in the eyes of God. We should prefer every sort of suffering therefore, rather than be guilty of a single vain thought, a thoughtless or profane word, or a trifling falsehood; for these every-day faults cost our Redeemer many sad sighs, and so wrung his Sacred Heart with anguish, as to force from him the bloody sweat of Gethsemane. The Most Holy One detests even the smallest sin; the Most Just God punishes in this world and in the next, him who transgresses his commands. It is gross ingratitude to our loving Jesus to consider venial sin as of no consequence, and to daily drink in iniquity like water; it is downright cruel, reckless, and malicious to dispose ourselves to commit grievous mortal sins, whereby we render fruitless his bitter Passion and death, crucifying him anew. For, since the God-Man died on Calvary to satisfy for our sins, so we, when we sin grievously, renew his ignominious death, trampling wantonly under foot his precious blood. Consequently, if we have resolved never to commit any sin, no matter how slight, we should to-day renew this our firm purpose, because mortal sin deprives us of everything, inasmuch as it renders useless the crucifixion and death of our Lord Jesus Christ.

Beloved Christians, we would need perceptions as pure as those of God himself, to conceive the full enormity of grievous sin. Let us, however, reflect, at least, upon the terrible evil of

I. *Mortal sin*, and of
II. *Habitual mortal sin.*

I.—That man is guilty of mortal sin who, with full consciousness and knowledge, and with perfect freedom of will grievously transgresses a commandment of God, or of his Church. For instance, he who knows that he is bound under pain of mortal sin to hear Mass on Sundays and holidays, yet who, through indifference and without legitimate cause, neglects to do so; or he who, through contempt for the precept of the Church, wilfully partakes of flesh-meat on forbidden days; he who understands that every sin against the Sixth Commandment is grievous, yet who willingly consents to impure thoughts, indulges in vile language or unchaste acts— all such are guilty of mortal sin. In short, mortal sin is a heinous transgression of the divine law which deprives the soul of sanctifying grace, and renders it subject to eternal damnation. It is called *mortal*, because it kills the soul and precipitates it into hell. When the sinner considers his sins in their relation to God, their malice becomes evident. Calmly and reasonably examined, what is mortal sin? First of all, it is disobedience in important matters, aye, it is open rebellion against God. Do we believe this? Let us reflect. Besides being our Creator, God is our Lord and Master, whom we are bound to serve and obey. All creation serves God, except the sinner who, in committing grievous sin, solemnly renounces his allegiance to God, substituting in stead the rule of his own evil will and bad passions. What audacity, what rebellion! The person who is guilty of mortal sin, says practically to his Lord: "I know I ought to serve Thee, but I now recognize Thee no longer as my Master! My own perverse will now takes the place of Thy commandment. I will not serve! I shall do as I please!" What temerity! Imagine you see a strong man, holding high in the air over a yawning abyss, a refractory boy. Would it not be the height of madness at such a moment for the boy to scoff at him who holds in his hands his very life? It is simply inconceivable; yet the sinner gives evidence of just such insanity. He knows that his life hangs by a mere thread which Almighty God at any moment may cut asunder, and yet he offends him, he mocks him!

Besides disobedience, there is also the grossest *ingratitude* in mortal sin, since all that we have and are is the gift of God. Even the irrational animal is grateful to his benefactor, but the sinner uses his gifts for the purpose of offending the Giver, sin being a misuse of temporal goods, and of the powers and faculties of the body and soul. What would you think of a beggar to whom you had kindly given an alms, if he were straightway to buy poison for the money in order therewith to end your life? Thus the sinner acts who converts the benefits he has received into means whereby to offend his good God. The Saints, filled with the love of their Lord, could not conceive the possibility of any one committing mortal sin, which they considered the climax of ingratitude.

Mortal sin is an expression of the greatest contempt for God, the Supreme Good, who is worthy of infinite love and of the highest veneration. When I sin grievously, I prefer to my Creator my own vile self, or some other despicable creature, some temporal advantage or sensual pleasure. We sometimes wonder how Judas could ever have been base enough to betray his divine Friend and Master for thirty pieces of silver—yet the sinner forsakes and sells his Lord for a much smaller compensation—he gives up heaven for some base pleasure, for a moment's miserable gratification.

Finally the grievous sinner makes void so far as in him lies, the merits of the redemption purchased by Christ. The man who commits mortal sin by his disobedience, despoils Almighty God of the glory which Jesus restored to him by his Passion and Death, and of which the sin of Adam had deprived him. Jesus Christ opened heaven for us, that we might there glorify God eternally ; but the sinner closes the celestial gates by his grievous offences and opens the portals of hell, wherein he will blaspheme his Creator for all eternity. Our Saviour has, as it were by his death on the cross annihilated sin, but he who offends God mortally causes sin to live again, that he may cause Christ to die anew.

It is useless, however, for me to attempt to depict the malice of mortal sin, which is as great, as incomprehensible as God himself. It is an offence against Infinity, consequently it is of infinite malice.

With regard to ourselves, mortal sin is followed with desperate consequences. The gravity of sin and its results are closely connected. Let us look up to heaven, there view sin and its consequences, Lucifer and his adherents would fain be like unto God, and this, their sin of pride, transformed them from angels into devils. Ponder well upon this. The supremely merciful and patient God instantly punishes with eternal torments the angels, those wonders of creation, and, for a single mortal sin, precipitates them from the heights of heaven into an abode of unutterable woe! He had never given them any previous example of his omnipotence ; he never paused to infuse a single ray of repentance into their hearts! How terrible must not mortal sin be! After their sin, our first parents, Adam and Eve, were driven out of Paradise, that place of delights, and exposed to the untold miseries, their sad inheritance being thenceforth transmitted to their posterity, to all generations. What a monster must not sin be which so afflicts man, the noblest work of God, and converts the earth into a vale of tears !

The eternity of the pains of hell will also serve to give us some idea of the gravity of sin. On former occasions, my dear brethren, we have carefully considered the subject of hell, and reflected upon what constitutes the everlasting suffering of the reprobate. We have weighed carefully, as well, the meaning of that small but momentous word, *eternal.* Can we think of those pains without trembling at the abominable malice of mortal sin, which merits such terrible chastisement?

If, lastly, the God-man in expiating sin, underwent the ignominious death of the cross, if the Most Holy expired upon the Tree of Calvary, between two thieves, tell me, dear Christians, what sort of an evil must mortal sin be which demanded such a sacrifice ?

Sin has caused all these sufferings, these punishments, temporal and eternal, what think you must be the condition of that soul, and in what deadly peril must it not be, that has heaped up sin upon sin ?

II.—As venial sin gradually disposes to mortal sin, so he who falls into a grievous sin seldom stops at the first offence. Unless a ray of extraordinary grace, a powerful movement to repentance overtake him in time, he will go on heaping up numberless crimes upon his conscience. Take, for example, the drunkard, who has no sooner steeped himself in the fumes of his brutal vice, ere he hastens to add to his sin of drunkenness, that of murder or impurity. Or that slothful Catholic who postpones his Easter duty; he will very probably soon omit attendance at Masses of obligation, or fail to observe the fasts of the Church. In short there are, unfortunately, very few who, having committed one mortal sin, stop there. Once blunted by vice in their spiritual perceptions, what concern is it of theirs as to their soul's salvation, as to the one thing necessary?

Beloved brethern, it is an article of faith that God gives to every man a certain measure of grace which is lost by sin. It varies in different individuals, and is an inscrutable mystery to us, but we know that it is accorded to each man in sufficient quantity to enable him to accomplish his salvation.

With a divine patience, God waits for some sinners many long years. In other cases, his chastisement descends upon them after their second or third fall into sin. It is certain that whenever the measure of God's grace is filled up, God's justice descends upon the guilty one. We have the testimony of Holy Writ upon this point. When the Scribes and Pharisees pursued our Saviour in order to put him to death, he said to them: "Fill ye up, then, the measure of your fathers." Our omniscient Redeemer foresaw their ruin on account of their stiffneckedness, and, therefore, he told them: You still have grace, the hour of divine vengeance has not yet come; but when you have put me to death, then is the measure of your sins full, and divine vengeance will overtake you.

This was literally fulfilled. St. Augustine hence concludes that divine forbearance waits until the measure of grace is filled up; but when this has come to pass, the sinner's punishment begins. Pardon is then no longer possible since no further grace is granted. What a fearfully alarming truth! To know that the measure of his grace must one day be filled up, but to be equally uncertain as to when it shall be accomplished, is, indeed, a fearful and melancholy truth for the sinner.

The prophet Amos, speaking in the name of God, declares that his patience will forgive three sins only, but to the fourth offence condign punishment shall be meted out.

Hearken, O sinner, to the divine voice, during this holy Lenten season, telling you: "I have already pardoned thee not three, but, perhaps, three hundred sins; thy measure of sin is now full; the forfeiture of grace is followed by eternal reprobation. I have been calling thee for three years, nay more, through the voice of my minister. Take advantage of this holy season and enter into thyself; make a good confession, cast off the old man, repent before it is too late! Desist, O impure man, from thy abominable vices! Be earnest in the matter of eternal salvation, for, after thy next sin, my patience and forbearance will assuredly end for thee. Amend thy ways, O careless trangressor of the percept of fasting ; perhaps thy next sin may bring down upon thy guilty head my wrath. Give up thy unjust practices, thou defrauder! Put a stop to thy excesses, thou wretched drunkard, lest thy first relapse serve to fill thy measure of sin and cast thee headlong into hell!

Whenever our Saviour healed a sick person, he was accustomed to say : "Sin no more!" thereby proclaiming sin as the cause of sickness. In the case of a man who had been ill for thirty-eight years, he added : when he had adjured him : "Sin no more," lest some worse thing happen thee!" What would he thereby insinuate? What could be more than to be sick for nearly forty years? Eternal reprobation, when the measure of grace has been exhausted. We should reflect seriously upon these words : "Sin no more lest some worse thing happen thee!" God sends to many the warning of a serious sickness, but it is disregarded. Other crosses and sufferings perhaps are laid upon them ; their dearest relatives are taken from them ; but all these gracious hints are ignored. Having rejected these, their final graces, matters, at length, culminated for them in eternal ruin. O! how often has not God called the sinner! He warns him to employ well his opportunities of salvation ; to amend a life of sin, but in vain ; his justice then overtakes and punishes such reckless contempt of his graces.

O sinful man! could you but penetrate the veil of the divine decrees, you might read in God's inner sanctuary these words, as dreadful, as awe-inspiring for you as was the handwriting on the wall to the guilty Belchazzar : "*I will wait patiently for one sinner ; five years for another ; but as for you I will take vengeance on you after the very next sin you commit!*"

Dare you accuse God of injustice when you know that grace is a gratuitous and unmerited gift from above? How many sins can you assure yourself you may commit, and go unpunished? How can you feel secure for a single moment?

Beloved Brethren, if we reflected as we should upon this grave truth, and upon the uncertainty of the hour of our death, could we continue to sin? Should we not utilize this holy time by amending our lives? Would that all sinners would avail themselves of it! Augustine, that great saint of God, once said : " How gladly would I speak to you of the certainty of your salvation, were I but sure of it myself! "

Let us be as careful in this matter as we are in our worldly affairs, and choose the right way ; for it is always the best. No man can be perfectly certain that he will save his soul. Our only security is in the avoidance of all mortal sin. One more deliberate deadly sin and the measure of our iniquities may be filled up! Let us therefore cry out with a firm and resolute will : " O God ! from henceforth no more sin, no more mortal sins ! Amen.

III.

HABITUAL SIN.

" A young man according to his way, even when he is old, will not depart from it."—Prov. 22 : 6.

As we have already seen, my dear brethren, one single mortal sin changed the Angels into devils ; the first sin of Adam and Eve entailed the most frightful evil upon them and their posterity ; and to expiate one single mortal sin our Redeemer had to undergo and underwent the ignominious death of the cross.

If one mortal sin, then, be so terrible in its nature and consequences, think you what must be the awful risk incurred when a sinner piles up many grievous sins upon his conscience ! The measure of grace he has received gradually fails him, and upon the commission of his next heinous offence, God's justice may descend upon him in eternal punishment.

" Had God's mercy not spared me," said David, in the depths of his contrition, "I had been long since in hell!" Consider this well, O sinner, for it applies precisely to your case. It has been the mercy and long-suffering endurance of your God that have, up to this hour, saved you; but what if this should be the last sin that he will tolerate in you ? Your measure of sin being, perhaps, filled up, and divine grace lacking you, what then ? Suppose you were to hear this : " Since you have contemned all my graces, my justice is now about to overtake you and punish you for that grievous sin you are even now committing !" Do you not realize that some of us, nay, perhaps many of those amongst us, have already reached this point ? Who, then, is so bold as to feel sure that he may yet commit ten or twenty additional mortal sins, and yet go unpunished ?

May not death overtake him whilst in the very act of sin, and precipitate him into eternal misery?

If, then, it is awful to commit one or several mortal sins, it is assuredly infinitely worse to form a habit of sin, for the habitual sinner has cause to dread, at any moment, that the measure of grace allotted him may be exhausted, and that his soul is trembling on the very verge of eternal reprobation.

Let us, therefore, to-day, consider the unfortunate state of the relapsing sinner, the dangerous condition of the habitual sinner. He is, indeed, to be pitied inasmuch as he may almost be said to be already of the number of the final impenitent. For

I. It is very *difficult*, although
II. *It is not utterly impossible, for the habitual sinner to be truly converted.*

I. It is very difficult for a man who is always falling back into his former sins to become converted. I ask you, who are habitual sinners, who repeatedly relapse into the same sins in spite of your apparent repentance, and oft-repeated good resolutions. In such a case, sin has become a habit.

You, O intemperate man, you, who perhaps spend your Sundays and holidays in drunkenness, not reflecting upon the offences you thereby commit against God, and the eternal punishment reserved for you; unmoved by the tears of wife and children, indifferent to the fact that they are suffering hunger and poverty through you; *you* are a habitual sinner. You have undermined your own health by your excesses, you are reckless about your reputation, which you yourself have ruined; you culpably and wantonly relapse into the very same sins, time and again. You, too, profligate, are a habitual sinner, you, who constantly gratify your impure desires, consenting to foul thoughts without a struggle or resistance, and actually seeking occasions of sin.

The habitual sinner comes but once a year to confession. After a hasty examination of conscience, and without having excited himself to true contrition, he confesses, without stating the circumstances which materially aggravate the malice of his sins. He always returns with the same catalogue of mortal sins, the same neglect of Masses of obligation, profanation of the Sunday by sinful pleasures, and brutal excesses. He looks upon these grievous transgressions as mere trifles, and if he finds that it requires an effort to renounce his evil ways, he at once shrinks from the sacrifice, and returns to his sins through habit. All those who thus close their ears to the admonitions of the ministers of God, and to the warnings of conscience, without struggling manfully against their besetting sins, all such may be classed as habitual sinners.

Our Saviour points out to us the difficulty of converting the habitual sinner. He makes it clear to us in three cases mentioned in the Gospel, wherein he raised the dead to life, that of the daughter of Jairus, the son of the widow of Naim, and, lastly of Lazarus, who had already been in his grave four days. St. Augustine says: "Death denotes sin, resuscitation, conversion from sin." He continues: In the case of the daughter of Jairus, Christ merely said to her: 'Arise!' To the son of the widow of Naim, he simply addressed these words: 'Young man, I say to thee, arise!' But when he stood by the grave of Lazarus, why did his eyes overflow with tears, why did he weep and exclaim with a loud voice: 'Lazarus, come forth!'—? Why this difference? Was it because the awaking of Lazarus required more of an effort to him, who is omnipotent? 'No,' replies the saint, 'our Redeemer would hereby give us to understand that the conversion of a sinner, who has been for a long time, as it were, buried in sin, is much more difficult than is that of a novice in crime; the maiden and the youth, who had but recently expired needed but a single word to resuscitate them, whereas Lazarus, who had been several days dead, required a loud cry from the Saviour to awake him."

Peter denies his divine Lord, and one look from Jesus makes him weep bitter tears of penitence? And why? Because it was his first offence. Would one glance suffice to convert the habitual sinner? Would that it were so, for then there would be no unhappy women in the world, whose husbands are drunkards and gamblers, no poor parents, whose children are spendthrifts and the ruin of their families! Truly, the condition of the man with whom sin has become a habit, is awful. All his faculties, his reason, his understanding and his will, are given up to his habit of sin. A slave to his passions, he no longer does what he wills, he is in bondage to habitual sin. His will is constantly growing weaker, his evil inclinations stronger. He frequently commits sins of habit, as though against his will, and driven thereto by some mysterious agency. It is just as if the Evil One held him by the hair of his head, compelling him to do that which no longer yields him any satisfaction or pleasure, for we find that the charm seems to desert that which satiates us. O, I have met people who, in their better moments, would shed scalding tears, and tell me: "I *must* commit these sins; they no longer afford me any pleasure, but I cannot do otherwise. I *must* continue them."

Alas! wretched slaves of passion! What a fearful state! St. Bernard, speaking of its hopelessness, says: "The frequent commission of sin grows into a habit, which, in time, becomes a necessity, rendering amendment of life an utter impossibility; despair follows, and this increases until eternal damnation is the logical result. O terrible truth!

Behold, O habitual sinner! what a fate awaits you! But, you will say, perhaps this is an exaggeration. Can you prove the contrary, and show me that more habitual sinners are converted than are eternally lost? Are you not yourself an example of how sin has become a second nature to you, and how, having abandoned all hope of changing your life, you say: "I cannot renounce sin!"—? You resemble a man lost in a snow-drift, who, being aroused from his deep and fatal sleep, is annoyed at being called and shaken. He rubs his eyes, and finding that his rescuer has withdrawn, at once falls back upon his icy pillow, and in a few minutes is asleep—asleep in the embrace of Death!

Thus the habitual sinner falls asleep again, even after having in his half-waking state made good resolutions of amendment. Referring to this class of sinners, the prophet Jeremias says: "When the Ethiopian changes his skin, so will you reform, who have through habit become sin-sodden." If the former change is impossible, so is it with him in whom sin has become a second nature; his conversion is extremely difficult. Perhaps you intend, O veteran in crime, to postpone your conversion till the hour of death? Will not repentance of heart then come too late to him whose tongue is rapidly becoming dumb forever? Is not despair more sure to seize upon him at the view of his past vicious career? As a rule, one dies as he lives. To, be sure, we have an example of conversion at the eleventh hour in the case of the good thief, but we have only one such case that we may learn never to despair of God's mercy. Dare the sinner count upon that mercy he has so frequently trodden under foot? Can he feel sure that, in that dread hour, he will have the grace of sincere repentance and be able to cry out: "Lord, have mercy upon me, a sinner!" Will not his last state probably be worse than the first. I assure you, O wretched man, you who have lived in the habit of some besetting sin for many years, who have never thoroughly reformed, but have returned each time to the sacred tribunal with the same list of heinous offences, yours will be a terrible fate, should you continue longer in your present course! But you may ask me: Can I not still amend, can I not do penance and repent, in earnest, of my past sins? Yes, for God's chastising hand has not yet descended upon you, and now, during this season of grace, he calls you. Reform, and even though your conversion be extremely difficult, it is not impossible.

II.—"God willeth not the death of the sinner, but that he be converted and live." To-day your Saviour extends his bleeding arms towards you, to embrace you, O penitent sinner, offering you his love and pardon. "If thy sins be as scarlet," cries out the God of mercy, "they shall become white as snow." The fountain of mercy is now open, and he is ready to receive you into his fatherly arms, if you approach him at this holy season with a contrite and humble heart. Look at the Prodigal Son, whom you here so closely resemble in his sins. Profit by his example.

This disobedient son asked, in his youthful levity and folly, for his patrimony, that he might spend it as he chose ; so, having received it, he departed from his father's house. He squandered his substance in riotous living, and in sinful excesses with companions, who, in the hour of adversity, forsook him. He sank so low that he had to stoop to the most menial labor, and even then, he lacked the necessaries of life. His miseries opened his eyes. Comparing his then wretched condition with his past lot in his father's house, he exclaimed amidst tears of repentance : "How many hired servants in my father's house have plenty of bread and I here perish with hunger!" He arose and went back to that father whom he had offended ; he confessed his guilt, and received, in return, grace and pardon. If you have imitated the Prodigal in your sins, begin now to imitate him in his repentance. You, too, have lost your inheritance, your state of grace, your adoption as a child of God. You, like him, have drained the cup of pleasure to the dregs, and then found yourself abandoned by your accomplices in crime. Alas! they had made you their slave, and torn you forcibly away from God, the eternal Fount of all true happiness, and now you run to and fro, like a fugitive pursued by your passions, or are kicked up and down like a foot-ball at the mercy of an avenging evil genius. Depressed and despairing, you involuntarily compare your present condition with that of your early days of innocence, when you diligently strove to serve your God. Take courage, poor prodigal! Change your course ere you have reached the brink of the precipice. You are no further removed from your heavenly Father than was Prodigal of the Gospel from his earthly parent. He calls out to-day : Return! or this may be your last moment of grace!" Exclaim then in sentiments of the most sincere penitence : "Father, I have sinned against heaven and before thee; I am no longer worthy to be called thy child!"

Look at Mary Magdalene, that model of penitents. She tells you : "I was at one time such a confirmed sinner. I was so lost and buried in sin that even the obdurate Pharisees considered me an outcast! You could not be more thoroughly immersed than I in intemperance, impurity, and obstinate resistance of God's grace. I confessed and repented at my Saviour's feet, and saved my immortal soul, obtaining mercy and forgiveness. If you have sinned like me, repent like me."

Why do so many recognize tremblingly their unhappy condition, yet, despite their passing good resolutions, refuse to renounce sin and become new men? They have not the necessary courage; they are too weak; they depend too much upon themselves; they are the slaves of human respect. If habitual sinners desire to be sincerely converted, they must take the first step boldly; they must, at a single stroke, cut off all the occasions that have heretofore proven their ruin, and by prayer and penance ruthlessly extirpate all vices from their hearts.

Hearken, O drunkard, to the voice of grace! Henceforth, not another drop must cross your lips to gratify your infernal passion. Listen not to the pleader's voice, begging for time, protesting that the process of reform must be a gradual one. This is mere stratagem of the devil and of your evil associates. Thus do they seek to tempt you again to ruin. Be firm, and hesitate not. And you, O impure wretch, from this day, no more sins! Habit cries out: "Not all at once! Avoid bad company, but do not break with them too suddenly!" Alas! what an infatuation! If your house were on fire, would you delay in checking flames? Would you say to the firemen: "Wait awhile, there is time enough yet to put out the fire?" Do you not realize that if you do not take immediate measures to extinguish the flames of lust, you will never do it? That which now looks difficult will later be impossible. Man, as we know, is by nature weak; but the habitual sinner is doubly so. Yesterday, he seemed determined to keep the good resolves he then formulated; to-day, his courage has weakened, and he cannot stand firmly.

I grant you that a severe struggle is necessary if you would conquer your vices; the way of virtue is in the beginning steep and rough; the kingdom of heaven suffers violence. Is this more than was demanded of the martyrs who, for the love of God, joyfully ascended the funeral-pile? Or who were torn limb from limb by wild beasts, or immersed in boiling oil.

No matter what may have been your past criminal career, you may, if thoroughly in earnest, be converted with the help of God. Now is the acceptable time, now is the season of grace; and Almighty God is ever ready to admit you to his friendship. I repeat that it is, of course, difficult, it demands sacrifices and strenuous efforts. But, begin now, the longer you wait the harder and more laborious it becomes. Do not try to do the great work gradually. Tear yourself at once from the trammels of your besetting sin! Cost what it may, even life itself, better lose all that earth can give, rather than forfeit the infinite treasure of life everlasting! If, however, you continue longer in your sins, it will be impossible later to arouse you, and you may sink into the fatal lethargy of despair and impenitence.

To thee, O Mary, I recommend all sinners; touch their hearts; obtain for them sincere conversion and final perseverance! O Refuge of Sinners! graciously hear us! Amen.

IV.

FINAL IMPENITENCE.

"The man that with a stiff neck despiseth him that reproveth him, shall suddenly be destroyed: and health shall not follow him."—Prov. 29 : 1.

Beloved Christians, in setting before you in my three past discourses the danger of deliberate venial sin, the terrible risk attached to the commission of a single mortal sin, and lastly, the unfortunate condition of him who defiantly heaps up sin upon sin, I have entertained the hope that all grievious sinners within reach of my voice, would turn to the Lord in humility of heart, before the justice of God could overtake them. If even venial sin offends our Creator, and as we have seen is severely punished even in this world; if, furthermore, mortal sin is terrible in its nature and consequences, since each particular one may serve to exhaust the measure of allotted grace and deliver over the offender to eternal reprobation; finally, if the conversion of the habitual sinner, although exceedingly difficult, is not impossible, all hope vanishes at the view of the obdurate sinner, immersed, so to say, in the ocean of final impenitence.

If it is hard for us to perfectly comprehend the enormity of mortal sin, language fails to express the horrible state of the obstinate sinner who commits sin upon sin, resolutely persevering in his impenitence, without a single ray of redeeming hope. This determined continuance in mortal sin is a sin against the Holy Ghost, which cannot be forgiven in this world or in the world to come; and this, not because the mercy of God cannot pardon any sinner who does penance, but because these stiff-necked men obstinately refuse to repent, and without repentance, forgiveness is impossible.

I fondly hope that there are no obstinate nor impenitent sinners among my hearers to-day, for such as these are not likely to be present, at least, at these Lenten devotions. I simply propose, my beloved Christians, to now place before your eyes such a portrait of this monstrous evil as may serve to preserve you from ever falling into it. If I can only, with God's help, inspire you all with a salutary dread of it, I may then feel secure as to your eternal salvation. Let us, therefore, now contemplate

I. *The terrible state of the obdurate sinner;* and
II. *The consequences and end thereof.*

I.—Obduracy in sin and final impenitence are that state of the soul in which man, without fear, piles sin upon sin, and without any real intention of future amendment. The worst of sinners, as we have seen, will have occasional seasons of regret for his past sinful course. At times he seems to understand his miserable state, and will even form good resolutions, which, however, he is too weak to put into practice. But when a man has reached this point of spiritual obduracy, he is blinded to his sad plight; he is totally separated from God; the measure of grace seems exhausted in his regard, and not a single ray of grace is sent from above to enlighten his understanding and to touch his heart. He sins without remorse of conscience; and in short, he already bears upon him the stigma of eternal reprobation, the natural consequence of sin. As the understanding of our first parents became darkened after their sin (we are told they hid themselves among the trees of Eden, and foolishly imagined that the omnipotent and omniscient Lord could not find them!); and as clouded intellect and obscured powers are in us, the results of original sin, so every additional sin of which the obstinate sinner is guilty, seems to increase his perversity, until he reaches that highest grade of obduracy, final impenitence. His sensuality entirely blinds him, his passions wholly enchain him, so that he can commit the most atrocious crimes, and flatter himself, at the same time, that they are mere human weaknesses.

This is, indeed a terrible state. We behold a faithful picture of it in Pharao. God sent to him his servant Moses, commanding him to deliver from slavery his chosen people, the Jews. Moses, armed with the power of working miracles, an infallible sign of his being divinely commissioned, received from him this insolent reply: "Who is this God whose command I must obey? I recognize no Lord over me, none to whom I must yield obedience; I shall not let Israel go." What blasphemous language! Obdurate and blind contumacy are here manifest. Now, as Moses could obtain nothing from this haughty king by mildness, he had to resort to means wherewith the Almighty God had furnished him, in order to force him to obey through fear. He caused Egypt to be afflicted with seven plagues; he changed water into blood; he filled the country with locusts that destroyed the crops; he scourged the men and cattle with frightful epidemics, yet still the heart of Pharao remained obdurate. Finally, by the command of God the first-born of each family was slain, and then at the prayer of the oppressed people, the wicked ruler let the Israel go. His obdurate heart, however, remained unchanged, and he pursued the chosen people as they quitted his dominions, and tried to force them back again. But he and all his followers found naught but ruin in the waves of the Red Sea.

If we turn our eyes from this hardened sinner of ancient times, we may recognize in some obdurate wretch of our own days the same lamentable characteristics of soul. Yes, there are modern sinners, who indulge in even more audacious lauguage than did Pharao. In their blindness they say that there is no God ; that nature produced itself; that the belief in eternity and the doctrine of future punishments, etc., are all well enough for weak intellects, serving only to keep them in check ; that what is called sin is only human nature, and that whatever nature urges one to do, can be no harm. Is not such language from the mouth of a Christian more impious than was the utterance of the heathen king of Egpyt? Do not the words of holy Writ apply forcibly to such obdurate sinners? "They have eyes and see not, ears and hear not." "The fool hath said in his heart : there is no God." All the truths such fools attempt to deny are taught them by our holy faith, but their vices have extinguished the light of their faith.

As Pharao would not listen to God's warnings and commands, but hardened his heart against them, so the obdurate sinner, to whom God's admonitions are addressed, upon whom his temporal blessings and benefits are poured out, continues obstinately in sin. He considers all who would lead him to amend his life as his bitter enemies. Like the Jews who, when our Redeemer presented to their gaze a picture of their own obdurate state, cried out in their blindness : "Now we know that thou art a Samaritan and hast a devil," so does the hardened culprit behave towards those who would admonish him of his sad condition.

When warnings and admonitions proved of no avail, Pharao was visited by chastisements that served only to make him more hardened. So, too, with our modern scoffer. After the divine benefits have been contemned, Almighty God sends down untold tribulations upon the unrepentent sinner. Poverty, disgrace, and manifold trials overtake him ; he is deprived by death of those nearest and dearest to him. God, in his infinite mercy and patience, endeavors to bring him to a sense of his wickedness. But, like a refractory son, who writhes in anguish under the rod of paternal correction, the hardened sinner grows furious at his continued trials and misfortunes as he terms them. He is envious of the happier lot of his fellowmen, and he persists in declaring his own tribulations to be the work of a capricious fate that maliciously and causelessly persecutes him. He has long since renounced his belief in an over-ruling Providence ; and in his foolish blindness, he now quarrels with the unlucky star which, he claims, nature or destiny has set over his "innocent" head.

Look about you, my dear brethren, and you will observe that prosperity and adversity alike seem unable to arouse the hardened sinner. In the face of either an adverse or successful career, the sinful wretch daily becomes more stubborn and impenitent, and more confirmed in his false views of God and religion. This is that state of blindness which is the result of, as well as the punishment of sin.

The traitor Judas presents a horrible portrait of final impenitence. What did not the love of Jesus do in order to prevent the Iscariot from accomplishing his unspeakable crime of Deicide? Our Saviour sought to soften his heart by admitting him to a participation in the Lord's Supper; and it was at that banquet of love that he admonished the false apostle of the awful sin he was about to commit. Hearken to those words: "One of you is about to betray me!" Jesus, in his mercy, further sought to deter him: "It were better for him," said the plaintive voice of Infinite Love, "it were better for him that he had never been born." Behold, the gentle Lamb of God casting himself on his knees before the traitor, and tenderly washing his filthy feet! Yes, and later, when in the Garden of Gethsemane, he receives from him the treacherous kiss, he embraces him, and whilst shedding tears, exclaims: "Friend, whereto art thou come? Betrayest thou the Son of Man with a kiss?" View on one side the excess of love and mercy, and on the other, the climax of obduracy and blindness! See, what a man is capable of, when final impenitence or rather the unadulterated malice of the devil has laid hold of his heart! Compare the abandoned sinner with Judas. Our Lord has warned him as often as he did his traitor apostle. Judas received but *once* the precious Body and Blood of the Man—God; the sinner has frequently received the holy Communion, yet he remains unmoved. Christ washed the feet of the Iscariot with water, but the sinner's soul has been cleansed and purchased by his precious Blood; and yet he continues stubborn. The Lord called Judas "friend;" he styles us his "brethren."

It is horrible enough when the unchaste, by their impurities, when the calumniator and the drunkard, by their relapses, add to the terrible weight which presses the suffering Redeemer to the earth, but when the impenitent calmly continue in their heinous crimes, despite every admonition, it is simply diabolical; it is the perfection of malice! Such an offender says practically to God: "I will offend thee, O Lord! I will remain in the mire of my sins; I will daily and hourly crucify thee anew!" Truly, this is the utterance of an incarnate devil! And what are the consequences of all this, and what the end?

II. Since the obdurate sinner renders his conversion impossible, the consequence of his crimes are despair and eternal damnation. In order to understand this more clearly we must consider that there are two virtues which keep a man united with God, and which, if he has separated himself for a time from his Lord, can still lead him back to the divine favor. These are the *love*, or the *fear* of God.

The love of God is opposed to every sin, for God is the Supreme Good. The fear of God avoids sin, because the all-righteous Judge will punish him who commits it. Consequently, where these two virtues exist in a man's heart, sin gains no admittance; much less is there any danger of obduracy in vice. Where divine love and fear are lacking, there are to be found disobedience and contumacy, in which case the individual's heart is hardened. We now ask: Can an impenitent sinner become converted? No, for his heart lacks these two essential virtues, the love of God, which avoids every fault, and the fear of God, which endeavors to do penance for past faults. How can a hardened sinner love God? He sins with the greatest indifference and boldness, just as though he did not believe in a God. He fears him not, for he is hardened in crime. His will is diametrically opposed to that of his Creator.

Is it possible for such sinners ever to become converted by the pressure of tribulations and misfortunes? Whilst the ordinary sinner beholds in these God's chastisements and his loving invitations to repentance, the obdurate man sees in them merely a cruel destiny, and maliciously upbraids Divine Providence for his bad luck. Had he humbly availed himself of these visitations of God's mercy he would never have reached the terrible state in which he now is. The prophet Jeremiah bewailed thus the hardened state of the Jews: "Thou hast struck them, O Lord, and they gave no sign of repentance; thou hast chastised them, and they received it not; it only made their hearts harder like rock, and they would not be converted."

Perhaps the admonitions of the ministers of Christ may cause the conversion of these obdurate sinners. No, they rage and fume against the priests and preachers of the church, as did the stiff-necked Jews against our Saviour. They fail to appreciate the priceless blessings descending upon them daily from the hands of God, and consider them all the result of chance or mere accident. O Pharao-like hearts, O impenitent sinners! on whom neither prosperity nor adversity has any effect, rush on in your sinful career, until Almighty God brings your life to a close by an improvided death!

Then, too, when a man commits a sin, but desires to rise after his fall, God sends him a ray of grace, which, if corresponded with, will eventually lead him to confession and true repentance. The sinner's amendment, in short, depends upon God's preventing grace, and his own co-operation therewith. Even the habitual sinner receives the one, and is capable of the other, up to the time when he has finally exhausted his measure of grace.

But, like the benevolent man who, having frequently seen the beggar on whom he has bestowed alms, squandering it for rum, finally determines to give the wretched creature no more money, so also God when he beholds the sinner resolutely rejecting or abusing the graces of salvation which he has so abudantly given him, sternly withdraws himself from that stubborn and impenitent soul, and showers on him no more spiritual blessings. Without the latter, the sinner has really reached the climax of obduracy. Without grace, neither penance or amendment are possible; hence, it follows that the impenitent sinners can never be converted, and that nothing remains for them but despair and eternal damnation.

This, as I have said in the beginning of my discourse, is that sin against the Holy Ghost which according to our Saviour's own words, can never be forgiven either in this world or in the world to come. The magnitude of this sin now becomes evident. God pardons the most grievous sin, provided there is a repentant heart, but the impenitent man wants no forgiveness; he cares nothing for grace, he has reached the climax of malice. But do not supernatural agencies still remain? Would not the working of some extraordinary miracle render possible the conversion of the impenitent? They do not deserve to have such wonders worked in their behalf, for they have persistently abused and outraged the grace of God. Besides, extraordinary miracles have already been wrought in behalf of sinners. But when? Why, at the death of Christ when all nature was thrown into confusion, when the sun was darkened, the rocks were rent, and the dead arose and appeared to many. Did the hardened sinners of those days become converted? Alas! modern sinners have still greater proofs than they of the divinity of our holy religion; they know that pardon without repentance is a moral impossibility, and yet they remain obdurate, and pursue a course which is sure to end in eternal reprobation.

Despair will seize upon the obdurate sinner as death draws nigh. His past life, with its terrible catalogue of crimes, will loom up before his horrified vision mountain-high; and the inexpressible anguish of that hour will contain a certain foretaste of the tortures of hell. Who is there, that would like to die like Cain or Judas? The renowned abbot Alexander, Prince of Hohenlohe-Waldenburg, relates in his diary the following, which occured to him in 1819. "A dissolute young man fell dangerously ill, the result of his excesses. Hearing of this, I at once called on him, and expressed my sympathy for his sickness. As I was leaving he begged me to call again. I promised gladly, and after a day or so, visited him once more. I found him suffering greatly, and terribly depressed. Pointing to two pistols which hung near his bed, he said: 'If this lasts much longer, I will put an end to the whole thing!' I was, of course, awfully shocked at this horrible speech, and I said: 'No! *that* you will never do; you are too noble for that. Why not have recourse to religion, which can comfort and console us in every circumstance of life?' 'Friend,' replied he, 'it is too late for me. When a boy, I was happy; I believed *then*, with childlike faith, but now, I have no faith!' 'But,' said I, 'our Saviour has told us: 'I am come to seek those who are lost.' He will, he can save you!' 'Let us drop this subject,' said the sick man, 'it is now too late. If there *is* a hereafter, it will be bad for me; if there is none, why trouble me with idle thoughts?' I tried again to do something for him when I next saw him, but his curses shocked me. I continued to pray for him, but a hemorrhage coming on suddenly, he died, breathing forth curses and cries of despair. Such was the sinner's death-bed."

V.

REPENTANCE.

"*But if the wicked do penance for all his sins, living, he shall live, and shall not die.*"—Ezech. 18: 21.

The Lord God appeared to Cain after he had committed the heinous crime of fratricide, and said: "Cain, what hast thou done?"

If there is no hand amongst us red with the blood of his brother, we must nevertheless admit, upon glancing back at our past lives, or even since the performance of our last Easter duty, that we have much to account for in our repeated venial sins, nay, perhaps, in some grave transgressions of the law of God. Some of us, alas! may have acquired a sad habit of sin, may have piled up iniquities until, at length, we find ourselves growing obdurate, turning a deaf ear to all calls to repentance, and beginning to tread the fearfully dangerous and downward path to final impenitence. But, during these days of grace, our Lord cries out to us by the mouth of his minister: "Christian, 'what hast thou done?' Unlike Cain, you have not offended me by one, but by numberless sins; you have thrust aside many graces that were calculated to lead you to repentance, and the amendment of your life; and now, you are nearing the brink of ruin. One step more—and your measure of sin will be filled up; one more grievous sin—and then, no more grace. You will be precipitated into hell's fathomless abyss!" O hearken, sinner, to the voice of God's mercy and love, exhorting you to amend your life! Heed this loving voice whilst there is time. For many, this may be the last call of God's love. It is not his justice which speaks to you, for that would perhaps condemn you; it is mercy, which is still willing to spare!

Behold, our good God now during this solemn season of penance, prayer and fasting calls and invites us to return from our evil ways. He addresses us now and brings forcibly before our eyes the enormity of sin, inasmuch as he presents to our gaze the suffering and dying God-man. Our loving Redeemer extends his arms upon the cross to embrace all, who return to him, to the end that his precious Blood may not be lost on any immortal soul.

Now, as we are all sinners, in a greater or less degree, we should all endeavor to obtain pardon by means of penance, the sole remedy for sin. "Unless you do penance, you shall all likewise perish." But, "if the wicked do penance for all his sins, living, he shall live, and shall not die." Let us then propose to ourselves this question: How must we do penance? I reply: If we would really repent and change our lives, we must

I. Know our sinful condition, and
II. Confess our sins and ever after keep them in remembrance.

I.—As the physician can have no reasonable hope of curing a bodily ailment, of which he knows nothing, neither can we hope without self-knowledge to effect an entire relief from sin, the disease of the soul. We cannot possibly do penance, unless we understand precisely our state, and the sins of which we have been guilty. A medical doctor will not prescribe a remedy for me, if I simply say to him: "Doctor, I am sick!" Much less can I expect a cure for my soul's indisposition by merely crying out; "I am a sinner!" The first step towards repentance then is an exact knowledge of one's sins. To attain this, we must examine our consciences. We must open up every fold of the heart, reflecting upon our state, and comparing what it now is, with what it should be.

We must consider what God demands of us each in our own place and condition in life, we must carefully search into all our thoughts, words, and actions since our last valid confession, examining diligently how we have kept the commandments of God and of his Church. See, whether we have carried into execution our good resolutions, or whether we have relapsed into our former bad habits; whether we have repaired our past shortcomings, and made restitution in cases where we have damaged others in reputation or property; ask ourselves whether we have continued to live at enmity with our neighbor, without making efforts towards reconciliation;

whether we have avoided the occasions of sin; above all, earnestly seek to discover if our past confessions have been made with due sincerity and contrition.

Next, let us reflect upon sin; on what it is, and on what are its effects, its malice, and its punishment—practically applying all these points to our own miserable state. We must think seriously of the ingratitude and disobedience shown to our good God by sin, of the loss of grace, of the forfeiture of our title as his adopted children, of our making void, as far as in us lies, the merits of the bitter Passion and death of our Lord Jesus Christ; and lastly, let us descend in spirit into hell, to which our vices are surely dragging us.

True repentance can never consist in a few hurried prayers, the careless recitation of the formula of an act of contrition, nor in the rapid accusation of one's sins to the minister of God. It involves a genuine change of heart, after a due and careful preparation. When you sin your heart and will turn away from God, you attach yourself to creatures, you prefer your evil inclinations to your sovereign Good; you bow down before those false gods, your wretched passions.

If you desire to do penance, then, you must detach your heart from creatures and return to God. You must detest that which you formerly loved; in a word, you must become a new man! Is it hard for us to abandon anything that has caused us temporal loss? Is it difficult to hate sin? Look you—suppose a certain man has robbed you of your good name, or by his lies and tricks has ruined your business, so that his malice has plunged you and yours into actual want. Tell me, how do you feel towards this open enemy? "Alas," you tell me, "I am filled with bitterness against him. Whenever I think of that man, whenever I see him, every indignity he has offered me looms up before me! Humanly speaking, it is hardly possible for me to forgive and forget the injury he has done me!" Well, now, take an example from this; how you should hate sin, your bitterest foe. It has robbed you not of earthly, but of eternal possessions; it has deprived you of the grace of God and of all the merits of your past good actions; it has transformed you, a child of God, into a slave of Satan. In view of all these points, is it hard to hate, and to hereafter avoid, sin, your sole enemy? Certainly not. We must continue the good work we have begun, by confessing our sins, and ever after preserving a salutary remembrance of them.

II.—It cannot be denied that confession, or the avowal of sin to a priest, is repugnant to man's natural self-love; it is highly disagreeable to be obliged to speak evil of one's self. But this self-accusation is absolutely necessary for the obtaining of the forgiveness of our sins.

Our Saviour has attached to the confession of sin its remission. This is clearly and explicitly laid down in the words he used at the institution of the Sacrament of Penance : " Whose sins you shall forgive they are forgiven, and whose sins you shall retain they are retained." Thus we see that whether our sins are to be forgiven or retained, they must first be confessed. For as an earthly judge could give no decision as to the guilt or innocence of a culprit without an exact knowledge of the facts of his case, nor a prudent physician prescribe for an invalid without knowing his symptoms and precise sufferings, so neither can the priest, the representative of God, judge of the sinner's guilt and of his dispositions as to absolution, unless the penitent fully discloses to him his sins, their number, and their aggravating circumstances. You will know, my brethren, that in the affairs of daily life, we cannot pardon our debtors without knowing who and what they are, as well as the exact amount of their indebtedness, so in the tribunal of penance, the representative of God can only judge of the matters laid before him, and bind or loose, according to the facts detailed to him by the penitent. It stands to reason that it would be silly to absolve or forgive what one does not know. It is equally so to expect absolution, unless all one's sins are laid open to the priest. Hence our Saviour attaches to the forgiveness of our sins the essential condition that those sins must be confessed.

Time and space will not admit of our producing from holy Scriptures, and from the Fathers and doctors of the Church, the many incontestable proofs that auricular confession of sin was instituted by Christ, that is has always existed in his Church, and that it never was introduced in the course of time by some cunning Pope or pious Emperor, as our enemies falsely allege. If it were not Christ's institution, the heavy burden it lays upon his representatives, the physical and mental strain it entails, the responsibility before God on the one hand and the humiliation, the discomfort, and the oppressive yoke (for so it seems in the eyes of sensitive and sensual humanity) it imposes on the other—all these would have combined together, and all Christendom would have risen up to protest against such a distressing human ordinance. On the other hand we well know that there is something within the human breast which urges a man to communicate to a kind and sympathising friend whatever may grievously and secretly oppress him. We well know that humble and penitent confession takes away half the sting from gnawing remorse. The peace and joy which open confession infuses, and the numberless conversions which follow it, all justify the practice of confession which our Redeemer himself commanded.

Consequently, our efforts to do penance are facilitated by the confession of sin at the command of him by whose sole power it is that our sins are pardoned. If we would receive forgiveness, we must be careful to make known all our sins to the representative of God. Oh! how guilty are those who, after a year's absence from the sacred tribunal, and after a hasty examination, accuse themselves only of a few petty defects, and become quite indignant, perhaps enraged, if the priest, in his desire to lawfully discharge his duty, and to have the confession of the penitent as complete as possible, questions them as to the performances of the duties of their state of life, etc. These persons surely do not reflect that, if through their own fault, any mortal sin is not confessed, their entire confession is rendered invalid, and that they receive the Sacrament of Penance unworthily! It is not quite likely that, after a year's absence from the holy tribunal, during which time they have been immersed in worldly cares and occupations, they have not given to the Sacrament that diligent self-examition, that conscientious preparation which so sacred a duty demands?

If we would do true penance, we mst confess our sins just as they are, without concealing anything of moment; we must accuse without excusing ourselves, as we know ourselves guilty before God. When sincerity is lacking, there is no genuine repentance. Alas! my brethren, this want of candor, this hiding and palliating sin is a dangerous rock, whereon many, otherwise good confessions, are wrecked! To this species of dissi, mulation may be attributed the fact that so many leave the confessional, that source of such untold peace to the sincere, without consolation or ease of mind. I am aware that it is self-love and the fear of being despised which urges many penitents to this course. Oh? if you have hitherto not been ashamed to commit sin, do not now hesitate to acknowledge it! If a wound is not wholly laid open for surgical treatment (no matter at what cost of pain to the patient) it supurates, and in time produces death; and if the disclosure of sin is somewhat bitter and painful, its results will be so much the more salutary and healing. Why this insincerity? What folly and madness! Consider that by your failure to disclose your sins, your confession and your communion are rendered unworthy; that your conscience will soon awaken and remorsefully reproach you; that the priest well knows the weakness of the human heart and compassionates it; that he never thinks upon nor divulges what is told him in confession; that what you now conceal will, on the day of judgment, be made manifest to the whole world; that from your fatal reserve you are opening your heart to the devil and taking your first steps with him on the awful road of final impenitence. Are not all these reasons well calculated to move us to the greatest possible candor with the minister of Christ, to an unreservedly honest confession of even our most henious crimes?

Whilst confessing our sins, our sorrow for having thus offended our living God should be uppermost in our souls. As you would not feel like pardoning your child for some offence against you, if he should merely refer to it without humbly acknowledging his guilt, and protesting that he will observe your commands better in future, so it is impossible for God to forgive us unless we confess with penitent dispositions.

Repentance begins with a knowledge of our sin ; as it is continued by penance and confession, it should therefore be rendered complete by a constant remembrance or our past offences.

Say that we repent, my brethren, after a good confession, and, that after performing the slight satisfactory prayers or works enjoined by the confessor, (and which cannot be compared with those of the early Christian penitents), an entire amendment of life follows. Shall we be satisfied with this? Ah! no, there still remain those temporal punishments due to our past sins. To this end, we should undertake voluntary penitential works. Again, our evil inclinations and unruly passions are merely suppressed, not exterminated. They must be battled with, or relapse will be unavoidable. Constant prayer, and frequent recourse to the holy Sacraments, extreme vigilance, and reflection upon our own weakness, and upon the magnitude of sin, will all contribute towards our permanent amendment of life. Our own experience tells us how easily we fall back, despite our apparent good resolutions. There is too much surface work in the lives of ordinary Christians. We should root out besetting sins from our hearts, and put our good purposes into constant practice. The great Augustine published all his sins in his work entitled *his* "Confessions," in order that he might always keep them before his eyes. Thus, it was, that he remained steadfast to the end. David and Mary Magdalene also knew that it was only by penance and constant remembrance of their sins, that they could render their conversion permanent. So should we act ; never forgetting our former sins, but always keeping up a continual warfare against our passions, we should work out our salvation in fear and trembling. The way of innocence I fear is lost to us. Let us then enter upon the difficult way of penance, and God's mercy will come to our aid, and enable us to persevere to the end. Amen.

VI.

GOD'S MERCY TO THE SINNER.

"And the lord of that servant being moved with compassion, forgave him the debt."—Matt. 18 : 27.

Now, that we are nearing the close of these Lenten conferences, my brethren, in view of how displeasing and how deserving of punishment all sin is in the eyes of God, should we not strike our breasts and bewail our personal sins with the profoundest sentiments of sorrow and contrition? Let us briefly recall the frightful condition of those who have committed but one mortal sin, the horrible state of the habitual sinner, and the still worse outlook for the impenitent, who are hardened in their crimes. To which of these three classes do we, as sinners, belong? Should we not carefully examine how manifold and grievous have been our offences, how frequent our relapses in the past? Alas! perhaps even now, we are living in a state of habitual tepidity, heedless of the daily mercies and bounties of our Lord, aye, even ungratefully contemning his graces!

Lifting our eyes to heaven, let us, my dear brethren, thank God this day for granting us this new opportunity of salvation. In spite of our repeated offences against him, he has patiently waited for our conversion, whilst, during the past year, he has suddenly called away many others to meet the punishment they deserved.

Shall we not be grateful for this unmerited favor of a prolonged life, for this respite which the divine mercy now offers us, and endeavor to propitiate our offended Saviour?

Mercy, mercy,—O touching, consoling word! Recognize, now, O sinner, the eternal anguish and misery into which sin at any time may thrust you, and, to-day, if you hear God's voice, harden not your heart! That tender voice calls you,—perhaps for the last time. Return, then, humbly and penitently to your heavenly Father, whom you have abandoned, and learn that God's mercy is

I. *Very great;* and therefore that it pardons
II. *Every sin,* even the most heinous.

I. I will pass over all the proofs of God's mercy that are to be found in his work of creation, and passing at once to that of the Redemption, I ask you: Why did the Redeemer of mankind come into this world? To show mercy to sinners. He saw, from his throne of glory, that by the sin of Adam and Eve, man had been separated from God, and that all posterity were burdened with that primal guilt. He saw also that mankind would be lost to heaven, for which it was created; and that, as children of Satan, all men would go to eternal ruin. In his tender mercy he resolved to leave his throne and save the guilty children of Adam. By expiating the guilt of our sins, he would make condign satisfaction to the divine Justice. What other object could the Son of God have had in view in his incarnation? Did he become man to increase his own honor and glory? Certainly not, for God is infinite perfection, and nothing can increase the glory of his intrinsic perfection. Whether his creatures be in heaven or in hell, the intrinsic happiness of the Deity remains the same; it can neither be increased nor diminished since God is unchangeable. Consequently, the Second Person of the adorable Trinity undertook the redemption of poor fallen humanity out of pure love and tender pity. If in our everyday life that Christian charity, which entails self-sacrifice, is so much the more meritorious, O, what must have been the immensity of Christ's love and mercy towards men, when he made such indescribable sacrifices for their sake! "He emptied himself" of the glory which he had in heaven from all eternity; he took upon himself the form of a servant. Coming down to this earth, this vale of tears, and becoming the poorest of the poor, he consorted with sinners, his bitter enemies, who by their crimes offended him anew, sojourned thirty-three years here, teaching and consoling mankind, reaping, in return, nothing but ingratitude, scorn, and calumny; and dying, at length, the cruel death of a malefactor! Alas! was not his every breath, thought, word and action offered up from sheer pity and compassion for unworthy sinners?

Jesus Christ shows us clearly the characteristics of divine mercy in his touching parable of the good Samaritan. The wounded traveler by the roadside is the true type of the Christian, wounded by sin. Our Saviour does not ignore the necessities of this poor sufferer as did the others who journeyed along the road. Neither does he, like the priest and the Levite of the parable, silently pass him by on the other side. True, he, our loving Redeemer, has often been offended, often, in his turn, been unhappily wounded by the sinner, and left lying neglected by the roadside. Yet, behold! he stoops from his high dignity to pour oil and wine into the sinner's wounds. Promising him pardon for his offences, he places him upon his own beast, yes, upon his own shoulders, to bring him back to the fold. The Good Samaritan of the Gospel gave two-pence for the maintenance and care of his wounded charge, but Christ, our Lord, pans out for the wounded sinner the infinite treasure of his graces in the holy Sacraments that the sick soul may be healed of its mortal malady, and relapse no more into sin.

O, my brethren, can there be a greater mercy than that which Jesus portrays in this parable? Have we not, each one of us, experienced his tender compassion in our individual needs? In our journey through life, how often have we not fallen into the snare of our enemy the devil, how often been grievously wounded by sin, stripped of our graces and merits, and left by the roadside, forsaken by all the world! Then our Lord took pity upon us; he sent us a ray of grace, moving us to repentance; and in the tribunal of penance he has healed our wounds, lifted up our prostrate souls, and strengthened and refreshed them anew by the reception of the Blessed Sacrament.

We have a still more beautiful example of the divine mercy in the parable of the Prodigal Son. O, *he* was not an ordinary sinner! He was obstinate as well as rebellious, and persevered in his sins. He squandered his substance, that is, the grace of God. He plunged himself into the most extreme poverty, into the depths of spiritual misery. His garments, that is, his robe of innocence, were torn by his vicious life. Hunger and want, the displeasure of God oppressed him sorely, and he was obliged to the most menial work, that is he basely served the devil. Wretched and forsaken by the world, he at length entered into himself and determined upon a different course of conduct. He would arise and go home to his father—ah! yes, to his loving and forgiving father! Obdurate as he had hitherto proven himself to parental admonition, deep as were the wounds he had inflicted upon his father's heart, O, all these were forgotten, all injuries were overlooked, when the aged parent saw his wilful son coming to him from afar. He hastened to embrace him, and when the wretched youth prostrated himself at his feet, humbly confessing his guilt, the compassionate parent raised him up, pressed him to his bosom and gave him the kiss of peace. There are no reproaches here for the guilty prodigal, no shrinking disgust for his loathsome condition! The father calls him his child: he gives him the most beautiful robe; he prepares a feast for him; he invites all his friends with him, for "I have found my son that was lost."

Behold, my friends, the unparalleled love of an earthly parent for his vicious but repentant son! And yet this is but a feeble image of the immeasurable love and mercy of God in behalf of poor sinners. Innumerable are the souls which the divine compassion has led by sufferings and tribulations to a knowledge of their wickedness, to penance and to amendment of life. Oh! how encouraging this reflection should be to the penitent sinner! Should there be any one here amongst you, my brethren, who, looking back with horror upon his past sinful life, and seeing how often he has strayed far away from his God, how many heinous sins now lie upon his conscience, and who asks himself, almost despairingly, "Can God forgive me?" I say to him: Have you more wounds upon your soul than the poor young man by the roadside had upon his body? Have you groveled in the mire of your sins more persistently than did the Prodigal of the Gospel? Have you served the devil for a longer time than Augustine did? Are you more deeply sunk in the slough of your vices than was Mary Magdalene? O, look up to the infinite mercy of your heavenly Father! To all these sinners that mercy granted pardon, and our Saviour calls out to you: I died for you upon the cross; I will not the death of the sinner. Take courage, the mercy of God is exceedingly great; it can forgive the greatest, the most heinous sin.

II.—It sometimes happens that a man has been for years an habitual sinner, deafening his ears to the calls to repentance which were vouchsafed him. Behold, he is seized at last with a mortal illness, and as he approaches the end of his life, he suddenly recognizes his miserable condition. Fain would he turn to God, but enchained by his abominable passions, he despairs of salvation, and cries out with Cain: "My sin is greater than that I should be pardoned!" This is the state of despair which ends in final impenitence. True it is that this man has lost and abused very many graces. He has lived as God's enemy, burdened his conscience with sin of every sort, and given scandal to all about him. Naturally, he feels convinced that he will die in his sins; but I say to him: You, too, may be pardoned! God's mercy is infinite, it pardons every sin, even the most grievous. Why despair because having lived many years in the midst of impurity? Reflect that even Mary Magdalene heard these words from Christ: "Thy sins are forgiven thee!" Perhaps you have retained ill-gotten goods, or have become rich by fraud and theft? Behold an example of an unrighteous man's repentance in the thief on the cross; and hear Jesus crying out to him: "This day thou shalt be with me in Paradise!" Listen to the great Augustine, who reminds you that he committed more and worse sins than you, and yet, through God's mercy, he became a great saint. "I will not the death of a sinner."

Our Saviour tells us of a servant that owed his lord ten thousand talents. This was an immense sum. The debtor prostrated himself before his master and begged and pleaded thus: "Have patience with me and I will pay thee all." And his lord had compassion on him and forgave him the debt. So, too, will the Lord of the universe do in your regard, O repentant sinner! St. Eusebius compares the ten thousand talents of the servant's indebtedness to our numerous offences against God. If the master acted thus towards his servant, may you not look for a like grace and favor from your merciful Lord! St. Jerome remarks: "No sinner need despair of salvation whilst his soul is in his body; he need never doubt the fathomless abyss of divine mercy, but he should do all in his power to deliver his soul from undue fear of being cast off. God's mercy surpasses human understanding; it may almost be said to save the sinner against his will, for the grace of conversion is often irresistible. "I was obstinate and loved thee not," says the great Augustine; "I loved sin, I left thee for thy enemy. But thou hast sought me out, and delivered me from the hands of my bitter foe, almost against my will." Oh! the incomprehensible mercy of God, which pardons all, even the most heinous transgressions! How have we merited this mercy? "Not unto us, O Lord!" To *thee*, my bleeding Saviour, to thee, we owe all these incomparable blessings! I have sinned and thou hast borne the chastisement thereof. And why? Through mercy for us sinners.

Oh! my dear brethren, let us reflect that it is only by penance we can obtain pardon. Many of you have already harkened to the call of grace and have become reconciled with your offended and outraged Creator. Oh! that having made this heroic effort, you may persevere, and may never again relapse into sin! But some are still holding back. Some still hesitate; they have not yet put their hand to the plough; they still continue in sin. O! would that these, too, would but shake off the heavy yoke of Satan and rise to a new life. I promise them they will be much happier after good and contrite confession. Let me not, I beg of you, call to you in vain. This may be, for many of us, our last Lent; if called suddenly away, would yours, my brethren, be an unprovided death?

O divine Saviour! thou didst die on the cross for sin! To thy sacred agonizing Heart I recommend all tepid souls; I conjure thee touch their consciences with the sharp goad of thy grace! Let them see and realize their unhappy state, that they may expiate their sins in a truly penitential manner whilst thy mercy is being offered them, and may not permit the precious blood to be spilt for them in vain. Amen.

VII.

THE THREE-FOLD SACRIFICE OF CHRIST.

" Who his own self bore our sins in his body upon the tree."—1. Pet. 2 : 24.

This is Good Friday—a *good* day, and yet, truly a day of woe and lamentation, for on it the Just One died the death of the greatest malefactor.

Jesus hangs upon the cross.

With the eye of faith we behold the thousands of insults, blasphemies, blows and buffets to which he has been subjected. Ropes and bands, thorns and scourges, nails and cross are the bloody instruments of our dying Saviour's martyrdom.

O, holy life! O, cruel death!

The sun is darkened, the earth trembles at the death of its Creator, the veil of the temple is rent asunder, the dead arise from their graves—everything expresses horror. To-day, my brethren, in memory of all this, our altars are stripped of all ornaments, the organ is silent, mournful dirges fall upon our ears; everything expresses sorrow for the death of the Son of God. Sin, which began in Paradise through the fruit of a tree, is atoned for to-day by the precious fruit of the tree of the cross. The sacrifice of Christ, in order to be fully satisfactory to the divine Justice must be three-fold.

1st. Sin perverted man's will; for this our Saviour atoned by his obedience and resignation in the Garden of Olives.

2d. Sin ruined man's body through his passions, and this injury was repaired by the fearful bodily sufferings which our Saviour endured in his own person in Jernsalem.

3rd. Sin brought everlasting death to man, and in order to avert this doom, our Saviour voluntarily suffered death on Calvary.

Let us therefore contemplate :

I. *Our Saviour's sacrifice of his will in* the Garden of Olives.
II. *The sacrifice of his body in Jerusalem*; and
III. *The sacrifice of his death on Calvary.*

I. In the Garden of Olives our Saviour offered up the sacrifice of his will by perfect submission to the divine will, thereby making satisfaction for the disobedience of our will. After the Last Supper with his disciples, our divine Redeemer goes with them in sorrowful silence, to the Garden of Olives. As a brave warrior hastens to the field of battle to await the appearance of the enemy, so our Saviour is impelled by his strong desire of perfectly fulfilling his heavenly Father's will, and of completing the work of our redemption, to hasten to the place in which his omniscience foresaw that the base designs of the Synagogue and the treachery of his faithless disciple would be carried out. He crossed the brook Cedron, and at the sight of its waters he recalls the words of king David, who had prophesied that the blood of the Messiah should be poured forth, like the waters of the brook, for the salvation of the world. He arrives at the Garden of Olives, whose trees remind him of the prophecy of Jeremias, foretelling that the body of the world's Redeemer should be tortured, beaten, and, as it were pressed down in the vat of inexpressible sufferings, in order to give to the world the oil of peace. He reaches the Garden of Olives, and here begins the sacrifice of his will for the redemption of mankind, who had sinned in Adam by refusing obedience to the divine commands in paradise.

Our Saviour kneels down; in the darkness of night, which is barely dissipated by the pale moon-beams, we behold him sorrowful, trembling, almost fainting, bowed to the earth in prayer. Whence comes this change in the Son of God, in the Lion of Judah, to whom nothing once seemed difficult or fear-inspiring? Dearly beloved, our Saviour is already engaged in the work of sacrifice; he is now offering up his will to that of his heavenly Father. Sometimes we, too, my brethren, are called upon to submit our will to that of another, but this does not trouble us if what our neighbor requires of us is reasonable and just. But the sacrifice of Jesus, by the wise counsels of God, must be filled with bitterness and pain in order to atone for sin. Consequently, although our Saviour submitted his will to that of his Father, yet there arose in his interior a violent, painful conflict. His human will shrank from the contemplation of his approaching cruel death, and nature trembled at the sight with dread and horror. Thus the Sacred Heart of Jesus, deprived of the power and aid of his divinity, became the prey of a thousand terrible thoughts and fears. Before him passed in prospective the long array of his approaching sufferings, the false charges, the manifold blasphemies and mockeries, the blows, the scourging, the crown of thorns, the nails, the cross. All these passed in review before his mind, oppressing his sensitive heart with the terrible vision of the future, and forcing him in advance to drain the chalice of suffering to its very dregs. O, who can describe this unspeakable pain, anguish, and torture of the God-Head? A bloody sweat bedews his body, yet he bows his blessed head, and meekly murmurs: " Father, not my will, but thine be done."—Luke 22 : 42.

Victim of obedience! What a resignation was thine to the decrees of the Eternal Father? Faintly, yet truly, was this submission of the will foreshadowed in the conduct of the patriarch Abraham. That holy man was commanded by God to sacrifice his only son as a proof of his perfect obedience. Isaac, the only son, must die a victim by the hand of his own father. What a conflict must have arisen in the paternal heart of the holy patriarch against this severe command of God! What overwhelming sorrow must he not have experienced as with his dearly-beloved son, he made the sad journey to the place of sacrifice, Mount Moriah! Of this you, dear parents, who have stood by the death-bed of your beloved children, may form some idea. You may imagine the unspeakable pain experienced by him, who was bidden by the Almighty not only to stand by the death-pile of his dear son, but to strike with his own hand the destroying blow.

Yet Abraham's trial was merely a test of his obedience. The consummation of the sacrifice was not required of him. In the Garden of Olives, however, our Saviour knew that his great sacrifice must be completed. O, be astonished at this stupendous miracle of self-immolation! Behold here the highest obedience, the grandest climax of love in the death agony of our suffering Saviour!

But the bitterest anguish of our Redeemer came from the knowledge that although he was about to die in atonement for sin, yet, in spite of his cruel death, millions of souls would yet be eternally lost through sin. He foresaw the betrayal of Judas and his eternal damnation, the denial of Peter and his danger, the flight of his disciples, and their disgrace, the blindness and malice of the Jewish nation, and their downfall; he foresaw how so many would despise his cross, and thereby, through their own fault, go to ruin. He saw in spirit the thousands of apostates who would fall away from the faith which he was instituting by his death; he saw the many heretics, who, in the mazes of error, would wander from the right path ; he saw the multitude of vices and sins with which *we*, my brethren, each one of us, ungratefully repay his immense love. O, it was our sins, the sins of those who call themselves Christians, that pressed him to the earth in the Garden of Olives! Those were the bitter dregs of the chalice which he must drain; that the bloody spear which pierced his heart. The climax of his action was in the thought that for so many ungrateful and blinded souls he would not only suffer and die in vain, but that his very sufferings and death would be the real cause of their damnation. There, in the dim shadows of Gethsemane, he kneels, overcome with this woful thought, deprived of all consolation and assistance, his heart convulsed with an agony which no human tongue can describe. Even heaven itself, his own royal kingdom, seems closed against him. The Eternal Father no longer recognizes his sole-begotten and beloved son. The Divine Victim trembles in every limb; the blood, which can find no room in his oppressed heart, forces its way to the surface, and falls in great drops, like crimson tears, upon the sinful earth. Alas! Even adamant would be softened to pity and compassion at the view of such exquisite torture! Oh! my Saviour, that our tears could but assuage thy sufferings, our blood flow instead of thine, gladly would we offer both tears and blood to thee! But no! Jesus Christ must needs expiate our sins, his precious Body must be sacrificed.

II. After our Redeemer had thus accomplished the sacrifice of his will, he continued the work of Redemption by undergoing the most ignominious treatment. Behold, how our Lord is bound by his enemies, and thus led to Jerusalem amidst blows and bruises, mockery and scorn! A few days ago "*Hosannas*" greeted him on every side; now the very same people denounce him as a seducer, a malefactor, and a traitor to Caesar. O, the inconstancy of the human soul! O, how fleeting and changeable is the fever of men!

Let us, in spirit, enter into the house of the high priest, and gaze upon innocence as contrasted with villainy. Black calumny, false witnesses, audacity, blows and stripes were all employed until, without examination or defence, Jesus Christ is condemned.

Jesus is worthy of death.

He, most Holy, the All-righteous; he, whose sanctity, charity and miraculous powers, these now-blinded people had so often admired; he, who on the summit of Thabor, was pronounced by a voice from heaven to be the beloved Son of God,—*he*, worthy of death. Behold, in the disciples having abandoned him at this supreme moment, a sad proof of the effects of human respect.

During that long night of his Passion, when he remained under the malign power of his brutal executioners, his sufferings were indescribable. "Prophesy unto us," said one guilty wretch, who had blindfolded the meek Lamb of God, "prophesy unto us, who it was that struck thee!"

The malice of the soldiery was diabolical; yet he bore all things with divine patience and silence. Finally, the morning dawned, that terrible Good Friday morning, which was to lead him to other and even more horrible torments.

Pilate, to whom he was brought, was convinced of his innocence, and yet this ruler, who sinned through fear of the people, commanded Innocence to be scourged.

Woe to him who falls through human respect, as did the Roman governor.

The blood of Jesus gushes forth in torrents, it colors the hard stones beneath the pillar, but it fails to touch the hearts of his murderers. They plait a crown of sharp thorns, and thrust it upon his divine head; his precious blood trickles down on temple and cheek.

Ecce homo! Look upon that adorable Face wounded and blood-stained for the love of us! But hark! what shrieks are those we hear: "Crucify him! Crucify him!"

III. The last sacrifice demanded by divine justice is about to be consummated. "It is expedient that one man shall die for the people." Jesus must die that we may live; he must expiate our sins, and "the wages of sin is death."

He takes up his cross and bears it, uncomplainingly, through the long streets of that deluded city.

As thou hast dealt with thy Redeemer, O misguided Jerusalem, so wilt thou be one day dealt with by thy enemies. They shall beat thee to the earth, and put to death thy children!

Weakened by loss of blood, Jesus falls again and again on his road to Mount Calvary. One would suppose the stony hearts of his enemies would have been melted with pity,—but, no! he is compelled by cruel blows and horrid blasphemies, to rise and resume his sad journey.

O, dearest Lord, we will run to thy assitance! What do I say? We, who are unwilling to bear anything disagreeable, a trifling mishap, some pain or imaginary insult, how shall we help thee, O Lord? Our pity consists in empty words, but not in deeds. Learn patience, O Christians! from your prostrate Saviour!

At length, he is stripped of his torn garments, thrown violently down by his executioners, and stretched upon the hard bed of the cross. The rude nails are cruelly driven into his tender hands and feet. He is raised on high; every nerve and sinew being strained and rent by the jolting and settling of the cross into the place prepared for it. Not a sign of impatience is visible in that adorable, gentle Face; neither sighs nor lamentations proceed from the pallid lips of the divine Sufferer. Suspended on high, enduring indescribable agonies of body and mind, he prays for his bitter enemies. The anguish of his blessed Mother at the foot of the cross adds the last drop to the torrent of torments that overwhelmed him.

At the end of three hours the chalice of affliction having been drained to the dregs, divine justice is appeased—the precious moment of redemption has arrived—the Paschal Lamb announces to redeemed mankind: "It is consummated! Into thy hands, O God! I commend my spirit!"

Beloved brethren, I have endeavored thus feebly to portray to you the three-fold sacrifice which our Redeemer offered for our sins. Let us endeavor to profit by it; let us imitate our loving Saviour, by presenting to our heavenly Father the sacrifice of our will, the sacrifice of our body and the final sacrifice of our life. Let us subject ourselves in every circumstance of life to the divine will, and avoid sin by a diligent mortification of our passions. Then, may we, indeed, hope, that our death will be but the beginning of eternal life.

Can we behold our suffering Jesus, and still remain in sin? O, ye proud ones, look at that blessed head crowned with thorns, and weep over your work. View those divine lips, saturated with vinegar and gall, O drunkard! and see what your excesses have done! Oh, miserly, avaricious Catholic, do you perceive those pierced hands and fail to recognize the result of your close-fistedness, your hard-heartedness towards the widow and orphan! O, unchaste creature, be ashamed of your shameful vices, when you do number those gaping wounds of your Redeemer! Alas! Jesus, our love, is crucified, and his crucifixion is *our* work.

May thy Passion and death, O innocent Lamb of God, interpose, hereafter, between us and sin, and prevent us from ever again yielding to those foul temptations of our enemy, by which he would have us renew again thy dreadful agony on the Tree of the Cross. Amen.

The Seven Last Words of Jesus on the Cross.

EIGHTH COURSE.

SEVEN SERMONS.

The Seven Last Words of Jesus Christ on the Cross.

THE FIRST WORD.

"Father, forgive them; for they know not what they do." Luke 23 : 34.

Once more, the holy season of Lent is at hand ; once more, it knocks gently at the portals of the heart, exhorting us to repentance, and reminding us to enter upon a new life, leads us from station to station of our Lord's bitter Passion, that, at each one, we may more firmly resolve to cease wounding his Sacred Heart. We have followed him again from Jerusalem to Golgotha ; and now, we behold three crosses planted on that bleak and gloomy hill. There are soldiers there, and a noisy populace shouting, like fiends, around the central cross. The innocent Lamb of God is fastened thereon ; the strokes of the hammer still resound, their echoes reverberate over valley and hill, and, penetrating to the uttermost parts of the shuddering universe, declare to it that, at last, the hour of man's redemption has arrived.

I hear all this once more—I behold these shocking scenes reproduced before my very eyes ! I see the rough nails quivering in the tender flesh,—yea, I see my Saviour dying *for me and my sins*, and can I remain insensible to the sight ? Shall I not mourn over my transgressions which have nailed him to the wood of the cross, and shrink with horror from the commission of every additional grievous sin ?

Some of you, my brethren, may have devoted the past week altogether to worldly pleasure and amusements ; many an evil word has been spoken, many an evil action has been committed, many a scandal has been given, and many a pure soul contaminated. Acknowledge it, at least, to your own hearts, acknowledge it here, in the presence of the Eucharistic God. Solemn and earnest are these days ; even the world of nature is grave and chill. The germs of the plants still slumber in the benumbed and frozen ground ; the genial rays of the vernal sun have not yet awakened them to new and beautiful life. The interior of this house of God, too, all sombre and solemn, should, with me, entreat you to employ well these forty days of Lent. Be obedient to the voice of the Church, which calls you to contemplate the Passion and death of your Redeemer. Do penance, and endeavor, each one of you, to become a new man ; so that when the Easter dawn gladdens the world, and the Church sings *"Alleluia"*—when it becomes Easter upon the hills and upon the plains, in the forest and in the fields, it may also become Easter in your hearts, as you celebrate your own spiritual resurrection with the risen Christ.

You may ask me : How can we profitably employ this holy season of Lent that it may become for us a time of penance, of change of heart, of amendment of life ? Allow me to place before your eyes a mirror in which you will clearly see *what you are and what you ought to be*. This mirror is not of precious metal or polished glass,—neither is there any thing novel about it, for it is to be found in the huts of the poor as well as in the houses of the rich. No doubt you have all looked into it in your turn ; for this mirror is *your crucifix*, it is our *Lord Jesus Christ upon the cross*. Not the dead representation, but the *living original*,—the Redeemer of the world agonizing on Mount Calvary, and giving utterance on the cross to his last most blessed words, the first of which :

"FATHER, FORGIVE THEM, FOR THEY KNOW NOT WHAT THEY DO," shall be the subject of our meditation to-day.

I. *"Father, forgive them, for they know not what they do."* The cross which bears the divine Sufferer is erected on Golgotha ; Jesus hangs upon it, and, in clear streams, his blood flows from his open wounds. It is noon ; the hot sun of Palestine burns upon the uncovered head of the Crucified. A soldier, at Pilate's command, has fastened on the top of the cross a tablet, which proclaims to the world in Hebrew, Greek and Latin, the crime for which the Redeemer suffers : *"This is Jesus of Nazareth, King of the Jews."* (Matt. 27 : 37.) At the foot of the cross sit four Roman soldiers, who, resting from their sanguinary work, pass the time of our Lord's agony in playing dice. They have just cast lots upon his seamless robe, which, like the garment of every condemned criminal of that time, belongs to the executioners. The inhabitants of Jerusalem flock around the cross, clamorous and scoffing: "Vah, thou who destroyest the temple of God and in three days buildest it up again, save thy own self : If thou be the Son of God, come down from the cross. He saved others ; himself he cannot save. If he be the King of Israel, let him come down from the cross, and we will believe him. He trusted in God, let him deliver him now, if he will have him ; for he said : I am the Son of God." (Matt. 27 : 40-43.) O Crucified Saviour, why dost thou not raise thine all-powerful arm and crush thy enemies in the dust like worms, or command legions of Angels to destroy those who so sacrilegiously scoff at their Lord ? Our agonizing Redeemer seems to turn his dying eyes sadly and lovingly upon us, as though he would reply : "What I suffer I suffer gladly ; I suffer voluntarily for the world, for my enemies, for *you*, my beloved children, and for all coming generations !" Then his eye, beautiful, even amid the dimness of coming death, seems to add : "Behold, my death is your life,—my wounds, your salvation."

But see, he opens his pale, dying lips. What will he say? Perhaps: "Woe to you, my cruel enemies !"—? Shall it be: "Accursed be you who have nailed me to this cross!"—? Ah! no; blessings, not curses, issue forth from those adorable lips, words of love, of pardon, of heavenly mildness, which is not of this earth : *"Father, forgive them ; for they know not what they do."*

Truly, these were divine words, worthy of the meek Heart of the expiring Son of God. Loving, blessing, pardoning, healing and consoling, he traversed this sinful earth of ours ; and forgiving his enemies, he departed from it. *Father, forgive them*, he prayed, as though to say : Father, behold *me* as thy sole victim, the holocaust of thy justice, pour out the vials of thy wrath upon me,—pain, torment, ignominy, abandonment, I gladly endure all, if thou wilt but forgive those guilty creatures, my enemies and yours. *"They know not what they do."*

O sinner, as you hearken to these pleading words of your dying Redeemer, do you not feel the hot blush of shame surging over cheek and brow ? Look into the mirror of Calvary, and behold your guilt in every open wound. All that implacable hatred could devise, infernal malice invent, or diabolical cruelty could employ, has been devised, invented, and employed by his enemies in order to increase his pains, and add a tenfold torture to his death, yet he prays : " Father, forgive them ; for they know not what they do ! "

My dear Christians, you, too, have your enemies. Will you return hatred for hatred,—will you maliciously revenge yourselves on them, or on one who, perhaps, has done you some deep and grievous wrong? Look up to the Cross. Your dying Saviour could crush his enemies, if he wished, but he does not. Will you not also say : "Father, I forgive this enemy of mine, as thou hast forgiven me."

When St. John Gualbert was but a youth, his brother was slain by one of his enemies. Burning with hatred and revenge Gualbert often lay in ambush for his enemy, in order to give him the death-stroke for his crime ; but the cunning murderer always evaded his grasp. Once, on a Good Friday, when Gualbert was riding alone it happened that in a narrow street, he met his brother's murderer, unarmed. Drawing his dagger, he fell upon the enemy, and was about to pierce him through, when the other, dropping on his knees, begged for grace and pardon for the sake of the Saviour who had died upon that day. Immediately, Gualbert lifted him up, embraced, and forgave him. God rewarded him for his generosity by giving him the grace of a religious vocation. From being a gallant gentleman of the world, he became a monk, and eventually, the Founder of a renowned Religious Order. Does not this example, O ! Christian, cry out : " Go and do thou in like manner ? "

Father, forgive them ; for they know not what they do,"—thus Jesus prayed upon the Cross for his enemies, thus he prays, to-day, FOR YOU, SINNER ! " Father, forgive him, for if he knew that by his sins he tears the crown of glory from my head, and presses the crown of thorns into my wounded forehead, he would not do it ; if he knew how grievously he offends you by his sins ; how he robs himself of all interior peace, and renders himself miserable for time and eternity, he would not, he could not, do it ! "

"*Father, forgive them,*" thus the dying Sufferer prays also for you, CHRISTIAN PARENTS, who bring up your sons, your daughters, not for God, but for the world. " Father, forgive such parents," he exclaims ; " for truly they know not what they do ; if they knew that I died, also, for their children ; that I purchased their salvation with my very heart's blood,—they would not do it ; if they knew what precious treasures are the souls of the little ones intrusted to their charge, how terrible the responsibility of guilty parents, how dreadful their future punishment, —they would never do it ! " Christian fathers and mothers, our dying Redeemer cries out to you from the cross: " *These children whom you call yours are mine, for I have redeemed and sanctified them !* "

II. "*Father, forgive them; for they know not what they do,*"—thus *we* also must pray for those unfortunate men who have devoted themselves to the destruction of Faith and piety ; for, if they realized the wrong they did in subverting the entire order of state and society, they could never bring themselves to perpetrate so cruel a wrong. Towards the close of the last century, the revolutionists of France, under various pretenses, had inaugurated the reign of lawlessness and licentiousness; and they sought for proofs that the unfortunate queen, Marie Antoinette, was hostile to liberty. One of the most rampant of these demagogues was the Jacobin, Herbert. Rushing into the apartments of the queen, he examined her books and papers, seeking proofs to establish the charges against her. He found nothing. A book lay upon one of the tables which he greedily opened, and there on a slip of paper, he found a pen-sketch, representing a heart pierced by an arrow, under which was the inscription: "Jesus, Son of God, have mercy on me!" Seizing it, he rushed forth with it to the tribunal, and there proved the guilt of the queen to her enemies.

Herbert, certainly, was true to his convictions. He who lives in the faith and fear of God cannot but shrink from the horrors of lawless revolution, but he who rebels against the divine law, will care still less for the violation of human laws. Render to God what is God's,—yea, but: Render, also, to Cæsar what is Cæsar's. Does not our Church teach that the temporal power is from God, and that the subject owes to it reverence and obedience? Has a good Christian ever been a revolutionist or an anarchist?

Where faith ceases, superstition begins; and he that departs from God, finally makes a contract with the devil. Have you not often experienced, that men without a spark of faith or religion are more superstitious than the very pagans? Napoleon I. was inimical to the Church; he robbed the Pope, and placed him between gloomy prison walls, yet often at night, he was wont to search the starry heavens for the guiding light of (what he was weak enough to consider) his "star of destiny." Does not France in our own days, begin to see the necessity of Christian faith and piety? Did not the representative, Brunet, formerly so hostile to the Church, vote in 1879, for the building of a temple to Christ in one of the public squares of Paris? Did not the notorious Ernest Rénan, who, a few years ago, employed his pen to disprove the divinity of Christ, not long since publicly declare that: "If France and the people of France expect ever to obtain power and respect, the state and the people must return to the way which they left, and must again become Christians and Catholics"?

"*Father, forgive them, for they know not what they do;*" thus the dying Saviour prayed, also, for the poor, deluded *victims of heresy and unbelief;* for those weak, misguided men who have been caught in the nets of the enemies of Christianity, and believe in false prophets. Forgive them, for they know not that they are dupes of Christ's inveterate adversaries; and that they serve only as tools for the promotion of their ambitious plans and pernicious schemes; if they knew it, they would not permit themselves to be seduced.

But you will say: "The world must make progress. *Excelsior* is the watchword of our time. Religion and the Church are opposed to progress, and are, therefore, assailed on all sides." Friend, the first point, I grant; the second, *never*. Yes, the world must make progress, for not to advance is to retrograde; there is, and can be, no standstill in material affairs. The human intellect may climb the dizziest heights, and count the very stars of heaven; it may descend into the depths of the earth, and bring forth its hidden treasures; it may search, inquire, discover, and invent. Be it so;—such is its task and its glory. But *the truths of religion remain, thereby, unharmed and unchanged.* You speak of progress,—but is there any progress possible in *Truth?* No more than dispute is possible that two and two make four; progress, in such a case, is equivalent to untruth and error; and in what God has revealed, what the mouth of eternal Truth has spoken, could there be any falsehood or vicissitude? Impossible. Name to me one tenet of our holy religion, *provided that it has been rightly understood,* of which *true* Science has ever proved the contrary with cogent and incontrovertible proofs; name to me only one article of faith that is contrary to reason. To-day one learned scientist may pretend to have reckoned to the year, the present age of this venerable world of ours; another may claim to have discovered the year and day when it will infallibly come to an end. But behold, to-morrow others, equally as wise and learned, may arise to prove the contrary, and produce counter arguments of tenfold weight and number. Who is right? Can truth reside in the domain of hesitation and doubt? Impossible, for *Truth* is *one.* Where union and unity are, there can be no hesitancy, doubt, or change, —yea, not even the faintest shadow of vicissitude.

Calmly and brightly the sun shines in the heavens, yet it moves not; the earth, moon, and planets surround it, ever in motion, ever winging their flight through their changing circuits. So, in immovable tranquillity and radiance, stands the Church in the midst of the confused turmoil of the world, and the variable fluctuations of the times. Clouds may obscure the splendor of the sun,—fogs and mists may darken, but they can never extinguish it. Persecutions may veil for a time, the splendors of the Church; heresies obscure her influence; but no efforts of men or devils can ever injure or destroy her. The rock in the ocean stands in the midst of angry waves; it trembles and groans under the stroke of the surging waters, but it falls not. Thus, also, the Church stands, and shall stand to the end of time, for she is built upon the Rock, Peter; and Jesus has given her his promise that he will never forsake, but remain with her all days, even to the consummation of the world. (Matt. 28 : 20.)

We must pray then : Father, forgive the enemies of thy Christ and of his Church, for they know not what they do : they know not what happiness, what repose, are imparted to the soul by faith and piety,—what consolation in suffering, what peace in death ! They have forgotten that religion is to man what the staff is to the steps of tottering age, what the rudder is to the ship, what the foundation is to the building ;—they have forgotten what the great St. Augustine once admirably said: "My heart longs for much, but it finds no repose until it rests in thee, O Lord !" At the foot of thy cross, O dying Jesus ! we prostrate ourselves in spirit, and adore thy infinite love. Thou who, in the agonies of death, hast prayed for thine enemies : "Father, forgive them,"—give us, also, the strength and grace to forgive our enemies from our hearts. Amen.

THE SECOND WORD.

"*Amen I say to thee, this day thou shalt be with me in paradise.*"
Luke 23 : 43.

Jesus hangs dying on the cross, whilst the heartless multitude stand about it, mocking and insulting him : "If thou be the Son of God, come down from the cross." Meekly, he prays for them: "Father, forgive them ; for they know not what they do !"—and, looking closer, we behold that he is not the only sufferer on Calvary. There are two other crosses there,—one on each side,—and on them are fastened two malefactors, condemned to the same punishment. The All-Holy One is exposed in the midst of criminals,—the guiltless among the guilty ! As Isaias had long before foretold: "He was reputed with the wicked." (Is. 53 : 12.) His enemies seeking to embitter his death, to the utmost, heap contumely upon their innocent Victim, and would fain make him appear the greatest malefactor of the three.

Glance for a moment, my brethren, at those criminals on the right and left of the Saviour ! The eye of the one glares with a savage hatred and despair. Gnashing his teeth with pain and rage, he makes herculean efforts to burst the fetters which fasten him to the cross,—curses and blasphemies flow from his lips : " If thou be the Christ, save thyself and us." (Luke 23 : 39.)—How different the appearance of the thief on our Lord's right hand ! Calm, resigned to the inevitable,—he is well aware that he meets the just reward of his crimes ; and he gazes with a strange compassion upon the pallid face of the divine Sufferer, whose every feature reflects a heavenly meekness. What are those remarkable words he has just uttered ? A prayer for his enemies ? Lo ! a ray of grace illuminates the darkness of the good thief's soul ; and hearing the blasphemous, insulting scoffs of his accomplice, he rebukes him, saying: " Neither dost thou fear God, seeing thou art under the same condemnation ? And we indeed justly ; for we receive the due reward of our deeds ; but this man hath done no evil." (Luke 23 : 40, 41.) Then he said to Jesus : " Lord, remember me when thou shalt come into thy kingdom." And Jesus said to him: *Amen I say to thee, this day thou shalt be with me in paradise."* (Luke 23: 42–44.)

I. The two thieves were alike in their crimes, alike in their guilt and punishment,—yet most unlike in their behavior, their repentance, their deaths ! Both hang near Jesus, every bone of their bodies racked with pain ; but on the left, is suspended a sullen, obdurate sinner, without remorse or purpose of amendment,—his evil memory vividly reproducing all the enormities of his past life. The secret ambush in dark forests, the open highway robberies, the assaults upon solitary, defenseless travelers, the naked, mangled corses of his victims, whom he has robbed of all they possessed—what dreadful visions are these ! Conscience urges him, at least, in these final moments of his life, to seek a reconciliation with the God whom he has outraged and offended. But in vain. As a savage beast caught in the snare, strives desperately to extricate itself therefrom, but only entangles itself the more in the meshes,—so this impenitent malefactor, though fastened hand and foot to the cross, tortured in body and soul,—adds tenfold to his torments by giving vent to the blasphemous rage which is consuming his very vitals. His venomous tongue utters such taunts as these to the agonizing Redeemer: " If thou be the Christ, as thou hast so often declared, prove it. Thou hast made the blind to see, the lame to walk,—thou hast helped others, help thyself and us !"

O, obstinate sinner ! behold here your counterpart ! Behold the terrible fate which awaits you, if you refuse to renounce your evil ways, and become converted to the Lord ! How indescribable are the tortures which remorse of conscience inflicts upon the impenitent !

Only the pure and undefiled know what it is to be happy: "A good conscience is a perpetual feast." As only he can truly enjoy life, who is sound in body, so he only can be truly happy, whose soul is in a state of robust spiritual health, whose conscience is free from the stain of willful mortal sin. The good Christian may be misunderstood, calumniated, persecuted,—but no earthly trials can rob him of his peace of heart; he knows that God's justice is eternal; and that, sooner or later, victory will be on the side of truth, innocence, and virtue. What do riches or honors profit the wicked? What do diversions or plays, wines or banquets, avail him? The splendid garments in which he arrays himself, the beautiful, elegantly furnished house in which he dwells,—all these fail to make him happy. He often envies the very beggar child at the church door, under whose coarse and tattered garments beats an humble heart, free from sin and injustice. He may lull, for a time, the ever wakeful voice of conscience, but silence it? Never! The expiring ember in the ashes needs only a gentle breath, in order to kindle once more into a bright flame, so the suppressed voice of conscience needs but a gentle breath from heaven to awake from its temporary stupor, and flame up accusingly before the avenging tribunal of God. It was conscience, and conscience alone, which, after the murder of Abel, drove Cain, from place to place, making him a wild and restless fugitive upon earth unto the end of his days.

A bad conscience is a worm that never dies, a fire that is never extinguished, a wound that is ever inflamed, and never heals. The ancient pagans fitly represented a man tortured by remorse of conscience, as one chained fast to a rock, upon whose liver an eagle and a vulture alternately fed at intervals. Alas! how terrible is the death of the obdurate sinner! Does not the wretched end of the impenitent thief on the cross reveal to us this truth? Does not the traitor, Judas, declare it, when he destroys his miserable life with the halter of the suicide? And in later times, does not the infidel Voltaire reiterate it with renewed force, as, with wild despair and a blasphemy on his lips, he gives up his black soul to the demon?

Ah! quit not the cross, my brethren, without having made a firm purpose of entering seriously into yourselves, of amending your life. Will you defer your repentance to the last fatal hour? Have you time at your command? Who can assure you that to-day may not be your last? God, it is true, has promised pardon to the penitent, but he has not promised to-morrow to the sinner. "No man can serve God and mammon." You must make your choice between Christ and the devil,— between sin and virtue;—and postpone not the affair of your conversion to your deathbed. Listen to a case in point. In the days of Queen Elizabeth, who persecuted the Catholics of England and confiscated their property on account of their faith, there lived a wealthy Catholic nobleman, who endeavored to make a compromise between his religion and his real estate. Outwardly, he pretended to apostatize, but inwardly, he persuaded himself that he was steadfast in the faith. That death might not surprise him in this sin, he always kept a priest concealed in his house in London, and another at his country-seat. Whether he should fall sick in the city or in the country, he thought he would thus always have the minister of Christ close at hand. But, one day, when the nobleman was on his way to his country-place, he was suddenly seized with apoplexy, and fell unconscious to the ground. The servant who accompanied him, hurried off to summon a priest: the good man came immediately, but, alas! he found,—*a corpse!* Does not this example cry out to you, my brethren: "Be prudent, lest the same thing happen to you?" No man can serve two masters. You know not the day nor the hour when the Lord shall knock at your door.

II. But, turning from this vision of the bad thief, from this revolting picture of obduracy, and despair, let us fix our gaze upon the good thief upon the cross, and learn from him lessons worthy our admiration and imitation.

We have dwelt upon the astonishment with which that poor suffering man heard the dying Redeemer pray for his enemies; and how having witnessed the heavenly resignation and meekness of the mangled Lamb of God, he caught from the divine repose and majesty of that adorable Face, a ray of grace which penetrated to his inmost heart. Enlightened in his interior, and inspired with the strength of faith, a voice seems to cry out from the depths of his soul: "This must be the Son of God!" No doubt the poor thief, straightway recalls his numberless crimes and evil deeds; he knows that his sins are many and very grievous,—but he also knows that the mercy of God is still greater. The blasphemies of his fellow-criminal fill him with disgust and horror; and having rebuked him severely, reminding him that the pains they jointly suffered were the just reward of their evil deeds, whilst our Lord was Innocence itself—full of confidence and hope, he turned to Jesus, saying: "Lord, remember me when thou shalt come into thy kingdom." (Luke 23 : 42.) In other words, he might have said: "I ask not to be freed from the tortures of the cross,—for what I suffer is richly deserved; I ask not for earthly goods,—(for my immoderate desires have brought me where I am); I only ask ardently for the pardon of my sins, and life everlasting. It is true, I am not worthy to say : Take me into thy kingdom—into that kingdom which thou didst declare to Pilate is not of this world, and into which nothing defiled can enter,—all that I ask is, that after thy entrance into that kingdom of glory, thou wouldst graciously remember the unfortunate sinner who was found worthy to suffer by thy side, and who has died full of sorrow and repentance for his sins!"

What an instructive and edifying example! If you have imitated the good thief in his career of crime, imitate him, likewise, in his sincere conversion. Be not obdurate, like his guilty accomplice; despair not, like Cain or Judas. Discouragement is one of the most fatal of sins. Not to despair is in itself a virtue, and bears with it a promise of final victory. He who pardoned the penitent thief on the cross is the same who pardoned David, Peter, and Magdalene; and he will also wash away *your* sins, my brethren, in the tears of your repentance. "He who is sorry for having sinned is almost innocent." Seneca. Though your offences be as numerous as the sands of the sea shore, they shall be blotted out from the Book of reckoning; though they be redder than scarlet, he will wash them white as snow. He will say to thee: "Thy sins are forgiven thee; enter thou into my kingdom, 'enter thou into the joy of thy Lord!'"

What joy and delight must fill the heavens at the conversion of a sinner! Christ himself declares it, saying: "There shall be joy in heaven upon one sinner that doeth penance, more than upon ninety-nine just who need not penance." (Luke 15 : 7.) Is he not always the Good Shepherd, who sorrowfully seeks the lost sheep, taking it upon his shoulders, and joyfully carrying it back to the fold? And, humanly speaking, O Christian fathers and mothers, is not that child dearer to you, whose life, assailed by a dangerous sickness, has long hung in the balance between life and death; and who has been given back to you, as it were, from the very jaws of the grave? After peril and imminent danger of death, life and health are always doubly dear.

The penitent thief dies with Christ; and calm and peaceful is his end. Yes, it is sweet to die in peace with Christ; through him the bitterness of death is changed into sweetness; and doubt and fear into the hope of eternal salvation. "O death, where is thy victory? O death, where is thy sting?"

But is not this happiness within the grasp of all? Will not the same Saviour who expired upon the cross, come to each one of you, my brethren, at the hour of death, in order to pour wine and oil into your wounds, consolation and peace into your grief-stricken heart? Will he not say to you by the mouth of his priest: "Son, be of good heart, thy sins are forgiven thee;" if thou departest from this earth, to-day, sooner or later, thou shall be with me in Paradise?

How great must be the perversity and obduracy, how terrible the blindness and unbelief of a man who, even on his death-bed, dares reject the proffered help of his merciful and loving Saviour! Yet many a priest has encountered such cases. On the other hand, great is the responsibility of those who fail to remind sick persons of their duty from false fear or undue solicitude for their bodily health;—or of those who call upon the divine Physician when it is too late to profit by his ministrations. Is this more the fault of the sick person, or of those who surround him? Certainly more the fault of those that attend the patient; since, often, unconscious of his danger, the latter lies in a stupor, incapable of thinking or acting for himself. Oh! how easy it is to die with Christ,—how hard, how terrible, to die without him!

Two malefactors hung upon the cross, but only one was converted. Does this not recall those words of warning addressed by our Lord to his disciples?—"Two shall be in the field: the one shall be taken, and the other shall be left. Two women shall be grinding at the mill: the one shall be taken, and the other shall be left."—(Math. 24: 40-41.) One of the thieves was converted in his last hour, that no sinner may despair; but, only one, that no sinner may presume. Hence, let this single example teach and encourage all who have deferred their conversion to the eleventh hour,—all who lie humble and repentant upon their death-beds,—to return to God in the bitterness of their hearts and with sincere sorrow for their sins; but let it, also, warn you, my brethren, not to defer any longer your conversion and the amendment of your lives; since death-bed conversions are very difficult and very rare. As a man lives, so he dies; he who lives in sin, as a rule, dies in sin.

The two thieves on the cross give us still another important lesson. The Lord desired the conversion of both; but, whilst one rejected the proffered grace of God, the other, accepting it, believed and hoped, and hence, had the happiness of hearing these words addressed to him by Christ: "This day thou shalt be with me in paradise." Here we have symbolized the religious history of the Jews and the Gentiles. As the thief on the left hand despised and rejected the Saviour, and was therefore rejected by him, in turn,—so it happened with the Jews; and as the good thief believed and was justified, so was it with the Gentiles. This symbolizes, also, the history of nations and of individuals,—both of ancient and modern times. Look at Africa and Asia; for centuries, Christianity flourished in those regions, and elevated the people to a high degree of prosperity and civilization; but when religion declined, when schisms and dissensions divided and weakened the true believers, the light of faith was taken away from Africa and Asia, and carried into Europe, to the Germanic and Slavonic nations; and ignorance and desolation settled down on the once favored lands. The garden of Christ became a barren wilderness; and the false creed of Mahomet now holds the people in the bondage of barbarism and superstition. Now, if among Christian nations, infidelity and immorality flourish like the banyan tree, if partisan hatred and fraternal dissension rend the seamless robe of Christ, if coldness and indifference paralyze the faith in Christian souls, and redeemed mankind turns away from the Crucified Redeemer and his holy Church,—may not those terrible words of the prophet be fulfilled to the letter: "If you be not converted from your evil ways and do penance, I shall come and take away the light from its place, and give it to others who are better, worthier, more faithful, and more grateful than you."

Prostrate before the cross of Calvary, my brethren, let each one of us cry out to the Crucified One: "O Jesus, I acknowledge my guilt, and I implore thee with the penitent David: 'Have mercy on me according to thy great mercy, and according to the multitude of thy tender mercies, blot out my iniquity.' Thou who hast said: 'A contrite and humble heart I will not despise,' reject me not when I approach thee with tears of sincere repentance. Make me learn from the murderer on thy left, how awful is the death of the impenitent sinner; and from the penitent thief on thy right, how tranquil and hopeful is the death of him who makes his peace with God, and expires in his love and friendship. Preserve us all, O God! from a sudden, an unprovided death; permit us not to die in our sins, nor without the consolation of the holy Sacraments. Give us the grace, during this holy season of Lent, to make a good confession and a worthy Communion; that we may appear before thee at Easter with clean holy hearts. And when, one day, our senses fail in death, our eyes grow dim, and the cold sweat of dissolution bedews our foreheads, assist us with thy holy grace, and grant us, each one of us, to hear the consoling words thou didst address to Dysmas on the cross: 'Be of good heart, this day thou shalt be with me in paradise!'" Amen.

THE THIRD WORD.

"Woman, behold thy son . . . . Son, behold thy mother."
John 19 : 26–27.

When Hagar, the Egyptian hand-maid of Abraham wandered in the wilderness of Bersebee, with her little son Ismael, suffering from hunger and thirst, and fearing that death was imminent, she sobbed aloud ; then saying to herself : "I will not see the boy (my son) die," she went her way, thus abandoning her child. Who can fitly portray her anguish. But, two thousand years later, we behold another mother, who is undergoing more terrible desolation. She stands upon Calvary, and she is Mary the Mother of Jesus. Unlike Hagar, we behold her surrounded by a brutal soldiery and a clamorous rabble, whilst high upon a cross, hangs her divine Son dying. She does not flee as did the Egyptian woman lest she should witness the expiring throes of her darling child, neither does she lift up her voice and weep. Although her heart is breaking, she stands erect, well knowing that her Son's sufferings have been decreed from all eternity, and that he endures them for the salvation of a guilty world.

But shall the Son depart from earth without addressing a farewell to that afflicted Mother,—without giving one word of consolation to her who, with motherly tenderness, had hitherto shared with him his every joy and grief? Behold, his thorn-crowned head moves,—his eyes, dim with blood and tears, cast down a loving glance upon his Mother at his feet,—upon John, his beloved disciple, the only one of his Apostles who had not fled. *"Woman,"* says he, *"behold thy son . . . . Son, behold thy mother."* Only a few words, my brethren, but O, how full of love and affection.

I. *"Woman, behold thy son,"*—thus the dying Jesus addresses his Mother. Why does he call her "woman"? Why does he not give her the tender name of *Mother ?* Be not scandalized, my dearly beloved. Venerable and highly esteemed among the Jews, was the name of woman ; it was a title given alike to high and lowly, rich and poor, married and single,—yea, even the mother was called "woman." Do you not remember how, at the marriage feast of Cana, in Galilee, when

Mary his Mother called the attention of her Son to the failure of wine, he said to her: "Woman, my hour is not yet come"—? Besides, the word "woman" has another deep and mysterious significance. If he had called her "Mother" upon Calvary, it would only have served to increase the anguish of their approaching separation. He addresses her as "woman," the valiant woman of the Proverbs, the strong, heroic woman who had been chosen from all eternity to crush the serpent's head. "Woman, behold thy son." What an admirable example of filial love is contained in these simple words! Suffering the most violent pains, surrounded by the chill darkness of the night of death, the affectionate Son does not forget the duties of a good Son towards his mother, but gives her a protector and guardian for the rest of her lonely days. "Woman," (this is the meaning of his words) "I must die that the world may live; I must depart from thee, but behold, I intrust thee, virginal mother, to a virginal son; I intrust thee to John, my beloved disciple,—to him, who at the Last Supper rested upon my breast; to him, the only one of all the chosen Twelve, who does not through fear forsake his master in death. Take him; and as I have ever been a true son to thee in the past, so will he, henceforth, discharge to thee in *my* stead, the duties of a devoted son!"

"Woman, behold thy son!" What *words of consolation* for Mary; but, at the same time, alas! what *words of bitterness!* Words of consolation, inasmuch as the Mother hearing once more the dear voice of her Son, knows that he is thinking of her, and caring for her future welfare even amid the agonies of a cruel death. But words of bitterness, since they convey to her the farewell of her only and beloved Son,—giving her John instead of Jesus,—the disciple as a substitute for his divine Master!

"Mother, behold thy son!" Oh, that the cross, to-day, might become a pulpit wherein your expiring Lord, the grand Preacher of the ages, might teach you, children, how to behave towards your father and mother; and especially, how to love and cherish your old, sick, or infirm parents. May you never forget that, after God, you owe all that you are and have, to your parents. How often have you been reminded of the Fourth Commandment in this holy place; how often have you been told to honor and obey your father and your mother! O, my son, my daughter, if thou wouldst be long-lived and prosperous upon the earth,—fulfill diligently this command of the Most High. To-day, your dying Redeemer upon the cross, presenting to you his own beautiful example of filial devotion, cries out to you: "Son, support the old age of thy father; and grieve him not in his life; and if his understanding fail, have patience with him, and despise him not, when thou art in thy strength ; for the relieving of thy father shall not be forgotten." (Ecclus. 3: 14, 15.) Does not God, in the Law of Moses, as well as in the Book of Proverbs, declare the fate of the wicked and ungrateful child ? "He that curseth his father, or mother, dying, let him die, he hath cursed his father and mother, let his blood be upon him." (Lev. 20: 9.) "The eye that mocketh at his father, and that despiseth the labor of his mother in bearing him, let the ravens of the brooks pick it out, and let the young eagles eat it." (Prov. 30:17.)

Truly, there would not be so much strife in families, nor so much misery upon earth, if children would always have the Fourth Commandment of God before their eyes, and faithfully fulfilled it. Does not daily experience convince us that the sins of children towards their parents are most terribly avenged ; and that the parent's curse often destroys forever the happiness of their ungrateful offspring? The hand of a wicked child raised to strike its father or its mother (as the saying is), shall find no rest even in the grave, but growing out of the earth, shall serve as a terrifying example to all future violators of the divine and natural law. Unto the fourth generation, does the vengeance of God pursue the unnatural child ; for the descendants of a disrespectful son or daughter mete out to their unhappy parents, the same measure of insult, disobedience, and dishonor, they, in their turn, had shown the authors of their being.

II. "Woman, behold thy son !" Having spoken these farewell words to his Mother, the dying Redeemer, turning to St. John, exclaims: "Son, behold thy mother." Behold, oh ! best beloved and most faithful of my disciples, dying, I leave not to thee earthly treasures. Poor and naked, I came into the world ; poor and naked, also, I go out of it ; but one precious legacy I *do* leave thee ; one priceless treasure I bequeath to thee at parting—my Virgin Mother ! I intrust her to thy care, that thou mayst be to her what I have always been during life,— a faithful, devoted son.

O Mary, Mother of Dolors, could these words completely comfort and satisfy thee? To John they were words of sweetest consolation ; since the confidence reposed in him by his divine Master was the highest honor that could be then conferred on him ; but to the heart of Mary, they were words of bitterness. Who can understand the magnitude of the grief which she experienced that hour ! Then it was, that the sword of sorrow, foretold by Simeon, pierced her desolate heart, urging her to cry out in the words of the Inspired Text: "O all ye that pass by the way, attend and see if there be any grief like to my grief!"

At the time when the Judges ruled in Israel, a great famine arose in the land. Elimelech, with his wife, Noemi, and their two sons went from their birthplace, Bethlehem, into the distant country of Moab, to escape starvation. They remained there ten years; and, in the meantime, the husband and children of Noemi having died, sad and sorrowful she sets out to return to her native place. Bowed down with sufferings and age,—care and sorrow depicted on her countenance,—she drags herself, once more, through the gate of Bethlehem. The women of the city, meeting her, ask in astonishment: "Is not this Noemi, the amiable?" "Nay, no longer Noemi, the amiable," she makes answer,—"but Mara, the bitter one, for the Lord has filled my heart with bitterness."

Behold, my brethren, in Mary at the foot of the cross, the amiable one, whose heart is, also, filled with bitterness. Amiable Virgin and Mother of grace, she has given us the Redeemer of the world;—but, alas! she is overflowing with bitterness, since, from the birth of her Son in Bethlehem until his death upon Calvary, her life has been one continuous series of the bitterest griefs. Every pain and trial of the Man of Sorrows was reflected in her sympathetic heart. Even when a child, she saw his life threatened by the bloodthirsty Herod; she witnessed the hatred of his enemies, the ingratitude of those whom he had come to redeem. But what was all this compared to the agony which she experienced during his cruel Passion and death? What must she have felt in that night of horrors when her divine Son was praying and sweating blood in the Garden of Olives,—when, at the various tribunals of his unjust judges, he was mocked, maltreated, scourged, struck, and defiled with spittle? But the chalice of bitterness was full to overflowing, when she stood at the foot of the cross, and beheld her beloved Child, mangled, bleeding, dying!

The precious Blood runs down in streams to the earth,—the divine Victim moves his thorn-crowned head from side to side, seeking in vain some alleviation of its pains. The sorrowful Mother sees all; she stands and suffers,—her heart beating violently, her limbs trembling. Lo! the fountains of her tears are dried up,—but no word or sound escapes her. She complains not of the dispensations of God; she demands not revenge nor condign punishment upon the inhuman executioners of her Son. She hears him pray for his enemies. She hears him promise paradise to the good thief; and she envies that repentant malefactor. It is granted to him, at least, to die,—to be relieved of his torments; only a few moments more, and he shall enjoy the delights of paradise with her Son, but *she* Mother of bitterness, must remain, for many years to come, in this land of exile, bewailing the loss of her beloved Son. And now, she hears the farewell which he addresses to her: "Woman, behold thy son." And a few moments later: "Son, behold thy mother." So near and yet so far, it is not given her to press her lips upon his, in a fond, parting kiss.

When Cambyses, king of the Persians, had defeated and taken prisoner Psametich, king of the Egyptians,—in order to punish him for his long resistance, he devised a certain plan whereby the royal captive might be made keenly sensible of his miserable condition. Placed in an open square, and guarded by soldiers, Psametich beheld his daughter led by, like a slave, bearing on her head a tub filled with water. Even the proud Persians wept at this humiliation of a royal princess; Psametich, alone, remained seemingly quiet and unmoved. Then, his son, the heir of his throne, was also led before him with an iron ring about his neck, like a slave. The king's eye remained dry, his tongue was dumb. All looked upon him with astonishment. Finally, his faithful servant was brought before him,—at which sight the king burst into tears. "Why," they asked, "do you now shed tears?" He replied: "The calamity that has befallen me and my children is so great that I have become insensible to it, but for the sufferings of others, there is still some sympathy and compassion left in my heart!"

Can we not say the same, my brethren, of the sorrows of the Mother of God? O mourner of this earth, weep if you can, for the flood of tears that streams from your eyes will mitigate your pain, and alleviate the oppression of your heart. Mary can weep no more; even the consolation of tears is denied her. Oh! the dumb, silent grief, the sorrow which has dried up the very well-springs of the eye,—is not this the most awful of all earthly woes?

III. "Son, behold thy mother. And from that hour, John took her to his own." (John 19:21.) From the Mother at the foot of the cross, I direct your attention to another mother in a like desolation. Many sons and daughters she calls her own, and loves them with a true and tender heart. But sad and grief-stricken is her countenance, bowed down her form,—not from age or infirmity, but from sorrow. Her children have, many of them, forgotten their mother, some have even raised their hands, in insolent audacity, to strike her. Who is this sorrowful mother? O Christian, it is your mother, the Church. "My son, my daughter, behold thy mother!" Jesus cries to you from the cross: "Behold my divine and spotless Spouse, despised, calumniated, mocked, persecuted by her enemies."

Is it not so? Has not the Church cultivated and trained the civilized nations of the earth; given a mother's tender care to the sons who now, in pride and disobedience, rebel against her? Cast a glance at the present age, my brethren, and behold the pitiable spectacle presented to your view! Mankind seems to be divided into three classes. One class are the pronounced enemies of religion of every form of divine worship. In their wild frenzy, they would fain subvert the whole existing moral order. Against Christianity, as the foundation of human society and civil laws,—against the dignity and authority of temporal and spiritual power, they openly rebel, or secretly plot and scheme. They fight with the weapons of falsehood and calumny; their chief agent, the Press, controls and poisons public opinion; and woe to the man who dares to oppose their atheistical views! He is either branded with infamy, or publicly ostracized. They seize upon every opportunity to sound the trumpet of unbelief, or scatter clouds of sophistical dust in the eyes of the unwary. Let a priest take but a single false step (man as he is,—and we are all weak), and immediately an outcry is raised by these critical censors,—as though they were purity itself, instead of whited sepulchres. To such, the words of Holy Writ are applicable: "Woe to you that make day night and night day, who call true false, and false true."

And the second class? They are the most numerous. They will tell you that they have nothing against the Church, faith and religion; but they are not what is called "enthusiastic Catholics." They go to church because their fathers and grandfathers went; because it is the custom, and they would be remarked if they stayed away. They do not calumniate faith nor its ministers; but if others, in their presence, indulge in railleries or scoffs at priests and pious practices, they suffer them to do so without showing displeasure by a single look or word. They are slothful, tepid Catholics, incurring the condemnation addressed to the Laodicean of old: "Because thou art lukewarm, and neither cold nor hot, I will begin to vomit thee out of my mouth."—(Apoc. 3: 16.)

And finally, the third class? This is the smallest; it is but a little flock (*pusillus grex*) of faithful, constant and courageous confessors of the faith, who fear neither reproach nor sneer, and who are ready at any time to sacrifice property and life for the Church of Christ. As St. John amid the horrors of Calvary took the afflicted Mother henceforth for his portion,—so, amid the trials and sufferings of this present time, the faithful Catholic casts his lot, unshrinkingly and unwaveringly, with his afflicted mother, the Church. Knowing that the storms of persecution must pass; and that Christ has assured his divine spouse: "Behold, I am with you all days, even unto the consummation of the world," (Matt. 28:10)—they console themselves in their tribulations with those other words of Eternal Truth: "Whosoever shall confess me before men, I will also confess him before my Father who is in heaven."—(Matt. 10:32.) To which of these three classes, my brethren, do *you* belong?

IV. "Son, behold thy mother," thus the dying Redeemer said to us all in the person of St. John. Yes, Christians, behold Mary, your mother! Standing at the foot of the cross, full of maternal love for you, she has sacrificed her only beloved Son for your eternal salvation. Every pang that she endures is for you. Eighteen hundred years have elapsed since that dreadful day on Calvary, yet her maternal love for you has not been extinguished. She has never ceased, and can never cease, to be the Mother of Jesus; and hence, she has never ceased to be your mother, the second Eve, the mother of all the living. Fly, therefore, to her, my brethren, to the Comforter of the afflicted, the Refuge of sinners, the Help of Christians, who has never yet refused consolation and help to her clients.

When, in the year 1522, the Turks conquered the island of Rhodus, which the Christian knight, L'Ise Adam, had long and heroically defended, the latter returned with the remnant of his fleet to the city of Messina. He was received with tears and loud lamentations by the inhabitants who had gathered at the shore; but, hoisting the flag of the only ship which had escaped the general destruction, he there revealed to their mournful gaze, the picture of our Lady of Dolors, to which was appended this inscription: "Our help in every tribulation and necessity!" Yes, my brethren, Mary is, indeed, our help in every tribulation and necessity, both of body and soul. Where is the mourner whose tears she does not hasten to dry? Where the suffering heart which she does not delight to comfort and to heal? Where, above all, the sinner who invokes her in his night of misery, and fails to receive light and peace, pardon and eternal salvation?

THE FOURTH WORD.

"My God, my God, why hast thou forsaken me?" Mark 15: 34.

Standing under the cross of Calvary, to-day, we again contemplate our bleeding Saviour, languishing in his last agony. Whilst the streams of his precious blood descend for the redemption of a sinful world, the meridian sun of Palestine glows upon, and burns, the defenceless Sufferer. Not the faintest breeze is abroad; but a dismal, unwholesome mist has settled down upon the plains around Jerusalem. The clamor of the mocking multitude becomes gradually weaker; only a hollow murmur from a distance, now strikes upon the ear,—interrupted occasionally, by the loud curses of the Roman soldiers.

Our Saviour has placed in safe keeping his only treasure upon earth—his beloved Mother. Nearer and nearer approaches the solemn moment of death. There, he hangs upon the cross, deserted by his Apostles and disciples, by his friends and followers. Helpless and alone, abandoned to all the tortures of an ignominious death,—even his Eternal Father has, at last, withdrawn his interior consolations. The Saviour of men must drain to the very dregs that bitter chalice of suffering, from which he had prayed, during his bloody sweat, to be delivered, saying: "O my Father, if it be possible, let this chalice pass from me!" (Matt. 26:39.)

The subdued murmur of mockery from the multitude is suddenly hushed. Some anxiously raise their eyes to heaven; others, with terrified gestures, point upwards. The sun's disk, which only a few moments ago, was bright and shining, grows gradually smaller and dimmer; the brilliant orb of day is wholly obscured; and gloomy night settles down upon the scene. Then, become visible the stars of heaven; a cold, biting wind blows over the landscape; the birds, affrighted, fly from their nests; the terrified beasts arise from their lairs; the cattle low uneasily in their stalls; even the scoffers around the cross are dumb;—an ominous silence ensues. Ah! comfortless, as is the face of nature, still more sorrowful and void is the heart of our Saviour. "*My God, my God,*" he exclaims, with failing voice, "*why hast thou forsaken me?*" Let us briefly meditate upon these words.

I. Alas! three long hours of torture have been passed upon this cruel cross, and the gaping wounds are every instant widening and becoming more painful. Terrible, however, as are these bodily sufferings, they are nothing in comparison with the intense torments of his soul. He sees, in spirit, the myriads of men, for whom his blood will have been shed in vain and the immense number to whom he will be a sign to be contradicted, and at this sight his heart is overwhelmed with anguish and he cries out : " My God, my God, why hast thou forsaken me ?" Incomprehensible words ! Has he not the fullness of the Godhead actually residing within him and is he not consubstantial with his heavenly Father? Yes,—but he now suffers as man and as such only is he, at this supreme moment, deserted by his eternal Father. Almighty God has withdrawn from him those interior consolations which he heretofore enjoyed.

He must suffer and endure all that any man can suffer, so that he may pay the infinite debt of sinful humanity. He does not sorrowfully exclaim at that moment : " My FATHER, why hast thou forsaken me ?"—but, " My GOD !" for the Son does not then see in God, his Father, nor the Father in him, his Son. The agonizing Christ on the cross is, to his Eternal Father, the representative of sin-laden humanity ; the sacrificial Lamb, whose death shall reconcile earth and heaven. In that mysterious hour, he stands to his heavenly Father in the relation of a servant, of a sinner, who must, therefore, endure all the dreadful desolation which the sinner experiences when he is deserted by God.

" My God, my God, why hast thou forsaken me ?" These words imply still more. They are the initial words of the Twenty-first Psalm. More than a thousand years before the birth of our Redeemer, king David had chanted them,—portraying in that special psalm, the sufferings and death of the future Redeemer. Now, hanging on the cross, our Saviour repeats the first words of this psalm, in order to remind the by-standers that the prophecy of David has been fulfilled in his Person.

" My God"—thus runs the psalm—" why hast thou forsaken me ? O my God! I shall cry by day and thou wilt not hear. . . . In thee have our fathers hoped : they have hoped, and thou hast delivered them. . . . But I am a worm, and no man ; the reproach of men, and the outcast of the people. All they that saw me have laughed me to scorn ; they have spoken with the lips and wagged the head : He hoped in the Lord, let him deliver him ; let him save him, seeing he delighteth in him. . . . I am poured out like water, and all my bones are scattered. My heart has become like wax melting in the midst of my bowels. My strength was dried up like a pot-sherd, and my tongue hath cleaved to my jaws. . . . They have dug my hands and my feet: they have numbered all my bones. They have looked and stared upon me: they have parted my garments amongst them, and upon my vesture they have cast lots." Has not this prophecy been literally and wonderfully fulfilled in the circumstances attendant upon the death of Christ? Is it not as if David himself stood upon Mount Calvary under the shadow of the cross; as if he actually saw the scorn of the multitude, the torments of the dying Redeemer?

O, my agonizing Saviour, thy dreadful dereliction on the cross, thy profound desolation and utter abandonment have never yet been equalled, and can never be surpassed! The martyrs, going joyfully to death for thee, longed, it is true, to suffer the most terrible torments. A St. Ignatius, on hearing the roaring of the lions that were about to devour him, exclaimed: "I am the wheat of Christ, which must be ground by the teeth of savage beasts, in order that I may be found as pure bread." A St. Lawrence, lying upon the glowing gridiron, cried out, when one of his thighs was already burned to a crisp: "Turn me over, for I am roasted enough on this side!" Other holy martyrs were covered with pitch, and set on fire, like torches; others again were slowly dismembered, singing triumphantly, in the midst of their torments, and kissing the instruments of torture. But the crucified Saviour was the Supreme Source of all their courage and constancy: they drew their superhuman strength and endurance altogether from the treasury of his infinite merits. Jesus, the strength of martyrs, alone, was really helpless and deserted in his agony. Abandoned by God and man, he was suspended on the cruel Tree of the cross, his soul inundated by a limitless sea of bitterness:—" My God, my God, why hast thou forsaken me?"

Behold! even inanimate nature, at that moment, bore testimony to the grief of her expiring Lord and Maker; even the lifeless rocks were rent as if with compassion for our suffering Saviour,—a reproach to the stony-hearted Jews who refused to acknowledge or pity him! In the chilly darkness which covered the earth, men and beasts trembled with fear and consternation.

Was this sudden darkening of the sun at noonday, a natural or a common occurrence? O my brethren, any one, in the least acquainted with the ordinary laws of nature, will not hesitate to declare it an extraordinary phenomenon. As is well known, astronomers can easily calculate (from a knowledge of the motions of the moon and earth), when a solar eclipse will take place. But, according to the testimony of the scientists, such a phenomenon could not have taken place during the week in which our Lord suffered. Why not? First, the darkness which fell upon the earth on that first Good Friday lasted from the sixth to the ninth hour,—three hours,—which, for a complete solar eclipse (as this must have been), is unheard of. Secondly, a solar eclipse can take place only at the time of the *new* moon, never at that of the *full* moon. Now, during the week of our Lord's Passion, the moon was at the full; since, after this week, came the Pasch of the Jews, who always celebrated that festival after the first vernal full moon. The fact of this mysterious darkness is confirmed by ancient and reliable witnesses: "In the fourteenth year of the 202nd Olympiad," writes the secretary of the Emperor Adrian, "a solar eclipse took place, greater than any that had hitherto been known; it was night at the sixth hour (noonday), so that the stars were visible."

"At the moment when Christ hung upon the cross," Tertullian cries out to the Romans: "When the sun was in the zenith, the light of day disappeared. You will find this event described in your annals." Yes, even the Prophet Amos prophesied it in these words: "And it shall come to pass in that day, saith the Lord God, that the sun shall go down at midday; and I will make the earth dark in the day of light." (Amos 8 : 9.)

The God of nature dies—and the sun is obscured; darkness covers the whole earth. If you permit the Lord to die in your hearts, my dear Christians; if you suffer the light of faith to be extinguished in your souls; or if you impiously quench the divine light in the hearts of others,—causing them to apostatize from Christ and his Church,— then will the awful darkness of an infernal night descend upon you, as well as upon the victims and sharers of your sin!

II. "My God, my God, why hast thou forsaken me?" Many amongst us, my dearly beloved, may have often repeated this sorrowful lament. Thus prays the poor, oppressed father of a family, whose daily companions are want and misery; and who vainly strives with his scanty means to feed and clothe his numerous offspring. "Why hast thou forsaken me, O God?" Thus, also, questions the desolate widow: "Thou hast taken away my staff, the bread-winner of my family, —my husband!" "Why hast thou forsaken me?" Thus wails the father, or mother, from whom death has snatched away a beloved child.

"Why hast thou forsaken me?" Thus moans, as well, the sufferer, upon his bed of pain. Have you just cause, O unfortunate ones, thus to complain? Alas! I cannot blame you for giving expression to your overpowering grief in sobs and lamentations. Nevertheless, dear friends, dry your tears, cease to complain, or, at least, do not give way to despair. Raise your eyes to the cross; he who hangs upon it might justly exclaim: "My God, my God, why hast thou forsaken me?"—for he was truly desolate and forsaken, which you are not. So long as you do not forsake God, he will never desert you; so long as you cherish in your hearts a true faith and confidence in God, no amount of temporal misfortunes can ever make you really unhappy. "'In thee, O Lord! do I trust,'" prays the faithful Christian, in the midst of his bitterest trials, "'let me not be confounded for ever.' Thou feedest the worms in the dust, and the birds in the air; thou clothest the flower of the field more gloriously than Solomon in all his magnificence,—thou wilt not then desert me, thy child; for thou hast promised to aid thy faithful servants, saying: 'Call upon me in the day of tribulation, and I will deliver thee.'"

Yes, truly, my brethren, God never withdraws his grace from a man unless the latter first forsakes him: and though he should appear to hide his countenance for a time, it is only to try our faith and hope in him. When, in the winter, it is cold, dark, and comfortless; when the flowers no longer exhale their perfumes, and the song of the birds is hushed,—tell me, my friends, is the sun to be blamed for all this? Certainly not; that brilliant orb still retains its place in the heavens, diffusing its light and heat with the same force as before: but, our side of the earth being turned from the sun for a time, its beams strike us less directly than before. Dearly beloved! the relations between the sun and the earth resemble those existing between God and man: he does not withdraw from me the sun of his grace, whose rays have ever the same power to warm,—but I, alas! turn aside from him, at times, and obstinately close my heart to those heavenly beams.

Tell me, my brethren, if you lived continually on sweets, would they not, at last, fill you only with disgust? As it is with sweetmeats, so is it with happiness. Sweets upon sweets sicken the body; and in the spiritual order, nauseate the soul. The heart of the ever prosperous man becomes cold; it forgets God, the Dispenser of all goods, until his hand is laid heavily upon it, reminding it of its weakness. "If we have received good things at the hand of God, why should we not receive evil?" said the patient Job. When, during the heat of summer the sun glows day after day, in the firmament, no wind stirs, and not the smallest cloud obscures the heavens,—many are delighted with the weather; but, lacking the fertilizing rain and the purifying thunder storms, the flowers wither, the grass is scorched, the crops are ruined, and sickness, scarcity, and famine arise. Continued good fortune in life is like a succession of cloudless summer days. Sunshine and rain, alternate joy and sorrow are the blessings of God's all wise providence. If things go badly with you, do not question, why God seems to forsake you, while every thing prospers with others;—why he loads the wicked with good things, and fills the lives of the just with trials and privations. Let me relate to you an incident, which I hope will recur to your minds whenever you are tempted to question the providence of God, and its mysterious dispensations.

When a certain holy Archbishop of Lyons was stricken with a dangerous and painful sickness, a monk stood by his bedside, administering to him spiritual consolation. Among other encouraging remarks, he made the following comparison: "God treats man as the physician treats his patient. So long as there is still hope that the disease can be cured, the doctor gives him the bitterest medicines; he cuts and burns, often inflicting on him inexpressible pain; but if, on the contrary, the patient is incurable, then, the doctor spares him all suffering; he gives him agreeable medicines; he allows him to enjoy any thing that pleases his palate; and seeks to render the few hours of life that remain to him, as cheerful and comfortable as possible." "Thus," said the Religious, "God acts with the sinner. If he be not utterly perverse and dead to grace, God sends him many tribulations in order to arouse his conscience, and lead him to a thorough reformation of life; but, on the other hand, if the heart of the sinner be hardened in vice, he leaves him to himself; he even sometimes, grants him honors, riches, and pleasures, in order to reward him for the few good deeds which he may have done in his life, and for which he has nothing to expect in the world to come." Do not these words serve to encourage us in our tribulations? Do they not explain to us many things in life, which have often puzzled us?

III. "*My God, why hast thou forsaken me?*" our dying Saviour cries out to his heavenly Father from the cross. "My child, why hast thou forsaken me?" he calls out to each one of us unfaithful Christians. "Why, O sinner! hast thou turned away from me, thy Redeemer, thy Benefactor? Why hast thou rejected me, the corner-stone of thy salvation? Why hast thou despised the benefits with which I have loaded thee? Why hast thou turned thy back upon me, who am the Light and Truth,—embracing, instead, the falsehood and darkness of the infernal Enemy ? Why, like Judas, hast thou betrayed and sold me, thy Master, for such contemptible rewards as the world could offer thee ? Why hast thou joined the irreligious rabble who, by their crimes, nail me again and again to the cross ? Why, like the lost sheep, hast thou deserted thy true Shepherd, who seeks thee, untiringly, day and night, among the thorns, in the desert, on the mountains, and in the valleys, although thou remainest deaf to his voice, and wilt not permit him to find thee ?"

As a parent chastises his child simply because he loves it, so hast thou often punished me, because thou lovest me. Give me strength to drink the few drops of bitterness which thou dost present me from thy own chalice overflowing with wormwood and gall. Here burn, here cut, but spare me for eternity.

THE FIFTH WORD.

"*I thirst.*" *John 19: 28.*

A solitary traveler wanders through the Great Desert ; the scorching rays of the sun beat down with intense fury upon the wide, arid plain. Weary unto death, and thoroughly exhausted, the fainting man drags along, sinking every moment, ankle deep, in the burning sand. Longingly, his eye searches the distant scene. Is he seeking, perchance, a tree, under whose grateful shadow he may stretch himself and rest his tired limbs ? Is he in quest of a green spot,—a human habitation, wherein he may find shelter from the beasts of the desert, or obtain some nourishment to appease his tormenting hunger ? No ; he is looking anxiously for a spring ; whereat to slake his devouring thirst, and refresh his burning tongue.

But, alas ! there is no well-spring in view. The hours drag on ; he becomes gradually weaker ; his limbs refuse their service—exhausted unto death, he finally sinks down, unconscious. " Water, O, for a drop of water ! "—these are his last words.

Yes, thirst is really the final and most horrible agony preceding dissolution. "I thirst," is the last word of the dying warrior, when, exhausted by loss of blood, he lies helpless and forsaken on the battle field; "I thirst," is the constant cry of the fever stricken patient on his bed of sickness; and so on, all through suffering Nature, down to the plaintive murmur of the dying flower, withered upon its stalk by a long continued drought.

But hark! the same pathetic cry resounds, to-day, from the cross on Golgotha, issuing from the pallid lips of the dying God-Man. To all the other inexpressible pains and torments endured in his extremity, are added those of the most violent and consuming thirst. A few moments ago, he bewailed, as it were, his entire abandonment and desolation, crying out : "My God, my God, why hast thou forsaken me?"—and now, knowing that all things were accomplished that the Scripture might be fulfilled, he said : "*I thirst.*" This fifth word of Jesus, my brethren, shall form the subject of our Lenten meditation, to-day.

I. Alas! what terrible exertions and labors has not the Saviour of men undergone during his Passion! Reflect seriously, my beloved, on all that he has suffered,—upon the sweat and blood he shed during that day and night of horror. Consider the many weary steps he has taken. Since the close of his Last Supper, not a morsel of food, not a drop of water, has passed his lips. After his bloody agony in the Garden of Olives; his three hours' exhausting prayer upon the ground,—his arrest, his tedious ordeal before Annas and Caiphas, Pilate and Herod,—he is scourged at the pillar, and crowned with thorns,—every drop of blood which escapes from his sacred veins, adding fuel to the dreadful thirst which is consuming him. Not an instant is given him for rest or refreshment; until, languishing, and ready to sink from exhaustion, they lay upon his wounded shoulders the hard wood of the cross. Dripping with sweat, he drags along under the burning rays of an oriental sun, falling again and again. Finally, arriving at Golgotha, the divine Victim is nailed violently to the cross; the blood pours forth unceasingly from his gaping wounds, whilst his naked body is tortured by the fierce rays of the sun; thus, he hangs three long hours on the Tree of the cross, suffering more than martyrdom, without even a drop of water to moisten his parched lips.

When they reached Golgotha, and the soldiers were about to nail the innocent Victim to the cross, some compassionate women offered him a draught of wine mixed with the juice of certain strong herbs,—an anodyne which it was customary to administer to malefactors before execution, so that, becoming stupefied, they might not be able to feel the torments of death. In the case of our Lord, however, his cruel enemies mingled gall and myrrh with the draught, in order to drench his mouth with bitterness. Consumed as he was with thirst, Christ refused to drink. He wished to resign his soul into the hands of his Father, and to complete the work of Redemption voluntarily, and in the full possession of all his faculties. Nearer and nearer, approached the consummation of that grand desire; vitality begins to languish, and death is eager to claim its prey. Still, like the weak flame of a taper, which blazes up brightly just before it is finally extinguished, so the vital powers flicker in the dying Saviour. Once more, before life ends,—the death sweat bedewing his pallid countenance—consumed with fever, yet still triumphant over pain of every kind, he cries out with a loud voice, " I thirst !"

II. "I thirst !" O, wonderfully mysterious words! They are addressed to you, O, Christians! " I thirst !" he exclaims : " I desire the consummation of that sacrifice of redemption which shall effect your salvation, and that of all mankind; I thirst to see you all, as believing children, assembled round my cross; to see you accepting the truths which I have taught, and which have the power of making you eternally happy. The water of divine grace streams forth from me, and I thirst to have you drink of this pure stream in deep draughts, —to the end that it may heal and strengthen you unto everlasting life.

"I thirst to do penance for your sins ; for yours, O *drunkard*, who by your intemperance, have, so often, robbed yourself of reason, the noblest gift of man ; and degraded yourself below the level of the brute. For your sins, I thirst, O miserable *glutton*, who sit at a luxurious table, gratifying your appetite with delicate meat and drink, and squandering in expensive wines the means your father accumulated by untiring industry for your decent support. For you, too, I thirst, *unscrupulous husband*, who waste at the tavern the money which your wife has brought you, or has helped you to earn. Instead of caring for her support, and that of her children, you condemn your family to utter want and wretchedness, spending days and nights away from them, in beastly drunkenness, or, if you return at all to your wretched home, rushing in upon its poor inmates, like a furious animal ; and cruelly visiting the consequences of your own sins upon your innocent wife and children. I suffer burning thirst, that I may thus do penance for you, O *disobedient Christian !* who cannot even abstain from flesh meat on Fridays—on that day on which I drank vinegar and gall, and on which I suffered and died for you ! For you, too, O *careless Catholics!* I suffer the pangs of thirst seeing that you cannot deny yourselves, or forego your worldly amusements and gratifications, even during this holy season, when the contemplation of my Passion should animate you to constant acts of mortification. Hence, I thirst, O drunkard! in order to make you temperate; O cold and slothful Christian! in order to make you zealous; O spendthrift! in order to make you economical; O idler! in order to make you industrious; O proud and arrogant one! in order to make you humble; O hard-hearted miser! in order to make you compassionate and generous; O profligate! in order to make you pure of heart; O angry and revengeful man! in order to make you patient and meek!"

III. "I thirst!" exclaims our dying Saviour to each one of us, my brethren; "I thirst for thee, and for the salvation of thy soul!" Let each one of us ask ourselves then, in return: "For what do *I* thirst? Do I thirst for thee, my Saviour? Do I thirst for heaven and its imperishable goods, or for the earth and its fleeting treasures!" Oh! what a miserable, pitiable creature man is! What a contradiction, what an inexplicable riddle even to himself! Alas! body and soul war constantly against each other. "The spirit is willing, but the flesh is weak." The soul aspires to God, and finds no peace until it rests in him; the body, on the contrary, is of the earth, earthy, and hangs like a leaden weight on the wings of the soul, dragging it down into the dust and mire of sin.

This is the meaning of those words of Job: "Man's life on earth is a perpetual warfare;" and of those other words written by the great Apostle of the Gentiles in his Epistle to the Romans: "I am carnal, sold under sin; for I do not that good which I will, but the evil which I hate, that I do." When I desire to obtain a transitory good, a fleeting pleasure, a worldly gratification, an hour of amusement, nothing is too difficult, nothing too arduous; at such times, I sacrifice money, goods, time, sleep, and food,—yea, I willingly travel thousands of miles,—because the coveted object is for myself, but when it is a question of doing something for my salvation, when serious questions, such as these, arise: In what state is my conscience? If our Lord, this very day, were to call me to judgment, how would I appear before him? Why do I not occupy myself with the important affairs of eternity, and continually elevate my soul to God in prayer?—Oh! then, I experience distaste and want of fervor; then, every exertion is too much for me, every moment devoted to God, too tedious! I am willing to spend money freely for a worldly object, a fleeting pleasure, but when there is question of giving an alms for the glory of God, or his church,—my purse is closed at once, and I have not a cent to spare!

"I thirst!"—thus our Saviour cries out from the cross; "I thirst!" Thus I exclaim continually;—but my thirst is not a natural, nor a healthy thirst; it is the diseased thirst of a fever-stricken man. I thirst,—not for God, but for the world; I thirst,—not for heaven, but for earth; I thirst, and although my Saviour invites me to drink from the fountain of living waters,—God himself,—I loathe that pure spring, and drink, in preference, from the foul muddy cistern of the world, which can hold no pure or wholesome water.

My Saviour! I seem to see thee, warm and wearied, sitting by Jacob's well; I seem to hear thee invite the sinful Samaritan woman to drink of thy saving waters. Ah! the same fountain which thou offeredst to her is here open to me! And thy words of sweetness and power are still echoing in my ears: "He that shall drink of the water that I shall give him shall not thirst forever! But the water that I shall give him shall become in him a fountain of water, springing up unto everlasting life." (John 4: 13, 14.) "Lord give me to drink of this water!" cried out the woman at Jacob's well. "Lord!" I exclaim in my turn, "thou hast often invited me to partake of this water, but I, ungrateful, miserable man that I am, have despised and thrust aside the draught that would have brought salvation to my soul! Ah! give me to drink, and forget my past ingratitude!"

IV. "I thirst!" exclaims our Saviour on the cross. Can he find no one to pity him? Do none hear his cry? O Mother Mary! when thou wert flying into Egypt, to protect thy divine Son from the wrath of Herod,—after a long search, thou didst find in the desert a fountain, whereat thou couldst slake the thirst of the Holy Child; now, when he is in the agony of death, thou canst not procure a single drop to cool his parched tongue. Yet, stop! Near the foot of the cross there stands a vessel; a sponge lies in it; perhaps, the executioners, who have been so cruel to him in life, will, at least, in death, offer him a cooling draught? Alas! poor Mother, thou seest that the sponge is colored with something resembling blood; the vessel instead of containing refreshing water, is full of vinegar and gall. Cruel men were accustomed to dip the sponge in this mixture, and apply it to the bodies of those who were crucified, to prolong their torments, by keeping up their vitality. A soldier now seizes the bloody sponge; he dips it in the vinegar, sticks it upon a branch of hyssop, and puts it to the Saviour's parched lips. "Hold!" exclaims one of the by-standers, "he calls upon Elias; we shall see whether he will come and help him!"

O, inhuman cruelty! O, pitiless executioners! Does your implacable hatred against the Innocent One extend even unto death? Can you deny to one who is languishing in untold agony, even the paltry gratification of a single draught of water? He cries: "I thirst!" and you give him unpalatable vinegar! And this, too, to him who permits his rain to fall upon the just and the unjust,—yea, even upon you, his enemies,—to him who protected your fathers when they were fainting in the desert, and permitted Moses to strike the rock that they might have drink! Do you thus repay your benefactor for his manifold gifts? Woe to you on the day of judgment, for our Lord will then exclaim: "I was thirsty and you gave me not to drink; yes,—instead of water, you gave me vinegar and gall?"

Yet, why exclaim against the rabble on Calvary? Let each one look to himself, my brethren,—and see whether he has not been guilty of the very sin which he condemns in others! "I thirst!" cries out our Lord in the person of your own neglected child: "O father! O mother! I thirst to know my God and my Saviour!" Do you gratify his pious desires? Do you appease his spiritual thirst? Do you lead him, in his tender childhood, to the fountains of living water,—to Catechism, to prayer, to Mass, and to the holy Sacraments? Do you not rather offer him vinegar and gall, instead of pure water? Do you not poison his innocent soul by your bad example, and by the evil principles you instil into his heart? Do you not, with sacrilegious hand, pull down all that the priest and the teachers have laboriously built up?

"I planted thee a chosen vineyard, O Christian soul! But if you continue to extend to me the vinegar of unbelief, instead of the wine of faith, then I will destroy this vineyard; I will tear down its fences and its wall; I will change it into a wilderness; and thorns and thistles shall grow therein; and I will command the clouds that they shall no more rain down upon it." Has not the Lord already fulfilled his threat? Has he not once before destroyed such a vineyard? Look at the Holy Land, where the Redeemer was born, suffered and died; in that hallowed spot, the vineyard of the true Church once flourished gloriously, and out of the press of its sweet, abundant grapes, the wine of paradise, the blood of the martyrs, flowed for ages in torrents. But, alas! the birthplace of the world's Redeemer is now a desert waste; Mahommedanism prevails, and pagan depravity and barbarism reign there, undisputed. The vineyard of the Lord is laid waste and destroyed. O, let us pray that this may not be our fate; pray that a like terrible destiny may not pursue the nations of Europe, if they continue to loathe the pure waters of truth,—if, despising the fountains of our holy Church they persist in offering to our thirsting Saviour, the bitter draught of infidelity and contempt! But, on the other hand, let each one of us, my brethren, exclaim from the very depths of a loving and believing soul : "As the hart panteth after the fountains of water, so my soul panteth after thee, my God!" Amen.

THE SIXTH WORD.

"*It is consummated.*"   John 19 : 30.

It is the ever memorable moment of our Saviour's death ;—the ninth hour, or (according to our mode of reckoning time), three o'clock in the afternoon. The earth is still covered with the darkness which settled down upon it at the sixth hour. It is spread like a mourning veil over the vicinity of Jerusalem ; it lies like a dread weight upon all creation. Even inanimate nature, the trees, the plants, the irrational creatures, seem to feel that the next moment may decide their fate ; the leaves hang sorrowfully upon the trees ; the flowers close their petals, and bend down their heads ; the wild beasts, affrighted, hide themselves in their forest dens, and the birds are hushed in their nests—for the Lord of all nature is dying upon the cross. The noisy mob on Calvary have also grown still ; the loud cries of mockery and scorn have died away ; a silence such as precedes a thunder-storm, prevails. O, my soul ! this terrible moment is that of my Saviour's death—it is the moment of my redemption !

"*It is consummated!*" falls from the pale lips of the God-Man, expiring on the cross. "It is consummated!"—a short sentence indeed, but an instructive, and important one. We will, in this sixth Lenten sermon, learn what it teaches.

I. "*It is consummated!*" Yes, my dear Redeemer, all is consummated ; the prophecies are fulfilled ; the sufferings and labors of thy earthly life are over. Past are all the insults and persecutions of thy enemies ; gone are thy night-watches, thy wanderings from place to place. The cruel blows, the scourging at the pillar, the crowning with thorns, are all at an end. The painful journey to Mount Calvary ; the torture of the nails, the slow martyrdom upon the wood of the cross ; the jibes of thy enemies, thy tormenting thirst ; the agonies of death,—all are over at last! Thou hast cared for thy only treasure, thy tenderly loved Mother; having intrusted her to the care of thy faithful disciple, St. John, thou art done with the world—now, all is past—all is consummated!

Oh! how deeply must thy heart have been moved, when, a few days ago, thou wentest up to Jerusalem to celebrate the Pasch for the last time with thy disciples! Then, in solemn, prophetic tones, thou saidst to them: "Behold, we go up to Jerusalem: and the Son of Man shall be betrayed to the chief priests and to the Scribes: and they shall condemn him to death." (Matt. 20:18.) Oh! what an ocean of sorrow must have inundated thy heart, when, after the Last Supper (in company with the chosen three), thou didst go to the Garden of Olives, to prepare thyself for the fearful trials of the following day. Trembling, thou didst then experience, in anticipation, the sorrows of death,—crying out to Peter, James, and John: "My soul is sorrowful even unto death .... The spirit, indeed, is willing, but the flesh is weak." (Matt. 26:38-41.) In thy agony, thou didst pray: "O, my Father, if it is possible, let this chalice pass from me!"—and, so great was thy suffering, that the very ground on which thou didst kneel, was saturated with the bloody sweat, oozing from every pore of thy sacred body. Behold! all the sorrows and torments of a lingering death, which caused thy human spirit to shrink back in horror, are now all past—the bitter chalice is drained to the dregs—"it is consummated!"

"Father, the hour is come!" thus thou didst pray before thy Passion, for thy Apostles, for us, and for all mankind,—"I have glorified thee upon the earth; I have finished the work which thou gavest me to do; and now glorify thou me, O Father, with thyself, with the glory which I had with thee, before the world was." (John 17:1, 4, 5.)

It is the instinct of every living thing to struggle against death. The drowning man instinctively clutches at the slenderest straw, in the vain effort to save himself. So long as the heart beats, and the eyes remain open, the invalid, the consumptive, yea, the very leper whose members are already beginning to corrupt, hopes to the last, for cure and deliverance. Even the beast of prey in the forest, the spider on the wall, the worm in the dust, all struggle desperately with the enemy which seeks their destruction. Death is, indeed, hard and bitter, no matter how poor or painful may be the life from which it releases us. Death is hard and bitter; and no one can make a greater sacrifice for another than to die for him. Yet the incarnate Son of God has done this! He has died the lingering death of the cross for me, and for my sins! All is over,—all is consummated! The redemption of our sinful race is accomplished; heaven and earth are reconciled; the gates of Paradise are opened, a new and everlasting covenant is sealed in the blood of the crucified Redeemer!

The Sinless One has been regarded as a criminal, for our sakes; the meek Lamb of God has been treated as a malefactor, esteemed even of less worth than the murderer, Barabbas; but now, sin is atoned for, the indictment against Adam, and his guilty descendants, lies cancelled at the foot of the cross; eternal justice is satisfied; all is over,—"it is consummated!" As the victorious general, after a bloody battle, raises the joyous shout of conquest, which all his troops thunderingly repeat, so, to-day, resounds the victor's cry from the cross: "It is consummated!" The battle with the prince of darkness is ended, the victory over sin and death is won!

"*It is consummated!*" Hear it, man, and rejoice! hear it, ye mountains, and re-echo the cry, bearing it on to the ends of the earth; hear it, ye fallen Angels—hear it, hell, and tremble; for it is a cry of horror for *you!* Hear it, ye souls of the just in Limbo,—it declares that the moment is at hand when the King of Glory will open the doors of your prison, and lead you into his kingdom! Hear it, also, ye blessed Spirits of heaven, for soon will you see your Lord seated again on that throne of glory, which he quitted for our sakes,—soon will the celestial halls resound with the canticles of innumerable Saints, begotten of the blood of the Redeemer, even as golden sheaves spring from the fruitful seed of wheat. The Cherub, who stands at the gate of Paradise, hearing this cry, sheathes his flaming sword, and hastens to rejoin the hosts of Angels, who rejoicing, array themselves to receive their returning Lord. Thanks, heart-felt thanks to thee, my dying Saviour, for delivering us from the bonds of darkness and the chains of hell, with that victorious cry : " It is consummated ! "

II. "*It is consummated!*" Our Lord Jesus Christ has consummated the redemption of a guilty world; but, is it completed, also, in *my* miserable soul? He has died for me—he has offered me his grace,—have I profited by it? He has stretched out his hand to me; have I grasped it? He has shown me the way of the cross; he has invited me to follow him therein,—have I done so, up to the present time? Oh! with shame and confusion I must accuse myself, I must confess my indifference, my disobedience, my indolence. I have rejected the food of life ; I have despised the Source of salvation. It was mercifully given me to choose between life and death, between fire and water, and I, (fool that I was !)—chose death rather than life, fire rather than water ; and only now begin to recognize my terrible mistake !

"*It is consummated!*" The grand mystery of Redemption is accomplished. But, for you, infatuated sinner ! ill advised son ! foolish daughter ! careless parent ! it is not yet completed. It is not yet accomplished for *you*, ye proud, envious, intemperate, impure sinners,—for you, unjust ones,—for you, usurers, who oppress your poor, suffering brethren, and who even take the last, hard earned penny from the desolate widow. Oh ! how will you answer for all these crimes in the Day of Judgment ? Shuddering, you will hear the solemn voice of the Judge, bearing witness : " As Judas betrayed me, as the Jews crucified me, so have you also betrayed and crucified me by your evil deeds. How often would I have covered you with the wings of my mercy,—how often would I have gathered you, as a hen gathers her chickens under her wings, but, alas ! you would not. You have despised my grace and my redemption ; receive now, the reward of your iniquities !"

Ah ! if we were not wanting in good-will, we might all exclaim with regard to our salvation : "It is consummated !" There are three hundred and sixty-five days in a year ; consider, then, my brethren,—if you would but daily strive to become better,—what a rich profit would be yours in a single year ! If you succeed in eradicating only one bad habit each year, what a perfect Christian would you not be at the end of ten, twenty or thirty years of life ?

III. "*It is consummated!*" Words of solemn warning, full either of terror or of consolation at the hour of death ! O poor, dying beggar, why do you tremble and grieve ? O rich nobleman, why are you proud and overbearing ? Behold ! death levels all distinctions ; those who in life were so widely separated, now slumber peacefully, side by side. When Elizabeth, the mighty queen of England, was in the zenith of her power, she exclaimed : "Give me forty years to reign and I renounce heaven !" but when she felt her end approaching, she cried out in terror, "Alas ! I would give all my treasures for another hour of life!" Then, turning away her face, she expired.

"*It is consummated!*" This is the exclamation of the just man upon his death-bed. He looks back upon his vanished years ; he recalls the trials which he has endured, the temptations he has overcome, the sufferings he has borne. He does not reckon now the tears which he has wept in the past, for he is about to enter into that happy Land where God shall wipe away all tears from the eyes of his elect. The sorrowful winter of life is over, an eternal spring approaches, enlivened by every celestial delight. All is consummated!

How dreadful are these words in the mouth of the dying, impenitent sinner! *"It is consummated!"* Yes, a life of crime and scandal is completed; but the work of salvation remains unfinished. The miserable, corruptible body has been royally pampered; but the soul, which should have been nourished by divine grace, has been starved and neglected. The unhappy wretch has taken every care to accumulate temporal goods by fair means or foul; but he has not lifted a finger to acquire the priceless treasures of eternal life. Now, with unavailing remorse, he looks back upon his past life; upon the long catalogue of his crimes:—but, alas! it is too late! In a few moments, all will be over; the life of the body will soon be finished, but the eternal misery of the soul will have only just begun!

On a cold New Year's Eve, a certain man stood at the window of his chamber, watching the snow flakes falling thickly upon the earth. His heart was as cold and desolate as the wintry prospect before him. His past life was full of transgressions of every kind; and now, old age has come upon him, and his hair is as white as the falling snow. The worm of remorse gnaws at his heart. "O, would I were a child again!" he sighs, "how much better and more wisely would I employ my time! How courageously would I walk forward in the path of truth and goodness! But now, it is too late! I see only an open grave before me, which will soon receive my guilty body. Oh! return, golden youth, return!" And behold! as he spoke the words, he awoke, and found it was all a dream, and that he was still a young man in the fullness of health and strength. But he had not received the warning in vain; he entered into himself, and became, thenceforth, an honest, upright man.

Take this admonition to heart: perhaps there is yet time for reformation. Abandon, at once, your past life of sin. Repent,—and God will pardon your offences; and when the night of death settles down upon you, you will not be forced to cry out, with the impenitent sinner, "Too late! too late! my life is finished; but now my misery is only at its commencement!"

If thoughtless souls would only reflect more frequently upon the end of all things; upon the consequences of one's actions, and upon that supreme moment of death, when all men will be forced to exclaim: "*It is consummated!*"—oh! from how many sins would they not be preserved! "In all thy works, remember thy last end: and thou shalt never sin." (Eccles. 7:40.) If the gambler, the spendthrift, the drunkard, would consider that their bad habits sink them in ruin and beggary; if the liar would reflect that his sins will draw down upon him shame and contempt; if the profligate would remember that he is destroying both soul and body by his lusts; if the thief and the murderer would call to mind that their crimes will bring them to prison, and, at last, to the gallows—certainly, they would shrink back in terror, before committing the first offence.

IV. "*It is consummated!*" Listen to these words, O man! when the desire of unjustly possessing your neighbor's goods arises secretly within you. Listen to them, you who keep company with a person who is dangerous to your virtue and morality; listen to them, you who go with companions to places which will cause your ruin: listen to them, and struggle to overcome yourself. By the grace of God, you will certainly come off the victor in the strife: and then you may joyfully exclaim: "The battle is ended, the evil desires are conquered, the victory is, at last, consummated!"

"*It is consummated!*" Let the Christian husband, who lives in discontent with his wife,—the rebellious wife, who has contracted an unhappy marriage,—listen to these words. Though the companion of his life be fretful, bad tempered, quarrelsome, the man must not forsake his home for the tavern, nor waste his substance in extravagance or dissipation. He must be patient with his unhappy partner—a kind, devoted father to his peevish children, remembering that the hour will soon come when he can exclaim: "The trials of my life are past. '*It is consummated!*'" And even though the wife should be aware that her spouse has broken his solemn vow of fidelity, let her persevere to the end. Honestly fulfilling all her duties as a good wife and mother, at last, she also may be able to apply to herself the words of our dying Saviour upon the cross: "Now, all is consummated!"

THE SEVENTH WORD.

"*Father, into thy hands I commend my spirit.*" Luke 23 : 46.

We are led, to-day, for the last time, to the cross upon Golgotha, at the moment when our Redeemer, freed from his agony, bows down his head and dies. O Cross of Christ! to-day, we celebrate thy glorious victory over sin and Satan; and to thee millions and millions of believing Christians now raise their eyes with pious confidence. whilst the priest chants : "*Ecce lignum crucis!*—behold the wood of the cross, on which hung the salvation of the world!"

My brethren, when a beloved relative, or friend, lies in the agony of death, with what eagerness, with what anxious solicitude, do we not apply the ear to the mouth of the dying person, in order to catch the final words, the last request! That child must be, indeed, ungrateful of heart, who does not treasure and venerate the farewell words of his dying father or mother.

It is Good Friday; and we, too, are standing at the death-bed of a Father. His couch,—alas! is hard and comfortless,—it is the cross; the Father who breathes away his life thereon, is the common Father of all—our Lord and Saviour, Jesus Christ! Behold! he opens his mouth, he speaks his final words! Attend to them, as they resound loudly throughout the universe: "*Father, into thy hands I commend my spirit!*"

I. "*Father, into thy hands I commend my spirit!*" The final moment of our divine Lord's agony has arrived. The three long hours of torture upon the cross have been endured, with perfect patience and consciousness. He has pardoned his enemies, and promised paradise to the penitent thief; he has provided for his mother with filial affection, and expressed his thirst for our salvation; now all is consummated; and since there is nothing left to him except his spirit, this, too, he, at length, resigns to his Eternal Father. "Father," he exclaims, "into thy hands I commend my spirit." Oh! this is not the low sigh of a dying man. No—it is the clear, powerful cry of the Sovereign Lord and Master who controls life and death, and who willingly and joyfully sacrifices himself for a sin-laden world. When our Saviour had drained the bitter chalice of suffering almost to the dregs, when his agony had reached its highest degree, and he hung upon the cross comfortless and desolate, he had exclaimed sorrowfully: "My God! my God! why hast thou forsaken me?" But now,—now he does not cry out: "*My God!*" No, he says, "*Father!*" for he is no longer the representative of sinners, using the language of a servant; he now speaks as the Eternal Son to the Eternal Father, as a loving child to a forgiving, reconciled parent. "Father," he would say, "behold, I have completed the work of redemption that you laid upon me; I have nothing more to give, by which I can prove my love and obedience to you, but my spirit; accept it, then; and, after three days, it shall be reunited with my glorified, risen body."

II. "*Father, into thy hands I commend my spirit!*" Thus spoke, at the end, the expiring Saviour; but in those words, he did not merely commend himself,—but me, and you, and all of us,—to his Eternal Father. After the Last Supper, before entering with his Apostles into the Garden of Olives (to gain there, in prayer, the requisite strength and solace to meet the sufferings of the following day), the High Priest of the New Law prayed thus: "Holy Father, keep them in thy name whom thou hast given me, preserve them from evil; but not for them only do I pray, but for those also who through their word shall believe in me." (John 17:11, 20.) As he prayed in that solemn hour, so, now, in the still more solemn hour of death, he exclaims: "Father, into thy hands I commend my spirit,—and with it I commend to thee all my brethren, the children of men. To thy mercy, I commend the sinner; to thy grace and pardon, I recommend the unbeliever; to thy power, I commend those who are weak and frail in faith and good works; to thy consolation, I commend thy sick and suffering ones; to thy protection, I commend all—both the living and the dead!"

III. "*Father, into thy hands I commend my spirit!*" When David fled before King Saul, and was obliged to hide in the mountains of Juda, dangers and death surrounded him; but he exclaimed confidently: "He who dwelleth under the shadow of the Almighty is secure and has nothing to fear." Yes, if God is with us, my brethren, who can be against us? "Into thy hands, O, Father," each one of us must, therefore say, "I commend my body and my life; I place myself under thy protection. Guide thou my going forth and my coming in; so that I depart not from the right path. Place thyself as a guard upon my tongue, and over all my words and actions, that all may be directed to thee, O my God!"

When your son, O Christian parents, goes abroad for the first time, into the great world, to seek his daily bread; when you lay your hand in blessing upon his head, and sorrowfully sigh "Farewell!"—tell me, to whom can you recommend him with greater confidence than to the protection of his heavenly Father, the omnipotent, the omnipresent God? And you, O wife, when your husband leaves home daily to earn a living for you and your children (perhaps at the risk of his own life), to whom, I ask, can you better intrust him than to the care of him without whose permission not a hair falls from your head, nor a single leaf drops from the tree of the forest? When heart and courage are sinking, who will support you—who will raise you up, if it be not the Lord, the Mighty One? And O, when you lie, pale and helpless upon your death-bed—what more beautiful last words can you then pronounce than those of your dying Saviour upon the cross: "Father, into thy hands I commend my spirit!"—?

Well for you, my brethren, if you can also cry out at that supreme moment: "Behold, O Father, I return to thee my soul, pure and spotless as thou didst give it to me in Baptism!" Well for you, if you can say with the faithful servant: "Lord, thou deliveredst to me five talents,—behold, I have gained other five, over and above." But still better for you, if it is granted you to hear this reply: "Well done, good and faithful servant, because thou hast been faithful over a few things, I will set thee over many things; enter thou into the joy of thy Lord." (Matth. 25.) Woe to you, on the other hand, if you must then confess with the slothful servant: "Alas! O Lord, I have not employed the talent that thou gavest me; I have buried it instead of returning it to thee with interest." Woe to you, if these terrible words are then addressed to you: "Take ye away, therefore, the talent from him, and cast him into the exterior darkness. There shall be weeping and gnashing of teeth." "If I had two souls," St. Augustine used to say, "O, my God! I might risk one of them in play; but as I have only one, I must work out my salvation with fear and trembling, that I may not lose it."

IV. "*Father, into thy hands I commend my spirit!*" Alas! these are the last, last words of our beloved, dying Lord! Behold, how his blessed eyes become dim and glazed; his face is overspread with the hue of death,—he inclines his head,—he breathes for the last time—he has given up the ghost!

It is all over! The awful tragedy has drawn to a close! The murder of the God-Man has been consummated! The servant has killed his

Master,—the creature, his Creator and Redeemer! The divine Heart that always beat with love for us, is stilled in death; the sacred lips, that breathed naught save words of consolation, are now cold and pallid; the beautiful eyes, that always beamed with love and meekness, are now dim and sightless; those hands, that loaded men with blessings and benefits,—those feet, which hastened, untiringly, from place to place, seeking the lost sheep of his fold, are now cold and stiff in death. But thy head, O Lord Jesus! is still inclined towards those whom thou hast redeemed; thy arms are extended, in order to embrace us, thy children, with tender love; only a few hours more, and thy sacred Heart will be pierced through with a lance, in order that my soul may hide there from the enemies of its salvation!

"O, Christian! what have I done to thee?" thus our Saviour mournfully addresses you. "Scarcely were you born, when I clothed your soul with the pure robe of Baptism; and when you had stained that white robe by willful sin, I washed it clean with my blood. I have planted you like a beautiful vineyard, but you brought forth nothing but weeds. You returned my love with hatred, my benefits with ingratitude! 'My son, my daughter, what have I done to thee? why art thou troubled? What is there that I could have done for thee, that I have not done? Answer me!'"

"*Father, into thy hands I commend my spirit!*" Hark! the universe rings with that awful cry. The foundations of the earth tremble; the palaces of Jerusalem are shaken; the strongest walls fall; rocks are rent; graves open, the dead come forth, and walk through the city, pointing with menacing fingers towards Golgotha, the dread theatre of a most horrible crime! In the temple of Jerusalem, they have just sacrificed the Paschal Lamb; when lo! the grand, costly veil before the Holy of Holies is rent in twain—a miraculous testimony that the wall of separation between heaven and earth has fallen—that the Old Dispensation has ceased forever, and the New Covenant concluded and sealed by the blood of the slaughtered Lamb of God! The sun, which has been concealed by thick clouds and darkness for the past three hours, comes forth, and illumines with its yellow light the hill of Calvary, revealing there the Cross, which still bears the lifeless body of the Lord Jesus. It sheds its beams upon the Sorrowful Mother of God, who uplifts her longing arms, as though she would fain snatch her divine Son down from his cruel bed, and clasp him closely to her maternal bosom. It shines also upon the faithful John, prostrate beneath the cross in an agony of grief; upon the wretched rabble, standing about dumb and anxious; upon the Roman centurion, who strikes his breast, exclaiming vehemently: "Verily, this is the Son of God!" Then, timidly and sadly, the multitude gradually dispense, whilst the dark clouds of night overspread the sky. Once more, it is lonely and deserted on Golgotha ; only the three crosses tower up gloomily against the horizon, bearing upon them the white corpses of the condemned !

V. My hearers ! we, too, have reached the conclusion of our Lenten meditations ; we, too, are about to quit, with the sorrowful crowd, the lonely mountain top,—leaving behind us the awful vision of the Crucified One ; but I cannot suffer you to depart from this sacred spot, without holding before you, once again, that mirror of Calvary, —the crucifix. But a few hours more, and the solemn season of Lent, the time of penance, of serious thought, will be at an end. You will soon return to your ordinary occupations, your absorbing business cares ; the world, with all its turmoil and strife, will surround you. Do not forget, I implore you, the holy impression of the past six weeks. Do not forget the sacred meditations made here, in God's blessed House,—the Seven Last Words of our dying Saviour upon the cross. Make, to-day, your practical resolutions for the future. You, who have enmity and revenge in your hearts, who cannot and will not forgive and forget, listen to our Saviour : "*Father, forgive them; for they know not what they do.*" You, who have repented of your sins, and have confessed them, or intend doing so during the Paschal season, hearken to the Second Word of our Lord,—"*Amen I say unto thee, this day thou shall be with me in paradise !*" You, parents, you, children, who discharge your relative duties slothfully and negligently, learn from the Third Word, your obligations: "*Mother ! behold thy son . . . Son ! behold thy mother !*" All ye afflicted ones, who suffer tribulations of any sort, and who are inclined to despair,—remembering that your Saviour has endured far more than you—listen to his Fourth Word : "*My God ! my God ! why hast thou forsaken me ?*" "O, dissolute man, gambler, drunkard, spendthrift ! learn economy, temperance, abstemiousness, from your Saviour's Fifth Word : "*I thirst !*" You, whose will is so weak in good, so strong in evil,— who find it so difficult to persevere in virtue's path,—continue faithful to the end, the final victory awaits you, for your Saviour, in his Sixth Word says : "*It is consummated !*" And you, O Christians ! young and old, learn to live piously, learn to die as Jesus Christ died, saying with him: "*Father into thy hands I commend my spirit !*"

My dearly beloved ! do not depart from Golgotha, do not quit the foot of the cross, with Magdalene, without having learned, like her, how intensely our Saviour has loved you, and how diligently you should return love for love. Do not go away without remembering that it was our sins that fastened him to the wood of the cross; and whenever you gaze upon the crucifix, hanging upon the wall of your room, recall all that your Saviour has done and suffered for your salvation; as often as you see a cross in a church, or elsewhere, reflect upon the SEVEN LAST WORDS of your expiring Redeemer, and endeavor to reduce their precepts to practice in your daily life.

A few hours more, and the Easter-bell will resound over mountain and valley, fields and forests! The joyful *Alleluia* will announce the risen Saviour. May it be, indeed, a blessed *Alleluia*, to you—the signal for your own glad resurrection from the sleep of sin, from the gloomy grave of spiritual death!

QUESTIONS OF THE SOUL.

NINTH COURSE.

SEVEN SERMONS.

LENTEN SERMONS.

FIRST FRIDAY IN LENT.

I. WHAT HAVE YOU DONE?

"*How canst thou say: I am not polluted? See thy ways, know what thou hast done;* AS *a swift runner pursuing his course.*" Jer. 2: 23.

According to the intention of the Church, my dear brethren, we should employ this holy season of Lent in weeping over and doing penance for our sins. But are we sinners, indeed? Ask the prophet Jeremiah, and listen humbly to the scathing reproach of his reply: "How canst thou say: I am not polluted? See thy ways, know what thou hast done; *as* a swift runner pursuing his course." Ask the Apostle St. John, and he, too, will tell you: "If we say, that we have no sin, we deceive ourselves, and the truth is not in us." 1. John 1: 8. In fine, my dear brethren, ask your own consciences, look at the record of your lives,—how polluted are both, and what a dark vision of sin stares you in the face! Are you going to continue your criminal and sinful career? Are you not resolved to relinquish your bad habits, to restrain your unruly passions, to avoid the occasions of sin, and to make good use of the means of grace for the amendment of your lives? O, how sad and deplorable will be the consequences, if you do not adopt the latter salutary course! Everything in this holy season urges you to do penance, and "we, helping, do exhort you" to make this holy resolution, and by putting it at once into execution, to bring forth fruits worthy of penance. To this end, I shall speak to you, my dear brethren, in these, my instructions for the Fridays of Lent, *on the sinners' return to God.*

The subject of my first discourse, (which I shall deliver briefly to you to-day,) is the question: "*What hast thou done?*" And in answer to that important question, I will proceed to show that you have

    I. Forsaken your God, and
    II. Offended your God.

I. In the Sacred Scriptures we find it recorded of the sinner, numberless times, that he has forsaken his God. "The beloved *forsook God* who made him, and departed from God, his Saviour." Deut. 32: 15. And again: "Woe to the sinful nation, a people laden with iniquity, a wicked seed, ungracious children: *they have forsaken God,* they have blasphemed the Holy One of Israel, they have gone away backwards." Is. 1:8. And in the prophet Osee, we read: "*They have forsaken the Lord* in not obeying the law." Osee 4:10. This forsaking God, means that the sinner turns away from God and walks in other paths than those prescribed by his divine law. Does that signify anything? Is it, dear friends, a matter of little or great importance? Listen and you shall hear. You have forsaken your God,

1. *To whom you are bound by so many ties.* Know, that a sacred, threefold bond unites man with his God.

a) *The bond of Creation.* "Let us make man to our image and likeness. . . . And God created him to his own image, and to the image of God he created him." Gen. 1: 26, 27. "The spirit of God made me, and the breath of the Almighty gave me life." Job 33: 4. God is your Creator, and you are his creature, the work of his hands. The book is the property of the man who writes it; the picture is the property of the artist who paints it; the marble image is the property of the sculptor who chisels it,—so, in a much higher and more binding sense, *you* are the property of God who has made you. What a holy bond between him and you,—and, yet, you have broken this bond by your sins, you have forsaken your God!

b) *The bond of Redemption.* "There is one God, and one Mediator of God and men, the man Christ Jesus: who gave himself a redemption for all." 1. Tim. 2: 5. "Blotting out the hand-writing of the decree which was against us; and the same he took out of the way fastening it to the Cross." Col. 2: 14. God is your Redeemer, and you are his redeemed ones, bought not with gold, or silver, or precious stones, but with the adorable Blood shed, (yea, even to its last drop,) from the veins of the only begotten Son of the Eternal Father. What a holy bond between him and you; and, yet, you have sundered this bond by your iniquities,—you have forsaken your God!

c) *The bond of sanctification.* "You are washed, you are sanctified, you are justified, in the name of our Lord Jesus Christ, and in the spirit of our God." 1. Cor. 6: 11. "By the justice of one, unto all men unto justification of life." Rom. 5: 18. God, your Sanctifier and you the sanctified; the breath of his infinite wisdom and holiness breathing continually the most precious inspirations and graces into your souls! What a holy bond! And, yet, you have torn apart this blessed bond,—you have forsaken your God. Will you, then, be able to say: "Of what consequence is sin?" O, how holy the bonds that unite you with your God! The ties which unite you to a friend, to your child, to your wife, husband, father, or mother are not so holy as these celestial ties,—yet, you would hesitate to break friendship with those dear ones whom you so tenderly love. And this God, to whom you are bound by divine bonds,—you nave forsaken him,—you have despised his love, and turned your back upon his laws. Is not sin something awful, if considered in this light alone?... But it has a worse aspect still. You have forsaken

2. *The God to whom you have promised fidelity.*

a) *In holy Baptism.* At the sacred baptismal font, my dear brethren, you promised before heaven and earth that you would never forsake your God during your whole future life. It is true, you may not have made this promise with your own tongue, with your own conscious will, but by the lips of your sponsor, who held you, a little speechless baby, at the font; nevertheless, the promise binds you just as strongly as if you had raised your hand to bear witness to the solemn oath. "The baptismal vows are inviolable, and though all other vows may be remitted, no one, either in heaven or upon earth, can loose and free a soul from its baptismal vows." St. Aug. Epist. 116.

b) *At your first Communion.* In that holy hour you ratified your baptismal vows. Think of that blissful moment when you were united for the first time, to the Body and Blood, Soul and Divinity of our Lord and Saviour Jesus Christ! In glowing love and innocence, you knelt at the foot of the altar, and promised to God and all the Saints, before the whole congregation whom you called upon as witnesses of your vows, that you would renounce the devil with all his works, the world with all its pomps, the flesh with all its temptations, and that you would remain faithful to God all the days of your life, allowing nothing to separate you from the love of Christ.

c) *On many other subsequent occasions.* You had heard, perhaps, a touching sermon;—you were saved from some great calamity;—you had received, perchance, some great and special benefit from God;—you were enlightened in prayer, you confessed and received Communion with unusually fervent dispositions. On all these occasions, you renewed that first holy bond of love with your God, you made the earnest resolution to give your hearts entirely to him; thenceforth, to love him sincerely and to serve him faithfully. Is it not so, my brethren?

And what have you done? Alas! I repeat the painful question. *What have you done?* Notwithstanding, your solemn promises, vows, and oaths, you have forsaken God; yes, you have forsaken him repeatedly and wilfully, by drunkenness, enmity, hatred, pride, impurity. And is *this* a matter of little or no importance? Is it a small thing for a soldier to forsake the banner of his country to which he has vowed loyalty and allegiance? Is it a trifling thing for a married person to dishonor and violate the bonds of matrimony which he solemnly promised to keep inviolate unto death? God bitterly complains of man, because he, thus, forsakes his Creator and Redeemer. "Be astonished, O ye heavens, at this; and ye gates thereof, be very desolate, saith the Lord. For, my people have done two evils. They have *forsaken* me, the fountain of living water, and have digged to themselves cisterns, broken cisterns, that can hold no water." Jer. 2: 12, 13.

II. What have you done? You have not only offended your Creator, your Redeemer, but, also, your Preserver and your Sanctifier. "You have grieved the Holy Spirit of God whereby you are sealed unto the day of redemption." Ephes. 4: 30. Sin is truly an offence against God; not as if God thereby felt or experienced pain, but, because sin is a contempt of God, a rejection of his sacred law, a rebellion against his adorable will. Hence, sin is also called enmity against God, as the Apostle says: "The wisdom of the flesh is an enemy to God." Rom. 8: 7. Moreover, it is a sacrilegious renewal of the crucifixion of Christ. "Crucifying again to themselves the son of God, and making a mockery of him." Heb. 6: 6. What have you done? You have offended God, yes

1. *Your great God.* The offence is aggravated by the dignity of the person offended. What a difference, my brethren, between an insult offered to a servant or one cast in the face of a king! The sinner offends a great God:

a) *Great in power and majesty.* "Thine are riches, and thine is glory, thou *hast dominion over all*, in thy hand is power and might, in thy hand greatness, and the empire of all things." 1. Paralip. 29: 12. "Who shaketh the earth of her place, and the pillars thereof tremble." Job 9: 6. "Who shall resist the strength of thy arm?" Wisd. 9: 6. "No word shall be impossible with God." Luke 1: 37. To be brief, dear friends, all the greatness and power of earthly potentates and princes are limited and finite,—God, alone, is *infinite* power and majesty.—He, alone, is:

b) *Great in glory.* "The Lord shall sit king forever." Ps. 28: 10. "His name, alone, is exalted." Ps. 148: 13. "There is none like to thee, O Lord, thou art great, and great is thy name in might." Jer. 10: 6. "King of kings, and Lord of lords." 1. Tim. 6: 15.—This God, great in power and majesty, and great in glory, before whom the pillars of heaven tremble, to whom heaven and earth are subject, and whom the Angels adore with hidden faces,—you, a poor miserable worm of the earth have offended.

2. *Your good God.* The insult is aggravated by the base ingratitude of the offender. If it be a cruel act to insult a stranger from whom you have never received a kindness or benefit of any sort, what can you say, my brethren, of a child, who strikes his father or his mother? And *you* have offended this infinitely good God, who is:

a) *So good towards all creatures.* "Thou, O Lord, art sweet and mild." Ps. 85: 5. God wills the true happiness of all his creatures and promotes their welfare in every possible way. He gives splendor to the sun, light to the moon and to the stars, color to the flowers, and a garment of soft feathers to the birds. "Thou openest thy hand and fillest with blessing every living creature." Ps. 144: 16.

b. *So good towards you in particular.* "What hast thou, that thou hast not received?" 1. Cor. 4: 7. Consider the wonderful and delicate mechanism of your body,—the immortal essence and beautiful powers of your soul; look back with tears of gratitude upon your past life, from the first moment of your existence to this present hour. Consider all that you have lived through; weigh seriously and carefully every inspiration, every blessing, every signal mercy he has showered upon you, and you will find that God has overwhelmed you with benefits without measure, without number; benefits, both spiritual and temporal, of which you were wholly undeserving, and which you valued or appreciated so little that you scarcely thought it worth your while to thank your great Benefactor for his gifts and graces. Like a father, he has carried you in his arms; like a mother, he has poured out his love upon you. "What is there, that I ought to do more to my vineyard, that I have not done to it?" Is. 5: 4. And *what have you done* in return?

You have offended this great, this good God, by every sin you have committed; by your pride, your anger, envy, lust, gluttony, and sloth. You have offended him not once and slightly, but grievously, and innumerable times. Look well, my brethren, into your life, into your thoughts, words and actions. O, what a horrid vision of sin stares you in the face! Are you not forced to cry out with the royal prophet: "My iniquities are gone over my head, and as a heavy burden are become heavy upon me." Ps. 37: 5. *What have you done?* O, let not this thought depart from your mind, though it should pierce your heart like a two-edged sword, though it should burn in its depths like coals of living fire,—cast not away this salutary thought, dear friends, till it effects, by the grace of God, a thorough and lasting conversion; till it leaves you, at length, firmly resolved to return to your God during this holy season of Lent, and to continue to do penance for your past ingratitude and sin, during all the coming days of your life. Amen.

SECOND FRIDAY IN LENT.

II. WHAT AWAITS YOU?

"It is a dreadful thing to fall into the hands of the living God."
Hebr. 10: 31.

Have you heard, my dear brethren, these words of the Apostle: "It is a dreadful thing to fall into the hands of the living God?" Ponder upon them with me, to-day, I implore you, for "his wrath no man can resist," Job 9: 13; and the arrows of his vengeance destroy all against whom they are directed. But who, (you ask,) will fall into the hands of the living God? He who departs this life in the state of mortal sin. O what a great evil is sin! Its black deformity was clearly set before you in my last discourse. I hope, then, you have complied with my request, and (never suffering those salutary thoughts to depart from your memories,) that you have pondered seriously upon the important subject. What have you done? You have forsaken your God, your loving and powerful Creator, to whom so many and such holy bonds bind you, and to whom you have so often vowed fidelity. . . . . What have you done? You have offended your God, your wise and amiable Redeemer who shed the last drop of his blood for you upon the cruel cross. You have sinned against the Holy Spirit, the great and good God, who has loaded you with inspirations and graces. . . . And now *what awaits you* in punishment of your infidelity, your disobedience, your malice? Think well on it, before it be too late. God must punish you; he is bound by his eternal Law to render to every man according to the works which he has done in the flesh, whether good or evil. What, then, awaits you for your sinful works?

    I. The judgment of an angry God,
   II. The hell of an avenging God.

The Eternal Lord and Law-giver will, nay, *must* enter into judgment with his offending creature. His outraged mercy demands the arraignment of the criminal at the bar of his infinite justice. Behold, then, O sinner, what awaits you: The judgment of an angry God. But what kind of a judgment is this? A judgment so terrible that its horrors, my brethren, are far beyond and above all human conception.

a) It is the judgment of an *infinitely holy God.* The Seraphim cried one to another, and said: "Holy, holy, holy, the Lord God of hosts, all the earth is full of his glory." Is. 6: 3. Being a God of infinite purity and holiness, he detests every sin in his innermost essence, and with an everlasting hatred: "Thou art not a God that willest iniquity, neither shall the wicked dwell near thee; nor shall the unjust abide before thy eyes. Thou hatest all the workers of iniquity; thou wilt destroy all that speak a lie. The bloody and the deceitful man the Lord will abhor." Ps. 5: 5–7. And you, O sinner, standing in judgment before this holy God,—what shall he see in your heart, in your life? Alas! how many stains, and spots, and indelible brands of hell! He sees your injustices, your adulteries, your drunkenness, your mortal sins against Charity, your sacrilegious Communions. The infinitely holy God sees all the crimes which you have committed from the dawn of reason up to this very hour. His angry gaze rests upon you,—you are doomed already to hell; the sentence is pronounced; you are, as it were, on your way to the place of execution,—the mercy of God, alone, stays for a little while the descending sword of his avenging justice. He can destroy you, body and soul, at any moment. Can you, then, be so careless, so indifferent, in the face of such momentous risks?

b. *An omniscient God will judge you.* Before an earthly judge you may sometimes succeed in concealing certain damaging circumstances,— and what you cannot conceal you may be able to palliate or excuse. But this, my brethren, is not possible before the all-knowing Judge. "Man seeth those things that appear, but the Lord beholdeth the heart." (1. Kings, 16: 7.) Yes, God beholds the heart, and he beholds it with the eyes of a God. "The eyes of the Lord are brighter than the sun, beholding round about all the ways of men, and the bottom of the deep, and looking into the hearts of men, into the most hidden parts." (Eccl. 23: 28.) And you, sinner, are in judgment before this omniscient God! His eye penetrates the most secret folds, the inmost recesses of your soul. All those bad thoughts and sinful actions which you have concealed from every human eye, all those corrupt desires which you have buried in the depths of your own bosom, are open and manifest before him, as though they were written on the unclouded sky with the beams of the meridian sun. How infinite, then, must be your shame and confusion before him!

c) *An inexorable God will judge you.* The time of mercy is passed, the measure of grace is exhausted to its dregs. Hence, God is inexorable in his vengeance. "You shall seek me, and shall not find me." John 7: 34. And you, O sinner, are in judgment before this inexorable Judge! Alas! what must be the feelings of a criminal when, in answer to his last petition for pardon, the terrible reply is given: "There is no pardon but with God!" Who will be able to describe the emotions of the weeping sinner, before the throne of God, when he clasps his hands in anguish and with torrents of tears implores mercy,—but obtains no mercy! O, how dreadful, dear Christians, is the judgment of an enraged God! Add to this, yet another circumstance which draws down more heavily still the fatal scales of divine justice.

2. *The judgment of that hour is forever decisive and irrevocable.* Whatever sentence the eternal Judge pronounces upon the offender remains pronounced for all eternity. From his sentence there is

a) *No appeal.* Here upon earth, a criminal may protest against the sentence pronounced upon him, and appeal to a higher court. It is only when the Supreme Court of the land has spoken, that no further appeal is possible. . . . It is very different, my brethren, in the Court of divine justice. There speaks the King of kings, (1. Tim. 6: 15); there speaks one most high, Creator Almighty, a powerful king, and greatly to be feared, who sitteth upon his throne. (Eccles 1: 8.) It is the Supreme Court of heaven that decides, and from its verdict there is no appeal. And as from the sentence of that divine Judge there is no appeal, so in the sentence itself there is

b) *No change, no shadow of alteration.* God judges, and his judgment becomes an eternal one. "The counsel of the Lord standeth for ever." Ps. 32: 11. "The will of the Lord shall stand firm." Prov. 19: 21. Therefore, there can be no alteration of the sentence. Let the victim of divine justice suffer the most intense and bitter agony, let his indescribable misery endure from century to century, the sentence of condemnation, once passed, abides forever, and will never be alleviated for the space of a single moment. "If the tree fall to the south or to the north, in what place soever it shall fall, there shall it be." Eccles 11: 3.

All this awaits you, O sinner! in the judgment of an enraged God. . . . You may doubt, or, perhaps, even discredit it; you may banish the thought of the judgment for a season from your mind; you may run from pleasure to pleasure, you may make yourself, for the time being, blind and deaf to the terrors which await you, but whether you prepare for it or not, the hour will come when you shall stand alone and defenceless before the throne of your God. "Every one of us shall render account for himself to God." Rom. 14: 12. "We shall all stand before the judgment-seat of Christ." Rom. 14: 10. "When one departs this life, he shall forthwith be placed before the jugdment-seat of God, and the most searching scrutiny will be made of all things which he has ever thought, spoken, or done." St. Aug. lib. 2, *De anima*, cap. 4.

II. Mortal sin is so great an evil that it deserves painful and eternal punishment. And such a punishment is really inflicted upon the sinner. God punishes him

1. With *a hell full of torment.* And the torment of hell is twofold:

a) *The torment of the gnawing worm.* The Prophet speaks of a worm which gnaws in the heart of the damned: "Their worm shall never die." Our divine Saviour repeats the same words: "Their worm dieth not." Mark. 9: 47. If a worm were generated in your heart, my brethren, eating into its very core day and night, what exquisite pain would it not produce? In the heart of the damned there lives a very poisonous worm, which continually gnaws the soul with its sharp teeth,—this is the worm of conscience, bitter remorse. It continually says: "What have you lost, O sinner? Into what infinite misery have you not plunged yourself! You might so easily have been a child of everlasting salvation, and, now, you are, forevermore, a child of infernal perdition!" The Fathers of the Church declare, that the torment of the gnawing worm is very painful. St. Bernard says: "This is the worm that never dies, the memory of past things. It never ceases to gnaw at the conscience, and, nourished by this indigestible food, it continues its life. I shudder at this biting worm and everlasting death. I shudder to fall into the hands of the living death and of the dying life!"

b. *The torment of the devouring fire.* "Which of you can dwell with *devouring fire?* Which of you shall dwell with *everlasting burnings?*" Is. 23: 14. "The end of them is a *flame of fire.*" Eccles 21: 10. "I am tormented in this flame." Luke 16: 24. "He shall be tormented with fire and brimstone." Apoc. 14: 10. "Depart from me, ye cursed, into everlasting fire." Matt. 25: 41. "The chaff he will burn with unquenchable fire." Luke 3: 17. "The Angels shall separate the wicked from among the just, and shall cast them into the furnace of fire." Matt. 13: 50. The Fathers of the Church use similar language. "There will not be so small a fire as burns upon your hearth-stone, and if any one would compel you to put your hand into it, you would rather give him anything than put your hand therein." St. Augustine in Ps. 49. "As often as I look at the earthly fire, I think of the fire of hell, and cannot sufficiently bewail the miserable condition of the damned." St. John Climachus in *scal. par. grad* 4. Behold, O sinner! this hell of torments awaits you, and it is

2. *A hell without end.* The enraged God said of old to his faithless people: "I will bring an everlasting reproach upon you, and a perpetual shame which shall never be forgotten." Jer. 23: 40. The Eternal Truth has declared that his sentence to the reprobate at the Last Day shall be: "Depart from me, ye cursed, into everlasting fire." Matt. 25: 41. "The smoke of their torments," says the Revelation of St. John, "shall ascend up for ever and ever." Apoc. 14: 11. We all know, my brethren, that a certain sort of fire was created to serve the use of man in his necessities,

but, alas! it is quite another sort of fire which serves the justice of God in his vengeance. The latter, unlike the former, does not consume what it burns, it continually restores what it feeds upon. No wonder, then, that those terrible and insatiable flames must burn for ever. Eternal will be the fire since eternal is its fuel,—the soul of the sinner and his unremitted sin.

O most dreadful of all truths! The judgment of an angry God and the hell of an avenging God, alike, await the sinner . . . This is the reward, or rather punishment of his momentary delights, his base brief joys, his loathsome, short-lived pleasures . . . This is your portion, O poor deluded ones, who disregard God and his holy law, who stretch out your hands to grasp the goods of others, who shamelessly dishonor your bodies by lust and carnal excesses. This your portion and inheritance, O drunkard, O proud man, O profligate father, O godless son! Fly, before it be too late, from the wrath to come; and, having immediate recourse to the tribunal of infinite mercy, seek by a sincere repentance to avert from your souls the irrevocable sentence of infinite justice, that you may never know how dreadful a thing it is "to fall into the hands of the living God." A blessing which, from my heart, I wish you in the name of the adorable Trinity, the Father, the Son and the Holy Ghost. Amen.

THIRD FRIDAY IN LENT.

IS THERE NO RELIEF?

"The mercies of the Lord that we are not consumed: because his commiserations have not failed." Lament. 3: 22.

How dreadful it is, my dear Christians, to be confined for years to a sick-bed of pain, to languish and to suffer, yet, not be able to die! How dreadful it is to be condemned to prison for life, and to remain day and night, in dismal solitude, between damp walls! . . . How dreadful to awake from a trance in one's coffin, and to cry out for help in vain! . . . But infinitely more dreadful is it, to be stricken by the avenging justice of God, and to weep, despairing, in everlasting misery. This lot befalls the unhappy sinner who departs this life in final impenitence. "Hell devours him who dies in his sins." (St. Greg.) But, is there no relief,—no escape? No, there is no resource for him who once has fallen a victim to hell,—there is no relief, nor hope of relief for such a one for all eternity. But for you, sinner, who are still living, there *is* relief. A solemn voice of olden times says: "The mercies of the Lord that we are not consumed: because his commiserations have not failed." Yes, his commiserations have not failed, there is hope, there is relief, yet

    I. In the heart of God, and
    II. In the bosom of our holy Mother, the Church.

I. There is relief for the sinner in the *heart of God*. Is it really so, you ask? Do not doubt it for a moment, for

    1. God wills not the perdition of the sinner.

a) His own word is our guarantee for this fact: "Thou hast mercy upon all, because thou canst do all things, and overlookest the sins of men for the sake of repentance." Wisd. 11: 24. "The Lord waiteth that he may have mercy on you." Is. 30: 18. "As I live," saith the Lord, "I desire not the death of the wicked, but that he turn from his evil way, and live." Ezech. 33: 11. "The Son of man came not to destroy souls, but to save." Luke 9: 56. "The Lord delayeth not his promise, as some imagine, but beareth patiently for your sake, not willing that any should perish, but that all should return to penance." 2. Pet. 3: 9. All these passages contain the words of God, the promises of God, so true and infallible, that the mere doubt of them would be sin. God wills not the perdition of the sinner.

b) *You have an example of it in your own person.*
We have heard that every mortal sin is an infinite crime, and deserves hell. Hence, God would act consistently with his justice if, after the commission of his first sin, he would fling man into the everlasting pool of fire. But, because he does not desire the death of the sinner, he withholds his avenging arm,—he waits and endures. . . . Have you not experienced this yourself, my brother? How old are you? Forty, fifty years, or, perhaps, older. How long is it since you fell into your first grievous sin? Was it not in your youth? And, yet, you are not in hell? To the first sin you added the second, the third, the fourth. And, still, you are not in hell? Your grievous sins have increased, doubtless, with years in number and weight. And, yet, O sinner! yet, you are not now in hell? Perhaps, a few days ago, perhaps yesterday, perhaps to-day, you have sinned wilfully and mortally. And yet, (I repeat it,) you are not now in hell? What does this prove? That God wills not your perdition; for, if he willed it, he could long ago have delivered you to eternal damnation. . . .

2. *God wills the sinner's rescue; he wills his salvation.*

a) *He reaches forth his hand to him.* All those passages of the Sacred Scripture, my brethren, which speak of the mercy of God, assert this consoling truth. They are countless; but I shall adduce only a few. "The Lord is patient and full of mercy, taking away iniquity and wickedness." Numbers 14: 18. "Thy mercy will follow me all the days of my life." Ps. 22: 6. "The earth is full of the mercy of God." Ps. 32: 5. "Praise the Lord, for he is good, and his mercy endureth for ever." Ps. 135: 1. Nay, more, my dear Christians, even to the sinner that is sunk in the lowest abyss of corruption and degradation, our merciful Father offers his helping hand. "If your sins be as scarlet, they shall be made as white as snow, and if they be red as crimson, they shall be white as wool." Is. 1: 18. And not only does he offer to the sinner his saving hand, but, O merciful condescension!

b) *He draws him, also, to his heart.* In the Sacred Scriptures we find the most touching examples of this divine tenderness and clemency in the conversions of Mary Magdalene, St. Peter, the penitent thief on the cross; and more especially in the parable of the prodigal son. The latter, having grieved his father very much, and wasted his entire substance by living riotously in a strange land, returns, at last, to his father's house in abject poverty and with a lacerated heart. And how does that good father receive him? "When he was, yet, a great way off, his father saw him, and was moved with compassion, and, running to him, fell upon his neck, and kissed him." Luke 15: 20. Was not this touching example sufficient in itself to convince the most incredulous of the tender patience of the Most High with his erring creatures? And yet, as if this parable of his marvelous clemency needed yet stronger confirmation, our blessed Lord saw fit to preface it with another consoling similitude: "What man among you, that hath a hundred sheep; and if he lose one of them, doth he not leave the ninety-nine in the desert, and go after that which was lost until he find it? And when he hath found it, doth he not lay it upon his shoulders, rejoicing; and coming home, call together his friends, saying to them: Rejoice with me because I have found my sheep that was lost! I say to you, that even so there shall be joy in heaven upon one sinner that doth penance, more than upon ninety-nine just who need not penance." Luke 15: 3–8.

O, my dear brethren, so great is the mercy of God which reaches forth a helping hand to the sinner and draws him to his sacred, burning heart, that it cannot be explained in the words nor conceived by the thought of man. (St. Chrys. hom. 2 in ps. 20.) This tender mercy of God is the only hope of the sinner, and if he has recourse to it in time, he will meet with a loving reception, and obtain entire forgiveness of his crimes.

II. There is help and relief for the sinner in the *bosom of the Church;* for, God has appointed her

1. *To receive sinners*

a) *With all love.* Our good God, my brethren, has established in his Church an unfailing fountain of relief and salvation for fallen man. He has given her, with the tender office of a mother, the commission to stretch forth her arms to sinners and draw them to the embrace of her maternal bosom; wherefore, she never ceases to call to those afflicted ones: "Come to me, all you that labor, and are heavy laden, and I will refresh you." (Matt. 11: 28.) And if they will but listen to her pleading accents, if they will but "run after the odor of her ointments," she will receive them with extended arms, and clasps them to her breast. "The Spirit of the Lord is upon me, because the Lord has anointed me; he has sent me to preach to the meek, to heal the contrite of heart, to give them a crown for ashes, the oil of joy for mourning, and a garment of praise for the spirit of grief." (Is. 61: 1–3.) God has appointed his Church to receive all sinners,

b) *Without any exception.* She does not say: "Come to me, you that labor and are heavy laden," but "Come to me, *all* you that labor and are heavy laden, and I will refresh you." Matt. 11: 28. Though the sinner be ever so miserable and loathsome,—he is lovingly received. Though he may have run for years in all the crooked ways of vice, though he may have lived in habits of the grossest sin all the days of his life,—he is lovingly received. Though he may have committed adultery like David, murder and rapine like the thief on the cross, yea, even treason and apostacy, like Judas; though, in fact, he may have trampled under foot all human and divine laws,—once truly repentant, my dear brethren, he is lovingly received. "Can a woman forget her infant, so as not to have pity on the son of her womb? And if she should forget, yet, I will not forget thee." Is. 49: 15. . . .

More than that. God has appointed his Church:

2. *To confer grace on sinners.* For that purpose he has given her

a) *The treasure of all salvation,*—to wit: the blood which our adorable Redeemer shed upon the cross. With this treasure all debts are paid. "Christ died for us; much more, therefore, being now justified by his blood, shall we be saved from wrath through him." Rom. 5: 9. "If the blood of goats and of oxen, and the ashes of a heifer being sprinkled, sanctify such as are defiled, to the cleansing of the flesh; how much more shall the blood of Christ, who, through the Holy Ghost, offered himself without spot to God, cleanse our conscience from dead works, to serve the living God?" Hebr. 9: 13, 14. "The blood of Jesus Christ cleanseth us from all sin." 1. John 1: 7. This priceless treasure of salvation is deposited in the Church, she has the key to it in her hands, and can take from its unfailing coffers, the wherewith to pay all our debts. A single drop of the adorable blood of Jesus is sufficient to outweigh the sins of thousands of worlds. Besides this, God has given her

b) *The power to loose from sin.* "And I will give to thee the keys of the kingdom of heaven. . . . And whatsoever thou shalt loose upon earth, it shall be loosed, also, in heaven." Matt. 16: 19. "Amen, I say to you, . . . whatsoever you shall loose upon earth, shall be loosed, also, in heaven." Matt. 18: 18. "Receive ye the Holy Ghost; whose sins you shall forgive, they are forgiven them." John 20: 22, 23. From these passages it is evident that the Church in her priesthood possesses the power of forgiving sins, and of reconciling the sinner with God. To those who walk upon earth is committed the administration of that which is in heaven; and the priests have received a power which God gave neither to the Angels nor Archangels. To these it was not said: "Whatsoever you shall bind upon earth, shall be bound also in heaven; and whatsoever you shall loose upon earth, shall be loosed also in heaven." The kings of this earth, it is true, have, also, the power to bind, but only the body. But the binding of the priests regards the soul and reaches into heaven. Whatever the priests do here below, is ratified by God above, the Lord confirming the sentence of his servants. (Chrys. *de Sacerd.* lib. 3, cap. 5.)

In conclusion, my dear Christians, let us seriously consider how infinite is the misery of the sinner, since the judgment of an angry God, and the hell of an avenging God await him. . . . But there is relief in the heart of Jesus, and in the arms and bosom of his holy Church. . . . Therefore, sinner, despair not. If all the demons of hell should cry out to you: "You are lost!" reply to them with humble faith and confidence: "I can yet be saved. The heart of God, my Father, and the arms of our holy Mother, the Church, are still open to receive me. Into that heart, the asylum of sinners,—into those arms, the refuge of the miserable and afflicted, lo! I flee with courage and contrite hope, and *there*, with the help of my merciful Redeemer, I shall find grace and everlasting salvation!" Amen.

FOURTH FRIDAY IN LENT.

HOW TO BEGIN.

"He that will love life, and see good days, ... let him decline from evil, and do good." 1. Pet. 3: 10, 11.

How glad, my dear brethren, is the shipwrecked mariner, who battles with the waves and is every moment in danger of perishing, if a rope is thrown out to him, to which he can cling! . . . How glad must not the sinner be, who is wrecked on this stormy ocean of life with the abyss of hell threatening at every moment to swallow him up,—if a strong hand is held out to him to rescue him from eternal perdition. Yes, there is safety, yet, for the repentant sinner in the heart of God and in the arms of the Church. But, how is he to begin the work of his salvation? St. Peter gives the right answer to this question in the following words: "He that will love life, and see good days, let him decline from evil, and do good." Alas! poor sinner, you have been aroused out of the sleep of sin by the depth of the abyss into which you have fallen, especially by the terrors which await you in eternity. Sighing you have called upon the good God to have mercy on you; you have implored him in the words of the royal Psalmist: "Have mercy on me, O God, according to thy great mercy; and according to the multitude of thy tender mercies, blot out my iniquity." Ps. 50: 1, 2. God *will* have mercy on you, poor afflicted soul, if you will but do what he demands of you; and that is

I. To abandon the *way of injustice,* and
II. To enter upon the *way of justice.*

I. What does it mean to abandon the *way of injustice?* Three things are required for it.

1. *To repent of sin.* So long as a man does not detest evil, he walks in the way of injustice; for his heart is attached to sin. Hence, the first condition of true repentance is sorrow, or contrition for sin. And this contrition must be

a) *Sincere.* It must have its root in the heart,—since, as the heart was formerly the seat of sin, it must now be the seat of contrition. "Rend your hearts," says the prophet Joel, "and not your garments." (3: 13.) "An afflicted spirit, a contrite heart the Lord will not despise." Ps. 50: 9.

The contrition of the mouth and of the lips is not sufficient. The heart must be crushed, must be *bruised*, (as is the literal meaning of the word,) by sorrow, and this sorrow must extend not only to one or two or three sins, but to all sins, at least, to all mortal sins committed. He who truly repents of his sinful life, makes no exception, he detests all grievous sins by which he has basely offended his God. The false contrition which includes only a few sins, and reserves to the penitent even *one* favorite mortal sin or evil habit, has no value whatever in the sight of the Most High.

b) True contrition must be *supernatural*. It must proceed from God, and have God, alone, for its object. Now, my brethren, your contrition proceeds from God if it is caused by his interior impulse, that is, by his divine grace; . . . it has God for its object, if you are sorry for your sins because thereby you have offended God, or, at least, because thereby you have lost heaven and deserved hell. This is the first and most necessary thing: *Be sorry for your sins!* "I know my iniquity, and my sin is always before me. To thee only have I sinned, and have done evil before thee." Ps. 50: 5, 6. "I am not worthy to be called thy son." Luke 15: 21.

2. *You must confess your sins.* "If we confess our sins, God is faithful and just to forgive us our sins, and to cleanse us from all iniquity." 1. John 1: 9. "No man can be justified from sins, unless he confess his sins." Concil. Trid. sess. 14, can. 6. 7. We must, therefore, my dear Christians, confess

a) *With confidence in the mercy of God.* If the sinner should believe that God either will not or cannot forgive him his offences, confession would be fruitless. Hence, the necessity for confidence in God "who overlooks (or forgives) the sins of men for the sake of repentance." Wisd. 11: 24. This confidence, then, my brethren, is necessary, and most especially necessary when the sins of the penitent surpass all measure and number. You must confess

b) *With a sincere self-accusation.* "You must confess, at least, all grievous sins, according to number, species, and necessary circumstances." Concil. Trid. sess. 17, can. 7. Confess, dear Christians, by laying bare the true state of your soul, without excuses, without palliation; confess as your conscience accuses you, and as you believe yourself guilty before God. This is the second thing. *Confess your sins!* "Be not ashamed to confess thy sins." Eccles. 4: 31. . . . Though it be ever so hard and painful to flesh and blood, overcome yourself for the love of God, and he, by his grace, will render the confession easy. . . .

3. *You must amend your life.* There would be no sincere contrition,

no firm purpose of amendment, in fact, it would be only a sham repentance, if, shortly after confession you commit the same sins you have so recently confessed. The devil leads some souls into hell by open, unrepented sin,—others by the snare of a false repentance. By returning to their former sins immediately after quitting the sacred Tribunal, they show that they, (as it were,) repent of their seeming repentance. Christ once risen from the dead died no more, so you, also, my brethren, having risen from sin, must sin no more, like Mary Magdalene, St. Peter, St. Paul, and a host of other sincere and holy penitents. You must amend your life, and for that purpose,

a) *Resist the temptation to sin.* After confession, the same temptations will assail you, sometimes more violently than before. You must make war against them, you must struggle against anger, pride, drunkenness, lust, the love of earthly things; you must fight with all vigor, and earnestness, and constancy, as if a kingdom were to be taken; as, indeed, it is,—for the kingdom of heaven is the prize. But in order the easier to stand in battle, you must relinquish the proximate occasion of sin, for as long as you remain in *that*, in spite of the holiest resolutions, you will most certainly relapse, since you undertake an impossibility, viz: to avoid sin without avoiding the occasions of sin. "Can a man hide fire in his bosom, and his garments not burn? Or can he walk upon hot coals, and his feet not be burnt?" Proverbs 6: 27, 28. Moreover, my dear brethren, you must

b) *Repair the damage caused by your sin.* The neighbor is often injured by sin. Justice requires that reparation should be made. You have stolen something, perhaps, from another;—know, then, that you cannot, and must not, keep it; you must make restitution. You have injured, perchance, the honor or good name of your neighbor, you must restore it. You have scandalized your fellow-men by word and example. You are bound to repair the injury which you have inflicted upon these immortal souls.

This is the third thing. *Amend your life, make satisfaction.* "Put away the strange gods from among you, and prepare your hearts unto the Lord, and serve him only." 1. Kings 7: 3. "Be converted, and turn from your idols," (your darling sins and passions,) "and turn away your faces from all your abominations." Ezech. 14: 6. "Turn from thy sins. Turn away from thy injustice, and greatly hate abomination." Eccles. 17: 21-23. The illustrious St. Gregory explains that "to do penance means to bewail the perpetrated evil, and to perpetrate the bewailed evil no more." (*Hom.* 34, in Evang.)

II. It does not suffice, my dear Christians, to forsake the way of injustice, but you must, also, enter upon the way of justice. *Decline from* evil,—this is very good; but it is not enough; it is only the beginning of repentance. Another condition is equally necessary for a sincere conversion: *Do good.* This is done

1. *If you do what God commands.*

a) You will do what he commands, my brethren, if you obey his expressed will, such as the Ten Commandments. "The Lord spoke all these words." (Exod. 20: 1–18.) And this law which was given by the Lord to Moses on Mount Sinai, was confirmed and explained by his Eternal Son who said: "Think not that I am come to destroy the law, or the prophets: I am not come to destroy, but to fulfil." Matt. 5: 17. His Church, too, tells you what he commands, through his representatives: "He that heareth you, heareth me." Luke 10: 16. The laws of the Church contain the will of God. God speaks through the mouth of his beloved Spouse. Obey, then, dear Christians, the precepts of the Church.

b) *Your own heart tells you what God commands, or what he forbids.* God has written his will upon every human soul, that she may know what is right and wrong. This is the precious gift of Conscience which he has given to every one of his creatures. "In every work of thine regard thy soul in faith; for this is the keeping of the commandments." Eccles. 32: 27. Walk the way of justice, my brethren. Observe carefully and perseveringly what God and your conscience tell you. . . . True, it is a great thing, and worthy of immortal reward, to thus do the expressed will of your Creator, but a greater thing it is, and belonging to eternal justice that

2. *You endure patiently the trials which he sends you.* All spiritual writers assert that the bearing of the cross is absolutely necessary for every one who desires to walk this world as a Christian and to perform the justice of Christ; for our Lord himself says: "If any man will come after me, let him deny himself, and take up his cross, and follow me." Matt. 16: 24. And again: "He that taketh not up his cross, and followeth me, is not worthy of me." Matt. 10: 38. Therefore, my brethren, strive to carry your crosses with cheerfulness and patience.

a) *The general cross.* The whole world sighs under misery. "Thorns and thistles," says the wisdom of Genesis (3: 18). "Sweat of the brow," says the same book of Moses (3: 19). Since every individual man is a descendant of sinful Adam who was forced in punishment for his disobedience to journey through thistles and thorns in this vale of tears, and to earn his bread in the sweat of his brow, every creature of God is subject to labor and sufferings. "Great labor is created for all men, and a heavy yoke is upon the children of Adam, from the day of their coming out of their mother's womb, until the day of their burial into the mother of all." Eccles. 40: 1.

b) *Particular crosses.* Every state of life has its difficulties and obstacles. The mother is tried, more or less, with her children; the wife, with her husband; the farmer, with his laborers; the poor man, with the necessities of his condition.—Bear, then, your cross, each one of you, my dear brethren, with patience and resignation to the will of God. "Join thyself to God, and endure," says the Wise Man, "that thy life may be increased in the latter end. Take all that shall be brought upon thee; and in thy sorrow endure, and in thy humiliation, keep patience. For gold and silver are tried in the fire, but acceptable men in the furnace of humiliation." (Eccles. 2: 3–5.) "Prepare thyself to suffer many adversities, and divers evils, in this miserable life," says, also, the pious À Kempis, "for so it will be with thee, wherever thou art, and so, indeed, wilt thou find it wheresoever thou mayst hide thyself." (Imitat. of Christ, libr. 2, c. 12, v. 10.)

From this brief discourse, my dear brethren, you now know what to do, and how to begin the work of your repentance, that you may obtain mercy and save your soul. Do not say it is too difficult. A thousand years employed in the most austere penance are incomparably easier to endure, than a quarter of an hour spent in hell. Begin, then, at once, and, (the grace of God assisting you to a happy termination of your labors and penances,) may it be given you all to realize in your own souls the truth of the passage which forms a consoling supplement to my text of to-day, that "the eyes of the Lord are (ever) upon the just, and his ears open unto their prayers." Amen.

FIFTH FRIDAY OF LENT.

DELAY NOT YOUR REPENTANCE.

"*To-day if you shall hear his voice, harden not your hearts.*" Ps. 94: 8.

The sinner, my beloved brethren, is often to be pitied. He perceives his spiritual misery; he knows that he stands upon the brink of hell, and that the next moment may precipitate him into its abyss, making him miserable for all eternity; and yet, he will not take hold of the hand of God, which is gladly stretched forth at all times, to rescue him from perdition. . . . And yet, he refuses to embrace that saving mercy. He will tell you, perhaps, that he intends some day to do so, but not now, later on, when he has grown older and wiser. What does the Spirit of God say to this? "Say not: I have sinned, and what harm hath befallen me? for the Most High is a patient rewarder. Be not without fear about sin forgiven, and add not sin to sin. And say not: the mercy of God is great; he will have mercy on the multitude of my sins. For mercy and wrath quickly come from him; and his wrath looketh upon sinners. Delay not to be converted to the Lord, and defer it not from day to day. For his wrath will come on a sudden; and in the time of vengeance he will destroy thee." (Eccles. 5: 4–9.) Again, St. Paul gives voice to a similar rebuke: "Despisest thou the riches of his goodness, and patience, and long-suffering? Knowest thou not that the benignity of God leadeth thee to penance? But according to thy hardness, and impenitent heart, thou treasurest up to thyself wrath, against the day of wrath, and revelation of the just judgment of God." (Rom. 2: 4, 5.) Therefore, my dear brethren, I cry out to you with emphasis—and Oh, that I could engrave these words with an iron pencil upon the tablet of your souls!—"*To-day if you shall hear his voice, harden not your hearts.*" Delay not to be converted to the Lord, for if you defer your conversion from day to day,

I. You risk everything, and
II. In the end, you lose everything.

I. *You risk everything.* What do you risk?

1. *The greatest graces.*

a) *The longanimity of God.* It is most certainly one of the greatest of God's graces to the sinner, when he bears with him with indulgence and patience. Consider only, my dear brethren, what an infinite outrage mortal sin is, and you will not be able to contain your astonishment that God defers its condign punishment even one single hour after its commission.... But God waits for the despiser of his supreme majesty, not only for the space of a single hour, but from year to year, and, often, on through the extended course of a long and sinful life. "I have always held my peace; I have kept silence; I have been patient," says the Mighty One, speaking through his prophet. (Is. 52: 14.) And, again, by the same lips: "The Lord waiteth, that he may have mercy on you." (Is. 30: 18.) Ponder, also, my brethren, the thrilling parable of the barren fig-tree: "Behold," said the master of the vineyard to his laborer, "behold, these three years I come seeking fruit on this fig-tree, and I find none. Cut it down therefore; why doth it take up the ground?" (Luke 13: 7.) Terrible command! full of dread significance for the slothful Christian! How long has God already waited for *you*, my brethren? For many years, perhaps for half a century. And you still delay to be converted to him? You will not yet confess your sins, nor avoid the occasions of sin, nor relinquish your bad habits, nor restore your ill-gotten goods? How presumptuously you play with the long-suffering patience of God! How quickly it may all end for you,—perhaps to-morrow, perhaps to-day. "The lord of that servant shall come in a day that he expecteth not, and in an hour that he knoweth not; and shall separate him, and appoint his portion with the hypocrites. There shall be weeping and gnashing of teeth." (Matt. 24: 50, 51.)

b) *The mercy of God.* Like his long-suffering patience, my brethren, the mercy of God is an inconceivably great grace. Ah, who is God, and who is the sinner? God, the Sovereign Creator, the Redeemer, the Sanctifier—God the infinite Power, the infinite Wisdom, the infinite and ineffable Goodness! Man, the work of his hands, the slave whom he has redeemed,—weakness, darkness, wickedness—worms, ashes, and corruption! Yet this great God, before whom a thousand years are as a day, and royal crowns like the dust in the road, offers mercy and pardon to that vile sinner, to the betrayer of his majesty, to the despiser of his most holy Name! Will you, then, dare to sport with this mercy of the Most High? The ancient prophet, inspired by *his* wisdom, cries out to you: "Return to the Lord, thy God; for thou hast fallen down by thy iniquity." (Osee 14: 2.) But you retort with the hard-hearted, stiff-necked people of old: "Command, command again; command, command again; expect, expect again; expect, expect again; a little there, a little there." (Is. 28: 10.) Will this long-abused mercy of God not be exhausted some time, my brethren, and, alas, when you least expect it? "Mercy and wrath are with him. He is mighty to forgive and to pour out indignation. According as his mercy is, so his correction judgeth a man according to his works." (Eccles. 16: 12, 13.)

You risk everything. What do you risk?

2. *The highest goods.*

a) *Your immortal soul.* Who would doubt that the soul of man is an infinitely precious good? Man's soul is God's image and likeness. (Gen. 1: 26.) And its value, its price, its ransom, the blood of a God, the blood of the Second divine Person of the ever adorable Trinity, made man for love of us. "Knowing that you were not redeemed with corruptible gold and silver from your vain conversation of the tradition of your fathers; but with the precious blood of Christ, as of a lamb unspotted and undefiled." (1. Pet. 1: 18, 19.) The devil is willing to give all the kingdoms of the world for the priceless pearl of one immortal soul: "All these will I give thee, if, falling down, thou wilt adore me." (Matt. 4: 9.) For your soul's sake, my beloved brethren, our Lord Jesus Christ has been crucified. And you will deliberately risk the loss of that precious, dearly-bought treasure! You are well aware that the unconverted soul, the soul in the state of mortal sin, will be lost for ever. Yet, as long as you delay to be converted to the Lord, this terrible danger threatens you; and threatens you, moreover, every day, every moment. Will you thus risk that other great good, to wit:

b) *Your salvation?* Can you doubt for a moment that salvation is a most excellent good? My dear brethren, it is the substance and the essence of all good; it is, in short, the highest good, completing man's felicity for all eternity. "They shall be inebriated with the plenty of thy house," says king David, "and thou shalt make them drink of the torrent of pleasure." (Ps. 35: 9.) "That city into which we are to enter," exclaims the great bishop of Hippo, "differs from our earthly habitation, as the light of the sun and of the moon differs from the light of him who created the sun and the moon." (St. Aug. *De civitate Dei*.) "In the eternal beatitude," adds the same learned author in another of his works, "you find everything you love;.and you can desire nothing that will not be there." (St. Aug. *De Trin.*) And *this* felicity, you have the blind temerity to risk? Faith teaches, my dear Christians, that man has no claim to heaven, so long as he lives in the state of mortal sin. From this it follows that, if you delay your conversion, you are continually in danger of forfeiting your eternal salvation.

II. If you delay to be converted to the Lord, if you defer your conversion from day to day, you risk everything and, *in the end, lose everything.* How is this?

1. *You may die suddenly and unexpectedly.*

a) *Think of the many dangers.* Nothing is menaced in this world as much as our natural life. Everything about us, dear brethren, has an occult power which, if exercised, can bring us to a sudden death. The sun, beautiful and bright as it is, may inflame your brain and cause apoplexy. If you walk by the sea-shore or go to bathe in its waters, a powerful wave may carry you away beyond your depth and drown you. If you traverse the streets of the city, and pass a building in course of erection, a stone or a board may fall upon your head, and crush it out of all semblance of humanity. A pistol-shot from some rough crowd at the corner may pierce your heart on your way home. The house in which you live may fall down, and bury you in its ruins. The staircase, as you go up or down, may break, and cause your destruction. In the midst of a thunderstorm, the lightning may strike and kill you. You may be thrown out of your buggy, and your neck broken on the spot. Travelling, you may lose your life by a collision on the railroad, or the explosion of a steamboat-boiler. But who, my brethren, could ever enumerate all the different kinds of death that continually menace life? "There is but one step (as I may say) between me and death." (1. Kings 20: 3.) "Remember," says the Wise Man, "that death is not slow, and that the covenant of hell," (the decree by which all are to go down to the regions of death,) "hath been shewn thee; for, the covenant of this world shall surely die." (Eccles. 14: 2.) In short: "It is appointed for men once to die." (Hebr. 9: 27.) Reflect, then, my dear Christians,

b) *How little security is yours.* Do you say to me: "Yes, but I am now young and strong"? *Youth* is no security against death. Young people may die, as well as the old. How many die in the bloom of youth and health? Does not the holy Scripture tell us of the death of the young man of Naim,—of the sad taking-off of the fair young daughter of Jairus? One cold frost in the early autumn blights the fairest blossoms and flowers of summer. *Strength* is no security against death. A violent storm breaks down the strongest trees. Nay, more, the great tall tree is a surer mark for the tempest than the frail little fern growing at its foot. Lazarus, the strong man, was striken down by mortal disease even in the midst of a loving and attentive circle of relatives and friends. Neither is health any security against death, my brethren. Here to-day, and away to-morrow. How many have gone to bed at night in good health, and have been found dead in the morning! How many have arisen in good spirits in the morning, have taken their breakfasts, and gone about their business; and, yet, were cold, and stiff, and dead the same evening! "Man knoweth not his own end," says the inspired Writer, (Eccles. 9: 12,) and again: "Boast not of to-morrow; for thou knowest not what the day to come may bring forth." (Prov. 27: 1.) "God," remarks a celebrated doctor of the Church, "has not revealed to us the hour of death." (St. Gregory.) And if you, in your turn, my brethren, should die suddenly,—(for what has happened to thousands of others, may easily happen to you;) if death should steal upon you unawares, "like a thief in the night," as our Lord has foretold,—and if it should not find you watching, you may lose everything and for ever! But let us suppose that a sudden death should not overtake you,—there may still be something else much more terrible in store for you.

2. *You may die unprepared,*

a) *Because of your own fault.* As a rule, sickness precedes death, my brethren, and sickness is an urgent warning from God, pressing you to be converted to him. But very often that salutary warning is in vain, because you do not realize your danger. You regard death as something far off, something remote, which may come to you at a future day, but not just *then*. You have every hope of recovery from your sickness; a fond delusion, in which those who surround you, your physician, your relatives, your friends, with cruel kindness encourage you. Thus it comes to pass that the reception of the last Sacraments is deferred,—perhaps, not even thought of. Finally, the solemn moment of dissolution arrives. The cheek grows deadly white—the death-sweat trickles down,—the eyes stare wildly; and, lo! the cry is made: "Behold, the bridegroom cometh; go ye forth to meet him." (Matt. 25: 6.) Alas! the lamp is empty; there is no time to fill it; "the door is shut." (Matt. 25: 10.) It is now too late to go in with the happy faithful virgins to the banquet of eternal bliss!—Or, my brethren, even if you know your danger, you may decline to make good use of it. Many dying persons cannot help but see that their end is near, but they refuse even in that supreme moment, to reach out their arms to their crucified Redeemer, they refuse to embrace the last pleading overtures of the mercy of God. Sham repentance or no repentance at all, are the customary characteristics of such miserable death-beds. And it is of such sinners that the Lord complains: "I knew that thou art stubborn, and thy neck is an iron sinew, and thy forehead of brass." (Is. 48: 4.)

Again, my brethren, you may die wilfully unconverted

b) *By the just judgment of God.* Sometimes it is decreed in the divine councils that the sinner perish. Many passages of the Sacred Scripture seem to indicate this. "It was the sentence of the Lord, that their hearts should be hardened, and they should not deserve any clemency, and should be destroyed." (Josue 11: 20.) "I will laugh in their destruction, and will mock." (Prov. 1: 26.) "You shall die in your sins." (John 8: 25.) O, my brethren, how terrible, how awe-inspiring, are these sentences? God always offers sufficient grace to the sinner, with which, if he earnestly willed it, he could save his soul. But he lacks the earnest, persevering will, and hence, the sufficient grace profits him nothing; he perishes in the end through his own fault. And if *you*, my brethren, should thus play with the grace of God, if you should go out of this world in the state of sin,—(and such may easily happen,)—you, too, will lose both soul and salvation. In hell, alas! the reprobate sinner may shed torrents of tears for those lost, those priceless goods, but nevermore shall he find the saving grace and mercy which he abused, and scorned, and outraged here on earth!

Therefore, dear Christians, delay not your repentance. Do not believe the devil when he suggests to you: "At a later period you may do penance for your sins." Do not believe the world which says to you: "Wait a little yet." Believe not even your own heart, when it says to you: "Later on." —But listen to these words: "To-day if you shall hear his voice, harden not your hearts." Amen.

SIXTH FRIDAY IN LENT.

HOW GLAD YOU WILL BE!

"*My soul shall rejoice.*" *Ps.* 34: 9.

A return to God, my beloved brethren, is absolutely necessary, if the sinner desires to escape eternal damnation. Either penance or eternal perdition. There is no middle way. "Unless you do penance, you shall all likewise perish." (Luke 13: 3.) "Do penance; for the kingdom of heaven is at hand." (Matt. 3: 2.) This return to God, however, is no child's play, but requires a determined will and many sacrifices. The longer conversion is deferred, the greater become the obstacles, the more rare is repentance; and finally, all is irretrievably lost. Therefore, in my last discourse I said: "Delay not." O, that you may attend to this call, dear Christians, and without delay, arise from the pit into which you have fallen! Then, you will be exceedingly glad, you will rejoice like to a person rescued from shipwreck, rejoice like to a man who is pulled safely out of a burning mine. And this shall be the subject of our last Lenten meditation. How glad you will be, how your soul will rejoice

    I. In every hour of life-long repentance, and
    II. Especially in your last hour.

I. "There is no health in my flesh, there is no peace for my bones, because of my sins." (Ps. 37: 4.) "Sleep is gone from my eyes, and I am fallen away; and my heart is cast down for anxiety." (1. Mach. 6: 10.) Thus sighs the sinner, finding voice in the words of the great penitents of the Old Law. But how different are his emotions the moment he returns to God! His conversion brings into his heart

    1. *Sweet consolation,* because

    a) *His sin is blotted out.* "The Lord is patient and full of mercy, taking away iniquity and wickedness." (Numb. 14: 18.) "If my people being converted, do penance for their most wicked ways, then, I will hear from heaven, and will forgive their sins." (2. Paralip. 7: 14.) "I have blotted out thy iniquities as a cloud, and thy sins as a mist." (Is. 44: 22.) "God is patient with sinners till they are converted, and this being done, he forgets the past." (St. Aug.) What blessed consolation for the sincere penitent! The guilt is blotted out. Though I have committed many and great crimes,—as soon as I truly repent of them, the guilt is blotted out. Though I have perpetrated a thousand sacrileges and outrages richly deserving of hell fire,—as soon as I turn to my heavenly Father, crying *Peccavi!* with sentiments of real and profound contrition, the guilt is blotted out. How you must rejoice, my dear brethren, at such a thought!

b) *You are reconciled to your God.* "Because they are humbled," says that merciful God, "I will not destroy them; and I will give them a little help; and my wrath shall not fall upon them," (2. Paralip. 12: 7.) "If that nation against which I have spoken," says he again, "shall repent of their evil, I also will repent of the evil that I have thought to do to them." (Jer. 18: 8.) "How great is the mercy of the Lord," cries out the Wise Man in amazement: "and his forgiveness of them that turn to him." (Eccles. 17: 28.) And, lo! in the parable of the prodigal son we read with grateful tears, dear Christians: "The father was moved with compassion, and running to him, fell upon his neck, and kissed him." (Luke 15: 20.) What a comfort for the converted sinner! He can say: "My God is reconciled to me; I can look up to him once more with confidence, and need not fear the arrows of his anger." But your return to God produces still another fruit. It brings a

2. *Sure hope of life.* By his return to God, the sinner becomes

a) *A child of God.* Grace, God's most beautiful and highest gift to man, is lost by sin. "If any one saith, that a man, once justified, can sin no more, or lose grace, let him be anathema," declares the solemn Council of Trent. (Concil. Trid., sess. 6, can. 23.) In the fifteenth chapter of the same session it is taught that *by every mortal sin, grace is lost.* To the repentant sinner, God gives again the precious treasure of his divine grace. Through a mystery which he alone can accomplish, he makes him the object of his complacency, and adorns him with the lost ornaments of the faithful son and heir. "Bring forth quickly the first robe and put it on him," said the father of the Prodigal, "and put a ring on his hand." "Born again," said our Lord to Nicodemus. (John 3: 3.) And "Behold what manner of charity the Father hath bestowed upon us," bursts forth the Apostle of love in admiration, "that we should be named and should be the sons of God." (1. John 3: 1.) Thus man is made a child of God, and for that very reason,

b) *An heir of heaven.* "And if sons, heirs also, heirs, indeed, of God, and joint-heirs with Christ," as St. Paul declares in his Epistle to the Romans. (8: 17.) The great inheritance which God has prepared for the children of grace, and of which Jesus Christ, our Elder Brother, has already taken possession, is heaven. "God hath appointed us to the purchasing of salvation by our Lord Jesus Christ," (1. Thess. 5: 9,) "unto an inheritance incorruptible, and undefiled, and that fadeth not, reserved in heaven for you." (1. Pet. 1: 4.) How rejoiced, therefore, will you be, my beloved brethren, in every hour of your repentant life! How glad will you be when you reflect that your guilt, (no matter how great,) is blotted out, and that you are sweetly reconciled with your offended God! How glad, when you reflect that you are a child of that great and good God, and an heir of heaven, a co-heir, in short, with our Lord and Saviour Jesus Christ. Indeed, whatever the world may present you as grand and delightful, cannot possibly bring you such consolation and comfort as these considerations afford. You should thank God every day for your conversion, my dear brethren, and praise his mercies. "My soul shall rejoice," exults the royal penitent of old. . . . (Ps. 34: 9,) "The mercies of the Lord I will sing for ever." (Ps. 88: 2.)

II. How glad you will be, how much you will rejoice in your last hour! For

1. *All things are set in order.* The last hour, no doubt, is an hour rich in tears. We have numberless examples of this before our eyes. But particularly bitter is this hour to the children of sin. Death knocks at the door in the midst of their unjust money-getting, of their impure and sensual diversions, and, alas! what fear and anguish and lamentation does not the sound of that skeleton hand evoke! "They shall be troubled with terrible fear," says the Inspired Text, "and shall be amazed at the suddenness." (Wisd. 5: 2.) How much, on the other hand, will you rejoice, O sinner! if now you arise from the abyss of sin and embrace a life of penance; for at the hour of death you will find all things set in order

a) *Before God.* You have confessed and bewailed your sins in good season, and the Lord has pardoned them. Every thing is now in order. What a consolation there is for the dying person in this pleasing thought: I go, indeed, to a God, "who is just in all his ways," (Ps. 144: 7,) "who rendereth to every one according to his works," (Matt. 6: 27,) but all my house is set in order. I go to a God, whom I have, indeed, offended by my sins, but with whom I have reconciled myself by repentance in time. Blessed be his mercy! my house is set in order,

b) *Before the world.* By your prompt conversion, long before the hour of death, you have also reconciled yourself with the world, and the world, too, has forgiven you. How consoling for the dying man is the thought: I am about to depart from a world, wherein I have repaired whatever damage or injury I have caused by my sins. I have restored the injured reputation of my neighbor, I have made restitution of the ill-gotten goods I once wrongfully acquired, I have blotted out, thank God!

all the scandals I have given. My house is set in order. How rejoiced is the steward who has his books and cash in order, when he is called upon by his master to render an account. No less will *you* be rejoiced, my dear Christians, when at the approach of death you find that all your spiritual affairs are set in order. Then

2. *The departure is easy.* You will leave the world

a) *With a joyous confidence in God.* "As I live, saith the Lord God," (by the mouth of his prophet,) "I desire not the death of the wicked, but that the wicked turn from his way, and live." (Ezech. 33: 11.) "The Son of man," said the Eternal Truth himself, "is come to seek and to save that which was lost." (Luke 19: 10.) For this reason, my brethren, the converted penitent departs this life with confidence in God who has forgiven his sins, and with confidence in the Redeemer whose blood has cleansed his soul from every stain. You will leave this world, dear Christians,

b) *With the joyous assurance of salvation.* It is true a man who has once fallen into grievous sin, can lay no just claim to heaven,—only "the innocent in hand, the clean of heart" can aspire to ascend the mountain of the Lord. And no man, my brethren, knows whether he be worthy of love or hatred. But on account of God's mercy and his promises to forgive the penitent, and reinstate him in all his rights,—the converted sinner may, nevertheless, expect eternal salvation with confidence.

How rejoiced will you be in the last hour, if you now return and do penance; for, then, your house will be set in order and it will be easy for you to die. In that last hour, you will look back with confidence upon the past, and rejoice that you, then, sincerely confessed your sins, abandoned the way of iniquity, and made your peace with God and the world, "before your feet stumbled upon the dark mountain." But you will also look forward with confidence into the future, dear Christians,—look forward across the precipice of the grave into eternity, where the crown of glory awaits you. With the Apostle of the Gentiles, you will joyfully exclaim: "I desire to be dissolved and to be with Christ." (Phil. 1: 25.) A good death will be yours, my brethren, if you die now to sin that you may live to justice. This death must precede and anticipate the inevitable death of the body, since the Psalmist has expressly declared: "Blessed are *the dead* who *die* in the Lord. Die to yourself and your sins, therefore, dear Christians, while the uncertain span of this life remains to you, and thus you will happily prepare yourself in time for that blessed life which lasts for all eternity. Amen.

GOOD FRIDAY.

THE DERELICTION OF JESUS UPON THE CROSS.

"*My God, my God, why hast thou forsaken me?*" *Matt.* 27: 46.

The bitter Passion and death of Jesus Christ, our Lord and Redeemer, ought to be, especially in this week, the chief subject of our meditation. If we review, with some attention, the life and Passion of our Blessed Lord from his birth to his burial, we will come, my brethren, to the sad conclusion that *all his sufferings have their ground and cause in the malice, or, at least, in the imperfection of men.* The malice of men assigned to the Son of God a stable for his birth-place; the malice of men drove him from his home into a foreign country; the malice of men pursued him in all his ways from youth to manhood; that same malice stretched forth and strengthened the hand of his enemies in order to apprehend, to strike, and to crucify him; and finally, that cruel malice tortured him, the innocent Lamb of God, even to the close of his bitter agony upon the cross.—*Only one suffering was inflicted upon him,* (without the intervention of men), *immediately by God.* And what is that exceptional suffering? It is that which on the cross forced from his Sacred Heart the painful complaint embodied in my text: "My God, my God, why hast thou forsaken me?" It is his being abandoned by God. And it is just this suffering which is least known to Christians, and, consequently, least esteemed by them: and no wonder; for it is really a mystery of which we would have no knowledge, whatsoever, if it had not pleased the Lord to raise the curtain, (as it were), on the cross and, granting us a glimpse of his interior, to reveal to us what occurred in that sanctuary of his soul during the time of his intense physical sufferings. But just because it is so little known, and so little regarded, when truly, my brethren, it is the most significant of all the torments of Jesus, I shall avail myself of this hour of devotion and spiritual recollection, in order to make with you a short meditation upon this touching mystery. I repeat, therefore: The abandonment of Jesus by God on the cross is **the most significant of all his sufferings since it was**

    I. The most painful;
   II. The longest endured; and
  III. The strongest proof of the love of Jesus for his Eternal Father.

I. In order, dear Christians, to get a clear idea or representation, (although it be, after all, but a feeble one), of the abandonment experienced by our Blessed Redeemer on the Cross, we must, first of all, consider that Jesus Christ was *both God and man*. We, my brethren, have only *one* soul in our body; Christ possessed in his body, not only like us, a human soul, but beside the human soul, the divine nature, which dwelt in him; so that he united in himself two natures, the human and the divine.

What took place at the moment when God forsook Jesus? The divine nature in Jesus Christ withdrew itself from the human soul in a manner inexplicable to us; it no longer operated upon it. His divine nature did not separate itself from the body and the soul, but it no longer administered any light or consolation to the human soul, so that it was as if the divinity had really and completely departed. *And what was the result of this apparent separation?* The result was that the human soul in Jesus Christ felt, in that hour of supreme anguish, as if she were really alone, entirely separated from and forsaken by God; she seemed to be be in the condition of one who had drawn down upon herself the displeasure and indignation of God and the wrath of heaven. She was seized with the tormenting thought that the face of the all-holy God was averted, and would remain eternally averted from her; that his heart was closed against her, and would remain closed against her for ever.

Now you will begin to realize, dear brethren, *that this suffering was the most painful of all the sufferings of our crucified Redeemer.* Not to mention that it was a suffering of the soul, (a purely spiritual pain); and that the sufferings of the soul, (spiritual, interior torments,) cause more vehement anguish than is inflicted by mere corporal sufferings, —I say, there can be nothing more terrible than the thought of being separated from God, the highest Good. This thought is something inexpressibly awful, even for a dying sinner who during his whole life cared nothing for God, despised and blasphemed him, wallowing for years in the mire of iniquity. How much more terrible, then, is this thought in every situation of life for a person who has always loved God with all the affection of his soul, and served him with all the sincerity of his heart; who knows and desires to know no other happiness, no other joy or pleasure, than to be eternally united with the Supreme Good? In order to bring only one example of this sort before you, my brethren, permit me to remind you of the violent temptation of St. Francis of Sales, who at one period of his innocent and holy youth, was disquieted by the thought that he was forsaken and rejected by God. O, how this poor soul, inflamed with the love of God, bewailed his distress and dereliction both day and night. Almost unceasingly, the bitterest tears flowed from his pure young eyes; the anguish of his soul was so terrible, that even the most painful death would have been welcome to him, in order to escape that cruel pain. How terrible, then, must it have been for Jesus to feel himself all at once forsaken by his Eternal Father; for Jesus Christ, who was always united with God, who always loved God with the most perfect love; who never had or knew any other will but God's will, who for the love of God, took upon himself all the tribulations of life—what words can describe the depths and intensity of *his* dereliction? As far as heaven is above the earth, so far his agony surpasses that of all his suffering creatures.

If the Saints sometimes experience a similar abandonment, although only in miniature, it appears to them more painful than the torments of hell itself. And yet, the Saints have the consoling consciousness that their being forsaken by God is only a trial of their virtue; that it serves to cleanse them from their sins and imperfections, and to qualify them more rapidly for heaven; to increase their merits in time and their reward in eternity. But even this consolation was wanting to our divine Saviour. And why? Because he had taken upon himself all the sins of the world, and had become the scape-goat of our iniquities. He saw in spirit all the sins, vices, crimes, and abominations which from the fall of the first man defiled the human race, and will defile it until the hour of the last judgment. And at the sight of these many and grievous crimes, he felt as if he, alone, had committed them, and was obliged to atone for them; unspeakable was his abhorrence of the turpitude of sin, unspeakable was his grief on account of the dishonor of God. In his woe and consternation, he felt as if the sins of the world formed an insurmountable barrier between himself and God; he felt now, (because he felt as mere man), as if he never could make sufficient reparation, or perfect satisfaction to the divine justice for the assumed guilt of sin; and for this reason, it seemed to him in that hour of tremendous agony, as if he were rejected by God. St. Paul plainly teaches this in his Epistle to the Galatians, when he says: "*Christ hath redeemed us from the curse of the law,* BEING MADE A CURSE FOR US; *for it is written:* CURSED IS EVERY ONE THAT HANGETH ON A TREE." (Galat. 3: 13.) "His body shall not remain on the tree, but shall be buried the same day; *for he is accursed of God that hangeth on a tree.*" (Deut. 21: 23.) Crushing, as it did, the Sacred Heart of our Blessed Lord with all its heavy weight,—in this curse chiefly consisted the torment and the horror of his being forsaken by God. Truly, we may boldly assert that though the other sufferings of his Passion,—for instance, his anguish on account of the blindness and malice of the Jews, on account of the weakness and fall of some of his disciples; the torments of his scourging, his crowning with thorns, his crucifixion,—were great and bitter, yet, in comparison with the torture of his dereliction, they were only as a refreshing dew. The abandonment of Jesus by his Eternal Father is in reality *a nameless suffering,* nameless in the full sense of the word; there is no name, there are no words, neither in the language of men, nor in the language of the Angels, sufficient to express its depths, its extent, its intensity.

II. But what increased and aggravated the pain of the abandonment of Jesus by God in an incredible manner, was *its long duration,* a circumstance which must not be overlooked and disregarded, if we do not wish to form an erroneous conception of this mystery.

1. This extraordinary pain did not begin only at the moment when Jesus cried out: "My God, my God, why hast thou forsaken me?"—for in that case, he would have said: *Why dost thou forsake me?* Neither did it take its inception when he was nailed to the cross, and elevated upon it on Mount Calvary. This pain, on the contrary, was *the first* which came upon him after the Last Supper, and the *last* which departed from him on the hard bed of the cross. That his abandonment by God took its inception on Mount Olivet, Jesus Christ, himself, gives us to understand both by word and action. Contemplate him only for a moment, my dear brethren, in his agony in the Garden. In what a pitiable state does he not appear! Enormous mountains of sin were crushing him with their abominable weight; he sighs, he sobs and groans; trembling and growing pale, he wrings his hands, and sinks prostrate on the earth. There he lies upon his face as if annihilated;—dissolved in the agony of his soul, he prays,—yes, prays for hours, fervently imploring the divine mercy and compassion; prays with such a fire of desire that the very stones on which he lay, (more tender than the obdurate hearts of sinners), might have been moved to love and pity for him.

And why all this intense suffering? Perhaps, out of fear of the corporal pains which were awaiting him during that night and the following day? That is impossible. We must not represent our Blessed Lord to ourselves as less courageous, less noble-hearted, than the holy martyrs. But no martyr, I believe, has ever bewailed his anticipated sufferings as Jesus did in the Garden of Olives. With him, therefore, it must have been another, a higher, *the* highest suffering in fact, that can be imagined, which terrified him on that occasion in such an extraordinary manner;—it must have been the pain of his abandonment by God. When the presence of God and the consolation of God are sensible, my brethren, the soul of the saint knows nothing of pusillanimity or hesitation. Remember St. Francis Xavier. Before his departure to Asia, he beheld in a vision all the hardships, tribulations, and sufferings which he was to undergo in his missionary enterprise. But with holy courage and enthusiasm, he cried out: "More yet, O God, more yet!" Should our Blessed Lord be surpassed by a saint in fortitude? What a senseless blasphemy! Therefore, because in the Garden of Olives he felt himself already forsaken by his God, he was plunged into that boundless abyss of sadness in which he said to his disciples: "My soul is sorrowful even unto death." (Matt. 26: 38.) Because in his agony in the Garden he was already forsaken by his God, he said: "O my Father, if it is possible, let this chalice pass from me." (Matt. 26: 39.) O Father, all things are possible with thee, "let this chalice pass from me;" a prayer which he probably repeated numberless times. Because at that hour he was already forsaken by his Father, hence that nameless anguish which seized his soul, hence the bloody sweat, which issued forth from every pore of his sacred Body. For this very reason, also, *an angel came down from heaven and comforted him;* for he would never have needed this exterior comfort, if the divine nature in him had not abstained from every comforting operation upon the human nature. But even the angel strengthened only the human will in Christ, without being permitted to communicate any light to his spirit, or any consolation to his heart.

2. In this terrible state of desolation and dereliction, our Blessed Lord endured all his sufferings in the houses of Annas and Caiphas, in the palaces of Pilate and Herod, in the streets of Jerusalem, and on Calvary's height. This was, so to speak, the seasoning or the soul of each individual torture. It is this that made all the other sufferings, true sufferings. If the blessed feeling that he still possessed the love and friendship of God in the highest degree, if the blessed feeling that, after a few hours, he would be admitted into the bosom of eternal glory, had penetrated him in a lively manner, it would have been an easy matter for him to suffer a thousand times more than he really suffered in his body. The Saints say, that there is nothing sweeter upon earth than to suffer for God in the consciousness of the love of God, supported and upheld by divine grace and consolation. But to suffer without any interior consolation, to suffer with the consciousness of being forsaken by God, is a terror of terrors. And in such a manner, Christ suffered from the beginning of his first agony on the cross. Therefore, every Christian must admit that our Blessed Lord suffered more than all men together can suffer; for though some martyrs suffered for a longer time, and endured, if possible, more cruel pains than he,—yet, while their bodies suffered, my brethren, their souls were filled with heavenly joy.

III. The abandonment of Jesus by God was not only the most painful, and long-continued of the sufferings of our Blessed Redeemer, but it was also *that wherein he manifested his most perfect love for his Eternal Father.* The proof of this is contained in the words: "My God, my God, why hast thou forsaken me?"

1. Consider attentively, dear brethren, *the time of his pronouncing this complaint.* It was not at the moment of his apprehension, nor of his scourging,—not at his crowning with thorns, nor his cruel crucifixion. During all the time that he was delivered to the power of men and of hell, not a word of complaint, on account of the terrible need of his soul, crossed his lips; no thought of complaint arose in the depths of his heart. The more severely God chastised him, the representative of sinners, the more humbly he submitted himself to his strokes. Only when the second

agony had already reached its highest point of torture, when the soul began to be separated from the body, and each moment threatened to be the last,—only when he thought that he would have to depart hence in this awful state of abandonment by God, only *then*, dear Christians, did he speak those heart-rending words: "My God, my God, why hast thou forsaken me?" When the chalice of all earthly suffering was emptied to the very dregs, then, at last, his bursting Heart cries out for the removal of that overwhelming agony which threatens to extend even beyond the grave, into the dread eternity.—But this complaint in that last dark hour was, nevertheless, my brethren, no cry of indignation or impatience, no murmur of rebellion,—it was only the natural expression of the most affectionate desire, of the most incomprehensible love of God. For with the words: "My God, my God, why hast thou forsaken me?" our Blessed Lord would say nothing else than: "I care not for all the sufferings of this world; even hell with all its horrors, pains, and inextinguishable fires would be endurable to me, my God, if I only were not forsaken by *thee!*" O what sublime language! What love! It is an incomprehensible language to us, re-echoed by many Saints in those sublime and heroic words: *"'Tis better to abide with God in hell, than dwell without him in heaven!"*

2. But, my brethren, let us not overlook the main point. Our Blessed Lord says: "My God, my God, why hast thou forsaken me?" Twice he lays a stress upon the little word "*My*", thereby indicating in the clearest manner the strong and tender sentiments of his Sacred Heart. Hereby he gives us to understand those sentiments, as if expressed in these actual words: "Thou, O God, hast, indeed, forsaken me, but still thou art my God, my Love,—I shall never forsake thee. And even though I should be forsaken by thee forever; if, on account of the turpitude of the numberless sins which I have taken upon myself, I should never more find any favor in thy sight, nevertheless, thou shalt ever be my God, the God of my heart, my love, my all; I will remain obedient to thee for all eternity; it is thy honor, thy glory, thy will, alone, that I seek in all things!" He is resolved to love God even in that terrible hour, when, as surety for sinners, he feels himself forsaken by, and separated from God, (as it were), forever. Truly, this seems to be the highest degree of love to which Jesus could elevate himself. This is that obedience of which St. Paul speaks, when he says: "Christ debased himself, taking the form of a servant; he humbled himself, becoming obedient unto death, even the death of the cross." (Phil. 2: 7, 8.) And in this, his boundless loving obedience, consists the chief merit of his Passion; in it consists his reparation for the outraged honor of God; in it, in fine, dear Christians, consists his atonement for the sins of the world.

3. To prove that it is not the fear of suffering, but simply the love of God and zeal for his honor that rules his heart, he immediately adds to his

complaint the words: "*I thirst,*" (John 19: 28); that is, "I do not refuse to suffer still longer; on the contrary, I have a burning thirst to suffer new, yea, even the most grievous and long continued sufferings for thy honor, O God, and for the salvation of men, my brethren."—He had scarcely declared in these words his readiness to embrace further torments, when the period of his painful dereliction and abandonment by God, had an end. The divine nature in him suddenly manifested again its sweet, comforting, and enlivening influence upon his human soul; a perfect ocean of delight was poured out over his blessed Humanity. The guilt of sin was wiped out; the divine justice was satisfied, and sinful man reconciled to his offended Creator. The God of mercy embraced his dying Son with infinite love, and pressed him, appeased, to the adorable, paternal Heart. And in that holy embrace, Jesus departed from this world with the joyous exclamation: "It is consummated.". . . . "Father, into thy hands I commend my spirit." (John 19: 30.—Luke 23: 46.) He had entered, my dear brethren, into the everlasting delights of Paradise.

But let us not forget, beloved Christians, that if Jesus suffered such tremendous and terrible torments, it was because he loved us poor sinners, because he wished to win a return of love from us. O, that we might fulfil the desire of his loving Heart, and, according to the words of the Apostle, *that we might no longer live to ourselves, but to him who has died for us!* But is it possible not to love so good a Lord, so amiable a Redeemer? Lacking this most natural, this most reasonable sentiment, should we not be regarded as monsters of men? Men without feeling, men without hearts, men, I should say, without the semblance of human nature? For in accordance with the law of our nature, love, everywhere, wins a return of love. If the infinite love of Jesus, alone, is unable to elicit from us a return of love,—must we not, with truth, be considered monsters of humanity? At the mere thought, at the bare possibility of such coldness and ingratitude towards our divine Saviour, the heart of St. Paul was so inflamed and fired with zealous indignation, that in the consuming ardor of his soul, he exclaimed: "*If any man love not our Lord Jesus Christ, let him be accursed.*" (1. Cor. 16: 22.) This curse shall be verified in us also, if we do not glow with gratitude and love towards him who, in his supreme hour of dereliction and abandonment on the cross, became, through tender love, anathema for us. Only a gratefully-loving heart will obtain a share of that fruit of love which ripened on the cross; only a gratefully-loving heart will be cleansed from its sins by the blood of Christ; only a gratefully-loving heart will not be forsaken by Jesus in temptations, in trials, in crosses, and in sufferings;—yea, my dear brethren, will never be forsaken, neither in life, nor in death, nor in the awful hour of judgment. Amen.

www.ingramcontent.com/pod-product-compliance
Lightning Source LLC
Chambersburg PA
CBHW030428300426
44112CB00009B/896